ANTI-CATHOLICISM AND NINETEENTH-CENTURY FICTION

SUSAN M. GRIFFIN

CAMBRIDGE
UNIVERSITY PRESS

CAMBRIDGE UNIVERSITY PRESS
Cambridge, New York, Melbourne, Madrid, Cape Town, Singapore, São Paulo, Delhi

Cambridge University Press
The Edinburgh Building, Cambridge CB2 8RU, UK

Published in the United States of America by Cambridge University Press, New York

www.cambridge.org
Information on this title: www.cambridge.org/9780521833936

First published 2004
This digitally printed version 2008

A catalogue record for this publication is available from the British Library

Library of Congress Cataloguing in Publication data
Griffin, Susan M., 1953–
Anti-Catholicism and nineteenth-century fiction / Susan M. Griffin
p.   cm. – (Cambridge studies in American literature and culture; 141)
Includes bibliographical references (p.) and index.
ISBN 0 521 83393 0
1. American fiction – 19th century – History and criticism.   2. Religion in literature.
3. Protestantism and literature – United States – History – 19th century.   4. American
fiction – Protestant authors – History and criticism.   5. Anti-Catholicism – United
States – History – 19th century.   6. Catholic Church – In literature.   7. Anti-Catholicism in
literature.   8. Catholics in literature.   I. Title.   II. Series.
PS374.R47G75   2004
813´.309382 – dc22   2003055896

ISBN 978-0-521-83393-6 hardback
ISBN 978-0-521-09352-1 paperback

To Douglas, Griffin, and Emma

Contents

Plates

Acknowledgements

This project has received support from University of Louisville Arts & Sciences Research, Research on Women, and Project Completion Grants, as well as sabbatical leave, for which I am deeply grateful. The Ekstrom Library staff, particularly Delinda Buie in Rare Books and those at Interlibrary Loan, were essential to the making of this book. Peggy Strain provided important research assistance in the early stages of the project. Jo Ann Griffin brought her "Girl Scout" virtues to my aid at its completion. My colleagues at the University of Louisville, Marc Bousquet, Debra Journet, Susan Ryan, Tamar Heller, and Nancy Theriot, all read drafts of chapters, giving valuable advice. I received research leads from Nina Baym, Ed Berman, John Crowley, Leonard Curry, Carolyn Karcher, Royal Rhodes, and members of the VICTORIA listserv. I was able to try out sections of this study at the University of Louisville Critical Theory Forum, the 18th- and 19th-Century Women Writers Conference, the Modern Language Association and Narrative conferences. Thanks to fellow panelists and audience members for suggestions.

Dale Bauer read the manuscript both in part and as a whole, offering astute and generous advice. I'm grateful too to Bob Levine, who invited me to talk about American nativist fiction, and who provided an enormously helpful reading of the overall project. Other anonymous readers for Cambridge University Press also helped me see how to improve the manuscript throughout, as did readers for earlier versions of this material published in *Legacy*, *PMLA*, *Victorian Literature & Culture*, and the *Roman Holidays* collection. Thanks to those editors for the opportunity to share my work and, too, for permissions to publish; and to Ross Posnock and Ray Ryan at Cambridge University Press for their encouragement and support. The scrupulous editorial assistance of Joanne Webb has been nothing short of invaluable. My deepest debt is to my family whose love and support have sustained and nourished me throughout these years of research and writing. Emma, Griffin, and Douglas – my great good fortune continues to astonish me daily.

Introduction

Rosamond; or, A Narrative of the Captivity and Sufferings of an American Female under the Popish Priests, in the Island of Cuba (1836); *Father Eustace: A Tale of the Jesuits* (1847) by Frances Trollope; *Six Hours in a Convent: or The Stolen Nuns!* (1854) by Charles Frothingham; *The Jesuit's Daughter: A Novel for Americans to Read* (1854) by Ned Buntline; *The Archbishop; or, Romanism in the United States* (1855) by Orvilla Belisle; *Overdale; or, The Story of a Pervert: A Tale for the Times* (1869) by Emma Jane Worboise. How did such narratives, with their eighteenth-century titles and seventeenth-century bigotry, come to be written and read in the nineteenth century? And there were many more, some obscure but others – like Maria Monk's *Awful Disclosures of the Hotel Dieu Nunnery* (1836) and Charles Kingsley's *Westward, Ho!* (1855) – wildly and widely popular. If these tales were to be believed (and any number of them were), across the United States and Great Britain and throughout the nineteenth century, women were being kidnapped from confessionals, imprisoned and raped in convents; Inquisitors continued to maintain and use hidden torture chambers; Jesuits practiced their time-honored treacheries; nuns posing as governesses corrupted Protestant children; priests hovered at deathbeds, snatching away family fortunes; Papal emissaries plotted to overthrow government power; Mother Superiors tyrannized over helpless girls, barring all parental intervention. While the belated presence of these "no-popery" narratives may seem puzzling, unlikelier still appears the readiness of writers like Sarah Josepha Hale, Charlotte Brontë, Benjamin Disraeli, and Henry James to borrow plots, characters, and imagery from the ready materials of anti-Catholic fiction.

In 1871, Harriet Beecher Stowe complained – perhaps disingenuously – that narrative fiction had become the primary genre for religious discourse: "Hath any one in our day, as in St. Paul's, a psalm, a doctrine, a tongue, a revelation, an interpretation, forthwith he wraps it up in a serial story."[1] *Anti-Catholicism and Nineteenth-Century Fiction* explores why this might be so. Why did fiction seem the appropriate form for religious controversy? Conversely, what did the images, plots, rhetoric, and characters of anti-Catholicism offer nineteenth-century novelists?

Reading widely and closely in Victorian anti-Catholic narrative makes clear that well-known stories and figures provide a narrative language for discussion and analysis of a range of cultural ideas and problems, including the roles of women, shifting definitions of masculinity, the status of marriage, education and citizenship, and literary professionalism, and, most importantly, Protestant self-critique. Stowe's metaphor is misleading, as her own example illustrates. *Uncle Tom's Cabin* powerfully moved its readership not by wrapping an intact sermon in a story but through what we might call a narrative theology. The social and political responses of Stowe's readership come about through engagement with her fiction as such: through the complex rhetorical manipulations of her narrative, the careful construction of emotional identification with its characters, the recognition of narrative conventions, the participation in plot tensions and anticipations.[2] Some anti-Catholic "novels" *are* little more than a doctrine wrapped in a fictional cover: minimally narrativized debates, designed so that the Protestant spokesperson may demonstrate (ostensibly to the other characters but actually to the patient Protestant reader) the errors of Catholic theology. Much of "Charlotte Elizabeth" (Charlotte Tonna's) fiction fits this "talking heads" description, as do books like Stephen Jenner's *Steepleton; High Church and Low Church: Being the Present Tendencies of Parties in the Church, Exhibited in the History of Frank Faithful* (1847). So, too, there are many nineteenth-century novels which include satiric depictions of a "Romish" character (Anthony Trollope's Barchester series is an obvious example). I have found more interesting those texts that make their arguments against Catholicism narratively – that is, in and through their plots and characters. Exploring what Jonathan Loesberg calls the "ideology of genre," *Anti-Catholicism and Nineteenth-Century Fiction* analyzes the plots and tropes of anti-Catholicism not as structures to be read through (as historians have too often done), but as fruitful objects of study themselves. Following Jameson, Loesberg argues for a possible congruence between the narrative structures of ideology and the generic and narrative structures of literature.[3] The formulaic conventions and formal variations of anti-Catholic fiction can be understood, then, as instances – rather than reflections – of the meaning-making that is ideology. This function is underscored when the plots and characters of anti-Catholic fiction find their ways into sermons, legal testimony, parliamentary proceedings, and newspaper reports. The narrative logics – what William Dean Howells calls the "foregone conclusion[s]" – of anti-Catholic fiction, are, as his own love story about an Italian priest and an American couple illustrates, meaningful as attempts to engage with historical circumstances, literary precedents, and a contemporary readership. I want to recover the analytic tools of formalist consideration and close reading too often missing from our contemporary criticism by showing their compatibility with – indeed, I would argue their necessity for – historical study. We cannot understand either the popularity or the uses of these narratives by ignoring the forms they take. This book therefore begins the work of describing the forms of anti-Catholic fiction, outlining standard plots like the escaped nun's tale, the priest–wife–husband triangle, the brotherhood of young men challenging an incestuous holy father's control of his daughter, and showing how these narrative structures, at various historical moments, respond to and shape the cultural, political, and legal issues of the day.

THE PROTESTANT IMAGINARY

Both Britain and America had long traditions of anti-Catholicism, but specific events revivified them in the nineteenth century.[4] One was certainly the heavy Irish immigration to England and the United States following the 1845 failure of the potato crop. A million and a half Irish emigrated during the decade, most to the United States and England. The resulting changes in both countries were marked. The Roman Catholic population of the United States burgeoned, so much so that by 1850 Catholics comprised the single largest Christian denomination in the country.[5] The Northeast, where many Catholic immigrants settled, became the primary source of American anti-Catholic literature. The shifts in the British Isles were significant as well. In 1841, 400,000 Irish-born were living in England, Wales, and Scotland; by 1861, England and Wales together counted 600,000 inhabitants born in Ireland.[6]

Powerful as anti-Irish feeling was at times in both countries, it does not fully account for – nor is it identical with – the anti-Catholicism of the period.[7] For one thing, the considerable German immigration to the United States in the second half of the century also included a substantial number of Catholics who roused nativist American suspicions. Traditional Anglo-American associations of Catholicism with Southern Europe remained strong, as evidenced by repeated representations of sinister Italian and Spanish clerics and of the corruption of the Renaissance Papacy and the horrors of the Inquisition.[8] Nor were attacks on the Catholic Church confined to the ethnicity of its congregants. A variety of events strengthened anti-Catholic sentiment in the nineteenth century: legislative changes in Britain, starting with the Catholic Emancipation Act in 1800 and including bills regarding support for Maynooth and the need for convent inspections; a series of sensational British legal cases like Metairie v. Wiseman and others, the Talbot case, Connelly v. Connelly, and Achilli v. Newman; and actions on the part of the Catholic Church, from the reinstitution of a Roman Catholic hierarchy in Britain to the sponsorship of the Leopold missionary movement in America. Significant, too, were changes within Protestantism itself, from the Tractarian and Ritualist movements within the Church of England to the growing heterogeneity of Protestant practices in both countries. Indeed, my argument is that what nineteenth-century anti-Catholic fiction tells us about are the Protestantisms of the period.

What did "Roman Catholic" mean to anti-Catholic novelists and their readerships? Roman Catholicism appears in England and America as foreign infiltration, as, variously, Irish, German, Italian, French influence. Yet anti-Catholic polemicists also simultaneously depict Catholicism as dangerous because it is a religion without a country; indeed, a religion inimical to nationhood. This threat is figured perhaps most vividly in Catherine Sinclair's appropriation of Eugene Sue's characterization of the Jesuits as the "Thugs of Christendom," an international brotherhood, sworn to secrecy and bent on world domination. Missionary activity in the American West, Rome's reestablishment of a church hierarchy in England (the so-called Papal Aggression) – activities like these confirmed Anglo-American fears that Catholic obedience to the Papacy was incompatible with either independent citizenship or loyal subjecthood. "CATHOLICS OWE NO ALLEGIANCE TO THE U. STATES," trumpets *Startling Facts for Native Americans called "Know-Nothings," or a Vivid Presentation of the Dangers to American Liberty, to be Apprehended from Foreign Influence* in 1855.[9] If Protestantism was understood as a defining aspect of "American" and "British," Catholicism was doubly dangerous, implying as it did both the immigrant's refusal to be converted from a prior nationality and membership in an anti-national organization.

This threat was given particular force by the Catholic Church's claim of authenticity – its self-identification as the unchanged and unchanging religion founded by Christ, the foundation for Catholic clerical authority and religious practices. Catholicism claimed to be, in every sense, the religion of "real presence." Protestants disputed the authenticity of Catholic belief and practices by describing Romanism as a religion of forms and surfaces: gilded decorations, ritualized behaviors, and mediated (through clergy or saints) relations with God. In contrast, Protestant religiosity was said to be distinguished by its wholeness and integrity: individual reading of the Bible and personal experience of the divine make for a religion that runs deep. Unlike Catholicism, a religion which is theatrically performed, real (Protestant) Christianity permeates the believer, makes for a genuine, homogeneous self. But the teleology of Protestant history, which linked the global march of civilization to progressive religious development, reaching its apogee in the Protestant nationalism of Britain and America meant that, as Protestants looked back at the past, they were forced to see the Catholic Church as in some sense originary. Indeed, so powerfully is the claim of Catholic priority felt that Protestant polemic assimilates the Church of Rome with Judaism. While the trajectory and meaning of this religious teleology was, of course, understood distinctly in the two nations, what was shared was the resulting defensive characterization of nineteenth-century Catholicism as anachronistic: William Sewell calls Roman Catholicism "virtually a restoration of Judaism,"[10] and the Jesuit appears repeatedly in polemical fiction as the Wandering Jew, an unregenerate, archaic figure, stubbornly clinging to the idea of an "Old Testament" patriarchal God of harsh judgment and physical punishment.[11] Catholicism is the primitive that Protestantism leaves behind: a religion of holy fathers who demanded unquestioning obedience, a cult fixated on the body, both as the site of penitential torture and as target of sensuous appeal (incense, candles, brightly colored statues). Attributing such qualities to Catholics, nineteenth-century Protestants defined by contrast, as well as buttressed, what they saw as their own more appropriately modern belief in a feminized Christ, internalized self-discipline, and evolved spirituality. Especially in America, the domestic ideal of the patriarch leading his household in prayer had given way to the mother reading the Bible with the child. Victorian Protestants replaced the Catholic image of the Virgin Mary with the figure of the Protestant mother, who serves not as mediatrix but as inculcator of norms – an inculcation that proceeds through love. Anti-Catholic writers contrast this domestic ideal with the church- and priest-centered worship of Catholics.[12] What Franchot calls "the antidomestic cultural architecture"[13] of the confessional and the convent are depicted as sites of patriarchal bodily punishment, retrograde refusals of the religious progress signaled by Protestant self-examination and a spiritualized maternal intimacy. Catholic secrecy is shown as at once attacking and substituting for Protestant privacy.

Yet what was perceived as the archaic absolute authority of the Roman Catholic Church and its clergy evoked, for some Protestants, not only a horrified retreat, but also a longing for submission. The Church of

England's status as a national church and the state orthodoxies of early America notwithstanding, Protestantism had, from its inception, emphasized the individual's unmediated relationship with God. If that tradition helps explain Protestant abhorrence of what was understood as Catholic clergy's power over parishioners, and, in turn, the Pope's ability to command absolutely, growing challenges to a hierarchical, institutionalized Protestantism in both countries suggests, in part, how such authority might appear as a felt need. These mixed emotions were fostered throughout the century by a variety of generational shifts – in theories of child-rearing and education, in workplace experiences, in mobility, in the situations of women, and in definitions of masculinity. Circulating around the image of the Catholic spaces as the site, and the Pope as the embodiment, of primitive externalized authority are nineteenth-century questions about individual autonomy. The depictions of the confessional by Hawthorne, Brontë, and James; the violent responses to the jurisdictions claimed by Archbishop John Hughes of New York and Cardinal Wiseman in England at mid-century; the extreme reactions to the papal declaration of infallibility in later decades all point to a regressive "attraction of repulsion."[14] James Parton, in a two-part article in the 1868 *Atlantic Monthly* on "Our Roman Catholic Brethren," describes Catholic's enviable "*certainty!*" Parton explains that "There is nothing they pity us so much for as the doubt and uncertainty in which they suppose many of us are living concerning fundamental articles of faith. A Catholic cannot doubt; for the instant he doubts he ceases to be a Catholic. . . . His priest is the director of his soul; he has but to obey his direction." Parton blithely predicts that Catholicism will become so Protestantized and Americanized in the United States that "we [are] all going to be Roman Catholics, then, about the year 1945."[15] For anti-Catholic writers, this is a nightmare vision, albeit one that they fear is far more imminent. Nonetheless, the "*certainty*" that lies in obedience also appears as a dangerous attraction in anti-Catholic writings. The authenticity of Catholic authority offers a possible antidote not only to potential historical illegitimacy of the Protestant Church but also to the felt inauthenticity of the nineteenth-century Protestant self. These mixed emotions surface in the lovingly detailed scenes of sexual violence endemic to the literature of anti-Catholicism, where the dynamics of recognition and authentication are played out in scenes of bodily mutilation and penitential practices. At work here, of course, is an inherited sexualized rhetoric of anti-Catholicism, its central topics (e.g., the convent as the site of sadism) and its traditional images (e.g., Rome as the Scarlet Woman).[16] Yet the catalogues of Romanism's tortures that pervade nineteenth-century anti-Catholic fiction are less expressions of an invariant psychoanalytic complex and more vehicles for the narrative analysis of contemporary cultural problems. The specific sado-masochisms of these texts, in fact, return us to the issues of obedience, autonomy, and authority central to what the Victorians saw as their rapidly and radically changing times.[17]

The nationalist religious teleology that marks Catholicism as a retrograde religion makes Catholicism Protestantism's – and thus, variously, Britain's and America's – past. Benedict Anderson describes the need to read "nationalism genealogically – as the expression of a historical condition of serial continuity,"[18] an understanding reflected in these novels' preoccupation with questions of origin, of legitimacy, of identity. Rapid demographic, legal, theological, and educational changes in Britain and America seem to have raised the old question of how Protestantism should maintain its authenticity in the face of Catholic priority with new urgency. Anti-Catholic novelists answer by telling the chronicles of Protestant America and Protestant Britain as originary family narratives, played out in inheritance plots, in stories structured by generational conflict, in the characters of missing or malevolent mothers and fathers, by depictions of incest and of triangular structures of desire. Fictions like Charles Kingsley's *Westward, Ho!* and William Sewell's *Hawkstone* position themselves as histories both national and psychological. *Hawkstone*, for example, attempts to trace the origins of religious and civil authority by telling a family narrative centered around what Sewell calls the primal sin, the sexualized rebellion against paternal authority, emblematized, he argues, by Oedipus.[19] Nativist American novelists in the 1850s depict United States history as a chronicle of sons' repeated attempts to bury and to resurrect their fathers. These historical warrants support my study's attempt, not to read through anti-Catholic fiction to psychoanalytic truth, but to think about why such stories "worked" for audiences and authors at the time and about what that work was.

Protestantism's Catholic past haunts the present in these narratives as the uncanny,[20] manifested in monsters both literal and metaphoric: the murdered and murdering father, the gang of thugs, the living dead, bloody bodies, vampires. As Homi Bhabha suggests, perhaps foremost among those "narratives and discourses that signify a sense of nationness" are those of "the *heimlich* pleasures of the hearth, the *unheimlich* terror of the space or race of the Other."[21] The enclosure of the confessional; the dungeons of the Inquisition; the Catholic realms of Canada, Cuba, and Ireland; the Spanish or Italian Jesuit; the Irish mob: all appear as familiar yet foreign presences making themselves at home in England and America.

What makes Catholics so uncannily threatening to Protestants in America and Britain is precisely the historical relationships of the two churches. Protestantism's legitimacy depends upon tracing its origins to, and differentiating itself from, Roman Catholicism. Catholics are thus what Catherine Sinclair calls "unknown relatives": at once familiar and unfamiliar, homely and foreign. Anti-Catholic literature recurrently figures the dangers of the Catholic who "passes" as Protestant: the Jesuit hidden in our midst, the spouse who leads a double (religious) life, the servant who reports family secrets to her confessor. The concept of "mimicry" proves useful in understanding nineteenth-century attitudes towards what were perceived as Catholic infiltration and corruption (dovetailing as it does with traditional Protestant accusations of Catholic superficiality and duplicity). Exemplary here is Sinclair's *Beatrice* in which Catholicism is represented as a kind of colonial counter-invasion. Polemical Protestant writers like Sinclair consistently depict all things Roman Catholic as false and partial – almost-but-not-quite-Christian: the maimed Bible that is the Breviary; the de-gendered celibate clergy – a man in a skirt and a woman shorn of her hair–; the pretty poison of illustrated children's books that secretly inculcate Romanism; the priest who substitutes himself for fathers both biological and heavenly. If the figure of the Confidence Man reflects uneasiness about identity and authenticity rampant in newly mobile, urban nineteenth-century America,[22] these reappearances of the Confidence Man's iconographic ancestor, the Jesuit, also bespeak the uncertainties of the period. Melodramas of conspiracy, as Robert Levine has shown, suit nineteenth-century writers who have a "sense of living in a culture that was unsettled and unsettling."[23] In both Britain and America, what the gaze of the mimicry man reveals, I argue, is the fissures within Protestant America and Britain themselves.

Through an oppositional logic, the Roman Catholic is presented as a ground for the national identities of America and Britain, and the American and the Briton. But what polemical writers consistently depict as the presence of Catholic influence in the Protestant home signals a dynamic that is more complex than the binary logic of a foreign Catholic "Them" versus a familiar Protestant "Us." The Catholic hegemony that Protestant polemic insistently "discovers" is belied by the very multiplicity of the Catholic groups and practices attacked: Jesuits, Carmelites, Irish immigrant families, Italian peasants, Spanish clergy, Archbishop Hughes, Cardinal Wiseman, Pope Pius IX. Similarly, the variety of Protestant identities in the period demonstrates just how limited the explanatory power of a strict system of binary opposition is in this instance. The Protestantisms that "Maria Monk," Sarah Josepha Hale, Frances Trollope, William Sewell, Ned

Plate 1   The Jesuit threat to American homes and liberties. *Stanhope Burleigh*, Helen Dhu
[Charles Edwards Lester], 1855.

Plate 2   "What, Not come into my own house." *Punch*, 1850.

Buntline, Charles Kingsley, and Robert Buchanan describe are distinct and diverse. Yet "Roman Catholic" serves as a useful construct through which they can write the religion that each sees as constitutive of national identity. In fictions written to muster and solidify the identity and unity of "their" Protestant audiences, anti-Catholic writers unwittingly reveal that, as Homi Bhabha maintains, "The 'other' is never outside or beyond us; it emerges forcefully, within cultural discourse, when we *think* we speak most intimately and indigenously 'between ourselves.'"[24]

Many Victorian parlors contained exotic art and furniture. Uneasily "folded into" the dominant culture, the foreign object at home marks "material and cultural victories" over the Other, at the same time that it (literally) opens the door to contamination by the foreign.[25] Even more threatening is the entry of the foreign subject into the home (Plates 1 and 2). Nineteenth-century fiction consistently imagines Catholicism's troubling presence in America and Britain as a family story. What should have been, from the Protestant point of view, a successive chronology – a religious and nationalized narrative of progress and modernity – is frustrated by Rome's stubborn refusal to die and be replaced. The old religion uncannily persists in the modern. And it persists as a foreign relative, a husband, a wife, a daughter, a father. Anglo-American Protestantisms are intimately and intricately imbricated with the Other against which they define themselves. The obsessive genealogies, the generational struggles, the family dramas that pervade anti-Catholic fiction bespeak Catholicism's enfoldment into the Protestant national identities of the United States and Britain. This very intimacy is what allows the efficacy of Rome and Romanism in nineteenth-century narration to extend beyond the writing of religion. The dangers and dramas of immigration and imperialism, for example, cannot be represented solely as wholly externalized attacks.

TALES OF AND FOR THE TIMES[26]

"[T]here is no better sign for the theology of the present day than its disposition to try itself by literary tests. Theology and Literature – the study of God and the study of Man – need to go hand in hand, and are only just beginning to know it."[27] Despite injunctions from nineteenth-century cultural critics like the 1856 reviewer quoted above, the novel of religious polemic has remained largely unread in the twentieth and twenty-first centuries.[28] This skeleton hidden in the closets of Anglo-American history was, in fact, an important part of the nineteenth-century making, remaking, and maintaining of both British and American national identities. In reading anti-Catholic fiction, we encounter the nation "*as it is written,*" to use Homi Bhabha's formulation – variously, locally, and changingly.[29] For, in writing anti-Catholicism, nineteenth-century authors were writing – often desperately – "Protestant," "America," and "Britain."

An important exception to this critical neglect of religious polemical fiction is Franchot's 1994 book, which established that "anti-Catholicism operated as an imaginative category of discourse through which antebellum American writers of popular and elite fictional and historical texts indirectly voiced the tensions and limitations of mainstream Protestant culture."[30] I have learned much from Franchot, and my debt to her work is strongest in Chapter 1, where I build on her discussion of Reed and Monk by analyzing how this standard plot circulates within the culture, tracing its permutations among some twenty additional such tales and moving on to look at how an elite editor and "domestic" writer made use of such sensational fiction. Thereafter the scope and trajectory of our studies diverge. I analyze British and American anti-Catholic fiction from 1830 through the turn of the century, stressing the importance of transatlantic exchange and comparison. In contrast, Franchot focuses exclusively on the United States, and her study stops with the Civil War. Nathaniel Hawthorne's complex engagement with Roman Catholicism plays a major role in her book; my analysis of antebellum American nativism explores the work of numerous less well-known writers.[31] Franchot sets her task as the tracing of "roads to Rome," that is, the paths Americans took towards conversion. My interest is in what opportunities the rhetoric and especially the forms (plots, characters, etc.) of anti-Catholic polemic provide to nineteenth-century writers of fiction and in tracing the ideologies of those forms.

Anti-Catholicism and Nineteenth-Century Fiction begins with the American antebellum escaped nun's tale and ends with British sensation novels of the seventies and eighties. Anti-Catholic literature, of course, both predates and outlasts this fifty-year span. However, before 1830, both the Catholic population in America and the resulting fictional response to it were very limited.[32] And, while gothic depictions of Romish evil were part of earlier British fiction, it is Protestant responses to the Oxford Movement that inaugurate Victorian forms of anti-Catholic narrative in the 1840s. At the end of the century, negative reactions to the homoerotic culture of Decadence certainly recognize its markedly Catholic aspects.[33] However, by the nineties, attitudes towards Catholicism had moderated somewhat. More importantly for this study, by the turn of the century, anti-Catholicism manifests itself less through distinctive fictional forms. Increasingly marginalized in mainstream Anglo-American culture, anti-Catholic rhetoric seems no longer to offer ways to depict and analyze contemporary social, political, and legal problems. I look briefly at how traces of that rhetoric surface in several turn-of-the-century fictions by way of conclusion.

An aim of this study is to reintroduce the range of nineteenth-century fiction.[34] John Sutherland's 1989 lament that "The tiny working areas of the 'canon,' the 'syllabus' and the paperbacked 'classics' are poor reflections of what the Victorian novel actually meant to Victorians" still rings true.[35] Many of the authors of the anti-Catholic novels treated in *Anti-Catholicism and Nineteenth-Century Fiction* are obscure (Charles Frothingham, William Earle Binder) or even anonymous, but some are among the most popular writers of their time – Catherine Sinclair, Frances Trollope, Ned Buntline. Others are influential cultural critics: Robert Buchanan, Eliza Lynn Linton, Sarah Josepha Hale, Charles Kingsley, William Sewell. Together, I would argue, their fictions constitute a substantial and revealing body of work.

If anti-Catholic fiction is a significant, albeit neglected body of work, it represents only partially the range of nineteenth-century attitudes towards the Catholic Church. Many Protestant reviewers and readers deplored the polemical excesses of anti-Catholic fiction. Harriet Martineau, for example, publicly criticized her friend Charlotte Brontë for going "out of her way to express a passionate hatred of Romanism" in *Villette*: "We do not exactly see the moral necessity for this (there is no artistical necessity) and we are rather sorry for it. . . ."[36] Martineau found anti-Catholic bias in *Household Words* as well and, as a result, stopped writing for Dickens's journal. Attacking the proliferation of popular stories about escaped nuns, the writer for the *Western Monthly Magazine* inveighs: "A prejudice so indomitable and so blind, could not fail, in an ingenious and enterprising land like ours, to be made the subject of pecuniary speculation; accordingly we find such works as the 'Master Key to Popery,' 'Secrets of Female Convents,' and 'Six Months in a Convent,' manufactured with a distinct view to making a profit out of this diseased state of the public mind."[37] And Catholics defended their faith against these slanders not only in pamphlets, speeches, sermons, and editorials, but in fictions as well.[38] My argument is not that every or even most Protestant readers believed that sensational nativist fictions represented Roman Catholicism with scrupulous fidelity, but that the popularity and pervasiveness of narratives of anti-Catholicism deserves attention.

Anti-Catholicism and Nineteenth-Century Fiction does demonstrate the cultural range of anti-Catholic fiction, pairing "Maria Monk" with Sarah Josepha Hale, Catherine Sinclair with Charlotte Brontë, incorporating the work of Henry James as well as "Harry Hazel ." The selectivity inevitable in such a study is also to some extent countered by the inclusion of materials issued by Harper's and Chatto and Windus as well as those "Published for the Author." In addition to their fiction-writing, a substantial number of these writers were editors and journalists in their own right: Sarah Josepha Hale edited the *Ladies Magazine* and then *Godey's Lady's Book*, Emma Jane Worboise, the *Christian World*, William Dean Howells, the *Atlantic Monthly*; Eliza Lynn Linton worked for the *Morning Chronicle* and the *Saturday Review*; Robert Buchanan was on the staff of the *Athenaeum*; Ned Buntline (Edward Zane Carroll Judson) created *Ned Buntline's Own* and George Lippard worked for the *Spirit of the Times*. Such positions point to the pervasiveness of polemical religious discourse, as well as to these writers' active participation in the lively literary marketplaces of their times. While this participation does not necessarily make their fictions more representative, it does demonstrate that books like Worboise's *Overdale* and Buntline's *The Jesuit's Daughter* are not simply the work of isolated iconoclasts.

Reintroducing new materials to our discussion of nineteenth-century fiction is one step; a second involves recognizing the generic qualities of specific anti-Catholic stories, which helps to illuminate the historical and ideological meanings of certain narrative choices in texts that we already "know." For example, readers of *The American* have long noted James's use of melodrama in that novel.[39] Chapter 6 examines *The American*, along with Benjamin Disraeli's *Lothair* and William Dean Howells's *A Foregone Conclusion*, in the context of the anti-Catholic literature from which it borrows, illuminating precisely what kind of melodrama James employs and the historical specificity of his decision to immure Claire de Cintré in the Rue de l'Enfer. Reading together a group of nativist fictions from the 1850s uncovers why a particular American incest story seemed politically and psychologically compelling at that moment.[40] Even what is perhaps the most canonical nineteenth-century anti-Catholic fiction, *Villette*, looks decidedly different when read in the context of British novels from the same decade that link Catholicism and colonialism, a reading pursued at the end of Chapter 4.[41]

This study also looks comparatively at anti-Catholic writing by men and women: William Sewell and Frances Trollope, Charles Kingsley and Catherine Sinclair, and Eliza Lynn Linton and Robert Buchanan. What Mary Poovey calls the "uneven developments" of gender can be seen in anti-Catholicism's intense engagement with the ongoing nineteenth-century cultural debate over gender definitions: in stories of escaped nuns that challenge the ideology of female spirituality; tales of incestuous priests that afford a safe venue for male generational struggle; narratives of Romish world dominance that exhibit anxiety about the mental and physical health of Victorian men. Not surprisingly, there are no fixed differences between male and female novels of anti-Catholicism. Individual works are, nonetheless, deeply marked by their authors' gendered experience and concerns. Attacking the Tractarian influence at Oxford, Sewell idealizes a celibate college of men; Trollope narrates a story of female self-education. Kingsley tells a story of male adventure and Sinclair a narrative of female domesticity, yet their similar portraits of Imperial Motherhood, as well as their anxious descriptions of invasion and counter-invasion, demonstrate the interpenetration of these genres, thus reinforcing the work of critics like Amy Kaplan and others, who have questioned the historicity of separate, gendered fictional forms.[42] Linton and Buchanan, public opponents on the woman question, attack Ritualism with remarkably similar plots yet decidedly different gender judgments.

Perhaps most unusually, *Anti-Catholicism and Nineteenth-Century Fiction* reads British and American fictions next to one another. Transnational work on the literature of the Americas, under the impetus of multiculturalism, is currently transforming and expanding American Studies, just as postcolonial theory and criticism are altering the contours of Victorian Studies.[43] Yet despite provocative arguments by critics like Nancy

Armstrong and Leonard Tennenhouse, Lawrence Buell, Paul Giles, and Robert Weisbuch, basic work on Anglo-American relations remains to be done.[44] The structure of contemporary literary studies and of English departments remains such that nineteenth-century novels are rarely read in their historical, transatlantic context. *Anti-Catholicism and Nineteenth-Century Fiction* joins the still-small body of work that recognizes the transatlantic nature of nineteenth-century literary culture. Giles and Weisbuch have provided powerful analyses of how canonical American authors resisted and reinvented British literary models. I emphasize a different dynamic – uncovering an important set of *shared* cultural assumptions and literary techniques in the work of a wide variety of popular writers.[45] Understanding such sharing is particularly important to the study of the novel, given how many Americans read British and British read American fiction in the nineteenth century, an exchange promoted by the lack of international copyright law. This Anglo-American reading audience is described in the overseas sales figures for works ranging from Maria Monk's 1836 *Awful Disclosures* to Benjamin Disraeli's 1870 *Lothair*.[46] A common British and American Protestant literary culture is vividly present in the literal intertextuality of anti-Catholic writing, its quotations, parodies, excerpts, allusions, and cross-references. The heritage of Protestant prejudice against Roman Catholicism, an Anglo-American tradition of no-popery, manifests itself multiply and diversely in these texts.[47]

Reading anti-Catholic fiction transnationally also helps highlight its respective nationalist characters. The stock figures of the Jesuit, the nun, the Irish working man, and the elite papist youth, are deployed variously in the creative maintenance of American and British identities, identities at once distinct and interdependent. For example, the Tractarians' presence at Oxford in the first half of the century raises Protestant fears about the next generation of male leadership in Britain. But antebellum American schooling is such that the fictional focus is on how Catholicized education imperils wealthy young *women*. So, too, the political and cultural implications of Catholic immigration and conversion differ for American citizens and British subjects. Although Roman Catholicism appears in nineteenth-century Protestant fiction as an ancient cult, the Roman Catholics who are attacked in these nineteenth-century fictions are what we might call new Catholics. British writers characterize hereditary Catholics, especially those of the upper classes, as nonthreatening. These "Old Catholics" are depicted as recognizably "English" in their sincere (if mistaken) religious belief – moderate and reticent in their practices, having no taste for the "Romish" practices and vigorous proselytizing characteristic of enthusiastic Victorian converts. Writers like William Sewell and Catherine Sinclair also describe Roman Catholicism as part of the problem of Irish immigration. However, the main focus for these two writers – and for British anti-Catholic fiction in general – is on the Romanizing of the Church of England, first with the Catholicizing reforms that John Henry Newman and William Pusey attempted to institute at Oxford in the forties, later with the changes in ritual, dress, and practices advocated by the so-called Ritualists beginning in the sixties. This is not merely the perception that the Church of England was becoming more Romanist in practices. Rather, the greater fear is that those within the English Church were in fact secret Roman Catholics bent on handing over sacerdotal and political power, as well as British wealth, to the Vatican.

The "new" Catholics that obsess American writers, on the other hand, are convent-educated Protestant girls and, increasingly as the century progresses, Irish and German immigrants. While a female-centered domesticity was a powerful force in both British and American Victorian cultures, the Church of England was never "feminized" to the extent that mainstream American Protestantism was. Thus, although escaped nun's tales are written in both Britain and America, American versions of the story are more numerous and successful, and even more ominous. Similarly, while British and American Protestants share the belief that Irish Catholic priests dictate their parishioners' votes, the relative newness and openness of the American political system and of the franchise in particular make Catholic votes appear more dangerous to New World democracy. The British see the Vatican's reestablishment of a Church hierarchy in 1850 as an affront to Victoria's sovereignty. Americans view the establishment of the Leopold Association (essentially a Vienna-based missionary society founded to strengthen Catholicism in the western United States) as an outright invasion. The opening of the American West brought with it the threat of widespread land-ownership by Catholics. While the British fear the infiltration of Oxford and the "perversion" of its students, Americans see themselves as battling a new parochial school system that will prevent the socialization of young immigrants into American (and implicitly Protestant) citizenship.

These historically and nationally distinct uses of standard narrative formulae make for certain methodological and organizational problems in writing about anti-Catholicism. Like anti-Semitism, anti-Catholicism seems to be at once timeless and historically specific. A rise in immigration, a Vatican decree, the liberalization of franchise requirements, the launching of a school reform program – each can evoke centuries-old images of lascivious priests, wanton nuns, Jesuit spies, and Inquisitorial prisons. The critical dilemma is how to address the variety and complexity of this literature, without rehearsing the same scenarios over and over. My solution is to focus on specific aspects of anti-Catholicism in separate chapters, basing my choices on the stresses or emphases created by particular historical and cultural events. For example, the Oxford Movement in the 1840s arouses British fears that Romanist priests are miseducating the elite male youth of England; accordingly my chapter on the Tractarians focuses on Protestant representations of the false Catholic father who destroys his sons. Such representations are not exclusively either British or anti-Tractarian – they surface throughout anti-Catholic literature – but national perception of the situation at Oxford makes them dominant in the fiction of the forties.

Indeed, I want to argue that one of the reasons for the popularity of anti-Catholic narratives is that they come to serve not merely as a means of attacking Rome, but as a flexible medium of cultural critique. I have already suggested that what anti-Catholic writers are doing is writing – that is, defining, defending, and criticizing – Protestant America and Britain. Anti-Catholic narratives can serve this purpose in this period in part because they are, by the nineteenth century, already traditional to Protestant cultures. Using plots and characters well known to their audiences, these writers can build on an assured set of recognitions, reactions, and readerly anticipations. The cultural shorthand[48] of anti-Catholic stereotypes and narrative structures provide nineteenth-century writers with a means of depicting and discussing the changes and problems of the day, ranging from the controversy over vivisection to the professionalization of American letters.

Anti-Catholicism and Nineteenth-Century Fiction thus studies local and diverse instances of anti-Catholic fiction. Despite shared tropes, characters, and actions, these texts cannot be understood as examples of some single overarching narrative. Even when a standard anti-Catholic plot is recycled in a Victorian novel, its function and meaning are not standardized. The narrative structures of anti-Catholicism prove malleable, adaptable to particular circumstances. Though we may recognize immediately the stealthy figure of the Jesuit, we cannot predict in advance how and why he will be deployed in response to an aggressive diplomatic move by the Vatican, a wave of immigration into America, or a set of changes in the marriage laws. While the need to counter Catholic claims that Protestantism was merely a loose conglomerate of individuals, with loyalty to neither a Church hierarchy nor history, means that writers of anti-Catholic literature tend to defensively represent their own religion as homogeneous and unchanging, the Protestant Imaginary explored in this study is, in fact, polyphonous, historicized, and evolving. Lauren Berlant uses the term "national fantasy" to characterize "how national culture becomes local – through the images, narratives, monuments, and sites that circulate through personal/collective consciousness."[49] In studying Anglo-American anti-Catholic fiction over six decades of the nineteenth century, I seek to explore and compare an important and pervasive structure functional in the fantasies of two nations.

ANTI-CATHOLICISM AND NINETEENTH-CENTURY FICTION

Chapter 1, "Awful disclosures: the escaped nun's tale," examines the "true" stories of American women trapped in convents. The evidence given by these "renegade Catholics" is intertextual, incorporating first-person testimony, affidavits, maps, floor plans, letters of support, and newspaper extracts. Treating the escaped nun's tale as a genre, my discussion moves beyond the two most famous narratives – Rebecca Reed's *Six Months in a Convent* (1835) and Maria Monk's *Awful Disclosures of the Hotel Dieu Nunnery of Montreal* (1836) – to discuss over a dozen examples, including *Rosamond* (1836) by Rosamond Culbertson, *The American Nun* (1836) by Lucinda Larned, *The Nun of St. Ursula* (1845) by Harry Hazel (Justin Jones), *Six Hours in a Convent* (1854) by Charles Frothingham, and *The Escaped Nun* (1855). So popular and pervasive was the escaped nun's tale that it even inspired parodies like *The Chronicles of Mount Benedict* by "Mary Magdalen" (Norwood Damon) (Plate 3) and the anonymously authored *Six Months in a House of Correction, or, the Narrative of Dorah Mahony, Who Was Under the Influence of the Protestants About a Year . . .* , which, in their comic exaggerations, outline vividly the contours and characteristics of the genre.

Calling upon images and ideals of domesticity throughout, condemning Romanism as the religion of antidomesticity,[50] this polemical narrative structure nonetheless throws into doubt nineteenth-century assumptions about the natural superiority of female spirituality. In addition to its manifest anti-Catholic function, the escaped nun's tale represents a dissent from the contemporary myth of the feminization of American religion.

From the examination of multiple narratives as a group the chapter then turns to the close reading of a text by an American writer of considerable prestige and power, Sarah Josepha Hale's domesticated version of the escaped nun's tale, "The Catholic Convert." Publishing "The Catholic Convert" in *Traits of American Life* (1835), Hale, long-time editor of *Godey's Ladies Book* (1837–77) and author of the feminist world history, *Woman's*

THE

CHRONICLES OF MOUNT BENEDICT.

A TALE OF THE URSULINE CONVENT.

THE QUASI PRODUCTION OF

MARY MAGDALEN.

[By Norwood Damon]

" But that I am forbid
To tell the secrets of my prison house,
I could a tale unfold, whose lightest word
Would harrow up thy soul ; freeze thy young blood ;
Make thy two eyes, like stars, start from their spheres ;
Thy knotted and combined locks, to part,
Like quills upon the fretful porcupine !
But this eternal blazon must not be
To ears of flesh and blood !"—SHAKSPEARE.

Vide page 154

BOSTON:

PRINTED FOR THE PUBLISHER.

1837.

Plate 3   Title page of *The Chronicles of Mount Benedict*, Norwood Damon [Mary Magdalen], 1837.

Record (1853), employs the escaped nun's narrative not to attack women's competency but to support her ongoing efforts in women's education. Hale's story demonstrates as well how domestic fiction can be grounded in the sensationalism against which it defines itself, echoing recent critical interrogations of the gender/genre divide that has at once enriched and limited studies of American fiction. Hale's story of the redeeming power of conjugal Protestant love – her attempts to refine and enculturate her audience into the ways of the republican family – effects its purpose in part by calling up the tropes and figures of anti-Catholicism.

While Chapter 1 details the making of a single genre in the escaped nun's tale, Chapter 2 focuses instead on how two well-known and widely read writers of the 1840s treat fictionally a British national crisis. "The dead father and the rule of religion: the Oxford Movement" reads William Sewell's *Hawkstone, a Tale of and for England in 184-* (1845) and Frances Trollope's *Father Eustace: A Tale of the Jesuits* (1847). Comparing these novels alerts us to the heterogeneity of British Protestantism and illustrates how anti-Catholic discourse can be used to a variety of ideological ends. Both writers see the "Romanization" of the Church of England by the Oxford Movement as perverting the education of Britain's male elite and thus the nation's future, and, like Hale, Sewell and Trollope propose Protestant pedagogy as the solution to Tractarianism's Catholic threat. Yet their programs divide along gender lines. Sewell plots a system of male colleges, the fictional counterpart to his *Christian Politics* (1848) and to his educational experiments as rector of St. Columba's and Radley public boys' schools. Trollope outlines female lessons in independence, describing in loving detail the mother–daughter tutorial relationship – the hallmark of sentimental fiction – so lacking in escaped nun's stories. Both Sewell's and Trollope's novels harbor disguised Jesuits plotting to steal inheritances, inquisitorial punishments, and secret Catholic spies. Yet Sewell, a High Anglican and former Tractarian, argues for Christian Paternalism and male collegiality based in obedience, while Trollope's Broad Church suspicion of popery, as well as her celebration of individual autonomy, cause this prolific woman writer to fantasize not only a "self-supporting" female but the possibility of female self-generation.

The escaped nun's tale has as its backdrop the ruin of a Protestant family. Sewell's and Trollope's narratives foreground families, working with what Catherine Gallagher and others have shown to be a structure standard to Victorian social analysis: the analogy between the domestic and the national. Telling stories of British families rent and perverted by Catholicism, they warn against Romanism's threat to Britain. The shadow of John

Henry Newman inhabits these texts, as a force destructive of British youth, but haunting the Protestant imaginary as well are its Catholic origins, which threaten to return as the figure of archaic patriarchal authority.

Chapter 3, "The foreign father and the sons of the sires: nativist novels of the 1850s," describes a second subgenre of American anti-Catholic fiction, analyzing a group of Know-Nothing novels by popular writers like Orvilla Belisle, Ned Buntline (Edward Zane Carroll Judson), and George Lippard.[51] While each of these fictions tells a remarkably similar story of father–daughter incest, they do not focus on the young woman as victim. Rather, like Sewell's and Trollope's work, they center around a male generational contest. The anti-Tractarian novels deal primarily with matters of elite education, while the American nativist novels are concerned with immigration and with the coming-of-age problems faced by middle- and especially working-class American males in the 1850s. American nativist novels frame the problem of Catholicism in explicitly and immediately political terms.

What fuels the plots of these sensational novels is a genealogical logic and, with it, competing Catholic and Protestant versions of history. The traditional figure of the grasping Catholic priest, hovering over the deathbeds of the rich, is given new life in the complex inheritance plots of these 1850s nativist novels. In dispute are not so much financial rewards as both the origins and the legacy of American citizenship and rights. Threatening that legacy are two sorts of Catholic clergy: the Irish immigrant priest, personified for American Protestants as Archbishop John Hughes of New York, and the sophisticated Jesuit from Southern Europe – the original Confidence Man. The primal father whom Sewell describes as Protestantism's repressed origin is also unexpectedly historicized here in the person of Alexander Borgia.

Uniting against these holy fathers – the trope here literalized in the incest plot – are nativist fraternal organizations, for example, the Order of United Americans, the United American Mechanics, and the "B'hoys" of New York's Thirteenth District Firehouse. As historians of the period like Friedman, George Forgie, and Michael Rogin have shown, the sons of those who fought in the Revolution experienced a troubled adulthood in this decade, struggling to reconcile loyalty to Washington and his fellows with their own identity as American men. The incest plots of these nativist novels play out that struggle, showing fraternal brotherhood united in their contest with the fathers over young women, at the same time confronting pressing public issues like public schooling, voting rights, land-ownership, and citizenship requirements.

The catalyst for incest plots of American nativist novels is the mother's absence, which destabilizes the Catholic family, opening a space for the father's desire for the daughter. The mothers who are missing from the American novels of the fifties are, however, central to two important British anti-Catholic novels from the same decade, explored in Chapter 4, "Mariolatry, imperial motherhood, and manhood." Pius IX's so-called Papal Aggression (the 1850 reinstitution of a Roman Catholic hierarchy in Britain) coupled with his declaration of the Immaculate Conception as dogma prompt Charles Kingsley in 1855 and Catherine Sinclair in 1852 to write novels that, like their American nativist counterparts, center around brotherhoods. But the brotherhoods described in these British novels are united less by antagonisms or loyalties to fathers and more by their allegiances to mature holy women. Men and nations are defined in *Westward, Ho!* and *Beatrice* by the women they worship. Pius IX's elevation of Mary via the dogma of the Immaculate Conception was understood as prefatory to his declaration of his own infallibility – the woman screening the man's bid for power. Kingsley and Sinclair dissent from this Mariolatry by reciting a counter-litany in praise of British imperial motherhood. These idealized British mothers serve, in turn, as representatives for Victoria, mother of her peoples.

Written during what Brantlinger calls the "Noon" of British imperialism, these two fictions represent foreign brotherhoods as rival colonial forces. Specifically, Kingsley, enraged by Britain's blundering in the Crimean War, recalls to his readership the imperial work of the English worthies of the sixteenth century. The outward colonizing movement of *Westward, Ho!* is countered by *Beatrice*'s depiction of what Deirdre David has described as colonial "counter-invasion." Sinclair figures Catholic immigration into Britain as an invasion of Scotland by Thugs – the nightmare image of the deadly colonial subject depicted in the numerous "Thug narratives" that circulated at mid-century. Further, both Kingsley and Sinclair suggest that the Catholic threat lies not only in outside forces but also within the British Isles themselves. Kingsley diagnoses the hysterical, twisted foreign sexuality of sixteenth-century Jesuitism as the dominating tendency of Victorian British culture and offers his hero Amyas Leigh as an embodiment of the native-born "muscular Christianity" that he prescribes as the antidote. And Sinclair, who subtitles her novel, "The Unknown Relative," describes Catholicism as a foreign virus that finds in Britons a welcoming host. British attraction to the physical tortures of Catholicism signals the lurking primitivism that Protestantism has never fully eradicated.

Chapter 4 ends by looking both back across the Atlantic and, as it were, upwards, to a more canonical fiction, enacting, in miniature, the strategy of my study as a whole. Kingsley's and Sinclair's concerns about the boundaries of both the nation and national character are paralleled not only by sensational American nativist novels about brotherhoods, but also by an historical novel focused on the feminine: Augusta Evans's 1855 *Inez: A Tale of the Alamo*. So, too, the affinity of what is today the best-known anti-Catholic novel of the fifties, Charlotte Brontë's *Villette* with works like *Westward, Ho!* and *Beatrice* furthers our understanding of how that colonialism informs Brontë's work.[52]

Chapter 5, "Under Which Lord? Ritualism, marriage, and the law," investigates the centrality of marriage, and in particular of married women, in the plots of anti-Catholic sensation novels published from the 1860s through the early 1880s. As Mary Poovey's and Mary Shanley's work on Victorian marriage reform has demonstrated, the married woman is situated at a site of – and serves as a term of analysis for – cultural tension and contradiction. Frederick William Robinson's *High Church* (1860), Charles Reade's *Griffith Gaunt; or, Jealousy* (1866), Emma Jane Worboise's *Overdale; or, The Story of a Pervert: A Tale for the Times* (1869), Eliza Lynn Linton's *Under Which Lord?* (1879), and Robert Buchanan's *Foxglove Manor* (1884) are all attacks on the Ritualist movement in the Church of England, characterizing Ritualism as a Romanizing threat to the British way of life and worship. The by-now familiar trope of the family as nation is here focused specifically on marriage itself as representative of Britain. That symbolic union is menaced by the confessor's intrusion. The confessional, as Susan Bernstein has suggested, appears in Victorian fictions as a rival to the marriage bed. In these sensation novels, the marriage triangle of priest–wife–husband serves as a vehicle for discussion of issues as seemingly disparate as the newly declared dogma of papal infallibility, the ongoing reformation of the British marriage laws, and the contemporary controversy over scientific vivisection.

The example of the anti-Ritualist novel thus illustrates not only the flexible utility of anti-Catholic rhetoric and plots, but also how religious controversy is never experienced as discrete from other issues of the day. This cultural ecology allows a range of apparently diverse issues to become grafted onto the familiar structures of anti-Catholicism. Looking at how religious polemic functions in examples such as these allows us to overcome the relative critical isolation of scholarship on nineteenth-century church history. Disputes over religious practices and church governance were not, as these novels vividly illustrate, confined within church walls.

Robinson, Reade, and the others frame their fictional discussions of Ritualism, dogma, marriage, and science within a specifically legal framework. This is not surprising, since so much of the battle over Ritualism was waged in the courts. What is striking is the way in which

Ritualism – perceived as Roman Catholicism in disguise – provides an occasion for the fictional exploration of the role of law in not only the religious but also the marital and medical lives of British subjects.[53] Questions of privacy, authority, and regulation are raised repeatedly in fictional depictions of the priest in the confessional, the scientist in the lab, and the husband in the home: are these private spaces or arenas subject to public regulation?

British sensation novels are appropriate vehicles for such discussions since they comprise a genre in which, as both nineteenth-century commentators and twentieth-century critics note, the gothic is made private and familial. (While the sensation novel's ties to its gothic predecessors have long been recognized, anti-Catholicism's part in that heritage has gone largely unremarked.) H. L. Mansel, for example, writing in the *Quarterly Review*, describes sensationalism's insistence on "proximity" (255). The promise to reveal the "skeleton shut up in [the neighbor's] cupboard," as the Archbishop of York disdainfully put it, is common to both American and British sensationalism.[54] However, the anti-Catholic American novelists of the fifties tend to depict the dangerous plots and practices of foreign invaders, while Robinson, Reade, Worboise, Linton, and Buchanan descry a more homely threat. Although the Romanist practices of Ritualism – confession in particular – are described as un-English, what is truly dangerous in these novels is how contemporary marriage unions seem to be split from within.

The comparisons between American and British anti-Catholic fictions that structure this book are taken up directly in Chapter 6, "Black robes, white veils, and foregone conclusions: Disraeli, Howells, and James," which reads Disraeli's 1870 *Lothair* through the critical and fictional responses of William Dean Howells and Henry James.

Disraeli's wildly popular novel is based on the story of the young Marquess of Bute's conversion to Roman Catholicism. Like the anti-Tractarian writers of the forties, Disraeli warns of Catholicism's threat to the British upper classes, although his focus is less on education and more on the Vatican's appropriation of British wealth. Written during the same period as the fictional attacks on Ritualism, *Lothair* makes a very different use of anti-Catholicism. Rather than deploy Protestant audience assumptions to psychologize Ritualism's secret Romanism and to analyze privacy and marriage, Disraeli represents Catholicism as a matter of political schemes. In this, his work appears less representatively British, resembling more the externalized actions of earlier American novels than, say, Sewell's or Trollope's explorations of the psychology of belief.

Although James chastises Disraeli for not making personal religious conflict into narrative structure, his *The American* and Howells's *A Foregone Conclusion* rest on similar choices. Howells and especially James, in depicting a character who is religiously and impenetrably Other, introduce the mysterious, the unknown, the uncanny. Howells's novel is haunted by the figure of the Italian priest, James's by the image of the veiled nun.

Reading *Lothair* as a key to the ex-Prime Minister's social, literary, and political situations, James suggests possibilities for understanding his own and Howells's decisions to draw on anti-Catholic rhetoric and plots in their contemporaneous fiction. Despite their growing success at establishing themselves as professional American men of letters, both writers, at this stage in their careers, experience their positions as precarious. In turning to anti-Catholic literary precedents, all three writers revert to an anachronistic mode, a gothic inheritance. For American writers of this generation, that choice translates into an encounter with romance, a troubling genre for Howells and James, the young champions of realism.[55] Thus, these postbellum writers consistently ironize their relationship to the scenes and plots and characters of anti-Catholicism. Anti-Catholicism here again serves a generational need: like the young nativist artisans depicted by Buntline and Lippard, Howells and James associate Romanism with their male predecessors. But Howells and James do not depict the invasion of Roman Catholicism into the United States; instead, their American protagonists encounter the religion of the past in the Old World. And, unlike the nativist novelists, Howells and James are concerned less with the political and more with the literary father. In encountering the European past, Howells and James confront American literature's past: Hawthornian romance.

Writing realist novels that invoke and ironize romance, Howells and James confront and explore the vexed status of the American male writer.[56] Popular antebellum anti-Catholic stories of artisan heroes are replaced by narratives of upper-class men negotiating uneasily the changing definitions of success and failure during and after the Civil War. That negotiation takes place, in part, through encounters with what antebellum Americans saw as the religion of antimodernism.[57]

CRITICAL HISTORIES

If Catholicism was understood in the nineteenth century as antimodernist, religious polemic itself came to be regarded as retrograde by literary critics in the twentieth. Fear of religious controversy has in recent years all but banned religion from the study of history in American schools. Fear of religiousness obscured religion from our study of nineteenth-century literary history. Nina Baym has argued powerfully that modern American studies designated a proto-modern canon of nineteenth-century literature based on the belief that dissent from mainstream Protestant culture was a condition of both greatness and Americanness.[58] We have moved from regarding the religious controversies of nineteenth-century culture as retrograde, recognizing, for example, religion's role as training ground for women's activism.[59] Indeed, in the introduction to an important collection on *Religion and Cultural Studies* Susan Mizruchi identifies "the boundary line of religion and culture at the turn of the twenty-first century . . . [as] a major site of intellectual action and interaction." Nonetheless, we are still recovering from that modernist legacy. The history of British literary studies is quite different – sharing little of the American anxiety about legitimation. Yet we have only to look at the limited group of works understood as comprising the Victorian novel to understand that nineteenth-century religious fiction remains under-read.[60]

My point is not, of course, that the religiosity of nineteenth-century culture has gone unrecognized – a whole body of scholarship belies such a claim. But the heterogeneity of religious writing, its denominational and generic diversities, its pervasiveness, and its imbrication with political, legal, cultural issues, all represent fruitful areas for future study. In particular, polemical fiction offers us vivid examples of the intensity and the diversity of the ways literature functions in the formation and maintenance of national imaginaries. Nineteenth-century observers point to fiction's roles in this work. Reviewing a group of "Religious Stories" associated with the Oxford Movement in 1848, a writer for *Fraser's* claims that: "now a very extensive literature of this kind has grown up among us, exhibiting the 'movement' and the 'developement' [*sic*] in all their phases and adding largely to the materials which must be mastered by the future Church historian who would qualify himself for describing the workings of the later controversies on the mind of our generation."[61] Nineteenth-century reviewers insist that the novel of religious polemic must not be viewed as an historical epiphenomenon – the secondary "result" of theological developments – but recognized as an integral and shaping part of cultural controversy. They argue as well that the forms of religious fiction are in themselves meaningful. In studying anti-Catholic fiction in its diversity, in charting its forms, recovering its historical specificities, and uncovering its cultural functions, I have tried to read some of those meanings.

CHAPTER 1

Awful disclosures: the escaped nun's tale

Between 1835 and 1860 Protestant Americans avidly read a series of reports by renegades from an ancient secret society: the church of Rome. Women's tales of escape from Catholicism were the most numerous and most notorious of these reports; especially in the 1830s and 1850s, the runaway nun was a prominent figure in the American cultural and political imagination. As Richard Hofstader suggests, the renegade's role in establishing truth goes beyond the spy's: the renegade not only conveys evidence but also *is* evidence. Her very existence confirms and reveals Catholicism's corruption. I argue that these female renegades reveal still more, for they disclose how questions of evidence were imbricated with the woman question in nineteenth-century American culture.

My study begins, then, by recovering multiple renderings of a standard anti-Catholic narrative, tracing some of the uses to which it was put in the United States in the 1830s–1850s. To suggest the pervasiveness of this plot in the cultural imagination of the time, I introduce a large group of polemical and sensational popular stories about escaped nuns. These formulaic narratives do not, on the whole, position themselves as "literary." Some were published anonymously, others written by aspiring religious, political, and journalistic figures. Two were international bestsellers. Ray Allen Billington in the 1960s and Jenny Franchot in 1996 have done pioneering scholarship on some of these narratives, in particular on *Awful Disclosure of the Hotel Dieu Nunnery of Montreal* by Maria Monk and *Six Months in a Convent* by Rebecca Reed. I hope to build on their recovery work in order to focus on the rhetoric and structure of these narratives, reading their ideologies in their forms and tracing some of the ways they circulate within the culture. Evidence of this circulation is seen most clearly in the parodies of the escaped nun's tale, revisions that attempt to reverse the polemical purposes of the "original" anti-Catholic narratives. At the same time, these parodies – *The Chronicles of Mount Benedict* by Norwood Damon, writing as "Mary Magdalen," and the anonymous *Six Months in a House of*

Correction, or, The Narrative of Dorah Mahony Who Was Under the Influence of the Protestants About a Year . . . – with their pointedly absurd exaggerations, are useful guides to the perceived standard characteristics of the tale.

The escaped nun's story proved useful to established writers as well. To demonstrate how this standard popular form traversed literary cultures, I turn to a single story by a well-respected editor and author of the time, Sarah Josepha Hale. Nina Baym's and Nicole Tonkovich's recent work on Hale and *Godey's Lady's Book*, of which she was the long-time editor, has helped to dispel twentieth-century perceptions of her as the insignificant "lady editor" of a frivolously feminine journal. For Baym, Hale is an important American woman writer of history, overtly engaged in the political act of nation-making. Hale's primary concern is the shaping of a cultured American middle class. Yet in order to do so, I argue, she draws on sensational, lurid stories of escaped nuns, reworking these scandalous materials into the fabric of genteel manners and mores. Hale's example here illustrates both the pervasiveness of anti-Catholic narrative forms and how they can be turned to differing ideological ends.

Starting my study with the escaped nun's tale is in part a matter of simple chronology – these stories flourished beginning in the 1830s. However, mapping the historical circulation of this distinct subgenre of anti-Catholic narrative also illustrates how the ideological meanings of a standard plot and characters can shift within a specific period. The doubts that the escaped nun's tale raises about its teller reveal how anti-Catholic narrative can be read as a form of Protestant self-critique that is distinctly national. And the questions of evidence that engage such stories introduce nineteenth-century polemical discourse's authenticity. How and why do these tales position themselves as true? What is the status of their female tellers? Are they only posing as trustworthy, miming the role of the real (i.e., Protestant) American woman? If they are genuine, how can they have been Catholic? The matters of gender and religious authenticity raised by the escaped nun's tale prove fundamental to the intertwined – and contested – histories of Protestantism and nationalism.

THE RENEGADE AS WITNESS

What made stories about escaped nuns so popular? Anti-Catholicism was widespread during the antebellum period in which escaped nuns' narratives proliferated. Fears that increasing immigration and a growing Roman Catholic population were threatening America's Protestant national identity fostered the formation of nativist groups in the 1830s and of the Know-Nothing party in the 1850s.[1] Protestant newspapers were, as Ray Allen Billington states, "with but few exceptions . . . given over" to anti-Catholic literature – primers, children's stories, travel books, novels, plays, verse, histories, gift books, almanacs, pamphlets, and sermons.[2] In *Confidence Men and Painted Women* Karen Halttunen shows how the weakening of family authority and of social deference that accompanied the shift from rural stability to urban mobility gave rise to cultural apprehensions about origins, authenticity, and sincerity. Those apprehensions were at work in Protestant suspicions about the secret society of Roman Catholics, as well as in uneasiness with the woman who was Catholicism's most notorious representative – the escaped nun.[3] So, too, the rise of Jacksonian democracy and the birth of mass culture guaranteed an audience for these anti-Catholic tales.[4] Horace Mann's argument that only public education could undo the work of Catholic families and parish schools and remake delinquent youths into law-abiding American citizens might seem to suggest that fears about Irish and German immigration are the ultimate source of these stories, which center on attempts to escape from institutions of (mis)education.[5] Certainly, most escaped nun's tales represent Catholic immigrants as contemptibly ignorant.[6] This range of political and cultural forces overdetermined the popularity of these narratives. But none of these factors explains why nunneries and nuns were the specific site of such high cultural anxiety. The protagonists of these stories are not confidence men or painted women or truant Irish boys or even vulgar immigrant girls but young Protestant women. Franchot maintains that convent narratives "voice the pressures of an emergent middle-class Protestant domesticity"; I argue that the evidentiary textures of these anti-Catholic texts reveal how those pressures are articulated in the figure of the Protestant girl.[7] Stories attacking Roman Catholicism serve also as a medium for Protestant self-fashioning and self-questioning.

While some escaped nun's tales were published locally, others were issued by mainstream publishers like Van Nostrand and Dwight, D. Appleton, and Harper and Brothers. Maria Monk's *Awful Disclosures* (1836) was by all definitions a bestseller: 20,000 copies sold within a few weeks, 300,000 by 1860. Rebecca Theresa Reed's *Six Months in a Convent* (1835) sold 10,000 copies in the first week and an estimated 200,000 within a month. When Rosamond Culbertson's *Rosamond* (1836) was published in book form after its serial run, a second edition had to be issued within weeks. The publishers of Charles Frothingham's *Convent's Doom* (1854) claim to have sold 40,000 copies in ten days. Frothingham's *Six Hours in a Convent* (1854) went through eight editions in a year, and there were thirty-one editions of Isaac Kelso's *Danger in the Dark* (1854) within the same period.[8]

Without question, these narratives represent an attempt by American Protestantism to combat Roman Catholicism's influence. Yet this general anti-Catholic purpose does not fully account for the fascination with the figure of the escaped nun or for the intricate construction and corroboration of her testimony. At the historical moment when American women were shaping Protestantism in their own image,[9] these publications called the testimony of the religious woman into doubt.

To her Protestant readers, the escaped nun simultaneously represented authenticity and unreliability: they knew what to expect from a woman who had been in a Catholic convent. While the escaped nun's story cannot claim the central place in nineteenth-century American culture that "woman's fiction" can,[10] it nonetheless constitutes an alternative plot of some importance. For example, George Bourne's *Lorette* (1833), the book that David S. Reynolds sees as the "prototype" of convent exposés,[11] shares Frank Luther Mott's list of "Better Sellers"[12] with Catherine Sedgwick's *Hope Leslie* and Susan Warner's *Queechy*, domestic novels that critics have recently made standard texts in studies of nineteenth-century American culture. The escaped nun echoes the emphasis mainstream writers of this period placed on women's spirituality. Yet her confirmation of this cultural dogma is narratologically structured to reveal an undercurrent of dissent. The multiple voices and forms and the visual, as well as verbal, rhetoric that the telling of the escaped nun's story entails work to destabilize the feminine spiritual, religious, and moral authority that which the domestic novel instantiates.

The very existence of the female renegade testifies to the awfulness of Romanism because who she is and what has happened to her tell her audience what Catholicism is. As Robert Levine suggests, "Lifting the holy veil of the unholy church, the first-person narrators of these texts . . . offered a restless reading public an intensely captivating experience with conspiracy."[13] The renegade nun is a victim of and a witness to popery's crimes. Yet perhaps, having chosen to enter the convent and take vows, she is also a perpetrator. The escaped nun attempts to bring the Church of Rome to judgment, but her story and her self end up on trial. Samuel B. Smith, a leading speaker for the New York Protestant Association and editor of the anti-Catholic newspaper *The Downfall of Babylon, or the Triumph of Truth Over Popery*, claims in his annotations to one escaped nun's narrative that "with all this mass of positive, circumstantial, and presumptive evidence, there is not a jury in the world who would not pass the verdict, *guilty,* against the Reverent culprits, who, in this Narrative, are brought before the bar of public opinion."[14] However, his own interventions in the narrative distinctly resemble advocacy for the defense – and the person he defends is the woman who reports the crime. As *Rosamond*'s publishers argue,

Our criminal courts allow in evidence a witness to criminate associates in crime under open promise of pardon to himself. And why should we turn a deaf ear to the evidence of one, testifying without any conceivable motive but the good of others, under no influence but that of truth – under pressure of no circumstances but such as are calculated to give the greater weight to her evidence?[15]

The woman's circumstances, motive, and criminality, must all be addressed. Since she constitutes evidence, the renegade must be subjected to examination and interrogation. Reading her narrative means glossing her silences and elisions and testing her authenticity, as well as attending to her more deliberate disclosures.

The escaped nun's story is a familiar one in the annals of anti-Catholicism, not only because nineteenth-century American culture was saturated with anti-Catholic materials but also because the story draws on older traditions: the gothic novel, American captivity narratives, and the literatures of British antipopery and French and Spanish anti-clericalism. The characteristics and contours of the escaped nun's tale are well defined: The narrative typically begins by describing how unsuspecting wealthy female Protestant students are enticed by beautiful music, lofty sentiments, charming rituals, and gorgeous decorations in Catholic convent schools. Often a priest (usually a Jesuit) obtains power over a girl through the confessional, eliciting her secrets, violating her innocence, perverting her emotions. Sometimes this leads to a kidnapping, in which the protagonist is bundled into a carriage in the dead of night and taken secretly to an unknown destination, which turns out to be a convent. Alternatively, girls educated in convent schools are lured into taking vows by being told that they can gain full access to the wonderful mysteries of convent life only by becoming nuns. This promise is borne out, since the young woman literally enters new areas of the convent once she takes vows. However, in the secret inner space of Catholicism, she finds not greater beauty and holiness, but an ugly life of austerity and deprivation. The refined pursuits of the upper-class young lady are replaced with mindless, repetitive devotions and demeaning physical labor. Under the guise of penance, the new nun is regularly subjected to physical and mental tortures ranging from minor penalties (being forced to lick the ground in the form of a cross is a favorite example) to more horrific punishments, like solitary confinement, starvation, and even murder. All communication with the outside world is cut off: letters are destroyed, visitors denied, false communications issued in the protagonist's name. Indeed, if those who love her manage to track the young woman down, the Mother Superior of the convent denies that she is present, sometimes claiming that she has died. Her privacy is systematically violated: captors invade her room, eavesdrop on her conversations, spy on her actions, and assault her person. Inmates are forcibly imprisoned in the convent. Secrecy is vital because convents amass wealth (wrested from those who become nuns) and provide a training ground for spies and teachers of Catholic propaganda, activities essential to Rome's goal of conquering the United States. If nuns are allowed to leave and tell their stories, Americans will abolish convents, and Rome's plot will fail. Therefore daring clandestine escape offers the only hope of release.

But, nuns must also be prevented from escaping because convents are priests' brothels.[16] Priests can enter them secretly, at any time of day or night, by means of concealed entrances and underground passages. The female inmates of the convent are either lascivious wantons or wretched victims of sexual and physical abuse. Those who refuse the priests' attentions are punished and, like the infants born as a result of priests' and nuns' illicit relations, eventually murdered. In the passages and rooms beneath the convent, dreadful penances are exacted, recalcitrant nuns imprisoned, and bodies disposed of (traces of lime mark the scenes of these latter crimes). In several versions of the escaped nun's tale, the protagonist becomes the auditor or reader of other nuns' sad stories of entrapment and torture. The gothic inheritance of the anti-Catholic novel is clearly at work in these multiple, framed narratives. As readers follow the heroine through the convent's maze of secret chambers and cells, they are in a narrative *mise en abyme*, enmeshed in the density, intricacy, and pervasiveness of popery's plots. For example, in *The Escaped Nun*, a compilation of nuns' stories, the author's personal history is interrupted for chapters at a time by the "History of the Orphan Nun of Capri" and the "Confessions of a Sister of Charity," both of which incorporate several individual narratives. These interruptions only add to the discontinuity and disorganization of the heroine's story, which bespeak the harried condition of Catholicism's victim, as well as her ingenuousness. The implication is that this is not a shameless woman's calculated bid for publicity and financial gain, but the work of a retiring female, shattered by her immurement in the convent.

The best-known escaped nun's narratives were Reed's *Six Months in a Convent* and Monk's *Awful Disclosures*, both of which had hundreds of thousands of American readers. The Charlestown burning in the first[17] and the outrageous story in the second helped make these two versions of the escaped nun's tale notorious. The Ursuline convent on Mount Benedict in Charlestown housed what was essentially a fashionable school for wealthy Protestant girls – in fact, only one-eighth of the students were Catholic.[18] Reed was an inmate of the convent and a teacher in the school for less than six months in 1831–32 before fleeing.[19] In 1834, Elizabeth Harrison also escaped, but she returned after a few days. Rumors in the *Mercantile Journal* and elsewhere implied that she had been taken back to the convent against her will. On August 10, Lyman Beecher, perhaps the most prominent of the American Protestant ministers at war with Rome, preached three provocative anti-Catholic sermons in three different churches.[20] On the night of August 11, 1834, the convent was burned to the ground by a mob. The Catholic population and press blamed Reed for having inflamed local Protestants with misrepresentations of her convent experiences. Her supporters countered in 1835 by publishing her narrative: "to vindicate her from unjust and unmanly aspersions which some friends of the Convent have indulged in toward her, and especially to advance the cause of truth."[21] The Catholic clergy, as well as the Protestant parents who had placed their daughters in the Ursuline school, responded to Reed's narrative, claiming the same objectives – vindicating beleaguered females and establishing truth.[22]

Awful Disclosures, an international bestseller, told the horrific tale of Monk's experiences at and escape from the Hotel Dieu in Montreal. According to Billington,[23] the narrative was actually the work of two anti-Catholic ministers, J. J. Slocum and George Bourne, who insisted they had written at Monk's dictation. In addition to "her" pronouncements in print, Monk appeared on public platforms, where she was joined by yet another escaped nun, Saint Francis Patrick, who claimed to have been a fellow inmate at the Hotel Dieu. Monk was supported by the Protestant Reformation Society and the *American Protestant Vindicator* newspaper, at least until two inspections of the Hotel Dieu Nunnery failed to substantiate any of her claims.

Reed's and Monk's first-person accounts of the horrors of convent life raised an immediate and sustained outcry. That the narratives' truth was contested underscores their political and cultural power: why else would high church officials like Bishop Fenwick of Boston have bothered to dispute their claims repeatedly? Public debate regarding the stories' veracity and the authors' identity and character took place not only in the religious press and pulpits, but also within and by means of the genre of the escaped nun's narrative. *Six Months* and *Awful Disclosures* spawned a group of answering fictions, some disputing, others supporting Reed's and Monk's claims to factuality. Examples include *Six Months in a House of Correction* (1835); Theodore Dwight's *Open Convents* (1836); Lucinda Martin Larned's *The American Nun* (1836); Mary Magdalen's (Norwood Damon) *The Chronicles of Mount Benedict* (1837); Harry Hazel's (Justin Jones) *The Nun of St. Ursula* (1845); Thomas Ford Caldicott's *Hannah Corcoran* (1853); Frothingham's, *Six Hours in a Convent* (1854), *The Convent's Doom* (1854), and *The Haunted Convent* (1854); and Lizzie St. John Eckel Harper's *Maria Monk's Daughter* (1874). Other fictions, not set at Mount Benedict or the Hotel Dieu, engage Reed's and Monk's claims less directly, but participate nonetheless in the cultural discourse of and on the escaped nun's tale and illustrate the ways in which this narrative traversed the culture. The 1833 *Lorette*, predating Reed's narrative by two years, was written by the same Bourne who aided Monk. Here I am less concerned with priority and more with the dialogue among the texts, including Culbertson's *Rosamond* (1836); Benjamin Barker's *Cecilia* (1845); Hyla's (Jane Dunbar Chaplin) *The Convent and the Manse* (1853); Josephine Bunkley's *The Testimony of an Escaped Novice* (1855); *The Escaped Nun* (1855); Kelso's *Danger in the Dark* (1855); and William Earle Binder's *Madelon Hawley* (1857) and *Viola* (1858).[24]

David Reynolds points out that, after Charlestown, "increasing emphasis was placed on the veracity of anti-Catholic" narratives.[25] As a genre, the escaped nun's narrative includes some texts that purport to be factual accounts and others that declare their status as fiction. (Of course, some "nonfictional" narratives – Monk's for example – have subsequently been proved to be hoaxes. Nonetheless, *Awful Disclosures* continued to be reprinted, read, and cited as an authentic history at least through the end of the nineteenth century.) My analysis focuses on supposedly nonfictional narratives (Reed's *Six Months in a Convent*, Monk's *Awful Disclosures*, Dwight's *Open Convents*, Culbertson's *Rosamond*, Caldicott's *Hannah Corcoran*, *The Escaped Nun*, and Eckel's *Maria Monk's Daughter*) but also relies on contemporary parodies of the escaped nun's story (*Six Months in a House of Correction* – advertised as a counter to the story told by "Miss Runaway" [Rebecca Reed] – and Mary Magdalen's *The Chronicles of Mount Benedict*), which exaggerate its characteristics and techniques. These "nonfictional" texts are significant for my analysis not because of any historically verifiable accuracy, but because of their claims to it. Indeed, these "true" accounts cannot be considered in complete isolation from their more frankly fictionalized counterparts, with which they share rhetoric, characters, plot, and structure. As Reynolds points out, Reed's and Monk's narratives both follow and set fictional precedent.[26] Indeed, in 1836 Dwight cites Monk's novelistic style as "internal evidence" of her veracity: "the story, short as it is, for simplicity and pathos is not unworthy the genius and talents of a Scott."[27] The narratives' titles foreground their participation in an intertextual conversation about the escaped nun: for example, Reed's *Six Months in a Convent* is imitated by Frothingham's *Six Hours in a Convent* and parodied by *Six Months in a House of Correction*; Reed's and Monk's narratives are deliberately invoked in the titles of Mary Magdalen's *The Chronicles of Mount Benedict*, Hazel's *The Nun of St. Ursula*, *The Escaped Nun*, and Harper's *Maria Monk's Daughter* and in the repeated use of the subtitle *A Tale of Charlestown in 1834*.

These texts anticipate challenges to the accuracy and authenticity of their evidence in similar ways. All the narratives, "fictional" and "nonfictional" alike, claim to be true. Further, in attempting to prove their own veracity, they rely on a common standard of evidence. Escaped nun's tales are regularly supplemented by documents authenticating their testimony and by corroborative footnotes, cross references, and appendices drawn from theological, historical, and even fictional works. While such documentation tends to be heavier in "nonfictional" narratives, it also plays a role in novels such as *Viola*, which includes footnotes citing Jesuit documents and anti-Catholic publications. (*Six Months in a House of Correction* mocks these corroborative efforts by including testimonials from a bishop, as well as fellow inmates and claims that "[t]he above will be signed by the whole Catholic population of Lowell and Boston, and endorsed by the Boston Post and Transcript."[28]) Typically, the escaped nun's lived experience is said to guarantee the truth of her depiction of Romanism, but so weighty is "experience" in judging "authenticity" that Frothingham offers his status as the *brother* of a nun as proof of the veracity of his "Convent stories." "The single fact that a near relative of his was an inmate of the Convent at Charlestown, in 1834, is deemed sufficient to substantiate all statements presented the public as facts," the preface claims without intended irony.[29] The title of Hazel's *The Nun of St. Ursula; or, The Burning of the Convent: A Romance of Mt. Benedict* may categorize the narrative as a romance, but it also ties the text to historical fact. Similarly, the illustrations depict both a fictional scene, "Cecile Taking the Veil", and a verifiable public event, the "Destruction of the Charlestown Nunnery, August 24th, 1834" (Plates 4 and 5).

These generic crossings and confusions suggest that the escaped nun's narrative was positioned as a "romance of the real," a term coined by George Thompson in 1849 to differentiate his sensational novels of American urban life from conventional idealized romances. In doing so, Thompson

CHAPEL OF THE URSULINES—CECILE TAKING THE VEIL.

Plate 4

THE

NUN OF ST. URSULA,

OR THE

BURNING OF THE CONVENT.

A Romance of Mt. Benedict.

Destruction of the Charlestown Nunnery, August 24th, 1834.

BY HARRY HAZEL,

Author of "*The Burglars, or the Mysteries of the League of Honor,*' "*The Belle of Boston,*" *etc.*

BOSTON:
PUBLISHED BY F. GLEASON, 1 1-2 TREMONT ROW.
1845.

JONES, PR., 42 CONGRESS ST.

Plate 5

assimilated his own fictional mode to contemporary investigative reports on slums, as Christopher Looby has shown. Both genres claim to uncover the fantastic truth, stranger than fiction, of crime and corruption in mid-nineteenth-century urban America. Looby's suggestion that the category of the exposé as "romance of the real" spanned nonfiction and romance in antebellum America[30] perhaps explains how escaped nun's narratives, from novels to newspaper reports, came to serve as evidentiary weapons in the fight against Rome. This is not a unique instance in nineteenth-century anti-Catholicism – both in the United States and Great Britain, fiction was regularly mined for the "facts" of Roman Catholic practice and doctrine. Novels like Eugene Sue's *The Wandering Jew* (*Le juif errant*, 1844–45) were a major source of epigraphs, examples, notes, and appendices for pamphlets, speeches, and essays. While maintaining the distinction between narratives that purport to be autobiographies and those that label themselves romances, I examine them together to underscore how reading an escaped nun's tale marshaled and confirmed recognized patterns of information for a Protestant audience. Tracing the profound intertextuality of the escaped nun's story suggests not only the ideologies that the narrative articulated and reinforced for its authors and audience but also the array of voices that cooperate and compete in the narrative's construction.

The escaped nun's narrative makes claims to truth based on first-person experience inaccessible to the general (Protestant) public. Even when the story is narrated in the third person, the point of view is that of the protagonist, whose scarred and debilitated body bears witness to her first-hand experience of the horrors of Catholicism. As Alexander Welsh demonstrates, in the late eighteenth and early nineteenth centuries, first-person testimony had been displaced by coherent narratives of circumstantial evidence "nearly everywhere: not only in literature but in criminal jurisprudence, natural science, natural religion, and history writing." Welsh describes how this shift in evidentiary standards affected the history of the novel:

Before the nineteenth century, novels were typically surrounded by a false frame of pretended documentation . . . that purported to account for the real-life existence of the narrative they contained. But increasingly, through the conscious practice of Fielding and others, the claim to represent reality in novels was expressed by their internal connectedness of circumstances.[31]

The works that I am discussing are still engaged in the transition that Welsh explores, some retaining first-person testimony (e.g., Reed's *Six Months in a Convent*, Monk's *Awful Disclosures*, Culbertson's *Rosamond*), others switching to third-person (e.g., Larned's *The American Nun*, Binder's *Viola*), still others combining both forms in framed narratives (e.g., Bourne's *Lorette*, Binder's *Madelon Hawley*).

How do these narratives prove that the proof they offer is valid? As the publishers of Rebecca Reed's story neatly put it: "It is therefore simply a question of personal veracity, and of internal and external evidence of truth."[32] Both the authenticity of the speaker and the accuracy of her information must be externally verifiable and internally consistent. From the outset, these texts insistently present themselves as evidence; maps and floorplans, often printed as endpapers, introducing and framing the text, provide testable assertions about the secret spaces in convents. Cast as a kind of ethnography, marked by "thick description," the narratives are incredibly detailed, documenting the minutiae of convent life, explaining strange customs, translating foreign languages, delineating elaborate rituals. Scholarly apparatuses often lend legitimacy: footnotes, depositions, extracts from other texts, appendices. In particular, narratives include page after page purportedly copied from works by Catholic clergymen. So marked is this tendency toward detailed, scholarly description that it becomes a principal source of humor in parodies of the escaped nun's narrative. For example, the narrator of *Six Months in a House of Correction* maintains that the tale's authenticity lies, like Rebecca Reed's, in its trivial details: "There is a minuteness of detail and a simple pathos in the narrative of Miss Dorah's adventures, which are in themselves unanswerable evidence of its truth." This same work also parodies mercilessly the ethnographic stance attempted by most Protestant exposés of the secret practices of Catholics. The most innocuous remarks and events are solemnly pronounced "significant": the word "doctor" is footnoted ("the doctor is a person who tends upon the sick"), and the phrase "No, not that" is said to "have a very deep meaning."[33]

Anti-Catholic texts claim to offer information impartially and to defer to their audiences' judgment of the facts. Monk and Reed, for example, emphasize that all the documents from both sides have been included. Monk declares that she has "no intention of attempting to enforce the evidence presented in the testimonials," that she will "leave every reader to form his own conclusions independently and dispassionately. . . . The Things I declare are sober realities, and nothing is necessary to have them so received, but that the evidence be calmly laid before the public." The introduction to *Hannah Corcoran* states that her story is being given to the public in order "to correct the many partial, inaccurate statements that have gone abroad, and to furnish the community with a narrative on which they may rely as being authentic."[34]

LETTER VI.

" My dear life!—It is a common saying with those of our nation, that when one has agreed to perform any thing with another
individual, and on the question being put, no answer is given,
the inference is, that silence gives consent: or, in other words,
that all is right, and we both agree in sentiment. Now, then,
my dear! how comes it, that so much as I have said to you, and
written to you, you have neither deigned to write me an answer,
or advance any thing satisfactory to me ?—From this I must infer,
that you have no intrinsic regard or wish for the person you thus
treat.—Perchance it may be your sickness occasions all this :—
yet I repeat, I am yours.

" N. B. Believe me, that I feel it most grievously, to be con-
strained to speak to you so clearly, and pointedly ; but it is because I love you.—I love you extremely ; and always shall ; and
I hope you consider me before any one else."

LETTER VII.

(This letter is of so indelicate a nature, that we have to suppress it. His deeply laid scheme required her utmost ingenuity
to baffle it, in order to save her reputation.)

SUPERSCRIPTION TO THE FOLLOWING LETTER.

" *Addressed to the most precious, lovely, and dearest girls,
my eyes ever beheld.*
" *You, whose names I do not know, but am anxious to learn.*"

LETTER VIII.

"My dear, loving sisters !—Lovely girls !—And pretty dears !
—I have already informed you that I have been at the brink of
the grave. No one would believe it, or would believe that I
could recover ; and I still remain very unwell and feeble, dis-
tressed with intermittent fever ; so that I am now fit for nothing,
my dears.—My health still continues very much on the decline ;

Plate 6   Censored "evidence." From Samuel B. Smith's "Introductory to the Letters,
Written by the Rev. Father Pies to Different Females," in Culbertson's *Rosamond* (28–29).

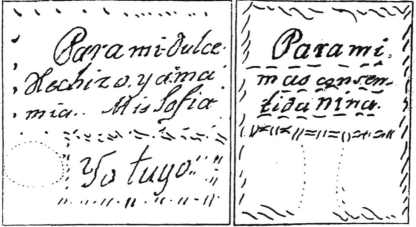

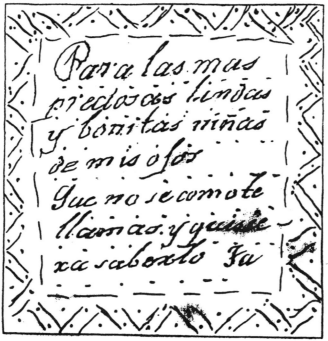

Plate 6 (*cont.*)

Implicit in such professions of completeness is the juridical assumption that "[c]ircumstances do not lie!"[35] Reed's publishers assume a stance at once dispassionate and prosecutorial in describing "the labor of seeing so many individuals, collecting such a mass of facts and testimony, and putting it together *correctly* . . . making this complete and unanswerable. We trust that, so far as the Narrative is concerned it will prove the 'End of Controversy.' "[36] As Welsh suggests, such statements are designed to show that "the representation is conclusive: if it purports to review all the facts that is because, in the opinion of the person making the representation, the facts when considered rightly all point in one direction."[37] Circumstances do not lie only when they have been carefully and conclusively managed: a fact or circumstance means nothing in isolation. The renegade, reporter, autobiographer, detective, prosecutor, and novelist alike make meaning by ordering facts into a coherent, inclusive, believable account.

Evidence is managed in the escaped nun's tale not only by meticulous, sometimes pedantic, inclusiveness but also by the strategic *omission* of information. In introducing *Rosamond*, the "ex-priest" Samuel Smith expresses his regret that a series of letters written to Rosamond by the priest who imprisoned her have been lost or perhaps stolen: "these would have been an inestimable appendage to the work." Smith calls on any reader who has come across these letters to turn them in, so that they can be published. However, letters from another priest to his mistress furnish "further evidence of the truth and accuracy of the Narrative." Yet even this evidence is incomplete, since some letters too foul to be published are omitted entirely; others are numbered and described but not reproduced (letter 7 "is of so indelicate a nature, that we have to suppress it"); still others have their obscenity hidden "under the original cloak of Spanish." Nonetheless, since some of the readership would not have known Spanish, "we have translated what we dare to present in that language, into Latin." Finally, although the handwriting is "almost illegible," two letters are given in holograph, printed so that "a blank in the fac-simile, makes that absence of what, in the original, would raise a blush on immodesty herself"[38] (Plate 6).

The cumulative effect of this editorial scrupulosity is to impress readers with the physical reality of the evidence and to convince them that real texts exist. Further, while rendering obscene material in Latin was by 1836 an editorial practice of long-standing, it is uniquely suited to Smith's anti-Catholicism. Smith sets up a continuum – horrible, fully accessible facts in English; worse, less accessible facts in Latin; still worse and even less accessible facts in Spanish; and inaccessible but by this point fully imaginable facts that are omitted – that invites reader participation in the pornographic construction of undeniable truth. So confident is Smith that his readership can supply images and narratives of priestly profligacy that he provides blank spaces for their inclusion. Because Culbertson's audience knows Rosamond's story in advance, the truncated text serves to mirror back its audience to itself. Its very incompleteness verifies the fullness of *Rosamond*'s – and Rosamond's – authenticity by lodging its truth in its Protestant readership.

Reader participation is also critical to claims of probability, the evidentiary criterion addressed most directly in the escaped nun's tales.[39] The appendix to Reed's *Six Months in a Convent* explicitly takes up the "[p]rinciples on which the credibility of personal testimony depends," citing John Abercrombie's *Inquiries concerning the Intellectual Powers, and the Investigation of Truth*:

> In receiving facts upon testimony, we are much influenced by their accordance with facts with which we are already acquainted. This is what in common language we call their probability; and statements which are probable, that is, in accordance with facts which we already know, are received upon a lower degree of evidence than those which are not in such accordance.[40]

This standard of probability makes escaped nuns' accounts instantly verifiable because they employ narrative patterns and character types from Roman Catholicism's past. Ancient anecdotes are given life both by being inserted verbatim into nineteenth-century texts and by being enacted in the nineteenth-century world of the novel. Binder, the ex-priest who describes the imprisonment of Madelon Hawley, makes clear that hers is an old story: "thus was chronicled another of those crimes which long since rendered the Romish Church notorious – which centuries ago, made black and fearful both the public and private history of her priesthood. Read there – if your eyes do not pale – the terrible catalogue of crimes."[41] In Culbertson's *Rosamond*, Smith quotes descriptions by Bernard of Clairvaux, Agrippa von Nettesheim, Nicholas of Clemanges, and Francois Eudes de Mezeray of licentious popish clergymen's veiling women to prostitute them,[42] and then shows Father Manuel doing precisely the same with Rosamond. If the narrative technique of multiplying nuns' life-stories as the protagonist moves further into the convent shows the pervasiveness of Rome's evil influence, the inclusion of these historical precedents demonstrates its perdurability.

The weakness of an evidentiary standard that depends on the audience's reading history comes under parodic attack in *Six Months in a House of Correction* and *The Chronicles of Mount Benedict* (Mary Magdalen). In *The*

Chronicles of Mount Benedict, the nun's tale is written to reveal not the horrors of Catholicism but the ludicrousness of Protestants' beliefs about Catholicism, beliefs founded on "the tales they read of popery as it was four hundred years ago." The author's literalizing of anti-Catholicism's assumptions broadly undercuts the argument that medieval chronicles can illuminate the evils of nineteenth-century Catholicism. *The Chronicles of Mount Benedict*, which opens in fifteenth-century Germany, tells of the persecution of the beautiful virgin Maria Ursula by a hard-drinking, lust-mad priest, Father Pertinax, and his companions. After all of these characters die, the action switches to the Vatican, where the Pope has returned from a hunting trip with Satan in Germany. His Holiness dreams alternately of extending his rule to America and of sating his lust for Maria Ursula. He decides to resurrect her and the others so that Maria Ursula can establish an (Ursuline) convent in America: "Now, by mine infallibility . . . I have nothing to do but to fit them out with incorruptible and infallible bodies." Thus equipped, Maria Ursula and Pertinax are sent "in some kind or other of a spiritual bark," which, "by some inexplicable delay," does not arrive at Charlestown until 11:10:03.25, 21 July 1826. The group then proceeds to Mount Benedict. The outrageous transition from "popery as it was four hundred years ago" to Charlestown in 1826 parodies the anti-Catholic "knowledge" that nineteenth-century Protestant audiences brought to their reading.[43]

Protestant knowledge about the woman who bears witness to the awful truths of Catholicism is shown to be problematic in other ways as well. To use the criteria outlined by Reed's publishers, the escaped nun's "personal veracity" is questionable because while her tale exhibits "internal and external evidence of the truth," her readership is already steeped in tales about the dishonesty of Catholics and women. Anti-Catholicism traditionally takes the honesty of Catholics as its target; nineteenth-century polemicists drew freely on this tradition. "They will stop at no falsehood where the good of the church is concerned . . . they will scruple at no forgery . . . it is a standing rule with Popish priests, in all their controversies with Protestants, to admit nothing and deny everything," states the "ex-priest" William Hogan, describing his own careful training in deception. He warns that Catholics are under specific dispensations regarding truth-telling to non-Catholics. Hogan warns Americans, "I too have been a priest, and I solemnly declare to the world, and to my fellow-citizens of the United States in particular, *that to keep no faith with heretics, but to destroy them, is one of the most solemn duties of a Catholic*."[44] Maria Monk tells of the Catholic distinction between a "wicked" and a "religious" lie. Escaped nuns' narratives are laced with quotations from the works of the Church Fathers which "prove" that Catholics are enjoined to use any means, however immoral and dishonest, to advance papal power. One of the appendices published with *Awful Disclosures* offers "additional evidence of the truth of Maria Monk's narrative" by citing five Roman Catholic theologians on "Falsehood," for instance, "*Sanchez*, a very renowned author, in his work on 'Morality and the Precepts of the Decalogue,' part 2, book 3, chap. 6, no. 13, thus decides: 'A person may take an oath that he has not done any certain thing, though in fact he has. This is extremely convenient, and is also *very just*, when necessary to your health, honour, and prosperity!' "[45] And the dispensation of the confessional is taken to mean that Catholics can lie with impunity since they will shortly be forgiven for the sin.

If all Catholic speech is suspect, gender is an added complication in the accounts of escaped nuns. The uneasy status of women's evidence is tied to a variety of cultural and narratological assumptions about women and the public realm, about women's consistency, loyalty, and sincerity, and about the dangers both of women's innocence and of their education. The most immediate problem the female renegade faces is that by telling her story publicly, she draws her modesty, respectability, and class standing into question. As Cathy N. Davidson notes, "Fame, for a woman, is by definition (gender definition), unfeminine, infamous."[46] The publishers of *Six Months in a Convent* work hard to absolve Reed of all desire for publicity: "We wish it to be distinctly understood that the publication is not made at the instigation, or on the responsibility of the author. On the contrary, she has very reluctantly yielded to the force of circumstances and the dictates of duty, which, in the opinion of her friends and the friends of truth, have left no other course proper to be pursued; and has placed her manuscript at their disposal."[47]

Similarly, Caldicott makes sure to mention that his subject, Hannah Corcoran, "consents to give these facts publicity from no other motive than the hope that they may be made instrumental." Samuel B. Smith insists "that no pecuniary inducement led to the writing of" Rosamond's story. These women claim that they tell their stories of victimhood in order to prevent other young females from becoming victims; they sacrifice their own privacy and modesty in order to protect the privacy and modesty of others. Monk claims repeatedly that she had no intention of publishing her story until she realized that it might provide a warning. Answering potential questions about "the propriety of publishing such immorality to the world," she pronounces concealment of sin the greater immorality and declares, "Although it was necessary to the cause of truth, that I should, in some degree, implicate myself, I have not hesitated to appear as a voluntary self-accuser before the world." The implications of public speech by women explain why the prefatory and editorial defenses of escaped nuns' modesty are so insistent. Though nunneries are what Franchot calls "antidomestic cultural architecture," false homes, perverse substitutes for the truly religious realm of home and family, the escaped nun's narrative nonetheless describes a woman deliberately breaking free from a private, protected, spiritualized realm.[48]

Even more compromising to this female testimony is the fact that it is given by a woman whose "honesty," that is to say, whose chastity, has already been compromised because she has been in a convent, one of the so-called priests' brothels. Disputes over the evidentiary status of the nun's story rapidly become disputes over the nun's sexual status. Norwood Damon, the author of the parodic *Chronicles of Mount Benedict*, underscores the escaped nun's "fallen" status by using the pseudonym Mary Magdalen. The epigraph to *Awful Disclosures* illustrates how even what appears to be the most neutral and verifiable of facts – the floor plan of the convent – is, at the same time, a figure for the most epistemologically vexed object of interpretation – the sincerity of the teller. Invoking that traditional Protestant figure for the Roman Catholic Church, the Whore of Babylon, Monk's epigraph figures the convent as the body of the scarlet woman: "Come out of her, my people, that ye be not partakers of her sin, and that ye receive not of her plagues."[49] If accurate, the floor plan that immediately prefaces this epigraph not only reveals the interior of the convent but also vouches for the escaped nun's authenticity as one who knows, who carries the truth of the convent out with her. With its false religious exterior and its hidden evil interior, the convent is implicitly contrasted with the sincere woman who has fled it. The good woman's inside matches her outside, a metaphor that gains resonance from the nineteenth-century belief, especially dominant in the sentimental culture of the 1830s, that underwrites the possibility of physical sincerity: when a woman blushes, pales, or faints, an "involuntary" feminine transparency allows her body to be read.[50] Yet, the escaped nun's residency in the convent inevitably raises the possibility of her own duplicity. For the epigraph can be read as identifying both the inner convent and the woman who was its inmate as the whore of Babylon.[51] Is she a true woman or a superficial imitation of one? Is hers a true story or a devious hoax?

The Catholic establishment attacked the escaped nun in the press and the pulpit. Having already broken faith, the apostate is not just potentially but definitionally unreliable. As Reed's publishers quote the Boston newspaper *The Jesuit*: "Whenever a Catholic changes his religion, his motives and conduct are to be *invariably suspected*, and his *honesty* to be *never trusted.*"[52] So miserable is the apostate, the *Jesuit* claims, that he or she inevitably commits suicide, a claim that Reed's backers immediately seize as evidence that Rome murders all who flee from its prisons. Larned's *The American Nun* addresses the more mixed Protestant response. The newly escaped Anna's plea for help is greeted with skepticism: "A runaway nun is not exactly such a companion as a clergyman of my age ought to be seen with," demurs her rescuer. "A deep flush overspread the wan face of Anna, and for a time she remained silent; then said, 'It is true, I have no vouchers for the truth of my story.'"[53] The apostate nun is a figure of shame. She has already proved herself unreliable by breaking her religious vows; now she divulges that which she has promised to keep secret.[54] The story that she tells only draws her integrity further into question. The Protestant clergyman who knows the awful "truth" about convents, who knows that the escaped nun's story of sexual misadventure is "true," is also part of the audience that distrusts any individual escaped nun's honesty.

Many of the gaps in the escaped nun's narrative are strategic attempts to prove the protagonist's innocence by demonstrating her lack of knowledge. The floor plan on which much of Monk's case rests designates not only the "[c]hamber where St. Frances was murdered" and the "[g]reat gloomy iron door," but also several spaces marked "unknown" and "secret apartments unknown." In recounting conversations with the Hotel Dieu gardener, the Sister of Charity in *The Escaped Nun* insists that she "did not know what to make of" his remarks and "had no idea of what he intended to hint at," yet the reader understands that the old man is raising poisonous herbs for the priests' murderous uses.[55] Like Henry James's Maisie, this innocent vessel carries awful truths to her audience. In *Rosamond*, the priest who has imprisoned the protagonist forces her to witness his rape of a fourteen-year-old girl. After a detailed discussion of the priest's plan and its consequences, Rosamond states "I could not support the horrible scene, but fainted."[56] Fainting at the crucial moment of sexual violation shields her from full knowledge of the crime. Since her own submission to the priest is never explicitly described, her unconsciousness suggests sexual innocence – or at least a lack of consent.[57] Smith, the annotator of *Rosamond*, follows the description of the rape scene with a four-page footnote in which he analyzes the rhetorical effect of this lacuna in the text. He argues that if Rosamond had meant "to *appear* refined," she would have emphasized the fainting from the start.[58] Smith claims that the order of the narration reveals Rosamond's artlessness and thus proves the sincerity of her account. Similarly, in several other versions of the escaped nun's story, the young woman is unconscious

when her vows are "taken": while her Catholic oppressors take her silence
as assent, her Protestant audience may interpret it as a form of resistance
that preserved honor and integrity.[59] Paradoxically, her refusal to speak as
a nun means that – perhaps – she can be trusted to report honestly and
sincerely as an authentic *escaped nun.*

These maneuverings between the reliable relation of facts and the insistent refusal to understand them present a novelistic pattern familiar at least
since Richardson: the heroine's innocence is threatened for pages and pages
of plot; if she is finally conquered, she dies, but if she escapes, she marries
and lives happily ever after. Of the escaped nun's narratives I have read,
only Maria Monk's breaks this narrative rule; Monk confesses that she is
the living mother of a priest's child. But even in this case the woman's
life-story becomes formulaic. Twentieth-century commentators inevitably
"prove" Monk's dishonesty by describing how her life-story ends: thirteen
years after the publication of *Awful Disclosures*, Monk was arrested in "a
house of ill fame" for robbing her male "companion of the moment," as
Billington puts it.[60] Such a conclusion has been read as refuting the evidence she presented over a decade earlier. By making the genre and plot of
Monk's life readily recognizable (it is that kind of story; she is that kind of
girl), her end determines her life.[61]

Monk's story concludes outside the confines of her book, but
within a familiar (didactic) pattern. This ending appears not only in
twentieth-century histories of anti-Catholicism like Billington's, but also
in nineteenth-century accounts. Lizzie St. John Eckel Harper, the author
of *Maria Monk's Daughter: An Autobiography* (1874), describes Monk as a
drunken, violent, abusive woman who dies, insane, in prison. In both her
narrative and her notes, Monk's supposed daughter maintains that *Awful
Disclosures*'s fabrications were framed to meet audience expectations:

A young girl of eighteen, with her disposition, unrestrained either by education or
religion – thrown penniless on the world, the victim of a licentious man, and driven
to seek refuge in a hospital – would naturally try to make friends among the visitors
and attendants, by representing herself as the helpless victim of circumstances. And,
in order the better to enlist their sympathies she would take care to shape her story
so, as to suit the prejudices and partialities of those, whose protection she sought.[62]

In this "true" account of her mother's story-telling, Eckel once again tells
readers a tale they already know. The fact that even the outrageous Maria
Monk is ultimately confined within the conventions of the fallen woman's
story suggests that the escaped nun's tale can be read as another version
of the seduction narrative, which attempts to define and control female

sexuality. Indeed, Monk states, "Many an innocent girl may this year be exposed to the dangers of which I was ignorant. I am resolved, that so far as depends on me, not one more victim shall fall into the hands of those enemies in whose power I have so lately been."[63] While Monk stresses her role as victim of priestly debauchery, other anti-Catholic writers focus more explicitly on female lasciviousness: "A destructive incredulity exists respecting the horrible impurity and deadly practice of Nuns, who are cloaked under various bewitching appellatives, and decorated in meretricious garbs expressly to ensnare and seduce our citizens," warns the author of *Female Convents*.[64] Somewhat more subtle are warnings about women's susceptibility to influence. Speaking of "the debauchery and wide spread iniquity" endemic to convents, Larned cautions, "[W]e are seldom aware how powerfully early impressions affect the mind, and how much they influence the character in after life."[65]

Yet the emphasis on questions of evidence, the attempts to bolster women's testimony with corroborative proofs from other (almost exclusively male) voices, and the ways strategies for validation undermine the women's reliability indicate that the escaped nun's tale is directed to other ends as well. A number of nineteenth-century responses to these narratives implicate the Protestant girl as a figure of cultural anxiety. Fanning the flames at Mount Benedict was a controversy among New England Protestants about religious choice: "all the hatreds bred of the struggle then going on between liberal and fundamentalist religion in Massachusetts were centered on the Charlestown convent."[66] By making the education of Protestant girls part of its mission, this Catholic institution provided upper-class Boston Unitarians with a means of circumventing the strict Congregationalism enforced in the public schools.[67] One of a number of articles about Charlestown that appeared in the popular weekly the *Christian Watchman*[68] argues that to judge the events, readers must focus on the convent's essential character as "a school for the education of many Protestant females."[69] In the letters appended to Moffatt's *An Answer to Six Months in a Convent*, fathers insist that they did not place their daughters in the Ursuline school to allow them religious choice. Repeatedly declaring, "I am not a Catholic," these men describe how they carefully chose the school and closely monitored their daughters' education.[70] A series of articles in the *Baltimore Literary and Religious Magazine* describing the escape of the nineteen-year-old Olevia Neal from a Carmelite convent claims that "[t]his is the fifth or sixth case in which some of the papists of Baltimore have attempted to possess themselves of the female children of protestants – by fraud, force, or seduction, within six years."[71] Emphasizing this image of the Protestant girl at risk, the writer warns that "families not Catholic . . . have a direct interest in all the affairs of a body, one of whose chief objects is to proselyte protestant children."[72] Contrasting "the stout man" with "a weak girl," one article complains that there are no laws to protect "a poor female [who] may be morally influenced by friends, deluged by proselyting nuns, seduced by cunning priests, betrayed by the workings of her own fancy, misled by the irregular exercise of some of the best feelings of the heart" and calls on Protestant fathers to protect and, if need be, to rescue their daughters.[73] Insistently, the Protestant press evokes the image of a vulnerable daughter in need of strong paternal protection and control.

I suggest that anti-Catholic stories about escaped nuns disclose misgivings about the new generation of daughters and their influence in the remaking of American religious practices. The tale that the runaway nun tells *is* a seduction story, but it is a *spiritual* seduction story that attempts to define and control women's religion. During the period when escaped nuns' tales proliferated, American Protestantism had moved from hierarchical, patriarchal Calvinism to an emphasis on the individual and the woman. In recent years, women's historians have charted the specific contours of this change,[74] tracing its relation to domesticity and sentimental fiction and revealing its role in empowering American women at mid-century. The escaped nun's tale reflects a significant cultural response to the feminization of American religion. Rather than focus on the mother as "God in human form," as Jane Tompkins puts it,[75] these narratives show the daughter at risk. What will happen if the American girl has religious choice? The escaped nun's story illustrates the young woman's incapacity to be trusted: her testimony is essential to unveiling the truth, but it also proves her vulnerability and fallibility. Indeed, the escaped nun makes a choice that proves her inability to choose. In the eyes of her Protestant audience, conversion to Catholicism means rejecting an independent, individual relationship to God. Entering the convent, a young woman abdicates her selfhood and cedes her autonomy to a corrupt and power-hungry priesthood.

Further underscoring such female incapacity is these texts' visible demonstration that women cannot be trusted to speak alone. Independent testimony from women cannot stand on its own as proof; it must be framed and intercut with other forms of evidence. While corroboratory documents add weight to the escaped nun's testimony, their erudition also implies that a lack of education in theology, law, and history makes American women unfit for religious conversation and controversy. Warning against exposing Protestant girls to convent educations, Larned in *The American Nun* chides "Children are *educated* by *influences*." Childlike, women are inevitably overcome by emotions, spiritually and sexually seduced. "The mystery which surrounds the Nuns, – their separation from the world, – their show of deep devotion and calm resignation, – their imposing, and to the young, attractive ceremonials of worship, – the thousand winning ways they know so well how to use."[76] American daughters do not – perhaps cannot – know enough to defend themselves from papist priests. Insufficiently instructed at home, women end up in that false substitute for domesticity, the convent. The escaped nun's tale awfully discloses not only priests' plots and women's prisons but also the fundamental weakness of the female self on which the future of American Protestantism rests. The fear that the woman who flees the convent is merely mimicking truth suggests that antebellum culture's faith in woman as the embodiment of faith itself may be superficial. The partial truths of this "Catholic" story, finally, do not verify the completeness of Protestant identity. The woman who gives evidence also serves as evidence – evidence that incriminates her self and her sex.

THE DARK STRANGER

The sensational escaped nun's narratives of the 1830s–1850s represent, along with their overt anti-Catholic purpose, a popular response to the contemporary feminization of American Protestantism. The writings of Sarah Josepha Hale, aimed specifically at shaping and responding to middle-class American culture, are also centrally concerned with the role that American females play in Protestantism. And I argue that she, too – albeit unexpectedly – uses the escaped nun's plot as a way to address this concern.

Hale's work also demonstrates clearly the nationalistic aims of anti-Catholic narrative. Set in Vermont, Hale's escaped nun's story is informed by her share in antebellum fears that Catholic missionaries were claiming the newly settled West and ends by sending her Protestant characters on a mission to American South. Writing against what she saw as the contemporary atomization of Americans, Hale uses a familiar plot to re-create the Republic.

The presence of such a popular, sensational discourse in Hale's writing may seem surprising, given her reputation as the genteel "lady editor" of *Godey's Lady's Book*. Nina Baym and Nicole Tonkovich have recently shown how Hale and *Godey's* were powerful forces in shaping and responding to American culture from the 1830s to the 1870s.[77] Recognizing the presence of lurid anti-Catholic plots and characters in Hale's domestic national literature allows us to examine a concrete example of how a popular rhetoric and plot can traverse a variety of discourses, eroding strict separation between "high" literature and "low" popular fiction, as well as between male sensationalism and female domesticity. The trajectory of the escaped nun's story thus epitomizes the argument of my study as a whole, demonstrating how the same anti-Catholic fictional structures come to be employed in a range of registers and to varying ideological ends.

Recognizing that "The Catholic Convert," the second piece in Hale's 1835 *Traits of American Life*, is Hale's version of an escaped nun's story allows us to understand an important political dimension of this period as well. While feminist scholars have long discussed the variety of ways in which Protestantism informed and fostered American women's culture,[78] only very recently has that culture's relation to and role in the virulent anti-Catholicism of the period begun to be explored.[79] Jenny Franchot's argument that antebellum anti-Catholicism provided American Protestantism with a means of bolstering its own identity as well as a medium in which to explore the tensions and contradictions implicit in that identity is borne out by Hale's practice. She employs the escaped nun's story to critique both the Catholicism and the newly debased Protestantism that threaten America. Hale's narrative offers rescue and redemption not only to the young woman seduced by Catholicism, but also to her "audience," a Protestant couple led astray by the selfishness and materialism that pervade post-revolutionary America. In "The Catholic Convert," Hale sets a contemporary version of an ancient tale in the American landscape in order to lead her readership, through association, to remembrance of lost values and a renewed nationalist feeling.[80]

As a reader and writer of Protestant millennial history – what Baym has called "History from the Divine Point of View" – Hale knew well the chronicle of Catholicism's crimes.[81] Further, Hale, who claimed that Ann Radcliffe's *Mystery of Udolpho* was the first novel she read (and that at age seven), was certainly familiar with the gothic tradition on which escaped nuns' narratives drew. And we do know of Hale's reaction to at least one antebellum story about an escaped nun, a reaction which offers an explanatory context for her own rendering of the plot in "The Catholic Convert." In the September 1834 issue of *The American Ladies' Magazine*, Hale expressed her outrage at the burning of the Ursuline convent at Charlestown, Massachusetts.

Hale dismisses the story of Elizabeth Harrison's escape and recapture as a recycled gothic plot: "This Monk Lewis story was mostly a fiction." Instead, Hale tells a different narrative of female victimhood, focusing on the "community of helpless women attacked" by male violence. Hale was well aware that this community was, in fact, primarily a Protestant one. While professing that "we certainly should not select a Catholic seminary as the place of education for our own daughters," Hale nonetheless defends the Protestant parents' decision to educate their daughters with the Ursulines: "Of all the protestant young ladies, and there have been several hundred educated at the Ursuline Convent since its foundation, *not a single individual has embraced the Catholic faith!*"[82]

In the November 1834 issue of *American Ladies' Magazine*, Hale returns to the subject, this time in order to defend herself from the Protestant press who had read her comments as pro-Catholic (as had Catholic journalists: the piece was reprinted in the Boston newspaper *The Jesuit* [September 6, 1834: 292–94]). Hale offers evidence of her staunch opposition to Rome: "The prevalence of popery would be, in our opinion, the greatest moral calamity – excepting the prevalence of *infidelity!* – which could befal our nation." Regarding the popular theory that the Pope and the Austrian government were funding Jesuits to infiltrate America and found convents and colleges such "as will enable these European tyrants through their partisan emissaries here, to overthrow and destroy our civil and religious liberties," Hale says, "it probably is true." Nonetheless, she argues that these schemes are the work of "priests and the despots of the old world," not of lay Catholics.[83] Hale again mocks the escaped nun story and reiterates her arguments against persecution. The bulk of the essay, however, takes the Charlestown controversy as an occasion for introducing one of Hale's favorite subjects: female education.[84] The chains and veils that concern her are mental ones: "The catholic religion does not allow the free exercise of mind – the nuns are shrouded in the veil of bigotry. . . . [I]t is not within the compass of their design to make woman an intellectual and rational companion of man."[85] That is, convent schools cannot produce *American wives.* Why, then, are more and more Protestant females being educated in convent schools? Because there are so few Protestant schools. Explaining, in the words of her title, "How to Prevent the Increase of Convents," Hale argues that Americans must offer superior and cheaper Protestant education for girls and women.

Hale continues with the topic in the December 1834 "Convents Are Increasing." Here, she turns to the Protestant mission that Ray Allen Billington, in his chapter on American nativism between 1835 and 1840, calls "Saving the West from the Pope." Arguing that "the Great West is the arena where the struggle between the Protestant and Catholic principles is mainly to be carried on," Hale warns that, without adequate funding for Protestant female education, the men of the West, themselves well educated in institutions like Lyman Beecher's Lane Seminary, will be condemned to marry convent-educated women.[86] The Protestant missionary work of such men will be all for naught, Hale insists, if they are not accompanied by educated female missionaries: "What avails it to send out Missionaries to heathen lands to preach to the men the religion of the Cross, while the women are training their sons in the creed of Juggernaut?" A single male convert is just that, but convert a female, and you convert an entire family. Hale's implication is that the missionary crisis abroad mirrors the problem of the wild, unsettled region at home. Unless American women are offered an educational alternative, "convents will increase, and Catholicism become permanently rooted in our country."[87]

The image of the convent provides Hale with a structure for discussion, not only of Catholicism's role in and threat to contemporary Protestant America, but woman's privileged place in the nation's making and preservation. Rather than accepting the nativist story of Elizabeth Harrison's experiences and repeating the conventional escaped nun's tale, Hale takes the Charlestown incident as an opportunity to tell a quite different story about why American women are in convents and about what must be done to rescue them.

Shortly after these three articles appeared, Hale collected and published *Traits of American Life*. But the escaped nun's story that she includes, "The Catholic Convert," was, in fact, originally published in the August and September 1830 issues of *Ladies' Magazine* as "The Unknown." It is the only piece that gets a completely new title when it is republished in *Traits*.[88] Predating, in its original form, the popular narratives by Bourne, Monk, Reed, and others, "The Catholic Convert" signals, with its changed title, the new focus on the Protestant–Catholic competition for souls that was dominating the popular imagination in 1835. What Hale's title leaves ambiguous, of course, is which way the conversion runs: is this a story of a convert to or from Catholicism? The ambivalence is significant, since, in her version of the escaped nun's narrative, Hale deliberately turns some of Protestantism's favorite attacks on Rome back onto American Protestants themselves. However, unlike the anti-Protestant parodies of the escaped nun's tale, Hale's rendering positions itself as staunchly Protestant. Her aim is the reinvigoration and refinement of American religious practice.

The story, set in Brattleborough, Vermont, opens with an insistence on the typicality of two of its characters: "Mr. Theophilus Redfield, and his wife Susanna, were . . . in their own sphere, a pattern couple: prudent, pious, and prosperous, gathering the maxims that guided their temporal course from the economies of Franklin, and their summary of religious faith from the Westminster Catechism."[89] This "pattern" couple, who serve as audience for the internal narrative that Hale will introduce, represents Hale's readership. Describing the Redfields as guided by traditional American and Protestant precepts, Hale immediately goes on to question the adequacy of any such set of rules. She asserts that the young should study instead "the works of Nature and the Book of Revelation" and that they should reason from their own sensory and emotional experiences, from what "their own hearts have felt." Accepting a religious theory "on trust," as the Redfields' post-revolutionary generation of Americans has come to do, actually means absolving one's self from individual responsibility and conscience.[90]

Hale's critical description of American Protestantism replicates a standard Protestant characterization of *Catholic* religious practices: deferring to a set of rules dictated by a priest, then turning to that same priest for absolution, the Catholic abdicates his or her own primary and singular relationship with God. Hale turns this critique against her pious Protestant characters, censuring the way in which they seek refuge in the letter of the law in order to justify their fundamentally unChristian economic behavior: "while they kept the Sabbath day with pharisaical strictness, the other six days were their own," days in which their lives are guided solely by the selfish standard of "pecuniary profit."[91] Class and economics are central topics throughout *Traits of American Life*. Hale's focus here on the Redfields' selfishness reflects the growing anxiety in antebellum America about the shift from self-sacrificing, communitarian republicanism to self-aggrandizing, market-based individualism.[92] In "The Catholic Convert," Hale frames this political problem in religious terms. The Redfields' lives and practices are guided by pragmatic, material considerations. As neighbors, church members, and citizens, they live in a realm of (economic) fact, where spirituality and sentiment hold no sway.

Having delineated the deficiencies in these typical Americans, Hale offers a remedy, albeit an indirect one. What will remake the Redfields into true Americans is a story. "Did you ever, reader mine, visit Brattleborough . . . ?" Hale asks, explaining that this site, like most of "our young country," lacks "the fallen column, the ivied tower and the desolate city." The Redfields completely disregard their Brattleborough farm's "beautiful situation and scenery," regarding it merely "as being worth so much cash." Nonetheless, the "strange circumstance" Hale is about to narrate has taught even the Redfields to see Brattleborough as "romantic" – clearly they are meant to set the "reader mine" an instructive example.[93]

Hale's efforts to "story" the American landscape here are repeated throughout *Traits*,[94] because, as she argues in "The Romance of Travelling," "the perpetuity of the Union" hangs on such literary work.[95] Landscape's educative role as a tool of political unification rests on its ability to evoke association, an ability that depends, in turn, on the stories told about it. The political efficacy of a literary landscape is made explicit in an 1845 *Godey's* column in which Hale proposes that the nation's sectional conflict can be overcome by American women writing to their children who had removed to the territories. Those letters, Hale instructs, should dwell on the shared landscape of the past, evoking "the feelings that humanize the heart and . . . [impart] the love of country to the patriot."[96] As Nicole Tonkovich explains, "In Hale's formulation, these local memories would function quite literally as *loci communae*, common places, performing the same function as did . . . rhetorical mnemonic device[s]."[97] Americans must come to recall the landscape's history as their own, and such memory traces are fashioned through reading. The writing and reading of a "United States" that Hale performs (and urges) figures vividly the work of nation-making that Benedict Anderson identifies as imagining a community, grounded in antiquity, yet sharing a simultaneous temporality across space.

Hale's writing is also exemplary of the workings of nineteenth-century anti-Catholic narrative generally. Summoning old readerly associations to the service of contemporary politics, the writers work to persuade and unite their audiences, shoring up and shaping national identities. The nineteenth century's growing religious, geographic, and cultural diversity, its increase in mobility and individualism, is countered, not by a return to the past, but by stories that reweave the interdependent meanings of "Catholic" and "Protestant."

In "The Catholic Convert," the story that will transform the Redfields' (and the reader's) feeling towards the landscape commences via the entrance of that narrative treasure-trove of anti-Catholic typology: the gothic. A late night knock at the Redfields' door reveals "a tall man, a stranger, habited in black, with a black handkerchief drawn up nearly to his temples, his hat pulled over his forehead."[98] This mysterious stranger, who refuses to reveal his name, offers the Redfields a large sum of money if they will accept a young woman and a boy as boarders for a year. There is one condition: the Redfields must not ask the boarders any questions, must not seek to discover their identities or origins. The couple agree, offering to regularize the agreement with a receipt and a written contract. However, "the dark stranger" refuses: "should I take a bond, you might, in the way of trade, consider it fair to take every advantage possible. But now, when I treat you with the confidence of a Christian, you will not fail in doing as you would be done by."[99] Echoing her opening critique of the Redfields, Hale distinguishes between a business arrangement whereby both parties pursue their own self-interests and a relationship that rests on mutual expectations of "Christian" behavior.

Fittingly enough, given this sensational beginning, the young woman, Mary, turns out to be a runaway nun of sorts. The shape of Mary's early life, formed by parental neglect, is one that will become familiar to readers of anti-Catholic narratives in the 1830s, 1840s, and 1850s.[100] Although both of her parents were Protestants, at her mother's death, Mary's grief-stricken father (Mr. Marshall, the dark stranger), committed her to the care of a Catholic woman, thinking "a creed was of very little consequence." Years later, he reawakens to his paternal duties and attempts to reclaim Mary and re-create a family home. But he is too late. Mary has been seduced into Catholicism. Using the intimacy of the confessional, a stealthy Jesuit priest has taught Mary to regard love for her "heretic" father as a sin; Mary "trembled and wept with horror and grief, whenever any parental tenderness . . . had called forth a return of [her] affectionate confidence." Invoking the sensational language of sadism and torture, Hale declares that such "religious bigotry and fanaticism . . . binds the soul in chains, which rust and canker, till a moral paralysis ensues, and all the natural and innocent feelings of the heart are turned to vile and cruel purposes." As in her "How to" article, Hale here participates selectively in the rhetoric of popular anti-Catholic literature in which, as Franchot notes, "captivity structured nativist perceptions not only of papal machinations but also of Catholic dogma itself."[101]

Having penetrated the family circle, the Jesuit steals into the family home: "notwithstanding all my vigilance, I could not prevent her confessor from seeing her and advising her; and he used his power over her to frighten and intimidate, till she resolved to enter a convent," Mary's father complains. Faced with what Franchot calls "the age's new experience of damnation: the broken parental heart,"[102] Mr. Marshall can thwart Mary's clandestine night-time escape to the convent only by fleeing with her to Brattleborough. Whisked away in the dead of night to a secret destination, Mary is separated by her father from the man who holds sway over her mind, heart, and body. The two fathers' actions are pointedly parallel: if Mr. Marshall carries Mary off to a secluded spot where the holy father cannot see or even communicate with her, he is merely countering the Jesuit plot that Hale's Protestant readers suspect – "knowing," as they do, that all Catholic priests use the confessional to obtain intimacy with and control over young women, that the next step is imprisonment in a convent, and that Jesuits are particularly expert in such matters.

Mary is initially described in a way that a nineteenth-century audience would read as "nun" and that illustrates Protestant ambivalence about sisterhoods.[103] Heavily veiled when she arrives, she confines herself to her room at first, creating her own convent cell within the Redfields' domestic space. When she does reveal herself, Mary's unearthly beauty marks her as at once intriguing and inhuman: "when her eyelids droop, it seems as if she was at prayer, and she looks so angel-like that it made me feel a little afraid to gaze upon her," she has "the pale unanimated beauty of a statue, rather than the loveliness of youth, health, and innocent happiness"; she prefers "the deepest solitude" to the company even of family, and appears at first to care for her brother out of duty rather than love.[104] Her Catholic training makes her an interesting figure of mystery – suggesting perhaps another reason for the escaped nun's tale's popularity. Mary's exotic attractiveness can be read as a veiled critique of Protestant ordinariness, a reading supported by the way Mrs. Redfield is gradually refined through her contact with Mary. Nonetheless, restricted to the Catholic (mis)education that, as Hale argued in her November 1834 *American Ladies'* article, "does not allow the free exercise of mind" and therefore cannot "make a woman an intellectual and rational companion of man," Mary lacks the attributes necessary to ordinary Protestant womanhood.

Colleen McDannell has traced in detail the differences between Protestant and Catholic domestic religion in nineteenth-century America. McDannell offers nuanced and specific support for the work of previous scholars (Baym, Cott, Douglas, Ryan, Sklar) who describe the way Protestantism increasingly located itself in domestic moral instruction. This "child-centered, mother-directed, and individual" moral pedagogy was iconized in the image of the mother reading the Bible to the child circled in her embrace. In contrast, McDannell shows, "social and economic conditions . . . kept Catholics from developing a middle-class domestic piety until almost the close of the century. Traditional Catholicism, with its preference for celibate life, church-centered rituals, and private piety, worked against the establishment of family religion." These differences were pilloried by Protestant propagandists, who typically depicted Catholic dwellings as unhomelike and Catholic women as unwomanly. "With a drunken Irish father, wild children, and a mother working in the mills, the Irish immigrant family was contrasted to the 'proper' Protestant family."[105]

Hale's criticism in *Traits* is directed less at the slovenly Irish and more at the antidomesticity she finds in the Catholic religion's celebration of celibacy and emotional asceticism. She will make her charge against Catholicism explicit later in *Woman's Record*, her magisterial history of women: "The Roman Catholic church degraded women, when it degraded marriage by making the celibacy of the priests a condition of greater holiness than married life."[106] For Hale, domestic sentiment is a model for and source of religious feeling. The perversity of the Catholic Church is that it takes advantage of the religiosity generated by human love in order to confine men and women to lives where such love is forbidden. The holy Protestant image of mother and child absorbed in what Richard Brodhead has called "disciplinary intimacy" or "discipline through love" was deliberately and explicitly constructed through contrast with images of archaic, patriarchal, external physical authority: the schoolmaster wielding a rod, the slave-owner brandishing a whip, the Irish father waving a fist, and, I would add, the Jesuit exercising a despotic, arbitrary authority, backed by the inquisitorial instruments of torture secreted in convents. But in "The Catholic Convert," Hale argues that, for a true woman, even what appears to be an archaic religion of external rules is actually a matter of feeling. Mary became a Catholic, not because a priest forced her into frightened compliance, but because the substitute mother that she loved was Catholic. Indeed, Mary's father's plan for wooing her away from Catholicism rests on his recognition of religion's emotional basis: "Her creed was that of feeling; she had been educated a Catholic; and it requires something more powerful than arguments or advice to overcome the prepossessions of our childhood. I knew, in short, that her feeling must, by some means, become interested for Protestants; that she must become attached to individuals of this religion."[107] Perversion comes about when the scheming Jesuit father not only educates her to believe that family love is sin, but also condemns her to a life in which she will never be a mother, will never re-create mother-love in her children. In a period in which the dominant domestic ideology held up mother-love as the model and basis for Christian feeling,[108] Mary's Catholic fate appears not only unnatural but immoral.

Hale's retelling of world history in *Woman's Record* represents Catholic women's rescue from the convent by Gutenberg and Luther, by the printing press and the Reformation. "It was by reading the Word of God that the nine nuns of Nimptsch discerned the contrast between the Christian life, and the daily routine of the cloister. They left their superstitions and returned to the duties God imposes on the sex," a return exemplified by the case of Catharine Bora, who married Martin Luther and became a mother.[109] Gutenberg saves the Catholic nun by allowing her to learn God's word directly; Luther, by introducing her to Protestantism and to marriage. Similarly, Mary is rescued from the convent (as it were), not by her father's direct combat with the priest, nor the Redfields' substitute parenting, nor

through theological arguments, but by the Protestant minister who, Luther-
like, initiates her into Bible reading and marriage. Mary's first step towards
normal Protestant femaleness comes from mothering her brother, a task
which draws her out of her solitary room and into intimacy with the
family. The second, and decisive, step comes with her love for Mr. Watson,
the young Protestant minister who teaches her to study Nature, the Bible,
and, eventually, their mutual love as the true sources of religious feeling. As
a female ruled by heart, Mrs. Redfield had recognized that her husband's
clumsy attempts to convert Mary by reason (i.e., by reading from Revelation about the "scarlet-coloured beast" [71]) would not avail. "She did not
think a girl so young as Mary would be much influenced by the reasonable-
ness of a proposition; she must be led by gentle persuasions, and by those
tender appeals that would move her feelings" (71). Mrs. Redfield therefore
invites Mr. Watson to board with them. The relationship's turning point
comes when, during a long walk in the countryside, Watson gives Mary
her first Bible:

A deep glow overspread his face as he put the sacred volume into her hand . . . "if
there be a sin, let it rest on my head" [cried Watson].
  "O, no! no!" said Mary quickly. "If it is sin, the Saviour will surely forgive it –
and I have so longed to read the Bible" – She paused and blushed – and after a
few more entreaties from Watson, consented to keep the volume. (75–76)

Clearly, this is a seduction scene. However, instead of a scheming, "celibate"
priest perverting the young girl in the closed, secret space of the confessional,
Hale represents the Protestant minister and maiden alike as awakening
to a new life of holy conjugal feeling as they read the Bible and explore
the American landscape. If the Catholic Mary resembles a cloistered, celibate nun, removed from human emotions, the Protestant Mary, at play in
Nature, is a healthy young woman, educating herself, eligible for love and
marriage.

The treasure buried in the Brattleborough landscape turns out to be a
romantic narrative of a rescue into domesticity through reading. "Mary,
the sweet nun, returned to the south, the happy wife of the Rev. Alexander Watson" (97). Like the young women who will help their spouses save
the West for America and from the internationalism of Catholicism, Mary
will accompany her husband as missionary to convert the South from its
twin apostasies of Romanism and separatism. Hale's writings represent
what Anderson calls the "deep, horizontal comradeship" that supports – in
truth, *is* – the nation as under siege in this period.[110] Speaking of American
women's antebellum engagement with the "work of history," Baym

demonstrates that "[o]nce the biblical focus of history is grasped, it becomes clear that the women's main aim in teaching and writing it was to further the advance of Protestantism, an aim which brought together religious, national, and gender loyalties in one surpassing commitment."[111] In "The Catholic Convert" Hale demonstrates how the story of an American girl's education enacts that multi-leveled commitment. The work of claiming (in the West), and reclaiming (in the South), America is, for Sarah Josepha Hale, woman of letters, one of female literacy.

Mary's rescue is the Republic's – and it is also the Redfields': New England must also recall its membership in a United States. At the close of the story, Hale focuses on Mrs. Redfield, the figure for the woman reader who is Hale's primary target. Mary's romantic narrative softens and refines the older woman, making her kinder and more contented. Telling and retelling "the strange story," Mrs. Redfield becomes "quite a lady" (97). Remembering, Mrs. Redfield reshapes herself from a money-hungry, garrulous gossip into the Victorian middle-class ideal.

"The Catholic Convert" ends with a vision of marital happiness, of a unified Republic, of a middle-class household refined by female gentility; it ends, that is, as domestic fiction. Yet that vision rests on its author's and audience's knowledge of sensational and anti-Catholic characters and plots. Franchot shows how the enduringly popular *Foxe's Book of Martyrs* "mythologized Catholicism into a virtual demon of antidomesticity."[112] Hale summons and then exorcises that demon's nineteenth-century literary manifestations: the nun, the Jesuit, the convent, and the confessional. The masked intruder returns as the Protestant father; the Jesuit is relegated to the past; the nun turns out to have been only a virgin, waiting to become a bride, yet *Traits of American Life* has its origins nonetheless in a dark stranger, "The Unknown."

CHAPTER 2

The dead father and the rule of religion: the Oxford Movement

Reading the escaped nun's tale we begin to see how anti-Catholic narrative functions in the imagining of a national community – or, rather, the often desperate and deliberate work of *reimagining* nationhood in the face of growing diversity, expansion, and secularization. The complex evidentiary status of the escaped nun's tale speaks to questions of authenticity and authority that continue to vex polemical religious fiction throughout the century. American convent narratives were widely read in Britain: Monk's and Reed's stories, published sometimes together and sometimes separately, saw over a dozen British editions before 1855 and were regularly quoted in anti-Catholic pamphlets and speeches. Religious sisterhoods themselves were a much-debated topic in Britain.[1] However, it is in the sensational novels of the 1860s to 1880s, with their discussion of marriage, that the convent seems to best offer an ideologically useful space in British fiction, a phenomenon to which I will return in Chapter 5.

If American writers formulate issues of nationhood early in the century by telling a story about the dangers and weaknesses of young women, British fiction of the forties depicts the vulnerability of young men, focusing on the appeals and dangers of paternal authority in an era in which family and educative models were rapidly changing. Polemical religious fiction targets the group within the Church of England, variously labeled the Tractarian, Puseyite, or Oxford Movement. Controversy over the Tractarians undoubtedly belongs to the internal politics of Protestantism; its connections to anti-Catholicism are, however, direct and various. For what the Tractarians were accused of was, precisely, secret popery. Well before Newman "went over" to Rome in 1845, many suspected that Oxford undergraduates were being converted to Romanism. Those suspicions were aired in Parliamentary addresses, newspaper columns, religious pamphlets, and popular novels, which saw Oxford as "the Thermopylae of the age,"[2] the crucial, and defining, point of a civilization's defense. If Oxford were to be lost to the foreign imperial force of the Vatican, Britain as such would cease to exist. While Sarah Hale campaigned to persuade Americans that young women's education was the key to a unified Republic, the British needed no convincing that their nation's future depended directly on the young men of Oxford who would become its leaders.

Unlike Chapter 1 which treated a large group of narratives, I will concentrate here on individual novels by two writers, *Hawkstone: A Tale of and for England in 184-* (1845) by William Sewell and *Father Eustace: A Tale of the Jesuits* (1847) by Frances Trollope.[3] Rather than focusing on the development of a standard plot, then, this chapter compares the way two writers with widely different political and religious beliefs respond narratively to a central moment in nineteenth-century religious history.[4] *Hawkstone* and *Father Eustace* are deeply gendered tales, reflecting their authors' respective professional and cultural situations. Sewell's institutionalized stations as a professional educator and scholar contrast markedly with Trollope's position as a woman writing popular books with broad appeal in order to support her family.

Reading these two novels closely illustrates how, even in the attempt to suppress what was seen as a foreign threat, the prevailing Protestant culture was far from monolithic. Historians of nineteenth-century Britain have, especially in recent years, traced the antagonisms within Protestantism, emphasizing in particular the challenge that evangelical religion represented to the established Church. Literary studies, however, tend to treat Protestant culture as relatively uniform and united in its attitudes.[5] Yet, *Hawkstone* offers a conservative argument in favor of paternalism and male collegiality as the solution to the religious and political problems of "England in 184-." Sewell argues that the Church of England must be returned to its position of authority as the true Catholic Church. Trollope, on the other hand, sees male institutional authority as oppressive, indeed deadly. Emphasizing individual freedom and judgment – in particular *female* freedom and judgment – Trollope opposes what she sees as the gothic rule of Rome with an open mother–daughter relationship, where the mother raises the daughter in independence. Unlike Hale in America, who suggests that girls need to be guided into marriage, Trollope argues that young women should be taught independence if they (and England) are to survive.

Anti-Catholicism depends upon an essentialist vision of the Other as timeless and unchanging. Given the recurring images, motifs, and narratives that comprise these constructions of cultural Otherness, the historian who describes them is in danger of losing sight of the differences among anti-Catholicism's uses and occurrences and, in turn, risks essentializing Protestantism. Looking at the local – at these two specific examples of the uses of anti-Catholic rhetoric, characters, and plot – works as a corrective. Reading *Hawkstone* and *Father Eustace* closely illustrates the intricacy, and idiosyncrasy, of two contemporaneous Protestant responses to what both perceive as a Romanist infiltration of England.[6]

My point is not simply that Sewell and Trollope create widely differing novelistic responses to the same theological, political, historical events, but that they do so while sharing a repertoire of rhetorical and polemical devices. Reading *Hawkstone* and *Father Eustace* side-by-side is therefore revelatory regarding the politics of narrative. Employing the same anti-Catholic plots, tropes, and images, Sewell and Trollope outline diverse – indeed conflicting – ideologies. High Anglicans like Sewell shared the Oxford Movement's emphasis on ecclesiastical authority rooted in apostolic succession, interest in the revival of observances and practices, and intolerance for schism and dissent. (William Sewell was himself a Tractarian until the appearance of Newman's Tract 90.)[7] In *Hawkstone*, Sewell responds to the threat of Roman Catholicism by calling for obedience to the received authority of the Anglican Church. In contrast, Broad or Low Church attacks on Tractarianism, like Frances Trollope's *Father Eustace*, tend to assume that any evidence of High churchmanship is proof of hidden popery and to emphasize the essential Englishness of individual autonomy.

While differing in their political and religious allegiances, both of these very different novels assume a central ideological framework that informed most nineteenth-century social theories: the belief that society's structure should mimic that of the family. As Sewell states in his *Christian Politics* (1848), "Domestic Society [is] the Type of Political Society" (56–57). *Hawkstone* is explicitly concerned with Rome's threat to both national and nuclear families:

"will not the vengeance of Heaven, sooner or later, in some frightful shape, fall upon those miserable men, who, under the name and garb of religion, are rending asunder, in this country, ties which God has joined, and tearing the children of this empire from their Father in the State and in the Church, as my child was torn from me!" [laments Sewell's hero Edmund Villiers] (2: 422)

Trollope, too, employs the trope of the (national) family, emphasizing the need for creative and created familial relations as a defense against popery.

The rhetorical and ideological equation of family and nation serves multiple purposes in anti-Catholic discourse. As the escaped nun's tale suggests, Protestant polemicists regarded the Catholic Church's emphasis on celibacy as invidiously anti-family. And, as Chapter 3's analysis of American nativist fiction will make clear, the Protestant teleology that both discovers and denies Catholicism as the starting point for Christianity, makes the topics of origin and inheritance particularly vexed. Here, I want to begin by focusing on the way that Sewell's political philosophy locates the origins of both civil society and religion as a family story of what he identifies as Oedipal guilt. However, the history that Sewell tells must itself be historicized within "England in 184-."

THE TRACTARIANS

Sewell and Trollope both tell their 1840s family stories specifically in response to what began as an attempt by a small group of Oxford divines to restore the historical authority of the Church of England. Constitutional changes had made the relation of Church to State the subject of widespread debate; a national church seemed about to become a thing of the past; democratic (and demagogic) politics threatened traditional hierarchies. Faced with growing popular sympathy for constitutional reform and with widespread theological and devotional latitudinarianism, the Tractarians turned to an intensive rereading of the Church fathers in an attempt to justify and clarify ecclesiastical authority. In the works of these early writers, the Tractarians found warrant for a return to the Church's original unity.

Ultimately, this reassertion of a primal and primary Church authority, transmitted through apostolic succession, led a number of Oxonians – most notoriously John Henry Newman – to submit themselves to papal rule and join the Church of Rome. As Walter Arnstein notes, these converts seemed to threaten England in a way that the growing population of impoverished Irish immigrant Catholics did not (the Irish problem is, however, figured fictionally in *Hawkstone* in the figure of Connell).

Although individual cases of conversion to Roman Catholicism were not unknown in early nineteenth-century England, it was in the 1840s that a trickle became in the minds of many Englishmen a flood. . . . The significance of the conversion process for Englishmen of the day lay less in the absolute number of the converts than in their intellectual distinction and their social status.[8]

Almost from the start, Keble, Newman, and Pusey, the leaders of the Tractarian movement, were figures of controversy – in ecclesiastical and political debate, in the national press, and at Oxford, where Newman, in particular, commanded an unprecedented student following. The threat to young English manhood seemed clear since, as Owen Chadwick explains, "By prestige and history Oxford university weighed heavily in

the establishment. It nurtured English statesmen, guarded orthodoxy, educated future clergymen."9

Both the crisis in ecclesiastical authority that motivated the Tractarians
and the cult-like power that they were rumored to wield over the finest
of England's youth propel the plots of *Hawkstone* and *Father Eustace.* For
Trollope, the figure of Newman conjures up the specter of the unchecked
patriarchal power that lurks in countless anti-Catholic polemics – that of
the suave, sly Jesuit General. Drawing on her readers' Protestant prejudices, Trollope pictures a young man so trained in obedience to the holy
father that he gives up all will of his own. In contrast to this careful,
thorough – and deadly – education of male youth in celibacy, Trollope
suggests that young women's "neglected" education may leave them free
to make the religious and familial choices that will ensure England's survival. In contrast to Trollope, Sewell, who shares the Tractarians' horror at
the Church of England's willingness to tolerate all diversity, regards such
religious individuality as threatening to national religious hegemony. He
describes, on the one hand, an Anglican minister destroyed by his failure
to wield his rightful religious authority and, on the other, an uncontrolled
throng of laborers. Yet, despite his conservative position on ecclesiastical
authority, Sewell, too, turns to anti-Catholic narrative strategies and characters, including yet another darkly plotting Jesuit, in order to demonstrate
that those at Oxford who turn to Rome are abdicating their Christian duties
as Englishmen. But Sewell's Jesuit differs from Trollope's suave, sophisticated strategist who fastidiously rules his international empire from Rome.
Drawing on an alternative stereotype of priestly corruption, Sewell describes
a crude, passionate, violent cleric with bloody hands. Indeed, through this
figure of an unholy father, Sewell suggests that Romanism threatens to
devolve modern Christian politics into an archaic state of nature.

WILLIAM SEWELL'S *CHRISTIAN POLITICS*

Hawkstone's anti-Catholic polemic rehearses the political philosophy that
William Sewell outlined in his 1848 *Christian Politics* and attempted to
implement in his years as an educator. Sewell's Christian politics is based
on the English ideal of a *limited* paternal authority. Described as "the age's
definitive statement on paternalism," *Christian Politics* prescribes a pluralis-
tic, local, and personal authority – "involving an authoritarianism that was
tempered by common law and ancient liberties."10 Both family and nation
are founded on obedience to the divinely sanctioned authority of rulers.
The worst crimes are those that sin against such authority: Sewell offers

the example of "Oedipus, the murderer of his father, and the marrier of his mother"[11] – an example that figures in *Hawkstone*'s family narratives.

Despite his reiterated emphasis on submission, Sewell acknowledges that civil and religious obedience must be voluntary – otherwise, authority is nothing more than a primitive despotism, like, he insists, that of the Papacy. The true Christian subject (and, in particular, the Englishman) must, at times, exercise choice. The question to be faced is "how can he guard himself from acting entirely on his own judgment; and leave the selection, as far as possible, in the hands of Providence?"[12] The answer, Sewell insists, is through the rule of law. Without legal authority, society devolves into anarchic democracy – as America's example demonstrates. In the "Hungry forties," labor unrest and Irish immigration made such a devolution seem possible in England. The decade saw economic depression, unemployment, frequent labor demonstrations, and cholera outbreaks; exposés and government reports presented the public with a nation in crisis. And immigration seemed to be eroding the (supposed) homogeneity of the English: the number of Irish-born in England grew from 290,891 in 1841 to 519,959 in 1851.[13]

In this context, the Oxford Movement's theological interrogation of Church and Government authority appears all the more dangerous. Anarchism, Sewell insists in *Christian Politics*, opens the way for the return of an archaic, violent, imposed rule, a rule depicted in *Hawkstone* in the figure of primitive father, specifically the Roman Catholic father. *Hawkstone*'s voice of reason, the holy Anglican minister Beattie, fellow of Oxford, and rector of the religious community that Villiers founds, explains that Romanism is "rather a retrogression in the development of His [God's] revelations than an advance. It is virtually a restoration of Judaism. It wants every mark which our blessed Lord set upon His own divine commission and ministry."[14] Invoking teleological Protestant history, Beattie warns that Romanism rejects the mild, loving discipline of the feminized Christ in favor of the archaic authority of the Old Testament patriarch. Popery is, Beattie insists, the tyrannical rule of a "maniac" – "uncompromising, universal, infallible." Implicit here is the image of the Papal Father as a savage despot, wielding an arbitrary and absolute authority. And the bloody religious history of the English monarchy, complete with its narratives of plotting, exile, and return, is surely a factor in this nightmare of an older, despotic authority who seeks to reclaim power.[15]

In *Christian Politics* Sewell outlines his solution to England's crisis of authority. England must turn neither to democracy (the rule by all) nor despotism (the rule by one), but to a graduated series of colleges, episcopal, parochial, and charitable: a group of clergy living fraternally together to support each bishop in his work; curates to aid each parish priest; and "Levites" to discharge "offices of charity, of education, of attendance on the sick, of superintendence over the poor." Each of these groups of "brothers" would be bound in obedience to a rule administered by a "head" whose authority is recognizably that of the limited paternalism that Sewell sees as peculiarly British: "though he retains in his own hands the one controlling, governing power, [he] governs by means of a body which enlarges his sphere of action, multiplies his faculties and senses, covers his defects, augments his means, and almost gives ubiquity and perpetuity to his being, within his little province." Herbert Sussman has shown how Thomas Carlyle, faced with the increasing public perception of the Tractarian Movement as effeminate and homoerotic, salvages his dream of monasticism by removing the male community of *Past and Present* (1843) to the twelfth century. For Sewell, who also offers an idealized male community as a solution to contemporary problems, the Romanizing of the Church and universities of England represents less an erosion in the boundaries of male attachment and more a dangerous individualism.[16]

Sewell had attempted to actualize the political theories of *Christian Politics* in a series of educational experiments. Fellow and subrector of Exeter, professor of moral philosophy at Oxford, Sewell founded two public boys schools, St. Columba's and Radley. There he sought to establish a public and private network of authority centered in the schoolmaster, whom Sewell called "sovereign."[17]

Lionel James argues that Sewell was "the earliest preacher and practiser of the ideal now accepted by all British schools of the school not as a barrack but as a wider home with the Head as the father and the staff as elder brothers." The earlier view of the boys and masters as natural enemies was replaced by the model family as described by Sewell: "The Head Master of a Public School has to . . . undertake to provide in that school for the due combination and discharge of the two parental functions – the strictness and firmness of a father and the tenderness and loving kindness of a mother." In his first address to the students at Radley, Sewell "spoke strongly of the affection which I had for them, the kindness, the more than kindness and confidence with which I longed to treat them – but I said I would make no secret I would be obeyed. And if affection was useless and punishment was needed I would scourge with a rod of iron."[18]

Sewell's pedagogy displays how educational philosophy and practice shifted – and often conflicted – in the first half of the nineteenth century. Nineteenth-century headmasters presided over the British public schools' change from a society of "free" boys, virtually ruling themselves, to a controlled training ground for moral "manliness" (Thomas Arnold is the most famous representative of this change).[19] When Sewell declares affection, he attempts to enact the "modern" ideal of self-regulation instilled through deep attachment to a specific individual.[20] The headmaster's declaration of love will earn the students' reciprocal emotions. Desiring to identify their wishes with the master's own, the students will develop an internalized discipline. Sewell himself describes this disciplinary gaze: "Constantly we shall be visiting the dormitory, coming upon you suddenly – (until we feel you have strength enough to resist the temptation of being left alone) coming among you at all hours, myself, the Fellows, the Prefects, and if we should find it necessary even our confidential servants," Sewell warned the Radley boys in a sermon.[21] What public school students and administrators alike would once have despised as spying is now preached as the gospel of socialization into self-control.

However, if this civilized and civilizing discipline fails, Sewell will revert to the old-fashioned means of compelling obedience: physical punishment. Sewell's discourse documents this shift when he moves from the language of love to what many nineteenth-century Anglicans would regard as the words of an angry Old Testament God ("I will scourge them with a rod of iron"). And, despite his lengthy descriptions of his affectional disciplinary system, Sewell's attraction to the rod seems clear: "To this hour some of the most delightful, touching, blessed associations I have are connected with the Whipping Room at Radley," Sewell recalls fondly in *Reminiscences*.[22] In the previous chapter, the contrast between Hale's story and the more sensational narratives it borrows from introduced the polemical distinction between a coercive Catholicism and the normalized discipline of a Protestantism entered into emotionally and relationally. Sewell positions himself on both sides of this roughly Foucauldian divide: training the boys in self-surveillance, but falling back on physical chastisement. Tension between these two forms of authority pervades *Hawkstone*, which declares an allegiance to loving discipline even as it delineates the sadomasochistic attractions of corporal punishment.

HAWKSTONE

Hawkstone is a novel of failed natural families, set in a nation where "No shelter is open in our Church . . . no homes in this country, which, when father and mother desert us, may take us up, and rescue us from the cruelty and mockery of the world, in the name of the father and of the mother of us all. Alas! – poor England!"[23] The novel depicts the newly industrialized town of Hawkstone as a religious, political, and cultural Babel, a community without a ruler, and, hence, without rule. Irish immigrants are everywhere; revolution is imminent. When the local lord, Ernest Villiers, returns to Hawkstone, his first act is one of symbolic paternal recovery: he heroically rescues a poor youth (in truth, his own child) from fiery death. Villiers's public goal is the reestablishment of religious authority in the form of the Anglican Catholic church, his private, the reclaiming of his role as father through the recovery of his lost son.

In the beginning chapters of the novel, the practices of traditional English Roman Catholics are presented as more attractive, seemingly more religious, than the lax relativism that prevails in the modern Church of England. Himself the son of the "ill-assorted union" of a holy Roman Catholic mother (the Lady Esther) and a nominally Protestant libertine father (General Villiers), Ernest Villiers's filial narrative figures Sewell's polemical ecclesiastical history ("On a small scale he was called on to solve the same problem, which England is called to solve upon a vast one"). Torn from his loving mother at an early age, Villiers is sent to Eton and Oxford, then summoned to Italy by his dissipated, "tyrannical," dying father.[24] Once there, he escapes the General's querulous demands whenever possible, leaving his father to the care of an unscrupulous servant, Pearce, who is a secret Jesuit. Instead of suffering by the side of his father, Villiers finds temporary happiness in love and secret marriage to a beautiful Italian Roman Catholic maiden, Pauline, who has previously rejected Pearce's attentions. Taunted by Pearce about this liaison, Villiers proudly proclaims Pauline his wife and strikes the servant, thus prompting the novel's revenge plot. By terrorizing and blackmailing the General, Pearce manages to displace Villiers as heir. Pauline dies soon after giving birth to a son, also named Ernest. Villiers returns to his father only in time to witness the General's agonized death. He then arrives home to find his son missing – kidnapped by Pearce.

Pearce deliberately raises the younger Ernest in an atmosphere of depravity, eventually placing him in the household of Connell, an Irishman who has, at Pearce's instigation, murdered a Protestant minister and fled to England. Connell, whose name marks him as a politically representative Irishman, is emotional, loyal, alcoholic, and easily led. He exemplifies what Sewell had, in the *Quarterly Review*, described as a typical Irishman: one who, without English discipline and regulation, falls prey to the religious and political demagoguery that Jesuits are only too ready to supply in Ireland and in England ("Romanism in Ireland"). Just as he encourages lawlessness in Villiers's lost son and among the Irish immigrants, so Pearce foments revolution and anarchy in the abandoned English working classes whom unscrupulous industrialists have left without guidance or sustenance. Both plots are part of the Romanist plan to annex England for the Vatican.

As this summary makes evident, Sewell casts his political analysis of 1840s England as a story about father and sons. Writing at a moment when religious and civil authority appear threatened by the heterodoxy of England's best youth and the lawlessness of the mob, Sewell seeks to analyze the origins of that authority. In *Hawkstone*, he insists that Villiers's (and, by extension, England's) crisis is propelled by a failure in obedience. In *Christian Politics*, Sewell offers Oedipus as the negative model of the disobedient son, whose "fate is held up as a picture of the deepest horror and suffering which ever befel mankind."[25] In *Hawkstone* the temptation to love a woman – Lady Esther, Pauline, Lady Eleanor (the Roman Catholic Englishwoman Villiers longs to marry), the Blessed Virgin – is represented as identical with the act of disobeying the father.

Perhaps the most explicit example of this rule is given when, directly after the General dies, Villiers, despondent at his filial failure, falls into a broken sleep and dreams of Pauline.

The delicate beautiful face came, indeed, and looked upon him as before, but it changed suddenly into the horrible and ghastly figure which he had witnessed on his father's deathbed. It seemed to utter on him fearful reproaches; to imprecate a curse upon himself and on his children, with the same voice with which his father had bade him depart, in the last words which he had spoken to him while alive. The eyes glared frightfully upon him; claws were stretched out to seize him; a cry – the cry of agony which had pierced him to the heart from his father's room – once more rang in his ears. . . .

We can recognize this as a conventional gothic scene: the beautiful, desirable woman is revealed as a corpse. Male heterosexual desire is coupled with fear of the female body as dead and deadly. But in Sewell's version the bride is revealed to be the dying father. In a classically Oedipal configuration, loving a woman is here figured as killing the father. Villiers realizes that choosing Pauline over his father was the original Oedipal "sin; and sin the beginning of all others – the dishonouring of parents, even of parents who are sinful themselves."[26]

Examining Villiers's love for Lady Eleanor also leads us back, through dreams, to the Oedipal triangle. Lady Esther, Lady Eleanor – mother and lover are associated not only by their alliterative names and their Roman Catholicism, but also by behavior and appearance. For example, entering his dead mother's rooms, Villiers finds "a female figure" kneeling in her place – yet what he is seeing is not the ghost of Lady Esther, but the body of Lady Eleanor. Later, when he is tempted to convert to a Roman Catholicism that he knows is false in order to marry Lady Eleanor, Villiers dreams warningly of a collapsing Anglican cathedral:

a black chasm yawned beneath the altar and swallowed it up; the worshippers and priests fled with cries of terror: and as there gathered round him in their place a host of frightful demon visages screaming in triumph, Villiers saw through a distant aisle a figure – a female figure – beautiful, pure, innocent, and holy – the figure by whose side he had watched over his uncle's bed – beckoning him to escape, and to escape with her.

Lady Eleanor is unnamed here, perhaps because she represents the female figure one might expect to see at the end of a church aisle: the Blessed Virgin (a figure with whom the Roman Catholic Pauline is also closely associated). With the cathedral dream, Sewell recognizes that, as the Church of England appears to be collapsing in 184-, Englishmen will be tempted to flee to the safety of Rome, here imaged as a woman. Villiers is saved from this "escape" only by a chance glance at the Prayer-book which is open to the text: – "Lead us not into temptation."[27]

What is striking is that the father whom Villiers has failed to obey is, the narrative clearly and repeatedly shows, unworthy. As the representative of contemporary English Protestantism, General Villiers is lax and selfish, particularly in contrast to the saintly, loving Roman Catholic parent that Lady Esther figures. Yet, Sewell argues that the God-sanctioned hierarchical structure of society is maintained not by the respect that any individual might earn, but by the reverence that institutions themselves command. In *Christian Politics*, Sewell addresses directly the problem of paternal weakness, saying that "This is the history of States, no less than of families; and the laws to be observed in this crisis are well deserving attention." No matter how strong the offspring becomes, the father's authority, Sewell insists, must be preserved, an argument with particular resonance for Britain's burgeoning empire and during a period of an increasing Irish population in England and Scotland. *Hawkstone*'s plot asserts again and again that "sons ought to bear with their father."[28]

Yet within *Hawkstone*, the son's disobedience is also a *felix culpa*. Following his dream that Pauline transformed into his father's corpse, "Every thing ended in remorse; and even remorse was sweet, for it was real, and true: it bore on no delusion. And as he bowed himself to the ground, and prayed, Villiers began to feel what religion is; he felt it in its first beginning – sorrow and shame." Oedipal sin institutes religion.

This self-abasement recurs throughout the novel, perhaps most strikingly when Pearce sets his foot on the kneeling Villiers's neck: "Villiers bore it all. He remembered the curse of undutifulness, to be made a servant of servants." After the dream of Pauline teaches him remorse for disobeying the father, Villiers's vocation lies in instituting religious rituals, founding religious communities, establishing religious practices. In doing so, he restores Christian civilization to Hawkstone. In the place of Romanist despotism and Irish democracy, Villiers restores the muted, shared, circumscribed authority of Anglicanism: "a church which, while it asserts its own independence and authority, can submit itself to the authority of another power as equally ordained of God," a church whose "first fundamental principles is obedience," a church, in short, befitting *Christian Politics*.[29] The religious organization that marks England as at once Christian and civilized has its origins, it turns out, in the father's absence. Sewell's language implies that the death of the General prompts the Villiers not only to find, but also to *found* religion. The individual paternal despot is replaced by an institutionalized authority.

There is, of course, another, more famous narrative that locates the origins of civilization and religion in the act of patricide: Freud's *Totem and Taboo*. Studying these two stories about fathers and sons together does not provide a psychoanalytic key to Sewell's anti-Catholic fiction, but, as with the Oedipus myth, opens out a set of fruitful resonances between the two theorists of self and society. Freud narrates:

there is a violent and jealous father who keeps all the females for himself and drives away his sons as they grow up. . . . One day the brothers who had been driven out came together, killed and devoured their father and so made an end of the patriarchal horde. . . . The violent primal father had doubtless been the feared and envied model of each one of the company of brothers: and in the act of devouring him they accomplished their identification with him, and each one of them acquired a portion of his strength. The totem meal, which is perhaps mankind's earliest festival, would thus be a repetition and a commemoration of this memorable and criminal deed, which was the beginning of so many things – of social organization, of moral restrictions and of religion. . . .[30]

Freud goes on to explain that, after killing the father, the sons feel guilt and remorse. "The dead father became stronger than the living one had been." As a result they outlaw any subsequent killing of the father (in the form of the father's substitute, the totem); religion is instituted as a form of "deferred obedience." The sons also give up their claim to the father's women, thus diffusing male rivalry. Rather than fighting among themselves for the father's individualized place, the sons elect to remain members of a group. The patriarchal horde is replaced by the fraternal clan. "Society was now based on complicity in the common crime; religion was based on the sense of guilt and the remorse attaching to it; while morality was based partly on the exigencies of this society and partly on the penance demanded by the sense of guilt."[31]

What Freud's later story allows us to recognize is that it is not just the savage mob rule that Sewell fears. If the democraticizing forces of the age succeed in toppling the civilized, circumscribed rule of English limited paternalism, England faces something worse than the horror of the horde. Disobedience invokes the return of the "violent and jealous" primal father.[32] When Villiers's disobedience kills the General, the result is not the son's autonomy but the institution of Pearce's tyrannical Roman Catholic rule. The overthrow of English, Anglican, authority opens a space for papal religious and political tyranny. This is the other face of Catholicism: not the seducing mother, but the punishing father. Inheriting the general's place, replacing Villiers as father by kidnapping the infant Ernest, orchestrating political, social, and religious unrest, Pearce becomes the author of both Hawkstone's history and *Hawkstone*'s plot.

Sewell makes the connection to the Oxford Movement explicit: Scorning the mild authority of the Church of England, which rules "not as a tyrant, but as a parent," young Oxonians "are clamouring for a sterner, stricter rule; for a more imperious, sweeping dogmatism; for a more uncompromising exclusiveness. And this they would call strength and power," little knowing what they ask. Sewell sets out to show them with the figure of Pearce. Drawing on English images of Catholic priests that date back at least to the Reformation, Sewell underscores the role that Pearce is meant to play:

the eyes small, and twinkling with deep lurking cunning, yet capable of concealing their expression, and his dress that of a butcher. But there was something about his whole appearance singular and almost unnatural, – a certain contrast between his dress and his manner, which was felt rather than understood, and an evident desire to make observations upon others, without being able to face others himself.

Even if the narrator did not say so explicitly, Sewell's nineteenth-century audience would recognize Pearce as a Jesuit: disguised, cunning, and brutal; the unseen watcher; the spy. The butcher's dress puns on the cruelty and violence Pearce carries from Rome (earlier in the book, the Roman Coliseum is made the scene of a sacrificial assassination by Jesuits). We can recognize as well that Pearce is a figure of the uncanny: he is and is not what he seems, the gap "between his dress and his manner . . . felt rather than understood." Reappearing at moments of crisis and in a variety of disguises (including, significantly, that of an ancient Jew), Pearce, the primal father, represents and resurrects the past: "Villiers himself felt a strange indescribable sensation thrill through him, and waken, as it were, a whole train of old and strange associations, which transported him to a distant clime." Like Oedipus, Villiers at once fails to know and knows his parent.[33]

The danger that this figure represents is illustrated by the manner of his death. The few mentions of *Hawkstone* that surface in twentieth-century studies of Victorian religious fiction[34] inevitably bring up its macabre description of Pearce's end: an "object of horror which they had found on entering the catacomb. . . . It was a body all but devoured by rats. . . . All over the pavement were traces of blood, as if this wretched man had fled from place to place before his ferocious assailants; and there were marks of bloody hands upon the walls. . . . The extremities were wholly gone. The vitals must have been attacked last."[35] I want to argue that the reason for this lovingly detailed sadism is not merely Sewell's hatred of Romanism and Jesuits nor the remembered dangers of England's disputed throne. The level of textual violence – excessive even in this melodramatic text – suggests that these factors converge with the threat of a more primal force; this is the violence with which the sons must assert themselves against the primitive father.

Hawkstone, then, suggests one of the reasons that Rome plays such a lively role in the Victorian imagination. Despite the fact that anti-Catholicism was often scoffed at during the Victorian era as embarrassingly outdated, the superstition of ignorant peasants, it maintained a stubborn hold on many.[36] Rome's presence in the cultural imagination of Victorian Protestants is overdetermined (and multifaceted), as both this chapter and my study as a whole demonstrate. The Oxford movement, Irish immigration, liberalism, changes in the law, Pius IX's actions, Cardinal Wiseman's declarations of authority – all worked at various times to activate inherited prejudices against Catholicism. What Sewell's national family narrative indicates is that the Roman Catholic father is still a source of cultural nightmare in part because he represents the return of Protestantism's past. Within the narrative of Protestant teleological history, Rome is the origin that modern, civilized Christianity has anxiously buried. In the *Quarterly Review*, Sewell described Romanism as the undead, warning: "We say again to the nineteenth century – *beware of Popery*. It was smitten down at the Reformation; in the next century it revived again. In the French Revolution it seemed at its death-gasp; it is now full of vigour." The French democratizing mob of the eighteenth century returns as the growing impoverished and immigrant population of the 1840s, both crowds that are perceived as demographically, symbolically, and, we might say, philosophically Catholic. In *Hawkstone*, as the image of the Jesuit as a Jew illustrates, Pearce's rule represents a religious devolution, the victory of the Old Testament over the New, a story of vengeance rather than love.[37] The Wandering Jew, with whom Pearce is repeatedly identified, figures the stubborn recalcitrance of the unregenerate who refuse Christian redemption and, with it, modernity.[38]

This figure from the past represents a special threat to Sewell precisely because Sewell himself is so drawn to the past. His political, educational, and fictional writings all make clear that he abhors the transformations that are taking place in the 1840s. In *Hawkstone*, as well as in *Christian Politics* and elsewhere, Sewell rails against what others call "progress": England's industrialization, the growth of a market economy, universal public education, growing religious tolerance and liberalism, the feminization, secularization, and institutionalization of social services. In opposition to such forces of modernity, Villiers deliberately encourages a return to agriculture, local trade, and cottage industries, and the restoration of charitable works to family and local church responsibility. But Sewell wants to take the return to the past only so far. He faces an historical dilemma much discussed in nineteenth-century religious polemic. Simply put: if originary Christian authority lies in Catholicism and the Catholic Church still exists, what is the warrant for Protestant authority? (See Chapter 3 for how these problems of origin and authority get configured in antebellum America.) In what sense is the Protestant an authentic Christian? How can the political theorist of Christian Paternalism dismiss Papal Authority? How can Sewell argue for tradition while attacking reversion to Rome? This is, of course, an instance of the general dilemma pointed out by nineteenth-century political thinkers facing the accelerated changes of the era. It is also, specifically, the problem that Newman himself faced: having begun by tracing the Church of England's legitimacy through apostolic succession, he ends by admitting Rome's prior and continuing claims.

Freud suggests that ritual is a way to recall yet contain the past. The Christian story of Christ's death is an example of how the sons' guilt and rebelliousness regarding the father are acted out as religious ritual: the sacrificial death of the son who is his father's substitute, a simultaneous expiation and reenactment of the original parricide. In *Hawkstone*, there is a nearly obsessive pairing of sons' and fathers' murders, the one substituting for the other. Villiers's "murder" of his father, the General, results in the disappearance of his son Ernest, the destruction of the boy's identity. Towards the end of the novel when father and son unknowingly battle one another; Ernest's foster-father Connell deliberately takes a fatal blow that Ernest

Senior (unwittingly) meant for his lost child. Earlier, Villiers encounters a disobedient young soldier under his command. Although (or perhaps because) the soldier's behavior is due to a lawless, lonely upbringing that duplicates that of the lost son Ernest, Villiers flogs his subordinate, yet it is Villiers who falls into a deathlike swoon immediately afterwards. At the end of the novel, the ruined Ernest is condemned to death, convicted on Villiers's unwilling testimony. Unlike the Irish Connell whose primitive attachment to his adopted son knows no limits ("Irishmen never forget their children"), Villiers's more evolved ethics mean that the institution of the law supersedes his personal loyalties. Reprieved only after he has taken poison, the son dies in his father's arms. That this filial sacrifice finally succeeds in warding off the primitive father's return is made clear when the masons open the family vault for Ernest's burial and discover an "object of horror" that Villiers identifies as the bloody remains of "the destroyer of . . . [my] child" – Pearce's body in Ernest's crypt.[39]

The Whipping Room at Radley, Villiers's self-abasement, the bloody torture of Pearce, the father-son dance of death – *Hawkstone*'s pervasive sadomasochism is characteristic of anti-Catholic discourse generally, whether it be the physical penances inflicted on imprisoned nuns or, more spectacularly, the tortures of the Inquisition. This topic will be discussed more fully in the following chapters; here, I would note how the figure of a sadistic paternal authority is associated with Catholicism's supposed refusal of the internalized disciplinary structures of modernity and Protestantism, its stubborn adherence to a regime of external, physical punishment. Yet, coupled with this denunciation of a primitive theological and political system, ruled by force, is a frightening and frightened attraction to that archaic power. Sewell shares the Oxford Movement's need to locate an historically legitimate source of religious jurisdiction. And, as *Christian Politics* makes clear, he sees England as facing a breakdown in its traditional institutions of legal, political, and cultural authority. *Hawkstone*'s convoluted narrative, structured around scenes of father–son misrecognition and discovery bespeaks a desire to know and be known, even if – perhaps especially if – that knowledge is experienced as pain.[40]

Like Freud at the turn of the century, Sewell in the 1840s bases his theory of civilization on the need to limit individual freedom and power. Freud argues that civilization – the rule of the "sons" – can allow only a partial restoration of the father's rights in the form of the patriarchal family. Sewell's plans for civilization appear even more circumscribed: replacing biological fathers with institutional ones. The salvation of England, Sewell suggests in *Hawkstone*, rests not on families headed by fathers, but in fraternal organizations governed by a paternal head. While Sewell does not disallow families, *Hawkstone* repeatedly documents the ways that marriage to women corrupts male scholars and clergy. Sewell reserves his most loving praise and detailed plans for the male communities where the disruptive force of heterosexuality is replaced by harmonious homosocial bonds. Elaborately described at the novel's close, these communities are filled, in large part, with young men from Oxford. For Sewell, then, the college is at once the point of entry for Romanism's subversive invasion of England and, potentially, the place of Christian England's last stand, what Villiers calls "the Thermopylae of the age . . . when the barbarous host pours down upon us with their gold, and tumult, and jargon, and parade, it is there that the few must take their stand who dare to resist the invader." Roman Catholicism is like the Persian horde – a foreign, barbaric "oriental"[41] paganism, glittering, decadent, and superficial. Sewell's historical typology here, like his use of the Oedipus story, exemplifies how Victorian anti-Catholic discourse interweaves the mythic with the history of Protestant and Catholic relations as it narratizes the present.

REVISING THE POPISH PLOT: TROLLOPE'S *FATHER EUSTACE*

While Sewell sees Oxford as the site of England's fight to the death, for Frances Trollope the Oxford Movement is itself deadly. Sewell locates male identity in institutions that have emerged to negotiate the threat of and need for an authentic, antique paternal authority, institutions in which he has a deep personal and professional investment. Frances Trollope's position as a popular female novelist writing to sustain her family obviously lies outside such institutions, yet her family history is such that she knows them intimately. Her fictional attack on the Oxford Movement goes to what Sewell's writings point to as the foundations of a national system of "Christian Politics": the struggle for authoritative (paternal) recognition that devolves into sadomasochism. Rather than writing an overtly political novel like *Hawkstone*, however, Trollope frames her analysis in literary terms.

Known throughout most of the twentieth century as "Anthony's mother," the popular and prolific Frances Trollope has received some recent attention in studies of nineteenth-century industrial fiction which discuss her *Michael Armstrong* (1840) and *Jessie Phillips* (1844). However, like most of Trollope's other novels, *Father Eustace* (1847) is largely unread by contemporary critics. Even Trollope's most recent biographer dismisses the novel as a recycling of hoary gothic plots, pandering to popular taste.[42]

Father Eustace does contain multiple gothic elements and capitalizes as well on the Protestant preconceptions of Trollope's English audience, taking advantage of the way the Oxford Movement had reanimated old prejudices. Seeking to explain the revival of a seemingly anachronistic anti-Catholicism in nineteenth-century Britain, Walter Arnstein notes that "numerous mid-Victorians possessed a highly vivid sense of medieval history. There was but a narrow mental gap between the Victorian Gothic and the true Gothic."[43] Rather than dismissing *Father Eustace*'s use of antique, well-known plots, I want to argue that it is by confronting the powerful, sadistic father and female victims of the gothic that Trollope critiques political and psychological theories such as those of Sewell that locate the originating structures of self and society in patriarchal violence. Taking issue with the Tractarians' invocation of what she sees as an anachronistic patriarchal authority, Trollope writes a story of female self-authoring. Pairing an exquisitely educated English youth with a "self-schooling" young woman, Juliana de Morley, Trollope is able to demonstrate the superiority of pedagogical, familial, and narrative structures generated by female autonomy.

Father Eustace's engagement with – and departure from – the gothic can be seen at the beginning of the novel when Juliana's father, Richard de Morley, dies. Exploring from turret to dungeon the family castle that she has inherited, Juliana follows a conventional gothic path. But, despite mocking allusions to brides entombed in iron chests and Udolphoean mysteries, "the adventure ended much as all other such adventures in the nineteenth century are likely to end"[44] – with the heroine deploring the horrors and tyrannical cruelties of the benighted past. Trollope's lighthearted dismissal of the castle's terrors seems to signal that her modern text will eschew the gothic's clumsy machinations. Yet *Father Eustace* challenges Juliana's easy assumption that horror and tyranny have no place in the enlightened nineteenth century. Trollope's often comic rewriting of the gothic exemplifies how many Victorian Protestant fictions both invoke and dismiss traditional tales of Roman Catholicism's historical power. What *Father Eustace* ultimately argues is that such narratives, whatever their subversive subtexts, finally rest on a willing acceptance of patriarchal authority.

With *Father Eustace*, Trollope not only suggests an alternative arc for the gothic and anti-Catholic narratives that are her models, but she also imagines a happier ending for her own family story. Like many women writers of her era, Frances Trollope found in the creation of fictional families a means of supporting her own children. Faced with her husband's financial failure, Trollope wrote some thirty-five novels, many of them centered around the dominant women characters who became her trademark.[45] Much of

Trollope's popular success stemmed from her ability to incorporate contemporary life into her work, whether she was writing satires of fashionable life, biting travel commentary, or fiction calling for reform. The Oxford Movement not only affords Trollope a timely topic, but also allows her to imagine a different fate for her daughter and herself.

Frances Trollope was vividly aware of the controversies surrounding the Tractarians. Her daughter-in-law records that Trollope conducted numerous dinner-party discussions about the Oxford scandals during the 1840s and met several times as well with Frederick William Faber, who had studied with Newman and converted to Roman Catholicism (Ransom suggests that meetings with Faber were the germ for *Father Eustace*). If Trollope's familiarity with the Oxford Movement was intimate, her personal connections with Oxford itself were also close. Both her father and husband had been fellows of New College. Her son Thomas Adolphus also attended Oxford, studying first at St. Albans under Whately and then at Magdalen, receiving his degree in 1835. While none of the Trollope men seems to have been seduced by or even much interested in the Oxford Movement, Frances Trollope's daughter Cecelia did become caught up with the High Church ideals of the Tractarians, writing a novel praising the strict observances of an Oxford-trained cleric, *Chollerton, a Tale of Our Own Times, By a Lady* (1846).[46]

In an era of strident religious controversy, Frances Trollope's own beliefs were comfortably moderate, a stance reflected in *Father Eustace*'s broad appeals to a relaxed, "ordinary" English Protestantism. In her writings, Trollope consistently criticizes religious extremism of all kinds; low as well as High Church dogmatism earn her scorn. Frances Eleanor Trollope commented that her mother-in-law: "remarks that it is a curious sign of the times, how very large a share High Churchism and Low Churchism have in the differences which divide men into two parties."[47] Trollope's best-known religious novel, *The Vicar of Wrexhill* (1837), attacks the practices of the evangelical clergy and criticizes the women who foolishly and self-destructively support them. Her depictions of popery in *Father Eustace* censure both the Church of Rome and those segments of the Church of England that have become, to her mind, Romanized. (Like Sewell, Trollope distinguishes between Romanist fanatics who are under the sway of Jesuit or proto-Jesuit confessors, and well-intentioned, if slightly misguided, traditional English Roman Catholics, who remain part of the general Christian community.)

What Trollope offers as an alternative to the popery that she attacks in *Father Eustace* is, of course, English Protestantism. Sewell's emphasis is on the Church of England's institutional status as the one true Catholic Church, the authentic preserver of Christian tradition. He calls for the Anglican Church to reject modern liberalism and diversity by reasserting its historical doctrinal authority. Trollope, on the other hand, looks not to the Church of England's Catholic origins but to the English national character as Protestant, individualist, and diverse. The legitimacy of her Protestantism does not rest on an historical chain of authority but upon its efficacy. For Trollope, "Protestantism" offers a gendered set of possibilities for self-making.

Father Eustace

Written in 1846–47, Trollope's *Tale of the Jesuits* features the General of the Society of Jesus, Antonio Scaviatoli, who functions as a gothic romancer, plotting the seduction of a beautiful young English heiress (Juliana de Morley) by a sensitive, handsome priest in disguise (Edward Stormont a.k.a. Father Eustace). Scaviatoli's design is for Eustace to win Juliana's love and effect her conversion to Roman Catholicism. The Jesuit General is sure that when Juliana learns, too late, that Edward Stormont is really Father Eustace, her despair will lead her to transfer the de Morley estate to the Society of Jesus and retire to self-imprisonment in a convent. The holy father's love plot is a perverse variation on the older gothic pattern wherein the young virginal heiress is first seduced/raped by a priest and then robbed of her fortune and imprisoned in a convent (the familiar story that the escaped nun was expected to tell).

What Juliana finds when she investigates her castle for the first time is not the imprisoned mother figure traditional to the plots of "female" gothic fiction,[48] but her father's secret Roman Catholic chapel. There, prompted by Father Ambrose's pictures of purgatory, she prays for her parent's soul and considers conversion to Roman Catholicism. "Then came the tremendous moment, when that grey-haired old man, whom, from her earliest infancy, she had been used to invest with a halo of mysterious holiness, declared to her, in the most specific terms, that she had the power either to loose or bind the soul of her father upon its passage from earth to heaven."

Trollope's language is provocative, indeed blasphemous. The power that her Protestant audience believes belongs to God alone is here imputed to humans, both lay and priestly: to Juliana and Father Ambrose. In referring to "the power either to loose or bind the soul," Trollope cites the text around which Protestant–Catholic debates about purgatory, indulgences, and confession all centered, thus invoking the touchstones of English anti-Catholicism: the corrupt and corrupting confessional, the selling of indulgences, and the idolatry of praying for and *to* the dead. Keble and Pusey's reintroduction of auricular confession into the Anglican church had reopened these debates and renewed these fears.[49] Trollope's Father Ambrose confirms the English Protestant suspicion that such idolatry of the dead consolidates priestly power here on earth: Having dictated de Morley's words during his lifetime, the confessor now speaks with the voice of the dead father, irresistible to the grieving daughter. Father Ambrose is then replaced by Father Eustace, whose intrusion into the castle begins with his literally taking the father's place at the organ, playing a requiem for de Morley. Both men act in obedience to the commands of the novel's central paternal authority, Scaviatoli, a figure linked by Trollope with John Henry Newman.

Antonio Scaviatoli was of middle stature, then, but not slightly built. His eye has extraordinary power when it was his will to use it; but, for the most part, it was not his will; for it was his habit to let his particularly long dark eye-lashes so completely conceal these eyes, that many people having business to contract with him, came and went almost without knowing whether he had any eyes or not.[50]

Anglo-American readers would immediately recognize the male with down-cast eyes as a Jesuit, hiding his secret knowledge and power. (That Newman was a secret Jesuit was well "known" in the 1830s – even *The Times* reported the allegation.[51]) At the height of the Oxford scandal, Scaviatoli's demeanour would also have been associated with what Newman and the other Tractarians called "reserve," a doctrine of reticence widely interpreted by Protestants as one of deception. "Reserve" was both a principle that allowed for the selective disclosure of religious information and a favored demeanor of "retiredness and absence of self." As David De Laura and James Eli Adams have noted, Newman's own speech, especially in the pulpit, was quiet and "subdued," a manner that dramatically – even theatrically – connoted personal reserve.[52] Like Pearce's disguises in *Hawkstone*, this performance of humility can be understood as pointing to the fundamental inauthenticity of Catholicism – a religion that does not penetrate below the surface.

Yet this very inauthenticity is so thorough that Scaviatoli literally embodies the perfection of what Trollope understands to be the Jesuit system. His words, his body, even his eyes – those windows to the soul – are completely, consciously controlled. Scaviatoli is also the exception within Trollope's

Society of Jesus: he embodies his own, not another's, will, "with vigour of mind and body, unbroken by penance, and unshaken by any terrors of discipline, either of this world or the next; recognising no authority that could make his spirit quail, or paralyse the native energy of his character." In fact, Scaviatoli's total control of his self is matched by the perfect obedience with which his will is met by others. Father Eustace has been trained "to abdicate all individual will, all individual judgment, and to live, think, speak, and act, wholly, solely, and without reservation, according to the judgment and the commands of your superiors." "No will but thine Scaviatoli!" Father Eustace repeats reverently. For Trollope's English Protestant readership, this pious intonation is both a parody of prayer and "proof" that Catholics practice idolatry. The General of the Jesuits has displaced God, both in his own eyes and in those of his Company.[53]

But if Scaviatoli acts as God, he is not the primal Old Testament deity whose authority is displayed through bloody violence. His is a more subtle "modern," disciplinary system of power. Sewell's coarse, sensual, grasping Jesuit is merely the agent of an international network; the refined, controlled Scaviatoli directs that network from his inner sanctum in Rome. Pearce disguises himself by changing clothes; Scaviatoli remakes himself and his followers. Expert in the scrutiny, study, and categorizing of human behavior, the psychologizing of the self, Scaviatoli is, in 1847, a figure of modern authority, one who uses the taxonomy of the confessional to create a culture of self-examination and self-control.[54]

What Trollope emphasizes, then, is that, while Scaviatoli is horrific in his unlimited and unchecked human authority, modern Roman Catholic power is – in true Foucauldian fashion – functional and systemic. Not the despotic General Villiers (or his counterpart Pearce) nor even the Superior General of the Jesuits, Scaviatoli, but the "self" that the Jesuits create is the most powerful agent of the Society's power. For what makes Scaviatoli's plot possible is the education of Edward Stormont into Father Eustace – an education in total obedience to a holy father.[55] Although he does his teaching abroad, Scaviatoli is further associated with John Henry Newman in his indoctrination of young Englishmen. In Scaviatoli, Trollope raises the specter of Newman as a Roman Catholic teacher who is educating English youth to death.[56] The Jesuits in *Father Eustace*, educated abroad, infiltrate England, bringing with them an underground educational system, at once a secret training and a training *in* secrecy.

Comparing the schooling of two orphaned English boys, Edward Stormont and Oliver Twist, Trollope claims that:

thanks to the light thrown upon the subject in the exquisite pages of Oliver Twist –
few amongst us are ignorant of the careful and skilful system of training, by which
a particular class of our metropolitan population are brought to such perfection in
the management of their fingers, that their movements are made as imperceptible
to feeling as to sight; and in like manner, if the whisperings from behind the veil
speak sooth, the COMPANY upon whom more eyes are now fixed than were ever
fixed before, not only instruct the young idea, but the young limbs also, how to
move onward, with as little disturbance as possible.[57]

By introducing *Oliver Twist*, Trollope allies her narrative with Dickens's
melodramatic exposés of contemporary life and looks back to her own social
problem novels, *Michael Armstrong* (1839) and *Jessie Phillips* (1843). While
she does not subject herself to the standards of the Blue Books, Trollope
does point to the factuality and topicality of her subject. A reviewer in the
New Monthly Magazine clearly accepted Trollope's narrative as accurate: "It
is impossible to peruse it [*Father Eustace*] and not feel that the care and
power thrown into it attest that there has been much groundwork for the
details."[58] Like the escaped nun's tale, Trollope's narrative both draws on
other fictions for evidence and itself becomes evidentiary.

In this case, the foreign, secret power of Rome is so pervasive that it is
written into the very bodies of Britain's youth. Behind the Jesuit's infamous
"gliding" step, Trollope suggests, lie years of indoctrination in total mind
and body control. According to Trollope, so complete is the Jesuit remaking
of individuals that it amounts to a second, unnatural creation: "not only
are the principles in which the unearthly disciples of Loyola are reared,
of so stringent a quality as to impede, and finally destroy, every natural
movement of the soul, but they are also made to be, habitually, of such
ready application, that no emotion can arise without bringing its antidote
with it." Internalizing these disciplinary principles, Father Eustace learns
an automatic, habitual revulsion from all of Edward Stormont's natural
feelings. As his superior says, "education has made him a good Jesuit,
though nature fights hard to turn him into a bad one." Scaviatoli knows
in advance that Juliana's goodness and beauty will awaken Eustace's ability
to love humanly, but counts on the young priest's programmed reaction:
"The glance of passion faded into the cold and paralyzing glare of abject,
spiritless despair."[59]

The self-control that Edward Stormont has learned under Roman
Catholic tutelage demands the suppression of adult sexuality. Tractarian
celibacy was an enduring source of scandal in Britain, generating attacks
ranging from cartoons in *Punch* to Charles Kingsley's sarcastic remarks

about Newman in *Macmillan's*, an attack that eventually led to the *Apologia*.[60] What Trollope sees as the Catholic perversion of sexuality is also displayed by the rapacious appetite of one of the novel's minor characters, a "female Jesuit," whose childish greed for sweets leads to her comic death. "All ladies accustomed to reside in convents are said to be particularly fond of preserved fruits, and indeed of sweet dishes of every kind," Trollope informs us.

With *Father Eustace* Trollope critiques the doctrine of obedience that the Tractarians found so compelling. Creeping under the shelter of authority, the infantilized Eustace and his ilk are taught that "the impious efforts of that fallacious earth-born impulse which men call conscience" must be "beaten down and trampled in the dust."[61] In a sermon on the folly of attempting "Knowledge of God's Will without Obedience" Newman condemned those who follow God's commandment merely because they agree with its morality, who fail to realize that they must "obey *because* it commands." Instead, Newman enjoins in another sermon, "Obedience The Remedy for Religious Perplexity," "To all those who are perplexed in any way soever, who wish for light but cannot find it, one precept must be given, – OBEY. It is obedience which brings a man into the right path; it is obedience keeps him there and strengthens him in it. Under all circumstances, whatever be the cause of his distress, – obey."[62]

In rejecting this doctrine, Trollope again parts company with Sewell, who distinguishes between the rule of law, wherein one obeys an individual as representative of an institution and the Jesuit rule of unchecked personal, physical (Papal, Pearcean) authority. Upholding the former, *Hawkstone* also lovingly details the masochistic attractions of the latter. Sewell acknowledges only reluctantly Englishmen's need to act independently when they can find no legitimate rule or ruler. Trollope's commitment to the liberal Protestant individual makes her suspicious of any system that devalues personal judgment. For Trollope, the rule of obedience is a death sentence. Taught "to abdicate all individual will, all individual judgment, and to live, think, speak, and act, wholly, solely, and without reservation, according to the judgment and the commands of your superiors," Eustace is only the facsimile of a living English man, "the living image of a helpless bigot, in whom this blind submission had stifled all the energy of moral freedom, and all the individual responsibility of manly honour." Like many other Victorian anti-Catholic texts, *Father Eustace* returns repeatedly to Ignatius Loyola's injunction: the Jesuit must make his "will 'dead as a corpse.' "[63] *The Spiritual Exercises* are, Trollope argues, a training in self-murder. Sewell's texts are haunted by the continuing suspicion that sons exist only through and in the father's recognition, that the uncertainties of modernity resurrect the desire for an authoritative Other. The self-abasement of a Villiers is explained and condemned by Trollope's description of the young Stormont who willingly – eagerly – allows the father to destroy him in order to gain approval. The ejaculatory vow "No will but thine, Scaviatoli!" is formulaic in its masochism.

Unlike Radcliffe's *Mysteries of Udolpho*, Trollope's novel does not finally explain away the dead body behind the clerical veil. Longing for an end to life, the increasingly "deathlike" Eustace makes a last visit to Scaviatoli, whom he has begun to distrust. Eustace's loss of doctrinal foundation is comically literalized when the floor opens beneath him and he falls into an imprisonment where he will "never see the light of day again."[64] He appears again in the novel only to finish dying, prematurely old, at Juliana's feet. This is the logical end of the sadomasochistic structure of male authority and identity that Trollope critiques. Banished from the father's presence, no longer able to locate his identity in the other's authority, Eustace no longer exists.

The figure of the Roman Catholic (or Tractarian crypto-Catholic) as blindly obedient abdicator of self is important in political polemic in the nineteenth century, whether the image is one of the cowed and superstitious Irish peasant (now turned British factory worker or American laborer) who acts and, perhaps most importantly, votes at his priest's direction (see especially Chapter 3) or, as we see in Trollope, the English youth educated into a living death. Along with Sewell's depictions of bloody bodies and the return of the murdered and murdering father, Catherine Sinclair's Thugs (see Chapter 4), and priestly dissectors of living women (see Chapter 5), Trollope's descriptions of Catholics as walking corpses, zombies whose bodies operate according to another's will, flesh out the gothic gallery of anti-Catholic imagery. These *unheimlich* figures – the archaic that haunts the present; the foreign disguised as the native; the dead that walks with the living; the automaton mimicking the human – attest to the Church of Rome's uncanny status in the cultural unconscious of Protestant Anglo-America. This is, I want to stress, an historical status, as well as one that must be historicized: "uncanny" must be understood here in terms of the relationship between the Roman Catholic Church and the Protestantism that evolved (or apostatized) from it; the institutional histories of Catholicism and Protestantisms; and the specific demographic, educational, legal, political histories of nineteenth-century Britain and the United States.

Trollope's plot demonstrates that the Jesuitical logic that she sees as central to Tractarian pedagogy in the 1840s leads to a (literally) dead end. But *Father Eustace* does not rest with the gothic fate of her male character. "Why are we not both dead?" Juliana asks Eustace at their last meeting. If, for Trollope, Romanist education keeps male youths from becoming men, first infantilizing and, then, effectively killing them, the tradition of the gothic entrammels female characters and creativity, as Trollope argues when she equates deference to the dead father with marrying a corpse and killing yourself. What Juliana learns when she finds out that Edward Stormont is a priest is that she is in love with a dead man, with a (her) father. The Jesuits hope that this will make her give up life too.[65]

So why is Trollope's heroine not dead, or at least dead to the world in a convent at the end of the novel? What causes the father's death plot to fail is the nineteenth-century mother and writer. Within *Father Eustace*, both archaic patriarchal authority and its gothic narratives are contained and countered by Trollope's story of female education. While Eustace's veneration for Scaviatoli is, throughout the novel, compared to the feelings of an unjudging, dependant infant towards his "never-to-be-doubted . . . mother,"[66] the *woman* who is a mother in *Father Eustace* makes no attempt to retain infallibility, to keep her child an infant. The priestly pretence to maternity is a grotesque parody – self-aggrandizing patriarchal power tricked out in the robes of female love and nurturance. The fundamental misogyny of this drag show is revealed in the Jesuits' virulent hatred of Lady Sarah, the ideal Protestant mother who not only fosters her daughter's autonomy, but also submits to being "mothered" by Juliana.

Trollope's fathers may give lessons in death, but her mother gives physical, emotional, and moral life. What Lady Sarah's mothering preserves, and what the infallible parental authority of the holy fathers destroys, is the basis of English Protestantism: individual conscience. Juliana de Morley may be, at first, susceptible to the Jesuits' machinations because of her desire to obey the wishes of her own dead Roman Catholic father. Yet because her Protestant mother has educated her in self-reliance and private judgment, Juliana is finally able to reject submission and, with it, spiritual and physical suicide. Immediately following Richard de Morley's death, Lady Sarah makes it clear that Juliana is mistress of both her estate and her self, with "perfect independence as to her own destiny." As Juliana reminds Lady Sarah, she is her mother's companion, not her subordinate. "I will not let you scold me for speaking to you with the freedom of a sister, rather than with the deference of a child, for it is you yourself, dearest, who have taught me to love you in both capacities."[67]

Lady Sarah's deference to her daughter is not an example of weakness to be avoided, but the source of the heroine's strength. Neither choosing dominance, nor accepting submission, Lady Sarah offers an alternative to the gothic model of self-making. We can see this differing dynamic at work in the scenes of Lady Sarah and Juliana reading side-by-side. In nineteenth-century Anglo-American culture the image of mother and daughter with an open book represents the making of self. Trollope clearly subscribes to this normative view of the mother's loving lessons as the "natural" and non-coercive means of subject formation.[68] Lady Sarah and Juliana each perform an activity iconic of absorption, yet they do so together. That Trollope shows not the mother reading to the daughter but two companionate readers indicates her belief in the younger woman's own self-making. Reading figures Juliana's autonomy, as her declaration that the only "submission" to which we are bound is submission to the will of God makes clear. That divine will is revealed, of course, not in popish priestly commands, but through the individual Protestant's reading of the Bible. It is not surprising, then, that Trollope marks the moment of Juliana's full recovery from her gothic trauma by declaring: "from that time she resumed her constant occupation of the library."[69] Under Roman Catholic rule, this room had been the space of perversion: Richard de Morley hid there from his wife and daughter, prostrating himself in the adjoining secret chapel; Scaviatoli staged clandestine meetings between Eustace and Juliana there, manipulating the unsuspecting couple's overwrought sexual and religious feelings, fashioning their guilt and desire. Juliana reclaims the room as the scene of Protestantism, a space in which she alternates between private reading and shared family prayer.

Trollope represents this Protestant scene as superior, not only to the patriarchal culture of physical coercion evoked by her gothic allusions, but also to its modern reincarnation in the guise of religious education in obedience. In both instances, Catholicism is seen as violating the integrity of the self. Drawing on her audience's belief that the Protestant's direct relationship with God and private reading of the Bible represent personal freedom from earthly authority, Trollope describes, reassuringly, the subject formation of the English individual. If, as Flint argues, the "spaces" of reading are where "subjectivity and socialization" meet,[70] Juliana's control of that space suggests Trollope's belief in her independence and choice.

Sarah Hale domesticated the sensational by having a husband educate a wife into Protestant womanhood. Trollope's feminist revision of the gothic is more radical, yet she can finally depict Protestant autonomy as available

to women only in an imaginary narrative realm. Before Eustace's revelation, Juliana is "puzzled as to the manner in which she was to bring
her little romance to its third volume." Her "self-schooling" finally allows
her to author the ending she wants, although not the one she (or Trollope's
readership) could have expected. Juliana spends her adulthood benevolently
plotting others' happiness. Having helped engineer her mother's remarriage
(to the local Protestant minister), she adopts her new stepbrother, renaming
him Julian de Morley (he calls Juliana "Mamma" and Lady Sarah, his biological mother, "Granny"); brings about the marriage of her best friend,[71]
who then bears a daughter, Juliana; gives her two namesakes in marriage to
one another; and lives to see the birth of their child Julian de Morley. In
short, Juliana figures the female writer who engenders a family in her own
image, creating new selves and a new story.

This imaginary ending wherein the daughter successfully authors her
own family narrative is particularly poignant if we consider the possibility
that Frances Trollope is writing *Father Eustace*, at least in part, to her own
daughter, Cecelia, whose Tractarian novel had just been published. By 1847,
Cecelia was already worn out by childbirth and beginning to show signs
of the consumption that killed her two years later. None of Cecelia's five
children lived to adulthood.[72] Trollope, with most of the rest of England,
saw Tractarianism as threatening the young male elite: it is, after all, Edward
Stormont who is destroyed by Rome. Nonetheless, the narrative of the
daughter's triumph over the gothic plot of Romanism and sadomasochistic romantic love may also be Trollope's wishful revision of Cecelia's
life-story.

Juliana's final rejection of the gothic and Trollope's revision of it also
resonate interestingly with another aspect of the Trollope family's dynamics.
After his financial failure, Frances Trollope's husband spent most of his time
immersed in writing an ecclesiastical encyclopedia which was to describe
"the denominations of every fraternity of monks and every convent of
nuns, with all their orders and subdivisions." In his *Autobiography*, Anthony
recalled that, despite his father's intense desire to see his sons educated, he
"could not give his time to teach me, for every hour that he was not in
the fields was devoted to his monks and nuns." Never completed, the
project generated no income. In contrast, Frances Trollope's books about
"monks and nuns," including this one,[73] were written early in the morning
before her family arose or while she sat nursing at their sickbeds and earned
sufficient money to support them all.

In *Father Eustace*, Frances Trollope, a woman who both mothered and
fathered her children by creating fictional families, writes a book in which

a young woman lays out her own family narrative. In rewriting Scaviatoli's gothic – and in rejecting the Tractarians' invocation of the fathers' history and papal authority – Trollope fashions a new woman's plot, one that, like the "impossible" ending of another famous anti-Catholic novel, Charlotte Brontë's *Villette*, overcomes both the narrative structure – and the cultural strictures – that imprison females.[74]

CHAPTER 3

The foreign father and the sons of the sires: nativist novels of the 1850s

Reacting as they do to the Tractarian scandal, William Sewell's and Frances Trollope's novels focus on education and describe a contest between all-powerful fathers and obedient sons. *Hawkstone*, in particular, was widely read in the United States, seeing at least four American editions. Reviewers understood the book as an informative account of the Oxford Movement.[1] Readers were drawn as well to Sewell's sensationalism; the *Literary World* enthused that "Some of the scenes in this work are highly wrought and absolutely terrific; as much so as any to be found in the works of Eugene Sue."[2] Sewell's vivid depictions of patriarchal violence prove especially useful when, in the 1850s, nativist American writers come to tell a somewhat different narrative about antagonism between fathers and sons. The story of the archaic father who keeps all the women for himself that Freud tells and that Sewell, remembering the history of British monarchial struggle, makes into an argument for the rule of (religious) law that he calls "Christian Politics" is recast in American fiction in terms of an unassimilated immigrant population. While *Hawkstone* and *Father Eustace* respond to theological changes in the education of a country's elite, the American narratives grapple with an historical and political shift in models for and experiences of working and middle-class masculinity. Like the American daughter's story in the escaped nun's tale, the saga of American sons' struggle for manhood is told through a standard plot, repeated again and again in a series of sensational popular narratives. If the nun's story suggests uneasiness about the feminization of American Protestantism and the figure of the American girl, nativist narratives about "the sons of the sires" describe the vexed political situation of young American males in the decade before the Civil War.

Analyzing the rise of nativism in 1850s' America, historians and literary scholars have argued that the figure of the foreigner offered a nation threatened by sectionalism a chance to unite.[3] Antebellum divisiveness has, in turn, been linked to the culture's strongly held image of the founding

fathers: the sons of those who fought in the Revolution, unable to successfully take their fathers' places, became a generation turned against itself.[4]
A group of nativist fictions deploy these two figures – the foreigner and
the father – in plots that attempt to adjudicate pressing questions about
the unity and integrity of Protestant America and to resolve male generational and gender anxiety. The introduction of a third character, the
foreign father, destabilizes the family configuration central to Protestant
bourgeois domesticity, opening up gender and genre possibilities. Differentiating between, yet insistently coupling together, foreign and founding
fathers, nativist novelists create a narrative structure that allows for the
depiction of both filial aggression and filial piety. *The Arch Bishop: Or,
Romanism in the United States* by Orvilla S. Belisle (1855); *The Convict: Or,
The Conspirator's Victim. A Novel, Written in Prison* (1863) and *The Jesuit's
Daughter; A Novel For Americans To Read* (1854) by Ned Buntline (Edward
Zane Carroll Judson); *Stanhope Burleigh: The Jesuits in Our Homes* by Helen
Dhu (Charles Edwards Lester) (1855); *The Countess: or, The Inquisitor's
Punishments. A Tale of Spain* by William Engolls (1847); *New York: Its
Upper Ten and Lower Million* by George Lippard (1853); *One Link in the
Chain of Apostolic Succession; or The Crimes of Alexander Borgia* by Edward
Hinks (1854); and *The Princess of Viarna: or, The Spanish Inquisition in the
reign of Charles the Fifth* (1857) all tell a story about America as a nation of
brothers united against an incestuous usurper from another time and place.

Michael Denning accurately characterizes dime novels as articulating
a "master plot . . . made up of nationalist, class-inflected stories of the
American Republic, inter-related, if sometimes contradictory tales of its
origins and the threats to it."[5] However, because he is bent on praising these
fictions as speaking for and to the artisanal working-classes and because he
overlooks the substance of antebellum religious controversies, Denning can
only regard the nativism of authors like Buntline and Lippard as embarrassing lapses. What this stance obscures is the strength and pervasiveness of
this particular story of America's origins, forestalling investigation of why
its telling seemed a way to solve contemporary problems.

Of course, these eight novels represent nothing like the spectrum of
opinion in 1850s America about Catholicism, Irish immigration, Protestantism, and the generational relations between men. Catholic newspapers
and journals like *Brownson's Quarterly Review*, the *Freeman's Journal*, and
the Boston *Pilot* challenged nativism directly and energetically, and editorials in a range of Protestant and secular publications were critical of
anti-Catholicism as well. My focus is, in fact, on the fictions' sameness –
the fact that seven different novelists wrote eight remarkably similar novels.
The marked similarity of these texts makes it clear that their authors felt

they had found a marketable formula. Buntline, who probably knew what American audiences wanted to read better than any other writer of the time, even reissued the 1854 *The Jesuit's Daughter* as *The Beautiful Nun* in 1866, changing only the single lines on the first and last pages that invoke the fictions' titles. These nativist novels' conformity to a standard plot tells us about one popular way in which the story of America's history was formulated and how what was perceived as a national crisis was worked out narratively. Following Loesberg's suggestive study of the British sensation novel, I want to view the historical and political situation in which these novels were written and published not as a determining "context" for these texts but as "an occasion for the materialization of a particular ideological narrative." Loesberg argues that "One reason for the popularity of sensation fiction was that those novels were telling a story, in one version or another, that all Victorian society was telling itself."[6] All American society in the 1850s was not telling itself a story about a contested national inheritance, but narrative elements from these sensational nativist novels can be found in speeches, sermons, and pamphlets from the period, indicating that such structures provided one viable means of meaning-making. The specific political content of that meaning was not always identical – even within the group of nativist novels I examine, authors' opinions on slavery, for example, varied widely – but the forms are shared. Insistently reproducing their story as a means of depicting contemporary American culture, nativist fiction-writers portray religious affiliation, filial psychology, gender identity, and national politics as inextricably intertwined.

The 1850s were a period of rising nativism in America, peaking in the phenomenal success of the American (or Know-Nothing) party in the 1854 and 1855 elections. The Know-Nothings carried Connecticut, Delaware, Kentucky, Maryland, Massachusetts, New Hampshire, and Rhode Island, with strong showings in Alabama, California, Georgia, Louisiana, Mississippi, New York, Pennsylvania, Tennessee, and Virginia. The party's popularity was such that candy, tea, toothpicks, buses, stagecoaches, and even a clipper ship were named after the Know-Nothings, who were predicted to win the presidency in 1856.[7] Increased Irish and German immigration had helped to feed a renewed anti-Catholicism: between 1845 and 1854 some million and a half Irish entered America, making up over 40 per cent of immigration totals between 1840 and 1844. The fact that, by the 1850s, the majority of immigrants were Catholic[8] seemed especially ominous. Perhaps most alarming was the active Catholic participation in politics – lobbying for support of Irish independence from Britain, campaigning to change the public school system. Archbishop John Hughes in particular involved himself and his flock in local New York politics.

The nativist campaign against what was seen as this Catholic "invasion" of America permeates its discourse, nonfictional and fictional alike. The savage, indigent Irish who mill around the background of Villiers's estate in *Hawkstone* are a much more immediate presence in American novels that focus on middle- and working-class protagonists and milieu. And the Irish clergyman, a minor cleric in Sewell's novel, becomes a politically powerful high-ranking prelate. While *Christian Politics* expounds a political philosophy, and *Hawkstone* and *Father Eustace* imagine idealized communities, fictions like *The Arch Bishop, The Convict*, and *Stanhope Burleigh* report on the Astor Place and Philadelphia riots and engage in current electoral campaigns.

Nativism flourishes at this point, not just as a result of rising immigration, but because there is a contemporary crisis in authority and identity that makes the threat of non-Americans particularly potent. Nativism offered "national homogeneity" to a country threatened by sectionalism and facing growing religious diversity and disaffection, and antebellum conspiracy plots worked to reconfirm and authenticate that American identity.[9] Bennett maintains that we must look past "old rhetoric" and "pornographic sensationalism" of the American anti-Catholic literature of this period to the added "diatribes against the authoritarian nature of the church" which reveal a debate about what constitutes authentic American citizenship and what counts as legitimate religious and political authority.[10] I agree that what Benedict Anderson defines as "nation" – the "imagined political community – and imagined both as inherently limited and sovereign" – is, at this "belated" period of American history, threatened both as to its shared commonality and its sovereignty.[11] Yet, I contend that what Bennett sees as the "old rhetoric" and "pornographic sensationalism" of anti-Catholicism, familiar as it may seem, should not be dismissed as meaningless convention.[12] Nativist novels address contemporary problems not merely through the insertion of authorial "diatribes," but also in their tropes, plots, and characterizations. My argument is that nineteenth-century texts advocate anti-Catholicism through – not despite – their detailed rhetorical, narrative, and literary structures. Thus, the national genealogy that becomes especially important in post-Revolutionary America is charted by the family story that structures all of the novels I am discussing. Anderson uses nineteenth-century America as an example of what he sees as "the biography of nations": no longer able "to experience the nation as new,"[13] the second generation begins to narrate the nation's history and, in doing so, develop a discourse of fraternity. American nativist novelists use the narrative of a contested heritage in precisely this way, addressing as they do so religious authenticity and its relation to nationalism. Their focus is profoundly gendered: these novels attempt to fix and define what it means to be not just American but, specifically, an American man – after the fact, as it were. The almost mythic figures and plots of anti-Catholicism prove singularly apt for characterizing the political and demographic situation of young men in 1850s America.

Every one of these fictions depicts bad Catholic fathers who fail to protect and provide for their female children. The ideology, practices, and physical culture of the nineteenth-century American Protestant home made Catholic homes and families seem lacking by comparison.[14] The Protestant image of the father as priest and the home as the center of prayer and religious instruction stood in contrast to immigrant Catholic culture in which the priest was a cleric called "father," worship took place in churches, and, so the stereotype ran, the father, instead of leading prayer at home, was drinking at the pub. These novels take the criticism of the Catholic father further, showing him as not just lacking but as inimical to the American way of life. Following the commands of Romanist priests, Catholic fathers act as foreigners. They disinherit their rightful heirs, diverting what should be family estates to Rome's coffers. Catholic fathers refuse to allow their daughters to marry the worthy young American patriots who love them, instead condemning the young women to convents, in which they are tortured, raped, and murdered. Cowed by the power of popery, un-American citizen-fathers blindly turn over their political, economic, and sexual power to despotic and demagogic priests. These "holy fathers" are usurpers: seeking, by way of a false paternity, to destroy the familial and the democratic structures of American life and, perhaps most ominously, to replace the Nation's Founding Fathers.

Calling priests "holy fathers" is not mere critical word play. Nineteenth-century Protestant commentators typically criticized the Catholic priest's use of the title "father" as false and presumptuous, claiming that it allowed clerics to intrude into intimacies that should be reserved for true families. In *The Jesuit's Daughter*, for example, the kidnapped Katrine O'Sullivan replies to her priestly abductor: "That is not the voice of my father – why do you call me daughter?" He retorts, "I am your spiritual father in the church – your earthly father you will see no more."[15] The image of a paternity gone awry is underscored by the fact that many of the "celibate" holy fathers in these novels are actually biological fathers, several of whom attempt incest with their own daughters.

Unlike American escaped nuns' narratives, these nativist novels focus, not on a woman's recounting of her story, but on the contest between the Catholic fathers (lay and clerical alike) who imprison her and the Protestant youths who seek to rescue her.[16] The young men are all native-born Americans, sons of patriots who fought in the War of Independence; often artisans, always ardent republicans, the young men uncover the priest's private sexual intrigue and challenge his public political demagoguery. The battle for possession of the woman is a battle for citizenship, for the republican rights that the new generation of American males have failed to inherit. "Our *rights* are in danger!" cries the collective voice of true Americans in *The Arch Bishop*, a novel which recounts how "one of their number, at the dawn of manhood . . . had been robbed of his betrothed, and when he turned to his country to plead his wrongs, had in the act been stricken down!" The author of *One Link in the Chain of Apostolic Succession* warns, "And yet Americans will sleep on, as if they knew not that their rights and liberties, *and privileges AS Americans*, are being daily and hourly encroached upon at a rate that threatens to soon strip them of all!"[17] This lost legacy of rights is also literalized in the novels' inheritance plots. Not only do virtually all of the novels depict priests as working to estrange dying wealthy fathers from their heirs, several also borrow from Eugene Sue in tracing the lives of competing legatees for a fabulous inheritance, a narrative convention that Michael Denning identifies as "a story of the battle over the legacy of the Republic itself."[18]

The antagonism between patriotic Protestant sons and "foreign" Catholic fathers in these texts corresponds to a mid-century cultural perception that the true American father was missing. Recent work in gender history has explored how generational shifts in definitions and experiences of masculinity worked to make fathers absent to sons during this period. The movement from a rural agricultural economy to an urban industrial one meant that the sons of the new middle class could no longer expect to work side-by-side with their fathers in or near the home. Carnes quotes an 1842 complaint that "'Paternal neglect' . . . had become epidemic."[19]

Americans were also conscious that the founding fathers had disappeared: by 1826, Washington, Adams, and Jefferson had all died. George Forgie has characterized the middle decades of the nineteenth century as the "post-heroic age," arguing that, as the sons of men who had fought during the Revolution reached adulthood, they had always to measure themselves against those "fathers of our country," whom they ritually invoked. Robert S. Levine describes the post-Revolutionary pattern of identification and imitation: "Subsequent generations aligned themselves with the Revolutionary generation through ritual reenactments of the nation-creating battle against conspirators." In nativist novels, narrators and characters alike repeatedly summon the images and voices of the now-absent founding fathers as incentives and models. For example, *The Arch Bishop* intones: "The beacon-like life of their forefathers was ever before them urging them on in the path of rectitude and prosperity, while the trumpet tones of Washington never ceased sounding in their ears, 'Beware of Foreign Influence.'"[20]

Yet, as in Sewell's filial narrative, with the disappearance of the father, loyal sons do not simply become him. The generational logic is not one of replacement but contest, for, even missing, the figure of the father retains its power. American writers in the 1850s, with their seemingly mandatory invocations of Washington and the other founding fathers, make it clear that fathers remained a powerful force. And physically absent as nineteenth-century fathers might be, they obviously maintained an important role in the family. The head of the household, the decision-maker, the source of financial support, the father was also the "chief disciplinarian."[21] The power of absent fathers is also apparent in the renewed attention Washington's life and death received in the 1850s, a period which saw the Senate purchase of the manuscript of the Farewell Address in 1850 (the sacred text of the nativists and the Ur-text of American countersubversion) and national fund-raising campaigns for the restoration of Mount Vernon and for the building of the Washington Monument, as well as the scandal surrounding the Know-Nothing takeover of the monument committee in 1854.[22] In fact, even the numerous antebellum depictions of the death of Washington illustrate, paradoxically, his forceful presence. Because Washington was perceived as emblematic of the United States, evidence of his deterioration would have seemed to imply that this new nation would follow the same cyclic course as Old World empires, rising only to fall.[23] Therefore descriptions of Washington's final days insist on his lack of physical and mental decay, so much so that he appears to be immortal. The select Senate committee's (1799) report to President John Adams, which insisted that Washington, "favored of heaven . . . departed without exhibiting the weakness of humanity," is echoed in innumerable speeches, essays, tributes, and poems in the following decades. Like the Virgin Mary, conceived without sin, Washington is spared death and decay as he is assumed into heaven. But how were the generation that followed to take their places as statesmen and leaders when the original leader remained intact? Faced with a father who never dies, American men could not count on the passage of time to solve the dilemma of their sonhood: "only the fathers were fully citizens in this political romance, for it alienated living communal power to a deified past."[24] Nativist discourse struggles to redefine nationhood apart from its makers, seeks to find a way to intertwine the identity of the U.S. with the generation of the 1850s.

This dilemma is exacerbated by the fact that the line of American succession was not left clear. On the one hand, to imitate Washington was to be rebellious, to break with the past and its loyalties so as to create a new order. On the other, custodianship of the founding fathers' legacy meant preserving the nation without change.[25] *The Jesuit's Daughter* is explicit in asking who were the true sons of the founding fathers. Constanza, who is being persecuted by the holy fathers of the Inquisition for loving a young man designated for the priesthood, appeals to her own powerless father to flee with her from Italy to America: "But father, I have heard that it is a vast country where freemen dwell. I know not whether he is King or Chief, but I have heard of a WASHINGTON whom they describe as Godlike; oh if once we were under *his* protection we would be safe!" Her father replies, "My child, there was a WASHINGTON, but he is DEAD!" To which Constanza responds with the key question, "Has he no sons, father, none to do as *their* father did?" In *The Jesuit's Daughter*, Buntline adjures those who allow Irish Catholic policemen to silence and arrest a Protestant minister in New York City: "And men who call themselves Americans, who are descended from persecuted, yet triumphant protestants, endure this! . . . Deny your fathers, disgrace not their names by saying that you are their descendants." *One Link in the Chain of Apostolic Succession*, which raises the issue of lineage in its very title, declares that either "[t]he disciples of the church of Rome, or the descendants of the revolutionary patriots, must eventually rule the United States," distinguishing between those who merely follow (disciples) and those who inherit legitimately (descendants).[26]

The question of what constitutes legitimate American descent pervades the nativist literature of the period, which is saturated with the rhetoric of founding fathers and loyal sons. It is a nationalist discourse, not only of origins, but also of evolution. The filial stance of the Native American or Know-Nothing party, which met yearly on Washington's birthday, is illustrated by *The Sons of the Sires; A History of The Rise, Progress, And Destiny of The American Party, And Its Probable Influence On the Next Presidential Election*, a nativist polemic published by Lippincott in 1855, that spells out the genealogical logic that informs novels like *The Jesuit's Daughter* and *One Link*. Declaring "THAT THE SONS OF THE SOIL SHOULD RULE THE SOIL," the author of *Sons of the Sires* describes the Know-Nothing party as a Christ-like infant, "scarcely born before Herods sent their murderous confederates to strangle it in its cradle. But having no notion to be dispatched so unceremoniously, it had grown to a giant, and set out on the march of its destiny, before the executioners arrived." This image of American nativism – and American youth, as well as America itself – as a young giant[27] under attack recurs in *The Arch Bishop*, at the funeral of George Shiffler, who has been shot down while bearing the American flag in a battle with Irish hoodlums: "This dead weight; this Papist Juggernaut, had gnawed at the vitals of the Old World . . . this vampire . . . with longing eyes looked to the vigorous, hale Giant of the New World . . . fastening upon the young Giant, began gnawing their way into his vitals."[28] Foreign, primitive, and parasitic Catholicism is represented as a gothic threat to the young America: the dead past feeding on the living. The logic of Westward evolution orientalizes Europe. *Sons of the Sires* elaborates on the allegory, detailing the nativist giant's pedigree:

The American party had its origin, therefore, not as its opponents affirm, in defective views of our government; nor is it the child of disappointed politicians, nor of the spirit of intolerance; but it is the offspring of those self-adjusting principles, and those elements of permanency found in our civil structure; or, in other words, it is the child of the people. It is not a bastard republican, but a born sovereign – a prince of freedom; an heir legitimate . . . very much in appearance like the pictures of the manly Washington; *i.e.* assuming that which no one doubts, that the spirit of the man externalizes itself in the person of the man.[29]

At first apparently parentless (in the biblical narrative, the Holy Family flees to Egypt together; this child escapes the "Herods" on his own), the young man is next said to be the offspring of the Constitution, the child of the people, and, finally, perhaps, the natural child of Washington. Oddly, in a book written in support of the American Republican party, the author associates the republican citizen with bastardy, in contrast to the young giant's legitimate royal succession. The implied distinction is between a succession claimed on the basis of an accidental, transient relation (by, for example, unscrupulous politicians who happen to get elected or by those new immigrants who, through the foolish generosity of American law, find themselves American citizens) and one that is organic, orderly, and inevitable.

The true son resembles the father, just as the father's appearance reflects his inner self; both are manifestations of the permanent "self-adjusting principles" of the Constitution. Such a theory of nationalist homogeneity serves an obvious purpose in a period of increased immigration. We can see a related logic and language at work in Buntline's *The Convict*:

"I say we must man our Ship of State with *Americans*, with Native born Americans, with the Sons of Sires who fought, bled and died for the establishment of freedom – with those whose feelings, whose family histories, whose hopes and very *existences*, are linked to the Union as the soul is to the body. It is well, and generous and just, to give a home on the farm which our forefathers left us, to the homeless and landless who come from abroad – but I deny their right to take up lodgings inside of the homestead, to assume the management and control of our blood-bought heritage – a heritage which *their* fathers strove with might and main to wrest from *our* fathers! Shall we forget this? shall we, though we permit the sons of the *murderers* who slew the martyrs of our Revolution, to come amongst us . . . ?"[30]

Equating family and national histories, emphasizing blood, insisting on the inextricability of true spirit and its physical manifestation, and focusing on property, Buntline's Ernest Cramer claims his heritage. But in America, this natural national patrimony rests on uncertainty: without a fixed line of succession based in blood, how can Americans ensure that their leaders are legitimate? If legitimacy lies only in being elected, then there is no guarantee that those in power in 1854 will be loyal to the past, that they will preserve the America of the founding fathers. Left to their own devices "politicians" may govern "defective[ly]" forgetting or ignoring Constitutional principles. The fact that the electorate was rapidly changing due to immigration made the likelihood of continuity even slimmer. Only if legitimacy lies in sameness, only if those in office are reproductions of Washington, can America retain its identity.

In 1850s America, this urgent question of political succession coincides with a violent debate over religious legitimacy. The proliferation of religious sects, the liberalization of Protestant theology and practices, the increasing secularism of American society, and accelerating non-Protestant immigration all seemed to undercut Protestant claims to have inherited the true, unchanging religion established by Christ.[31] The problem of apostolic succession confronted by the ex-Tractarian William Sewell is, in antebellum America, a matter for popular public debate. The most vocal and aggressive critic of Protestant religious legitimacy was John Hughes, Archbishop of New York, the best-known and most-hated Catholic prelate in America. Dagger John,[32] as Hughes was called by his many enemies, is the subject of *The Arch Bishop*, the dedicatee of *One Link*,[33] a character in *Stanhope Burleigh* ("Hubert"), *New York* ("the Prelate"), and *The Convict* ("Eminence"),[34] and vilified in *The Jesuit's Daughter*. Not only do the nativist novelists attack Hughes personally in their prefaces and through more-or-less disguised representations of him as "the pugilist of the Pulpit,"[35] but they also attempt to undermine his claims to an authority

based in apostolic succession by tracing, instead, the lines of American political inheritance. The trajectory of Hughes's career – an Irish immigrant who
arrived in the United States as an uneducated laborer and rose to become
the highest-ranking American Catholic – instantiated nativist complaints
about the rapid growth of "foreign" power in the United States. Hughes
was adamant about both the rights of Catholics in American democracy
and the anti-democratic character of Catholic church discipline.[36] In *The
Convict*, Buntline explicitly declares that the unquestioning obedience to
ecclesiastical authority that Hughes demanded is a usurpation of American
sons' legacy of rights. Trollope's anti-gothic and anti-Oxford argument that
the doctrine of obedience destroys the self is recast here in terms of local
New York politics. The prelate whom Buntline calls "Eminence" declaims,
"In the Church, we, who are its heads, ask naught but *obedience* – implicit
faith and obedience. God has given us the heretics for a spoil, and their
land for a heritage."[37]

Perhaps Hughes's most forceful presentation of the Catholic claim to
authority based on apostolic succession was "The Decline of Protestantism,
And Its Cause," a public lecture delivered on November 10, 1850,[38] in which
he countered Protestant histories of evolutionary progress with a narrative
of religious devolution. Looking at this lecture, and the Protestant response
to it, helps clarify the issues of inheritance, authority, and legitimacy at stake
in nativist novels. James Gordon Bennett of the *New York Herald*, Hughes's
longtime nemesis – and most astute audience – noted the timeliness of the
Archbishop's polemic:

King Solomon has said that there is a season for everything. History bears him
out . . . Barnum from time to time has opened upon us with a black whale, a Fejee
mermaid, a Buffalo hunt, Joyce Heth, Santa Anna's wooden leg, a sickly ourang
outang, a spotted negro, a giant or a dwarf, a Calvin Edison or the fat boys, a
double-headed calf or a pig with five legs, so that with him the season is opening
all the time. Bishop Hughes has opened the religious campaign of the season with
a powerful argument on the "decline of Protestantism." . . . . There is a season for
everything and every season must have an opening.[39]

Deftly locating Hughes's sermon in a variety of popular antebellum discourses, drawing on the languages of the religious marketplace, cultural
consumerism (high and low), military campaigns, and – for good measure –
recreational hunting, Bennett suggests why Hughes was such a powerful
figure in the American popular imagination.[40]

Speaking in Saint Patrick's Cathedral, Hughes argued that, having broken
with the historical church founded by Christ, Protestantism inherits none of

its legitimate, institutional authority. Indeed, it defines itself by its difference from, not its identity with, Christ's church. Hughes maintained that he had studied Protestant authors of every denomination back through Luther, yet the only definition of Protestantism he could garner was that it was a religion based on (1) the rejection of, initially, Catholic, but, implicitly, all human authority and (2) the right to read and interpret Scripture for one's self. In these principles, Hughes locates the sources of Protestantism's "decline," claiming that the Protestant can believe and even preach whatever he wishes because "If he preaches error, what right has any authority on earth to rebuke him? He can answer, 'Look at your charter. Is it not the privilege of the Protestant – is it not my right?'" The Catholic voice of authority is opposed by the Protestant charter of rights. Hughes's use of the language of civil rights is also meant to be ironic, since he goes on to point to Protestantism's "civilly shackled condition," arguing that the Protestant Church enjoys power only where it is a "state-slave" serving the government's purpose – provocative imagery in antebellum America.[41]

Nativist novelists' responses to and depictions of Hughes are also illumined by Reverend Joseph F. Berg's "In Answer to the Lecture of Archbishop Hughes on the Decline of Protestantism," a sermon preached on November 26, 1850, in Philadelphia, which shares many foundational assumptions, as well as rhetorical strategies, with fictions like *The Jesuit's Daughter*, *One Link* and *Stanhope Burleigh*. Berg begins by making Protestantism an inherent aspect of just government "You can have no just government, no equitable laws, protecting the sacred rights of person and property . . . without Protestantism." Law and government are not primary; they protect rather than create rights. For the American Protestant, what is "sacred" is neither divine presence nor ecclesiastical nor civil institutions of authority but "the rights of person and property." Berg answers Hughes's claim that Protestantism is a state-slave by sexualizing the political allegory, taunting that the Catholic Church is the "*State Mistress*": "She is the despot that sways the mind of the judge, and wields the hand of the magistrate, that compels the very monarch upon his throne to bow reverently before her claim of temporal supremacy."[42]

Both the Catholic and the Protestant polemicist attempt to gauge Protestantism's current status by writing a gendered religious chronology which they represent as imbricated at every point with civil and national histories. The test of theological truth, and, with it, national authenticity, is ecclesiastical origin, located in a male founder. Berg disputes Hughes's genealogy of Protestantism, arguing that, rather than beginning with Luther in 1517, Protestantism actually dates back to Paul and the year 66, "when an inspired

Apostle *protested* against . . . apostacy." What Hughes calls the rejection of authority and the beginning of diversity Berg depicts as keeping faith. The self-defining act of Protestantism is not, as Hughes claims, defection but protest against "infidelity."[43]

For Berg, the history and thus the identity of Protestantism rests on a chronology of sameness – not an institutionalized apostolic succession, but a succession based on unchanging, shared belief. This defense makes it all the more imperative that Berg refute Hughes's claim that Protestantism has no distinct, fixed identity. Yet, the minister ends by acknowledging: "we often make too much of our denominational peculiarities. . . . The external pressure of infidelity and Popery may be one means of bringing them [Protestants] more closely together; but the principle of union must be *in* us, in order to lead to permanent and living results."[44] Mimicking Protestantism's divisions even in his pronouns ("we . . . them . . . us"), Berg's language reveals the weakness of his position. Nonetheless, he uses this closing exhortation to imply the superiority of Protestantism's inner light to Catholicism's external ecclesiastical structure.

Berg's appeal to "the principle of union" illustrates how the rhetorics of religious controversy and national politics interpenetrate as antebellum America struggles with diversity and sectionalism. Nativist literature argues that the true sons of the sires are men who have inherited internalized unchanging constitutional principles, not those whose claims to citizenship are a matter of misguided law and corrupt government; so, too, true American religion is passed on as a personal legacy of faith, not a rule of obedience imposed by those who hold ecclesiastical office. The by-now familiar distinction between Protestantism as an authentic religion that permeates the person and Catholicism as a superficial set of behaviors dictated by a punitive Church hierarchy allows for the linking of national and religious authenticities. Like Washington's "heir[s] legitimate," Paul's Protestant descendants embody their paternity, preserving its purity.

What nativist novelists claim is that this line of Protestant American inheritance leads, not to a single heir apparent, but to a brotherhood of Young America. The "desire for insidership, for admittance to a purposive community" that Robert Levine identifies as central to American nativist writing is here satisfied with a fraternal vision. More aggressive and secularized than Sewell's – and certainly Trollope's – British collegians, the sons of the sires, the true Americans who oppose the upholders of apostolic succession, are all depicted as citizens who, working with a group of other young men, seek to restore their nation to its former republican glory. Rather than the institutional solution offered by the British educator, American writers propose a grass-roots political activism. While the nativist novelists differ in their class allegiances,[45] each depicts the brotherhood of true Americans as uniting men of all ranks and stresses the fraternity's artisan membership. Individual heroism both depends upon and leads to group action. In *The Jesuit's Daughter*, Oby Kelsey, the fatherless support of his mother and sister, is a member of New York's Thirteenth district's firefighters, "Americans of the right stripe, full blooded Natives . . . the better class of mechanics" ("We ain't no *gentlemen*. We're only firemen!"). The girl he loves, Katrine O'Sullivan, is kidnapped when the Irish police break into his house, but he and the Thirteenth rescue her at the last moment from a burning convent (her sister, who has not managed to find an American lover, is murdered). In *The Convict*, the orphaned hero, Ernest Cramer, a member of the Order of United Americans and of the United American Mechanics, rescues, with the help of his friend, a young woman who has been kidnapped in order that "Eminence" can seize her mother's fortune; Cramer must also battle the Jesuits in order to keep his wife his own. *The Arch Bishop* represents Paul Gordon and George Shiffler, both fatherless mechanics, as belonging to the Order of United Americans which is praised for including "the millionaire and the day-laborer side by side" and, especially, many successful self-made men. The title character of *Stanhope Burleigh*, the sole child of his widowed mother, is on the other hand, "rich – and born rich" and has studied law at Harvard. Yet even this privileged son discovers the common fate of the American male when he loses his beloved to Catholic priests. Praising the Order of United Americans, Burleigh vows to "meet oftener hereafter" with his oppressed fellows.[46]

The three of these novels that are set in the Old World describe precursors of the American republican fraternities, groups of young men united against the holy fathers of the Inquisition, thus claiming a legitimating history for contemporary American religious politics. The genealogical logic of sameness that allows Reverend Berg to claim Paul as a proto-Protestant is at work in this identification of Old World proto-democracies.[47] At the start of *The Princess of Viarna*, the oppressed lower classes have formed a criminal but benign brotherhood (à la Robin Hood's Merry Men). When a true leader returns, the fraternity of thieves unites with those persecuted by the Inquisition. Together, they rescue the jongleuse Zelda (who is actually Blanca, the Princess of Viarna) from the convent and fight to overcome ecclesiastical tyranny and restore legal sovereignty. Unfortunately, the emperor of Spain, Charles V, is so weak that he abdicates in favor of the Church. As a result, the freedom fighters look to the New World, where apostolic and royal successions will be replaced by a dynasty both republican and Protestant:

"In that rich and golden realm, long after the scepter of the seas hath passed from the enervated, crime-stained hand of Spain, will arise a new race – children of martyred sires. . . . In that new home will be developed the mystery of man's self-government, and the astounded universe will behold nations without kings, religions without priests." When the aristocratic relatives and friends of *The Countess* fail to save her from Bartolme, the head of the Inquisition, the military comes to the rescue. The soldiers who break into the Inquisition's dungeons are so outraged at the horrible instruments of torture that their officers cede their authority to the troops, allowing them to mete out justice on their own. The common men torture the Inquisitors with their own tools and finally blow up the building. In *One Link*, Hernaldo Zinna, an artisan, runs the meetings for his "brothers" in the laboring classes, who are attempting to fight the ecclesiastical violation of their homes and their women. He is driven mad, not by the capture and torture of his beloved, but by the Inquisitors' most fiendish plot: they arrest all of his brotherhood and, ignoring his plea to "die with my comrades," leave him "Alone!"[48]

The readers of all of these novels would certainly have been familiar with the phenomenon of a secret or quasi-secret fraternal organization, working towards political ends. Several authors of nativist novels were actively involved in such fraternities. Buntline, who had a life-long relish for secret societies, was a founding member of the American Party, and has even been sometimes credited with originating the "Know-Nothing" name. Edward W. Hinks, a well-known general in the Civil War, publisher (and author?) of *One Link*, also published the weekly newspaper, *The Know-Nothing and American Crusader*. Lippard, according to David Reynolds, "founded a secret brotherhood that revered him as the 'supreme Washington.'"[49]

The most famous and successful of the nativist fraternities were the Order of United Americans and the Order of the Star-Spangled Banner. Founded in 1844, the OUA had a membership of at least 50,000 by 1858. The OSSB, founded in 1850, is the group to which the term "Know-Nothing" was first applied; this secret society even had a junior division for younger nativists called the Order of the American Star and nicknamed the "Wide Awakes."[50]

Nativist brotherhoods were part of a more general rise in fraternal organizations over the course of the nineteenth century. While Anbinder's statistical study of four Know-Nothing lodges disputes the characterization of the membership as predominantly young and artisanal, the popular conception of the group was, however, as these novels demonstrate, precisely that. Carnes argues that the proliferation of fraternal societies filled the gap left by absent fathers, enacting ritual initiations into manhood, providing both substitute fathers as well as a masculine peer group of brothers, and allowing males to break free of female domestic influence.[51] What the novels I am reading describe, however, are fraternal organizations that are inimical to fathers, that stress not an internal hierarchy of elders but a shared brotherly identity. Their hatred of the father unites them as brothers. The conflict that Sewell attempted to buffer institutionally, through male educational communities headed by an elder of limited authority, is fought out on the streets of New York and Philadelphia.

Yet these groups also claim to be united as faithful sons of the sires. What reconciles filial loyalty with filial aggression is the novels' insistent differentiation of the American father from the foreign one.[52] The native son's identification of himself as American relies on the existence of the Catholic Other. Virtually every rhetorical attack on a Catholic father is accompanied by an invocation of Washington. To give just one example: the narrator of *The Arch Bishop* says of the title character, "had he served his country with half the zeal he has served his foreign Master, his name would now have been enrolled beside that of a Washington, a Lafayette, a Clay and a Webster." The foreign father's Otherness is doubly underscored in comparisons between the subtle lies and secret missives of the Jesuits and the noble public words of Washington, for the words quoted are inevitably those of the Farewell Address, with its "Warning against Foreign Influence."[53] The "foreign influence," in turn, is said to be wary of Washington's influential example: Buntline inveighs against the plot by the Jesuit General (Hughes) to "deprive the free children of a Protestant country of the Bible of their fathers, . . . read in the Camp of WASHINGTON," and even ban the History of the United States from the schools because "it speaks of the education of Washington."[54]

As this example implies, the history of Protestant democracy deployed in these novels speaks to the contemporary controversy about public schooling. Archbishop Hughes was an active and vocal opponent of the public school system, arguing – accurately – that the socialization of immigrant boys into American citizens that educators like Horace Mann saw as the task of the public schools was a deliberate campaign to break religious and family ties seen as un-American. A primary tool employed in this patriotic "normalization" of Catholic youth was the teaching of Protestant teleological history.[55] Hughes led a political campaign on the school issue. Insisting that what was needed was state support for Catholic schools, he petitioned the legislature and organized an independent ticket (the so-called Carroll Hall Ticket) in the 1841 election for senators and assemblymen of 1841. The strong feelings regarding schooling are represented in, for example, *The*

Arch Bishop, in which the Catholic clergy are so opposed to such education that they demand that all Catholic parents withdraw their children from American schools, insisting that a pious illiteracy is better than literate heresy.

However, the primary interest of this group of novels is not in the educating of Catholic immigrant youth, but on the threats to young "native" Americans. In a period in which America's nationhood and Americans' identities are being (re)claimed by narratives of succession, that threat comes from the foreign father who rewrites the past in order to establish himself in the present. The Jesuit's ultimate aim is to supplant the true father. In *One Link in the Chain of Apostolic Succession* (1854), we are told that during the past twenty-five years, "the good old principles of republicanism and Protestantism that animated the heroes of the revolution have been gradually crushed out, and their places usurped by those of a decidedly opposite nature." This priestly displacement of the founding fathers is literalized in *Stanhope Burleigh*. Burleigh (himself identified as a "noble child of Washington") walks along the gallery of portraits of his male ancestors, stopping before "the finest-looking fellow in the lot," the original American father who came over on the Mayflower. As Burleigh recalls this brave history, "his ancestor's face . . . disappeared, but in its place he saw the wily image of Jaudan, the Jesuit."[56]

Loyalty demands that nativist brotherhoods unite to unseat such usurpers. Indeed, proof of filial faithfulness would seem to necessitate nothing less than taking over the father's place. Earlier I argued that antebellum depictions of Washington's death bespeak his powerful presence. Yet we may also hear the lament for the loss of Washington that echoes throughout these novels as an insistence on his *absence*. *Stanhope Burleigh*'s dedication "To the Young Men of the Republic" illustrates how the invocation of Washington legitimizes the sons by simultaneously associating them with him and substituting them for him:

A New fpirit has gone over the land! – the fignal fires of feventy-fix have been rekindled! – a new light has sprung from Wafhington's tomb!

Ye, who in the generous fervor of youth, are bearing the torch of alarm through every valley, and making it blaze on every hill-top of our beloved country – to you who have ftudied the Paft, and will control the Future of this ocean-girt land of Freedom, this book is dedicated.

The pointedly archaic spelling, used nowhere else in the novel, assimilates the speaker's voice with those of Washington and the generation of the founding fathers. Yet the novelist hails not Washington's presence or even rebirth but the "new" spirit and light that Washington's burial enables. National identity comes to rest, as Benedict Anderson has suggested, on the ability to speak not to but *for* the dead.[57]

If the death of the founding father and the usurpation of his place by the foreign father create a space for the sons' legitimate empowerment, what actually triggers their aggressive actions are the physical attacks on females that these novels vividly detail. For example, in *The Jesuit's Daughter*, the unscrupulous Irish politician O'Sullivan sacrifices his daughter Ursula to the convent where priests and their male minions maim her with a thumb screw and a red-hot brand, drag her hair out by the roots, and finally resort to the water torture that drives her mad.[58] In *The Countess*, Bartolme, the Jesuit head of the Inquisition, orders Blanchette's death by "the Virgin" (an Iron Maiden): "the arms enclosed her form, while the fair image was changed into an instrument of torture, armed with a thousand sharp knives, which pierced her flesh in all directions, cutting her body into innumerable pieces." Soon after, Bartolme himself is put to death by the same "Virgin," the blades still clotted with Blanchette's blood. Such violence is typical, but even in the few more restrained novels, Catholic fathers kill young women. In *Stanhope Burleigh*, Genevra is condemned to nunhood by her father and forced to take the veil by priests: "Jaudan [General of the Jesuits], as her spiritual Father, gave away the pure virgin bride to Christ; and O'Sullivan, as the officiating priest, pronounced the vows which were to bind her to the Bridegroom forever."[59] At the moment when her hair is about to be shorn, Genevra screams and dies. This popish rape of the locks carries with it no Popeian irony. Recurrent in these novels are lingering depictions of women's hair being cut in the convent or pulled out during torture, imaging the simultaneous sexual violation, de-sexing, and exposure of women.

The sadism of these scenes is multi-functional. Repeated instances when the torturer's instruments are turned against him make clear that, most simply, violence against a woman serves as justification for violence against the father-figure. The sensational sadism of *Hawkstone* that found such an avid readership in America is here recast: staging sexualized scenes of the father's violence towards the woman that the son desires, these novels plot reversal and revenge. And certainly we can recognize the misogyny of this pornographic torturing of young women.[60] But I want to suggest as well that in these depictions of the fathers' minute attention to the details of sadistic torment we can glimpse the sons' displaced desire for paternal recognition. The masochism that Sewell and Trollope attribute to the Tractarian generation – and that Trollope's heroine explicitly refuses – is cast in these nativist novels' multiple, exhaustive, and inventive inflictions of pain. If the masochist's pain lends vicarious access to another's power, nativist novelists represent this exchange even more vicariously: the daughter's body becomes the vehicle for the father–son encounter, a way for the younger man to imagine acknowledgment by the elder, acknowledgment that seems the only avenue to the empowerment of this disenfranchised generation. The Sires' sons fear and desire to be claimed as such.

This reading is reinforced by the insistently Oedipal structure of these nativist plots, which lead from literal incest back to the remembered primal scene. In *One Link*, Alexander *Borgia* forces his daughter Lucretia to commit incest in order that he may avenge himself on a woman who rejected him long ago. *The Arch Bishop*, *The Convict*, and *Stanhope Burleigh* all depict close relations between priests and their daughters that raise suspicions about the young women's purity, distort the daughters' femininity, and hamper their courtships by young men.[61] Bartolme of *The Countess* lusts after Blanchette, who is, unbeknownst to both, his lost daughter. In *The Jesuit's Daughter*, Sister Genita, about to elope with Father Alessandro, is given over to the Inquisition by the jealous Constanza. After watching Genita's torture on the rack, Alessandro and Constanza discover that her broken and exposed body is that of their long-lost child. Alessandro exacts vengeance by murdering the now broken-hearted mother, and then takes his place on Genita's rack. Throughout these fictions, the holy father's unholy instinct to incest is represented as a resurrection of the past. Musing over the priest's attraction to the woman who is his daughter, Buntline waxes philosophical:

Can there be a memory, a lost remembrance, that yet hovers up from the mystic realms of that which have been, hovers about the temple wherein love consecrates the present by its glorious prophecies of the future. . . .

We shall see – we shall see – as we always have seen, when it is too late.

We shall see, when, possibly, the spectral phantoms of a realized destiny point toward us in mockery, as rise from the graves of our buried hopes.

From the grave of hope, pointing with their long skeleton fingers, jeering us – jeering at our frailty.[62]

Buntline's flamboyant determinism is, perhaps, idiosyncratic, but his depiction of incest as the return of the repressed is not. Fathers are explicitly said to be attracted to what amounts to the reincarnations of their youthful loves, the wives whom their clerical ambition has caused them to deny: "there is something very mysterious, very mysterious in the influence this young girl exerts over me" a priest says of his as-yet unrecognized daughter, "It seems to me more like the influence which my beloved Agnes [the girl's lost mother] used to exert over me than any passion I have recently felt. . . ."[63] With almost comic literalness, the father's desire for the daughter replicates his original coupling with the mother, repeating the son's primal exclusion. Like the figure of Pearce in *Hawkstone*, this is the archaic father who keeps all the women for himself.

What points to the overdetermined nature of this figure – its place in the political unconscious – is the fact that nativist novelists represent him not in the obvious intruder of the period – an Irishman fleeing the potato famine – but by a character who is a foreigner to the novel's place *and* time. While Irish lay fathers may give their daughters over to lascivious priests, and the Irish-born Archbishop Hughes character may plot and leer, both incest and authority are typically reserved in these novels for a sophisticated, subtle, well-educated Italian or Spanish cleric, usually a Jesuit. For nativists fighting to preserve Anglo-Saxon purity in an America threatened by immigration and split over slavery, the Southern European priest serves simultaneously as an inherited foe, as a worthier opponent than the Irish peasant, and as a dark-skinned racial "Other." This mysterious, powerful, mobile character marks the intrusion of a different discourse into novels that "realistically" depict antebellum American life. Buntline and the others position their narratives as factual, topical exposés, including attacks on pro-Catholic newspapers and their editors by name, descriptions of the Astor Place riot, detailed reports on city and state election strategies and results, and the names of those involved in the Philadelphia violence of 1844. As Reynolds has shown, Americans did not lack contemporary cases of corrupt clergymen or "reverend rakes" – cases that undeniably had their effect on these novels. Yet the availability of such examples makes the use of an anachronistic, gothicized, popish prelate – an Alexander Borgia – all the more pointed.[64] What is certain is that these nativist novelists tell their stories in two registers and that the "romance of the real" that they construct thereby brings a rich set of associations to bear on contemporary problems.

Priests are also figures from the past because, as we have seen, Protestant polemicists, combating Catholicism's claim to priority, argued that Roman Catholicism was an anachronism. According to Protestants, the Catholic claims to authority that were outlined in Archbishop's Hughes's sermon (that it is the true Church, unchanged since the days of Peter) make it unfit for religious rule: not only has the Catholic Church not evolved into modernity, but its lack of progress means that the past crimes of the Church continue into the present. Hence the logic of describing the Catholic threat to nineteenth-century America by depicting sixteenth-century Italy or Spain, a technique employed as well as parodied in the escaped nun's tale, and returned to in these nativist novels. Hinks declares "Such *were* the thoughts of Alexander Borgia, Pope of Rome; such *are* the thoughts of the Catholic priesthood of the nineteenth century, from Archbishop Hughes down to the lowest and most fallen specimen of manhood that exists as a priest of Romanism." Similarly, *The Princess of Viarna* is dedicated to "The Protestant Community" as a warning "that, although the Spanish Inquisition is nominally extinct, the religious spirit which created it, not only lives among us, but ardently struggles to re-erect, in every quarter of the globe, its blasphemous tribunal." In novels set both in the past and present, then, unreformed and unredeemed Rome haunts the nineteenth century as the undead.[65]

Depicting the uncanny repetition of primal scenes of sexual violence, rivalry, and identification, American native novelists locate incest at the explanatory center of male identity. Within nineteenth-century narratives, whether nativist novels or Freudian case studies, the uncovering of incest seems to solve the mystery and enables the making of coherent historical constructions.[66] But, rather than resting with incest as a timeless source of psychological truth, we can explore *why* an incest plot seemed, to antebellum Americans, a satisfactory way to explain maleness. In other words, we must recognize that these historical narratives themselves have both a history and an historical function. Drawing on a variety of discourses (theological, literary, economic, oratorical, traditional as well as contemporary), nativist novels, in telling these family stories, participate in the cultural debate over America's and Americans' identity. An incest plot appears explanatory to antebellum nativists because of the gendered, religious, and political uses it serves in mid-century America.[67] Incest was a traditional libel on the priesthood, which Reformation attacks on clerical corruption and celibacy only intensified. Antebellum Americans' belief that mother-centered domesticity was the mark of the modern made the violent rule of the clerical father, his sexuality unrestrained by marriage ties, all the more horrific and threatening.[68] And the situation of the post-Revolutionary generation of young men struggling to redefine nationhood and their role in it gave this image of a powerful paternal rival from another age specific resonance.

One particular example of the nativist father–daughter–son plot helps clarify the historical functions of these charges of paternal primitivism in 1850s America: that of the Borgias. As Bullen has shown, in both popular and scholarly nineteenth-century representations, Pope Alexander VI, Rodrigo Borgia, was the touchstone for Catholic corruption. *Every one* of

the nativist novels I have been discussing offers Borgia as an acknowl-
edged example of papal immorality (usually referring to him as "Alexander
Borgia" or, occasionally, "Roderick Borgia"). Like her father, Lucretia Borgia
was a Victorian icon of archaic depravity, her female example underscoring, by contrast, the evolved morality, superiority, and powerlessness of the
nineteenth-century Protestant angel in the house.[69] By repeatedly describing Catholicism as the religion of the Borgias, nativist novelists associate
the Catholic clergy with incest.

Two novels go beyond this guilt by association, however, and deal directly
with the Borgias' family story. In *One Link in the Chain of Apostolic
Succession*, Hinks represents Lucretia as a young woman whose natural,
loving nature is violently perverted by a father who extorts her sexual compliance as the price of her betrothed's life (a bargain which the totally
corrupt Alexander Borgia fails to keep). The Pope acts out of hatred, not
love: he is seeking revenge against the woman he believes to have been
Lucretia's mother. In response to her father's unspeakable actions, the
daughter becomes a hardened, violent, vengeful woman. Nonetheless, the
novel's ending suggests that she may yet be rehabilitated by the love of a
good man, opening the way for a story of the younger man's redemptive
replacement of the holy father reminiscent of the minister's rescue of the
young "nun" in Sarah Hale's "The Catholic Convert." Hinks has rewritten
Lucretia Borgia, the emblem of the evil female aggressor into her father's
victim, an ambiguous figure like Beatrice Cenci.[70]

In Lippard's *New York*, Lucretia Borgia is even more morally ambiguous, a
figure of both Catholic corruption and American patriotism. Esther Royal-
ton, the illegitimate mulatto granddaughter of a great American statesman,
dresses as Lucretia Borgia (in a white dress with a scarlet sash and trim,
wearing a lily and carrying a poniard) when visiting a house of pleasure.
Her companion, the politician Gabriel Godlike, who is dressed as Roderick
Borgia, attempts to rape her, but she fights him off with the dagger, declaring her parentage:

"For know, that while there is a taint upon my blood, that there is blood in my
veins which never knew dishonor, the blood of ___ ___, whose grandchild stands
before you! . . . You a statesman! you a leader of the American people! Faugh!"[71]

As a result of this encounter, Godlike is handed over to a vigilante tribunal.
The true American daughter recognizes the present-day politician as a false
pretender to the father's place. But, by making the daughter the visible
sign of America's suppressed history of miscegenation, Lippard's rendering
of the Lucretia Borgia story in *New York* differentiates between founding

and foreign fathers (Godlike could never measure up to the "leader of the American people!") even as it associates the two (in fathering an illegitimate "taint[ed]" daughter, ___ ___ acts as Alexander Borgia). The fathers of the Union also fathered slavery, and, with it, the sectionalism that makes Americans foreign to one another in 1853. How can the Union be saved and fratricide avoided? By the young men of the present uniting against these emanations from the past.

Lippard's depiction of the Borgias is representative, not in its abolitionist stance – he is alone among these nativist novelists in showing that the American history that is told in hagiographies of the founding fathers occludes the black woman's story[72] – but in the association between founding and foreign fathers to which it draws such sensational attention. Insistently disavowed throughout other nativist novels, the compulsive coupling of the two fathers, as well as their polarization into good and evil, nonetheless implies a splitting and displacement, a safe way for one generation to express hostility towards those who preceded them. Like the echoing laments over Washington's absence, the repeated pairing of founding and foreign fathers creates an acceptable path for sons to keep faith yet seize power.

The Borgia plot underscores the feeling that all of these novels express: that the American male's path to their manhood is barred, that the present is abrogated and the future blocked. The sons inherit neither voting rights nor property rights nor rights to women of their own.[73] The novels vary in the way they bring these plots to closure: in some cases the sons succeed; in others, the foreign fathers prevail. *Stanhope Burleigh* ends with the title character thwarted in his attempt to marry:

"ALMIGHTY GOD, WITNESS ME! FOR I SWEAR IN THY PRESENCE, AND BY MY LOST AND MURDERED GENEVRA, THAT MY HEART AND MY HANDS, MY LIFE, MY FORTUNE, AND MY SACRED HONOR, ARE FREELY OFFERED A SACRIFICE TO MY COUNTRY."

. . .

The cold, grey twilight had now brought in the dawning of a day, that was to save the Republic of Washington.[74]

Even when he leaves the son defeated, the foreign father offers him a way to imagine becoming an American man. Stanhope Burleigh, unable to save his bride, vows to marry and save the nation that Washington has (at last!) deserted.

CHAPTER 4

Mariolatry, imperial motherhood, and manhood

With the exception of *Stanhope Burleigh* (London: Blackwoods, 1855), none of the nativist novels discussed in the last chapter was, as far as I have been able to ascertain, published in Great Britain. However, there was British support for American nativism, as in an 1855 *British Quarterly Review* article praising *The Sons of the Sires* and warning, "Everywhere [in the United States] is Catholicism, in its worst character of Jesuitism, straining all its power to obtain the empire which, with a fatalist kind of confidence, it sees prepared to its hands." Counterparts for the American nativist fraternities of the 1850s can be found in British novels from the same decade which describe both a noble brotherhood of true Britons and a secret Catholic society, bent on espionage. Concerned, like the nativists, with maintaining national identity in a period of expansion and immigration, British novelists shift the 1840s' focus of anti-Catholic sentiment away from Oxford to the threatened borders of Britain's growing empire, at the same time that they register Catholicism as a threat from within. Herbert Sussman has argued powerfully that monasticism offers British writers at mid-century a vehicle for discussion and representation of male identities: "Concerns about relationships among men in the present were posed as historical accounts of these all-male religious communities of the past." Similarly, Charles Kingsley, in *Westward, Ho!* (1855), and Catherine Sinclair, in *Beatrice; or the Unknown Relatives* (1852), describe male brotherhoods from long ago and far away. Kingsley writes an Elizabethan adventure story, Sinclair what I will argue is a "Thug narrative," a militant narrative of foreign exploration and its domestic counterpart. Kingsley – canon, one-time Christian Socialist, chaplain to Queen Victoria, professor of Modern History at Cambridge, tutor to the Prince of Wales, religious controversialist, and novelist – publishes his immensely popular novel of Elizabethan adventure,[1] which argues that nineteenth-century England needs to recall the original greatness that it achieved by defeating Catholic Spain. This anti-Catholic narrative provides a venue in which Kingsley can voice his concerns about

Britain's military weakness, as evidenced by the Crimean War, as well as his anxiety about the health and hygiene of British bodies. Sinclair, a well-known Edinburgh public lecturer and philanthropist and author of some twenty-nine books, uses the anti-Catholic *Beatrice*, one of her bestselling works, to argue that the growing heterogeneity of the British Empire threatens its very identity. *Beatrice*, too, focuses on the weaknesses of modern British bodies, depicting their vulnerability as emblematic of that of the British Empire.

Both Kingsley and Sinclair offer images of a holy English mother whom they describe as crucial to national definitions of maleness and femaleness. Unlike the American anti-Catholic novels of the 1850s, with their focus on holy fathers foreign and founding, these fictions defend against the threat of *the* Holy Father, Pope Pius IX, by debunking Catholicism's Marys and deploying an image of Imperial Motherhood.[2] This strategy makes sense in context of the complex gender constructions involved in British understanding of the Papacy at mid-century. In one of many sermons attacking Pius IX, the traditional image of the Whore of Babylon was invoked:

> Her curses and imprecations we can defy and despise; but when she would embrace us in her polluted and blood-stained arms, we recoil at once. To yield for an instant to her arts . . . were defilement and disgrace to ourselves; were a betrayal of our native land; were casting contempt on the ashes of our sires; were disloyalty to our Queen. . . .[3]

To succumb to Romanism is to break with Britain's history. A nation formed of and by the "sires" – a figure shared with American nativism – is here further defined by means of the female. This sexed and sexualized construction of Britain and its enemy contrasts the corrupt female seductress with the pure female ruler. Rather than the "belated" nationalism of the American generation, British writers of the period evince an anxiety about Britain's imperial identity. Instead of summoning (and dismissing) the ghost of Washington, Kingsley and Sinclair invoke the memory of Elizabeth I, the presence of Victoria on the throne, and the normalizing figure of the middle-class mother.

Reacting as they do to the so-called Papal Aggression – the reestablishment of a Catholic Church hierarchy in Britain – Kingsley's and Sinclair's novels express concerns that are specifically British. While Americans too saw the Immaculate Conception as a part of the Romish campaign for world domination, and while American literature certainly has its share of Protestantized Madonna figures,[4] the narrative pattern to which 1850s U.S.

nativist fiction conforms is indicative of transatlantic historical and political difference. However, popular as they were, Buntline's and Belisle's plots are not the only fictional form that fictional American anti-Catholicism told at mid-century. I close my discussion of British nativism in this chapter by glancing briefly back across the Atlantic to an American novel that offers a domestic alternative to the violent clashes of fathers and brothers explored in the last chapter: Augusta Evans's 1855 *Inez: A Tale of the Alamo*. Describing what she sees as an important episode in the history of U.S. expansion, Evans centers her anti-Catholic narrative on female experience. And, finally, I balance my extended analysis of the popular, but surely uncanonical, *Westward, Ho!* and the today virtually forgotten *Beatrice* by looking at what is probably the best known and regarded novel that attacks Roman Catholicism in this decade: Charlotte Brontë's *Villette*. Charlotte Brontë's virulent anti-Catholicism is far less anachronistic and iconoclastic than has been recognized. Her narrative participates both generically and thematically with a body of contemporaneous fiction.

PAPAL AGGRESSION AND THE IMMACULATE CONCEPTION

"An Italian flag has been unfurled within the heart of our great metropolis, and bold defiance bid to our laws and religion, therefore all must now be actively true to the flag of Old England."[5]

In the 1850s, Pope Pius IX seemed to present a series of direct political threats to Britain. Foremost amongst these was the so-called Papal Aggression. Since the time of the Reformation, England had been treated by Rome as a mission, governed by the Vicars Apostolic. In 1850, Pius IX reestablished the English Catholic hierarchy, appointing Nicholas Wiseman cardinal, and designating English bishoprics. Wiseman, a "Romanized" convert, whose confrontational manner contrasted greatly with the private, low-key demeanor of the older English Catholic families, wrote a pastoral "Out of the Flaminian Gate," which injudiciously declared, "till such time as the Holy See shall think fit otherwise to provide, we govern, and shall continue to govern, the counties of Middlesex, Hertford, and Essex, as ordinary thereof, and those of Surrey, Sussex, Kent, Berkshire, and Hampshire, with the islands annexed, as administrator with ordinary jurisdiction."[6]

Outrage was immediate and widespread: what Pius IX called a "restoration" was labeled "the Papal Aggression." In response, Queen Victoria is said to have asked "Am I Queen of England or am I not?" On October 22, *The Times* reacted with indignation: "If this appointment be not intended as a clumsy joke, we confess we can only regard it as one of the grossest acts of folly and impertinence which the court of Rome has ventured to commit since the crown and people of England threw off its yoke." The Prime Minister, Lord Russell, declared, "There is an assumption of power in all the documents which have come from Rome – a pretension of supremacy over the realm of England, and a claim to sole and individual sway, which is inconsistent with the Queen's supremacy, with the rights of our bishops and clergy, and with the spiritual independence of the nation" (See Plate 7). November 5, 1850, saw Guy Fawkes celebrations of major proportions where "The Pope, Wiseman, assorted dignitaries and hundreds of Jesuits were burned in effigy" (Plate 8).[7]

In 1854, Pius IX declared that the Immaculate Conception was dogma, an action that, like Kingsley's and Sinclair's novels, deployed an image of the feminine to political ends. Church historians have read Pius IX's pronouncement of Mary's singular status – uniquely conceived without sin – as a strategic assertion of papal authority and the logical step towards his proclamation of papal infallibility in 1870.[8] By creating dogma, Pius IX asserted that the Papacy has historically had the power to do so and thus paved the way for that power's formal recognition and codification as infallibility.

Drawing on the work of Marina Warner, Julia Kristeva has suggested in "Stabat Mater" that Pius IX declared the Immaculate Conception dogma in order to counter contemporary gender disequilibrium. Yet, this strategic elevation of a woman by a priest was not perceived at the time as a conservative attempt to keep women and men in their places. The Immaculate Conception is, Warner makes clear, doubly gendered in that it represents Mary as Christ-like (sinless and hence divine), reading her life story as his: that of a redeemer chosen above all others to save humanity through a life of suffering.[9] Through her role as Mater Dolorosa, the sorrowful mother, she becomes both Maria Regina, the Queen of Heaven (at once mother, spouse, and daughter of Christ), and the second Eve, whose sinlessness undoes Original Sin. Such claims for Mary were precisely the focus of the historical Protestant resistance to Mariolatry in general and to the Immaculate Conception in particular. Protestants claimed that Catholics were guilty of idolatry, of *worshipping* Mary, of making a woman equal to God. Indeed, the Catholic practice of appealing to the Blessed Virgin's tender mercy was taken as evidence that papists believed Mary to be more loving and charitable than God Himself. Further, the English were well aware that the dreaded Society of Jesus had, from its inception, actively promulgated belief in the Immaculate Conception as a means of directly challenging the Reformation.

LORD JACK THE GIANT KILLER.

Plate 7   Lord Russell combats Cardinal Wiseman. *Punch*, 1851.

THE GUY FAWKES OF 1850
PREPARING TO BLOW UP ALL ENGLAND!

Plate 8   Cardinal Wiseman as Guy Fawkes. *Punch*, 1850.

Many feared that the papal attacks on Britain from without would actually be welcomed by segments of the British population. Indignant as they were at the "Papal Aggression," Queen Victoria and Lord Russell both suspected a simultaneous and more powerful threat from within. Russell warned,

> There is a danger, however, which alarms me much more than any aggression of a foreign sovereign.
> Clergymen of our own church . . . have been most forward in leading their flocks "step by step, to the very verge of the precipice. . . ."
> What then is the danger to be apprehended from a foreign prince of no great power compared to the danger within the gates from the unworthy sons of the Church of England herself.[10]

Accompanying these fears about the legacy of the Oxford Movement was the fact that famine had greatly increased Irish immigration in the late forties: "Probably 400,000 Irish entered England in the ten years 1841 to 1851."[11] Between the flamboyant practices of the new Catholic converts and the ever-growing presence of the poor Irish, the face of Roman Catholicism in England changed rapidly in this decade. Not only Protestants, but even the older English Catholics saw these new forms and figures of Catholicism as foreign to England, rejecting what they saw as imported "Roman" ideas about church authority and ritual and feeling no affinity with the Irish poor.

Catherine Sinclair's call in *Beatrice* to rally around "the flag of Old England" illustrates how these events were perceived as militating a return to an original – albeit mythical ("Old England") – national homogeneity and unity. Yet her narrative, as well as Kingsley's, repeatedly discovers the differences between an insular nation and an expanding empire.

THE BROTHERHOOD OF THE ROSE

Charles Kingsley, like William Sewell, was initially attracted to Tractarianism at Oxford. He was particularly drawn to the possibilities for asceticism offered by Catholicism and seems to have had a special interest in the physical discipline of self-flagellation. Kingsley later rejected this disdain for the body as what he called "Manicheism" and found in his feelings for Fanny Grenfell, his future wife, the basis for a theory of Christianity centered in marital love. Biographers have speculated that his own early preoccupation with Catholic asceticism fueled the vehemence of his anti-Catholicism in later life.[12]

In the twentieth century, Kingsley has been remembered largely for his challenge to Newman's integrity (Newman answered with the *Apologia*, thereby reviving his own reputation and permanently damaging Kingsley's) and as the proponent of "muscular Christianity."[13] Susan Chitty's biography and Peter Gay's 1986 work on Victorian love return to us another Kingsley,[14] this one the champion of married love, of a Christianity rooted in physicality and sexuality – what John Maynard calls "Kingsley's Sexual *Via Media*."[15] And Patrick Brantlinger has recovered Kingsley's attempt in *Westward, Ho!* to urge a more aggressive military policy in the Crimea. James Eli Adams's study of the styles of Victorian manhood has shown the complexity and richness of Kingsley's "typicality." Focusing on *Westward, Ho!*'s anti-Catholicism allows us to see the relationships among all of these "Kingsleys" – the religious controversialist, the champion of imperialism,[16] and the promoter, and personification, of a newly defined "manliness."

Westward, Ho!'s swashbuckling plot seeks to advance the English empire by re-embodying English men and women. The Protestant polemical image of Roman Catholicism as an archaic religion of the body – sensual in its worship yet disdainful of the flesh, sadomasochistically obsessed with penance and punishment, fostering lasciviousness through "celibacy" – becomes, for Kingsley, a vehicle for critiquing what he sees as a *modern* loss of the healthy physicality that is quintessentially "English." Adams reminds us that "Perhaps more than any other middle-class writer, Kingsley placed the male body into widespread circulation as an object of celebration and desire – a project recognized in the contemporary tag, 'Apostle of the Flesh.' " In 1855, the war in the Crimea gives point to Kingsley's concerns. Kingsley's dedication of *Westward, Ho!* to the bloodthirsty James Brooke, the white rajah of Sarawak and George Augustus Selwyn, the "fighting Bishop" of New Zealand, along with his public (e.g., *Brave Words for Brave Soldiers* [1855]) and private (e.g., a pamphlet written to Thomas Hughes and John Ludlow in 1855) writings on the Crimea, make his desire for aggressive British military action clear. The connections that Haley and others have shown between the idea of the healthy male body and the politics of empire are nowhere more evident than in the conjunction of gendered bodies and imperialist ideology in Kingsley's historical romance.[17]

Following the historical studies by his brother-in-law J. A. Froude,[18] Kingsley describes the Elizabethan era as a period of new-found intellectual, religious, and individual freedom.[19] To Elizabeth's "worthies," England "owes her commerce, her colonies, her very existence." Indeed, Kingsley claims that the "epic" defeat of the Spanish Armada defines England and Englishness. Kingsley, like the American nativists, defines and authenticates national identity by locating it in antiquity, in this case in an action and era of imperialism. In *Westward, Ho!* Kingsley offers a program for Victoria's burgeoning empire based on the revival of this genuine English manhood, a male identity structured by its choice among female figures of worship.[20]

Kingsley's insistence on the cultural and ideological functions of the image of ruling female is illuminated by the work by Margaret Homans, Adrienne Munich, and others, that has begun to recover the ways in which "Victoria was central to the ideological and cultural signifying systems of her age." More specifically, Nicola J. Watson has explored the relations between Victorians' cultural constructions of Elizabeth I and their images of Victoria as what Macaulay called "a milder, better Elizabeth."[21] In *Westward, Ho!*, the man who was to become, four years later, Victoria's chaplain, splits her attributes as wife/mother and ruler between two female characters in order to explore how women's private and public roles are essential to Britain's identity as an empire. In doing so, Kingsley displays, albeit unwittingly, his own and his culture's ambivalence about Victoria's complex and in many ways contradictory personage.

Anti-Catholicism provides a medium for the safe expression of that ambivalence. Victoria's representatives, Mrs. Leigh and Elizabeth I, stand in marked contrast to the woman whose worship defines continental maleness, the Virgin Mary. For Kingsley, Catholic maleness is identified with the most notorious brotherhood dedicated to Mary: the Society of Jesus and, especially, his character Eustace (a name which had, by this time, become a code word for "Puseyite"),[22] a thin, pale, lascivious misogynist who yearns, perversely, for Rose Salterne, the local beauty. Rose is also beloved in healthier and more straightforward ways by all of the young men of North Devon, including the Leigh brothers, Amyas (a "giant" in stature and strength) and Frank (a more refined courtier). In order to prevent civil war in their community the young Devon men form the "Brotherhood of the Rose," vowing loyalty to their beloved and whichever man she chooses. Rose is the occasion of the normative heterosexuality that sustains homosocial bonds; Kingsley makes it clear from the beginning that she herself is unworthy of any worship. What truly sustains and defines the two models of maleness is their relation to the mature women who command them: for the Catholics, Marys secular and divine – Mary Stuart and the Blessed Virgin; for the Protestants, Mrs. Leigh and Elizabeth I. Just as the image of the Immaculate Conception displays Pius IX's aggressive bid for papal infallibility, the women for whom Kingsley's brotherhoods do battle allow him to define "Protestant," "English," and "Male." *Westward, Ho!*

moves antiphonally between a male adventure plot and the depiction of female attributes, creating a litany that contests and corrects the tenets of Mariolatry.

MATER DOLOROSA

The Jesuits of *Westward, Ho!* preach countless sermons on Mary's sorrows, in which they accuse Elizabeth I of substituting her name for Mary in the Litanies, and exhort their listeners to "choose between her and Elizabeth." Kingsley counters with his own sermon *not* on "the supposed woes of the Mary who reigned above," but on "a Mary who reigned . . . below, whose woes were somewhat more palpable to the carnal sense," Mary Stuart. The sufferings of *that* Catholic Mary are, Kingsley argues, well deserved; he describes her as a cold-hearted wanton, a sexual and political intriguer.[23]

Devotion to the Virgin, centered in the Immaculate Conception, is what Kingsley sees as "Manicheism," a religion, he argues, based upon contempt for the body and disgust with sexual, physical, earthly love. Mary can be seen as emblematic of such dualism, as Marina Warner explains:

The Immaculate Conception remains the dogma by which the Virgin Mary is set apart from the human race because she is not stained by the Fall. And if on one plane the perfection of Mary is defined as the conquest of the natural laws of childbearing and death, then the prevailing idea of perfection denies the goodness of the created world, and of the human body, and postulates another perfect destiny where such conditions do not obtain. This is dualistic, and the Virgin Mary is a symbol and an instrument of that dualism.

The counterpart to this Manicheism is the cynicism and "seeming" that Jesuits, according to Kingsley, teach their pupils: "That all love was lust; that all women had their price; that profligacy, though an ecclesiastical sin, was so pardonable, if not necessary, as to be hardly a mortal sin." Since, for Catholicism, Kingsley argues, love of woman is antithetical to spiritual love, Mary Stuart is the logical counterpart to the bodiless, inhuman Blessed Virgin Mary; Mary as whore and Mary as virgin.[24]

In his letters, Kingsley argues expressly that the Catholic dualism of body and soul dissolves gender categories and undoes family structure. Rejecting the body, Romanism locates holiness for both sexes in a feminized "soul," fostering what Kingsley calls "the desire to be an angel," that is, "a woman, unsexed."[25] Catholic men and women alike aspire to a womanhood stripped of sexuality. Similarly, the dogma of the Immaculate Conception, by making Mary inhuman, threatens Christ's embodied humanity.

Kingsley's explicit critique of what he sees as Catholic splitting of soul from body resonates with other Protestant condemnations of celibacy. From the escaped nun's tale of the 1830s through the marital triangles of 1880s sensation novels, the figure of the Catholic priest troubles gender distinctions and disrupts families, acting as, variously, the holy father who seeks to usurp the place of biological parents, the incestuous father who claims the daughter for himself, and the clerical rival for the husband's place. Kingsley's own later attack on Newman linked duplicity and celibacy: "Truth, for its own sake, had never been a virtue of the Catholic clergy. Father Newman informs us that it need not, and on the whole ought not to be; that cunning is the weapon which Heaven has given to the saints wherewith to withstand the brute male force of the wicked world which marries and is given in marriage."[26] Kingsley's slur is consistent with his overarching theory of national character: heterosexuality, health, and Protestantism are basic to Englishness; these components blend into an essential integrity in which the body and soul perfectly reflect and express one another: "sound mind, sound body." As Bruce Haley has shown, most Victorian analyses of what was perceived as a modern, national loss of health, were psycho-physiological in their assumptions. Catholic celibacy – which asserts a disjuncture between soul and body – is, then, necessarily (and, Kingsley would argue, historically) linked with deceit, yet another proof of Romanism's inauthenticity.

Rejecting the dualism that, he claims, undergirds the perverse power of the Catholic clerisy, Kingsley proposes an alternative hierarchy, placing at its apex the earthly married mother, in this case, Mrs. Leigh. In contrast to the Manicheism and asceticism of Rome, Kingsley preaches the holiness of marital love. So ardent is his faith in the Christianity of sanctioned sexual love that he believes in the erotic union of married couples in heaven. *Westward, Ho!*'s interest in Mrs. Leigh begins when her active sexual life is over, when she has become the mother of sorrows. Yet, unlike the Blessed Virgin, Kingsley's Holy Mother has a body. Hence the rather startling scene wherein Amyas discovers his mother praying in her night-dress and kneels by her side. After they pray together, her arm about him, they exchange a silent glance of complete understanding ("There was nothing to be spoken, for there was nothing to be concealed between these two souls as clear as glass," and one of her tears drops on his forehead. Afterwards, Amyas notices "her little bare feet . . . peeping out from under her dress" and bends to kiss them over and over again.[27]

The appearance of such a blatantly Oedipal moment should come as no surprise. As we have seen, the Catholic Church's claims of historical prerogative position it as nineteenth-century Protestantism's primal father.

Anti-Catholic narrative becomes, therefore, a vehicle for the representation of generational struggles, a means of expressing cultural uneasiness about the loss of unified religious and political authority. But what Kingsley describes is not merely an Oedipal scene. Sewell may fear the mother's seduction and the son's regression, Buntline may describe the father's lust for the daughter as a reinscription of his possession of the mother, but patriarchs play little role in Kingsley's adventure story. Despite the fact that *Westward, Ho!* responds directly to the political actions of Pope Pius IX, that powerful cleric has no avatar in the novel. (Recall, by contrast, the multiple representations of Archbishop Hughes.) This scene of mother–son intimacy suggests Kingsley's alternative strategy. The loving details of Mrs. Leigh and Amyas's commerce (the physical closeness; the mutual, nonverbal knowing; the tears) evoke the Kristevan "semiotic": a perfect, physical, pre-Oedipal, prelinguistic union. This image of mother–son love is the ground for Kingsley's sentimental manhood.

Yet it is also a scene that must be kept at a safe distance. When Amyas exclaims, "You have such pretty feet, mother!," the son's words prompt the mother to hide her body and to invoke the father, "Your dear father used to say so thirty years ago." Kingsley makes it clear that to be an Englishman is, in part, to subscribe to the law of the father – to leave the mother, to go out into the world and do battle, to "be worthy of our name." "[S]ubstituting a Virgin Mary, who is to *nurse* them like infants, for a Father in whom they are men and brothers," Catholicism robs men of "independence, self-respect, and self-restraint," Kingsley argues. Complete union with the mother is for non-men: Mrs. Leigh tells Amyas that his dead brother, the delicate courtier, Frank "has often come to see me in my sleep; but you never came. I guessed how it was – as it should be." Amyas, "busy with the men," must come and go. Kingsley quotes Lovelace's lines ("I could not love thee, dear, so much, / Loved I not honour more") approvingly, for the true Englishman abhors "that silly fashion of the French and Italians, to be hanging ever at some woman's apron string."[28]

Nonetheless, rather than a complete, Oedipal proscription of the mother's body, Kingsley describes the periodic renewal of the "semiotic" union as sustaining the adult son. During their separation, Mrs. Leigh repeatedly appears to Amyas. Guilty at Frank's death, he mistakes her maternal gaze for a monitory one and dreads returning home to her judgment. When mother and son meet in the flesh, however, she insists on hearing the details of Frank's martyrdom: "Tell me all about my other son, that I may honour him as I honour you." For Kingsley, to be a mother is "to have no self, and to live not only for her children, but in them." Mrs. Leigh exists not as an internalized disciplinary monitor, but as audience for the narrative of her son's life, resembling here the nineteenth-century English mothers who, in works like *Tom Brown's Schooldays*, nobly sacrifice their boys to England, women also emblematized in Victoria's incarnation as "mother of her nation."[29]

Hence, the ideal Kingsleyan female figure is precisely the sorrowful mother who grieves over her son's pain and death. While Kingsley works hard to distinguish Mrs. Leigh from Catholicism's Virgin Mary, the resemblances between these Pieta figures persist. Kristeva analyzes the function of the "maternal masochism" enshrined in the Mater Dolorosa, speculating that Mary's tears signal the return of the semiotic, that non-time before and after death. Among her functions, then, the Sorrowful Mother provides a way to manage death, to, in effect, live forever. It's important here to distinguish the "perverse" sadomasochism that Kingsley attributes to Catholicism from the idealized maternal masochism that he presents as normative. In the latter, the struggle for recognition that is at the heart of relationships of domination is replaced with a fantasy of the (m)other as selfless self.[30]

In *Westward, Ho!*, as in so much of Victorian culture, femininity itself is represented as being created or released by the sorrow (so much, but not all: compare Trollope's idealized mother–daughter love in which acknowledgment and independence are mutual). This representation will soon become concretized in the "imperial tears" of the widowed Victoria;[31] yet in 1855, Victoria, less comfortably perhaps, is not the sorrowful mother but the happily married woman. What Kingsley presents (predicts?) is that suffering and sadness are the female's heritage: religious persecution cast a permanent pall over the life of Mrs. Leigh's Protestant mother, "and the skirt of that dark mantle fell upon the young girl." Habited in the raiment of sorrow, the body of Mrs. Leigh bears witness, with her tears, to her son Frank's death and embraces a new "daughter," Ayacanora, whom she will tutor in sorrowful femininity.[32] At the novel's end, the mother places the daughter in her son's arms: " 'Amyas, my son,' said the silver voice of Mrs. Leigh, low, dreamy, like the far-off chimes of angels' bells from out the highest heaven; 'Fear not to take her to your heart again; for it is your mother who has laid her there.' "[33] Kingsley's heavenly mother teaches that immortality lies not in denial of the flesh, but in the body, in a physical, marital union that is a return to the mother's dream-time.

MARIA REGINA

Throughout *Westward, Ho!*, Kingsley exposes the political strategy behind the Jesuit assertion that the Queen of the Seas is the Queen of Heaven:

claiming the seas (and the New World) in the name of Mary is actually Papal Aggression and Spanish Aggrandizement, an attack on Victoria's and Elizabeth's roles as rulers of an earthly empire. If Mrs. Leigh is the Mater Dolorosa of Protestantism, Elizabeth I, as Virgin Queen, represents Kingsley's direct challenge to Maria Regina. Mrs. Leigh is the private woman *par excellence*; Elizabeth is the public one. Kingsley simplifies the complexities of Victoria's cultural meanings, in which private and public selves remain inextricably and complexly mixed. In his depiction of Elizabeth, Kingsley is influenced by J. A. Froude's revisionist history, including his two essays on "The Morals of Queen Elizabeth" (1853). Like Froude, Kingsley seeks to defend Elizabeth's honor against a whole history of Catholic slurs (e.g., the Jesuit-trained Eustace's remark that at least *his* virgin queen is undefiled). Kingsley champions Elizabeth as virgin and queen by uncovering the politics of Mariolatry. He meets challenges to Elizabeth's virginity by describing the sexual profligacy of her Catholic counterpart. Nonetheless, both Froude and Kingsley take care to stress Elizabeth's human sexuality, making it clear that her virginity is a political choice, not an incapacity. Froude quotes Elizabeth herself on the subject:

these things ["the honour of a husband"] have I thought upon when I was a private person, but now that the public care of governing the kingdom is laid upon me, to draw upon me also the cares of marriage may seem a point of inconsiderate folly. Yea, to satisfy you, I have already joined myself in marriage to an husband, namely, the kingdom of England.[34]

Here the image of Elizabeth resolves the contradictions inherent in Victoria's position as wife of Albert, progenitor of many, and yet meant to, somehow, serve as England's spouse and mother. Both the Catholic marriage of Mary and Christ and the Protestant one of Elizabeth and England are expedient, but the one is blasphemous, the other properly secular.

Given Kingsley's idealization of male action and a sorrowing, passive femininity, one might expect his critique of Maria Regina to include an attack on female rulers. However, Elizabeth's champion in fact proposes an *anti*-salique law, so that only queens might reign: "Then would weakness and not power be to man the symbol of divinity; love, and not cunning, would be the arbiter of every cause; and chivalry, not fear, the spring of all obedience," declares Frank. The female monarch stands in contrast to both the mother without a self and the Holy Father, who uses power and cunning to enforce obedience out of fear. Men who serve a woman remain men, voluntarily choosing to defend her weakness.[35] Again, Kingsley foreshadows the image of Victoria, unavailable in 1855, that would later become so dear to British troops – the lone woman waiting in England whom they protect with their battles abroad.

ALONE OF ALL HER SEX: THE SECOND EVE

The first woman's temptation and fall results in humankind's sinfulness. Because of Eve, woman becomes her (the) body; in her role as child-bearer, she endures and displays both sexuality and suffering. As Mother of the Redeemer, the Virgin Mary undoes the work of Eve. Unlike all other humans, she is without sin. Unlike all other women, she is chaste, intact.

Through the characters of Rose Salterne and Ayacanora, Kingsley challenges Mary's claim to the role of Redeemer, of Second Eve. Both Rose, the metaphoric queen of Devon, and Ayacanora, the New World "goddess," each seemingly unique among women, are humbled in the course of Kingsley's narrative. Rose's pride leads to her death, and Ayacanora is transformed into the ideal, imitative, imperial subject.

Rose is named after the flower that emblematizes both Mary's peerlessness *and* female sexuality. Implicit, too, for Kingsley's mid-century audience, is one of the epithets for Victoria – "The Royal Rose of England" – used commonly at the time of her coronation.[36] Kingsley parodies Catholicism's cult of the Virgin by describing how the local yokels "treasured up the very parings of her [Rose's] nails"; there is not one "who would not have gone to Jerusalem to win her." The ludicrousness of such religious "sentimentality" is made all the more obvious when we recognize that this merchant's daughter is the Eve in the garden of North Devon. Seducing not only the local young men, but also Catholic "foreigners" in the persons of the Jesuit Eustace and the Spaniard Don Guzman, Rose is an "apple of discord." Her ringlets are described as "entangling the soul of Eustace Leigh within their glossy nets." When the best of her admirers – the Brotherhood of the Rose – scatter to fulfill their public duties, "Mistress Salterne was left alone with her looking-glass." As in Eden, the "serpent" – Don Guzman – who tempts Rose appeals to her pride by offering secret knowledge. "That temptation of having some mysterious private treasure, of being the priestess of some hidden sanctuary, and being able to thank Heaven that she was not as other women are, was becoming fast too much for Rose, as it is too much for most [women]," and Rose falls, fleeing with the Spaniard to the Americas.[37]

Kingsley is insistent on this matter of the Fall, as Maynard has noted. Even when it turns out that Rose has been married, not abducted, by the Spaniard, she is still described as fallen: "if she sinned like a woman, she died like a saint," cleansed of that sin by the fires of the Inquisition.[38] For

Kingsley, then, the sin of being "like a woman" is not sexual activity but the desire to be "not as other women are." The story of how Rose falls by believing herself alone of all her sex illustrates the illogic of Catholicism's claim that Eve's Fall can be undone by Mary's divinity. How can Mary's unique superiority redeem Eve's sinful desire to be uniquely superior? In recalling the image of the unmarried Victoria, Rose's narrative also hints at the ambivalence that greeted the young Queen's rise above other women.

In Ayacanora, Kingsley retells Eve's story again, this time offering his version of female redemption in what Adams has identified as belonging to the Victorian genre of the male "tropical fantasy" of a free space beyond discipline and apart from history. When Amyas discovers the savage girl in a New World Garden, "she, unabashed in her free innocence, gazed fearlessly in return, as Eve might have done in Paradise." His attraction to her is checked when two of his men go native with Indian "wives." Finding them, Amyas falls silent,

partly from noble shame at seeing two Christian men thus fallen of their own self-will; partly because . . . a solemn calm brooded above that glorious place, to break through which seemed sacrilege even while he felt it a duty. Such, he thought, was Paradise of old; such our first parents' bridal bower! Ah! if man had not fallen, he too might have dwelt for ever in such a home.

The temptation to rest here with Ayacanora, "to forget kin and country, and duty and queen," "glided in like some gaudy snake." Satan and Eve conspire to seduce men into living privately, as "free" individuals, in what appears to be a timeless realm. However, when a jaguar suddenly pounces on one of the Indian women, Amyas, "like a true-born Englishman," is reawakened to Christianity, civilization, community, and work. The Genesis story becomes historical, not mythological. (Christ may appear as a tiger in Blake's England; in colonialist South America, he is a jaguar.) He resumes his role in the human history that follows the Fall,[39] returning to help lead "that great sea-fight which was to determine whether Popery and despotism, or Protestantism and freedom, were the law which God had appointed for half of Europe, and the whole of future America."[40]

Amyas also takes on the rehabilitation of Ayacanora herself, who is described throughout as his "burden." Ayacanora clearly images the imperial subject – the white man's burden, the "good Indian, siding with the forces of progress."[41] (Her European genealogy – she is the lost daughter of a Spanish nobleman – allows Kingsley to tell this Pocahontas story without the problem of miscegenation.) A skilled huntress and a fierce warrior, Ayacanora scorns the company of the Indian men, who worship her as a

"Daughter of the Sun." She even manages to steal the one source of knowledge forbidden to her, a magic trumpet, sacred to males. Yet, this New World womanhood is sacrificed to her love for Amyas. "Her proud spirit [is] utterly broken, for the first time, by the terror of that great need [for Amyas], and by a bitter loss [of the male fetish, the trumpet]." Taught by Amyas that nursing is "fitter work for a woman than fighting among men," she learns to aspire to be "an Englishwoman, and a martyr." By the time of their arrival in England, Ayacanora's engenderment is complete: "the self-help and daring of the forest nymph had given place to the trembling modesty of the young girl" who clutches at Mrs. Leigh's skirt.[42]

Purged, like Rose, by "the sacred fire of sorrow," this second, human Eve lives on to redeem Adam as well. In the final scene of the novel, the scent of apples recalls the New World paradise that he has lost to Amyas, who has been blinded by lightning as punishment for his avenging rage against Don Guzman. When he drops an apple and, unable to recover it, bursts into tears, Ayacanora hands the fruit to him, and, with it, her sorrowing weeping self. With the English apple, woman offers man the human knowledge of sin and sorrow, "fruits meet for repentance." The sins of the Garden are undone, neither by fleeing history nor by transcending humanity and sexuality, but, Kingsley insists, by marriage. The last words spoken in the novel are "What God has joined together, man cannot put asunder." *Westward, Ho!* ends with the once-powerful male leaning upon the woman who began as his beloved burden. Kingsley's final scene gives holy sanction to the marriage of England and her colonies, and shows how the recovery of England's authentic youth (figured in the young Amyas) will provide for an aging empire: "the heroes who from that time forth sailed out to colonise another and a vaster England, to the heaven-prospered cry of Westward-Ho!"[43] This inspirational history, will, he hopes, alter Britain's dismal performance in the Crimea, remedying his nation's degeneration into effete modernity.

"THEY PRAY TO A WOMAN, THE IDOLATROUS RASCALS! AND NO WONDER THEY FIGHT LIKE WOMEN"

Even in *Westward, Ho!*'s sixteenth-century context, Catholicism appears anachronistic, a primitive rite that has no place in the era of the Reformation, scientific discovery, and political freedom. For Kingsley, like other anti-Catholic writers, Roman Catholicism is an attractive and repulsive religion of sadomasochism, one that holds special appeal and terrors for the ex-Tractarian whose pornographic religious drawings focused on the penitential. And a Jesuit-ridden Catholicism clearly represents not just the past, but also an aspect of Kingsley's nineteenth-century culture. For example, Eustace is described as likely to become a Jesuit because of his "vague hysterical fear of the unseen," the very quality, Kingsley argues, that those in the nineteenth century benightedly admire as "religious sentiment." Kingsley's contention that Catholicism's dualism broke the natural unity of soul and body, fostering an unhealthy self-consciousness, also makes it emblematic of what he sees as a contemporary malaise. Unlike Amyas, who "never thought about thinking, or felt about feeling," all of Eustace's expressions of emotion are, Kingsley argues, prototypically modern – artificial, manipulated, even macabre.[44]

Kingsley's critique of Victorian culture is a dream of real men, wielding power naturally and instinctively, without guilt or remorse. The corporeal rhetoric of *Westward, Ho!* uncouples imperialist action from its effects. Sexually and physically inadequate, the Catholic conquerors can only make themselves manifest on the bodies of their victims, as Kingsley documents with his repeated descriptions of the tortured corpses of the New World natives. This figure of perverse sexuality, unable to sustain healthy bonds with either men or women, modulates by the nineties into a specific identification of the Catholic male as the homosexual. Kingsley's characterization of Eustace and his ilk in 1855 displays what Herbert Sussman identifies as the "increasingly troubled, edgy response"[45] to male brotherhoods at mid-century. What his emphasis in *Westward, Ho!* on the sadism of Catholicism's colonialism highlights, however, is his belief that British imperialism is embodied not in those it colonizes but in the persons of the explorers, in the massive physique of young England, Amyas Leigh. The Spaniard's sadistic need for dominance, for the self-affirmation that comes with another's submission is contrasted with the autonomy of the authentic Englishman, complete in himself, who does not need the recognition of the foreign "Other."

Yet this insistence on the cultural primacy of the healthy male body makes the novel's closing description of a crippled Amyas, leaning on his imperial female "burden," unsettling.[46] Kingsley's insistent distinction between men's worship of woman as Queen of Heaven and men's loving loyalty to woman as mother and Queen on earth cannot quite explain away this powerful image. Ayacanora, the booty that the English worthy carries back from his New World service of Rose and Elizabeth and the anglicized substitute that Mrs. Leigh gives to her son in marriage, figures complexly the results of the island nation's expansionist campaigns. Kingsley's celebration of what he sees as the beginnings of England's Empire hints at the cost of Empire to England. His critique of the sexual and political beliefs and practices that underwrite Catholic mariolatry rests on a counter-litany of English womanhood. Invoking Mrs. Leigh's, Rose's, and Elizabeth's inspiring and sustaining virtues, Kingsley seeks to restore Britain's health, yet his wildly popular narrative of Protestant England's glorious origins reflects as well contemporary cultural uneasiness with Gloriana Victoriana.[47]

THE THUGS OF CHRISTENDOM

Catherine Sinclair's 1852 *Beatrice; Or, the Unknown Relatives* was, like *Westward, Ho!*, widely read throughout the second half of the nineteenth century; its preface was even reprinted separately as a tract, *Modern Superstition*, in 1857. The prolific Sinclair's best-known work was a collection of tales for children, *Holiday House* (1839), since lauded as "the first work of children's fiction in English that included realistically human child characters and was intended to entertain as well as instruct."[48] While I would hesitate to use the words "realistically human" in describing *Beatrice*'s wild tale, Sinclair's psychological studies of persons under duress are at times penetrating. And, I will argue, her genuinely anti-Catholic narrative articulates Britain's and especially Scotland's political, legal, and economic situation at mid-century.

Sinclair's novel shares with *Westward, Ho!* the representation of Romanism's spread in Britain as a counter-force to the work of Empire. Kingsley's remedy for the weakness within modern British men lies in recalling the founding of the Empire in England's early forays against external enemies. In order to defeat what has now invaded from within, Britons must remember and repeat their history of conquering without. *Beatrice*, on the other hand, attempts to shore up a unified, homogeneous British identity by descrying and describing foreign "Others," only to uncover how the foreign has already infected contemporary Britain.

Beatrice, set in the Scottish Highlands, describes the period that leads up to the Papal Aggression (1820s–1840s) – the last line of the novel announces mockingly the imminent arrival "in scarlet from Rome" of "The Cardinal Archbishop of Edinburgh and Glasgow." Sinclair seeks to analyze the practices and beliefs that have allowed that "aggression" to occur. In locating her analysis of religious and political conflict in the Scottish Highlands, she participates in the romanticized ethnography of the area begun earlier in the century by Sir Walter Scott, depicting an exotic, picturesque, and primitive place: her characters are forever adjusting their tartans; natives, many of whom speak in dialect, are fiercely loyal to their clan and its chief (first Sir Evan and later Allan McAlpine). This touristic stance makes

Scotland at once a foreign realm and, because of its deep connection to the past, a location for the true Britain. Royal attitudes towards Scotland, and in particular, the Highlands – emblematized by Victoria's occupation of Balmoral Castle in the 1840s – helped foster this simultaneous exoticization and nostalgia. Murray G. H. Pittock describes the complex ways that what he calls Celtic Primitivism serves the idea of Empire, arguing that "the dissolution of the illusion of imperial solidarity has a symbiotic relationship with tensions over the notion of unitary Britishness itself."[49]

The Highlands represent as well a British location vulnerable to invasion by the foreigner: Spanish Catholics, Italian-trained priests, and Irish migrant workers. Part of this vulnerability comes from the local gentry's military service – a McAlpine stationed at Gibraltar marries a Spanish woman, setting the plot in motion – although that same military service outside the British Isles teaches others like Sir Evan McAlpine (hero of the siege of Kittoor) and his old manservant McRonald how to fight against foreign incursions at home. At work here is the pervasive fear of counter-invasion that Deidre David descries in nineteenth-century Britain: the ways in which the conquered peoples of the Empire infiltrate the culture, economy, and space of England. Counter-invasion is figured most literally in *Beatrice* by the importing of a mob of Irish reapers at election time.

This tension between Other and self, between periphery and center, corresponds neatly with the Protestant perception of the Catholicism as at once foreign and familial, a correspondence that Sinclair exploits. *Beatrice* makes explicit what earlier anti-Catholic fiction implies: that the "Otherness" of Catholicism is especially fearful because it awakens something alien within the British themselves – as the novel's subtitle, "The Foreign Relatives," intimates. The primary way in which the "foreign relative," the alien familiar, is represented in *Beatrice* is in the figure of the Thug, an image that had recently arrived in British culture from India. A friend who is attempting to free Sir Allan McAlpine from Jesuit control declares:

"Conscience tells you loudly, McAlpine, that you have a part to act for yourself in life, and Father Eustace, backed by Mr. Ambrose, says you have not. . . . Are not your limbs given you to walk with? Are not your eyes given you to see with? and has your Creator given you an intellect and conscience that are not your own? Those who would urge the extinction of these are the Thugs of Christendom."

Earlier in the novel, a Protestant Bishop sermonizes: "Let your deepest fears, then, be reserved and your most anxious precautions taken against those Thugs of Christendom, who murder the soul by steeping it in crime as an act of devotion."[50]

THE POPE IN HIS CHAIR.

With Mr. Punch's Compliments to Lady Morgan.

Plate 9   Rome's Orientalism. *Punch*, 1850.

In calling Jesuits "The Thugs of Christendom," Sinclair means not that they are common or even criminal louts, but that they belong to the European equivalent of an Asiatic death cult. Both the contemporary horror of Thuggee and the more traditional revulsion at popery turn out to be complementary aspects of a sort of imperial panic. Neither inside the borders of England's isle, nor within the expanding perimeter of the Empire's lands, are loyal subjects secure against deceivers.

In making Catholic priests unnatural – perhaps even supernatural – villains, Sinclair draws on the gothic tradition of Radcliffe and Lewis, as well as the nineteenth-century examples of Sewell's *Hawkstone* and Trollope's *Father Eustace* – indeed *Beatrice* explicitly cites the latter's authority, as well as following Trollope (and Kingsley) in naming her priestly villain Father Eustace. And British anti-Catholic rhetoric from at least the thirties on denounces Roman Catholicism as comparable to "Hindooism" in its "paganism." (See also *Punch's* 1850 depiction of Rome's Orientalism [Plate 9].) With the figure of the Thug, Sinclair is able to adapt Sewell's and Trollope's portraits of Roman Catholic priests as the mysterious, duplicitous agents of a pagan, primitive cult so as to address the particular fears that faced Protestants after 1850.

The secret Hindu cult of Thuggee was discovered and subsequently prosecuted by British officials in India during the 1830s. At first, British authorities, including Colonel Walter Sleeman, who was to become Superintendent of Thug Police, scoffed at the idea that such practices could be occurring secretly in the regions under their rule. Contradicting as it did firmly held beliefs about British superiority and Indian ineptitude, the story of Thuggee was literally unimaginable. Yet, once the investigation was begun, the unimaginable proved irresistible. Not only did narratives by Thug informers form an evidentiary base for prosecution, but they also provided sensational reading for the British public. In the 1830s, readers avidly followed the story of Thuggee in the popular press, the reports and memoirs of Sleeman and other British officials, and Phillip Meadows Taylor's immensely popular 1839 novel *Confessions of a Thug.*[51]

Drawn from essentially the same sources, each of these narratives describes a string of remarkably similar stories of strangling and theft. Here is the tale that the British audience embraced so eagerly: "Thug" is Hindi for deceiver. Thuggee was said to be a Hindu cult, dedicated to Kali (or Bowanee/Bohwanie), goddess of destruction. Its membership was male, consisting of full-fledged Thugs and young boys in various stages of training. This brotherhood worshiped by killing, specifically by strangling (the group was also known as "Phansigars" or stranglers), a relatively slow means of dying and thus one particularly pleasing to Kali, who delighted in terror. Devotees led normal lives ten months out of twelve, often serving as trusted servants of the colonial British. During the traveling season, they would take to the high roads, win the trust of a group of travelers, and then strangle and rob them. As Rapoport points out, the Thugs' method of murder necessitated this practiced deceit – strangling demands a certain intimacy.[52] This skill in deception at close range extended even to Thug burial practices. Victims were thrown into shallow graves, but their bodies were carefully slit open so that no later swelling would uncover them. Time and again in Thug narratives, British officials learn that a cache of corpses lies literally beneath their feet.

The figure of the Thug becomes a powerful – and useful – one in the British political rhetoric of the period. As David points out, Carlyle styles Chartism "thuggery" in 1839, and the term also begins to be used to describe English working-class street gangs.[53] Given this general connotation of a dangerous group from the edges of society that threatens order, it is clear how "thug" could come to be used, loosely, as a designation for "Jesuit." But the resemblance between the Society of Jesus and the cult of Thuggee was, in fact, much more precise in the Victorian cultural imagination. The characterization of Catholicism and its practitioners as primitive and superstitious is, as we have seen, traditionally Protestant. Following the "discovery" of Thuggee, first French and then British writers begin to specifically characterize that primitivism as Thug-like.

In equating Thuggee and Catholicism, Sinclair is following Eugene Sue, whose 1844–45 novel, *The Wandering Jew*, was widely read in England.[54] Sue cites directly Count Edward de Warren's "British India in 1831," which in turn quotes Sleeman's published reports. Driven from India by the British, Sue's Thugs spread their deadly practices worldwide – the conquered people of the East launch a counter-invasion of the West. The Thug leader Faringhea, whose name is taken from Sleeman, articulates a European nightmare, the return of colonialism's repression: "Exile will widen our domains" (1: 22). Sue's descriptions of Thuggee are clearly meant to be characterizations of Jesuitry.[55] Thugs are said to be "devoted to each other, even to heroism, blindly obedient to their chiefs, who profess themselves the immediate representatives of their dark divinity, regarding as enemies all who do not belong to them, gaining recruits everywhere by a frightful system of proselytism – these apostles of a religion of murder go about preaching their abominable doctrines in the shade" (1: 20). This dark religion works to destroy what are, for Sue, the fundamental human institutions: family and nation. "For us," the Thug declares, "there must be neither country, nor family. Our family is composed of our brethren; our country is the world" (1: 22).

After detailing the murderous practices of both the Thugs and the Jesuits at great length, Sue makes the analogy explicit: "I have found, brother, that you are like myself, a son of the *'good work,'*" exclaims Faringhea when he meets his first Jesuit (1: 69). He explains that the Thugs, like the Jesuits, are an ambitious male brotherhood, sworn to unquestioning obedience, who forsake marriage, family, and country to labor worldwide in the service of their respective queens, Kali and Mary. Most importantly, their "*good work*" is the same – the making of corpses. As evidence of their shared brotherhood, Faringhea cites the text so beloved of anti-Catholic writers: Ignatius Loyola's deathbed directive that the Jesuit should be as a corpse in the hands of his superiors. When Sue's Jesuit villain protests that members of his Society kill only the mind, the will, and the thought, the Thug returns: "And what are bodies deprived of soul, will, thought, but mere corpses? Come – come, brother; The dead we make by the cord are not more icy and inanimate than those you make by your discipline" (1: 69). Indeed, Faringhea quickly becomes a convert to Jesuitism, having recognized that "Bohwanie is to the holy society [of Jesus] what the child is to the man" (2: 182).

Sue's novel is deeply engaged with class politics. The Wandering Jew of his title (Ahasuerus, the shoemaker who refused to succor Christ) has called down God's punishment not only on himself, but also on the working classes who are his descendants. Both the Thugs and the Jesuits seek to exploit the misery of the lower orders, inciting class hatred and violence with the ultimate aim of recruiting the bitter and disillusioned to their ranks. In contrast, Sue proposes a socialist harmony extending across class and gender borders.

The analogy between Catholics and Thugs that Sue spells out in his fiction seems to become available to British writers with the Papal Aggression of 1850. In both "Popery: British and Foreign" (1851) and "Petition of the Thugs for Toleration" (1853), for example, Walter Savage Landor explicitly equates Catholicism with Thuggee. In the former, Landor argues that "popery" has now infected and corrupted the Church of England as well as the Church of Rome. The "Petition," ostensibly written by Thugs, argues that they, too, deserve religious toleration in England, since their religion is clearly more moral than Catholicism. In this and in "A Brotherhood of Ancient Britons" (a mock plea for tolerance of the Druids), Landor represents the attempted manipulation of liberal British laws by groups patently unworthy of representation, showing the ways in which Catholics pervert the rhetoric of toleration.[56]

Sinclair, too, uses the figure of the Thug as a tool for analyzing the political and class components of religious controversy. Like Sue, Sinclair describes Jesuits' relations with the poor as deceitful and self-serving, a means of undermining nationhood and family and of consolidating the international power of the "brotherhood." And she shares Landor's view that Jesuits manipulate the language of "rights" and "toleration" in order to obtain political power, an argument prominent as well in the discourse of American nativism. Invoking justice and equity, Sinclair's Jesuits seek to alter the social, legal, and political conditions of British Catholics. What they really want is "not religious equality but political predominancy."[57] Landor and Sinclair regard the reinstitution of the Roman Catholic Hierarchy – the Papal Aggression – as revealing the true aim behind the increasing rights and visibility of Catholics in Britain.

The plot of *Beatrice* details the political aggressions of the Papacy, as well as offering strategies for defense. The novel is set in the Scottish Highland village of Clanmarina, home to two rival aristocrats, the Protestant Sir Evan McAlpine, chief of his clan, and the Roman Catholic Earl of Eaglescairn, who is ruled by his confessor, Father Eustace. The McAlpine household comes to consist of Sir Evan, his aunt, Lady Edith Tremorne, and his nephew, Allan. To these are added Beatrice Farinelli, survivor of a Spanish shipwreck on the shores of Clanmarina, whom Sir Evan and Lady Edith raise as one of the family.

In Sinclair's Clanmarina, the Catholic priest deliberately keeps his flock in ignorance and poverty, opposing all education, as well as any attempts at economic initiative or independence. Visiting the Catholic sections of the village is like traveling to a primitive land – and that land is clearly Ireland, figured here as a foreign realm within Britain's borders. The parish priest, Father Eustace, is described as "Irish" in his behavior, and his parishioners' "wretchedness" is said to "exhibit[] a perfect exaggeration of Irish misery, in its most priest-ridden districts, and from the same causes – an absentee proprietor and a resident Popish 'Father'!"[58] There is a literal Irish invasion as well, when the priest imports both a candidate (Mr. O'Grady, a "straight-from-Tipperary Irish Papist") and a gang of "reapers" in order to sway the local election.[59]

Sinclair's polemic has some basis in historical reality. At mid-century, "old" Catholics lords and their peasantry could still be found in pockets of the Scottish Highlands. Conditions were, as Sinclair describes them, often primitive and almost feudal. Beginning in the 1820s, a regular steamboat service allowed migrant workers to cross over from Ireland. In the 1840s, the potato famine made for a major influx of poor Irish into Scotland, largely to the industrial, urban south-west.[60]

In *Beatrice*, the contemporary movement of Irish "primitives" into Scotland and England is associated with Roman Catholic clerical infiltration into British homes and polling places imaged, in turn, as I have suggested, as a counter-invasion from India. Throughout *Beatrice*, Sinclair raises the specter of Thuggee, repeatedly equating Catholicism and "Hindooism." Describing the presence of convents on British soil as scandalous, Sinclair extends the analogy: "we have as much right to permit Suttee in India, as to allow women in the United Kingdom to take these wicked vows" (xxii). Catholic penitential practices are compared to the self-mutilation of fakirs; a conventual ceremony to "some secret Hindoo rite";[61] Catholic prostration before the Pope to Brahmins falling down before their idols. Beatrice claims that the local priest's power is such that he could successfully introduce the Juggernaut among his parishioners, a near-literalizing of this pervasive anti-Catholic trope. Sinclair represents Romanism as a pagan, primitive "religion of dead men's bones" that demands human sacrifice. Drawing on Sue, she depicts Mary's Society of Jesus as, like Kali's Thuggee, a fraternity of trained assassins. At the direction of their Jesuit confessors, victims commit a slow suicide, forswearing their families, rejecting their bodies, abjuring prayer to God, retreating into the isolation and silence of the convent, surrendering their wealth, ceding their moral judgment, relinquishing their legal status, and abdicating their wills.

In calling Jesuits Thugs, Sinclair invokes a potent popular image, a range of audience associations, and a narrative structure. The story of Thuggee can accommodate both the traditional accusations of British anti-Catholicism and Sinclair's immediate political concerns. Outwardly, *Beatrice* seems unconcerned with colonialism. I want to suggest, however, that the internal divisions Sinclair describes in Scotland (Protestant vs. Roman Catholic, a secret Italian-Spanish invasion, the problem of Irish immigration, Scotland's own status as a "foreign relative," the uneasy coexistence of Episcopacy and Presbyterianism) express a larger anxiety about the identity and integrity of the Empire, an anxiety signaled by and embodied in the figure of the Thug. Linda Colley has argued that the forging of Wales, Scotland, and England into Britain in the eighteenth and early nineteenth centuries entailed the imaginative creation of a British "Us" defined against the external threat of a foreign "Them"; Britons "came to define themselves as a single people not because of any political or cultural consensus at home, but rather in reaction to the Other beyond their shores." That formative "Other," Colley shows, was Catholic France, and the patriotic British identity that she explores is emphatically Protestant. In 1853, Sinclair suggests that the integrities of both Protestant Britain and Protestant Britons are acutely threatened from without and within. The reestablishment of the Roman Catholic hierarchy raises fears of, first, a papal colony located within Britain's boundaries, and, then, of a shadow empire, with Britain itself as a papal colony. Sinclair's Lady Edith quotes the General of the Jesuits as saying, "From this room I govern not only Paris, but China; not only China, but the whole world, without any one understanding the manner in which I achieve so colossal a power." She goes on: "No body of police is equal to them. They form a spiritual army at war with the individual interests of all mankind. . . . Shall free-born Britons allow such coils to be thrown over their hearts and their homes?"[62]

The Jesuits' campaign against nation and family is successful precisely because of the brotherhood's ability to go, like Thugs, undetected. The Thug is dangerous because he can "pass" as the colonial subject: the surface of the trusted servant and, metaphorically, the subdued landscape, hides a violent criminal and violated British bodies. At work here is what Homi Bhabha has described as colonial mimicry, the creation of "a reformed, recognizable Other, as *a subject of difference that is almost the same, but not quite.*" Thus, for example, Charles Grant's "Observations on the State of Society among the Asiatic Subjects of Great Britain" (1792) calls for the "'partial' diffusion of Christianity": enough religious reform to effect social control, but not enough to raise issues of equality and liberty. Mimicry points both to what Benedict Anderson describes as "the inner incompatibility of empire and nation" and to a corresponding split within the colonizer himself. For the logic of creating an "almost-British" subject means that the "real" Briton is subject to the disconcerting, returning gaze of the subaltern: "the look of surveillance returns as the displacing gaze of the disciplined, where the observer becomes the observed and 'partial' representation rearticulates the whole notion of *identity* and alienates it from essence." Mimicry becomes menace. Bhabha shows that what is menaced is the loss of wholeness, of *presence* – "the body and the book loose [*sic*] their representational authority."[63] The Hegelian contest of recognition and refusal played out between master and slave is here reformulated in postcolonial terms.

In simultaneous avowal and disavowal of the loss of imperial integrity, colonial fantasy focuses on the racist stereotype, which functions as both phobia and fetish: "The return of the oppressed – those terrifying stereotypes of savagery, cannibalism, lust and anarchy which are the signal points of identification and alienation, scenes of fear and desire, in colonial texts."

A similar dynamic can be read in Sinclair's paranoid representations of the atavistic Jesuits who sneak into the British Isles and reduce its inhabitants to "ape[s] endowed with speech." The foreign element of Roman Catholicism can insinuate itself into the British family and thus the British nation because of the power of mimicry, the ability to be at once like and unlike, to be, in effect, unknown relatives.[64]

In *Beatrice*, fears of the hidden Jesuit are played out in the exchange and refusal of the gaze. Sinclair spends much time describing what she calls the Jesuitical "custody of the eyes," the priestly practice of keeping one's gaze fixed on the ground, of never looking directly into another's eyes. Ostensibly, these are acts of modesty and discretion, which display humility and avoid temptation – the demeanor of "reserve" adopted by the Tractarians. However, as elsewhere in anti-Catholic literature, the Jesuits in *Beatrice* alternate between hiding their eyes and fixing their victims with a "mesmerizing" gaze. Sinclair implies that the Jesuits keep custody of their eyes not in order to protect their own purity, but to mask their real identities. Jesuits may disguise themselves as British, but their eyes will always reveal their difference. In turn, the British, when faced with the Jesuit's gaze, lose their ability to see. *Beatrice's* converts all acquire a blank, trance-like gaze. Jesuitism is said "to put out the eyes of . . . [Allan's] soul," rendering him "a mere breathing image." The penances inflicted on Bessie, a local girl, leave her blind in one eye. "We Protestants walk in blindfold security," the enlightened Beatrice declares, "because, judging from ourselves, we cannot believe in underhand treachery."[65]

What the returned gaze of the almost-but-not-quite English subject recognizes is how the British have turned a blind eye to their country's and their own internal instability. Scotland provides the Scottish Catherine Sinclair with proof that Britain is a Union, yet the case of Scotland inevitably suggests the differences between a nation and an empire. Pitting a "native" Protestantism against a "foreign" Catholicism, she glosses over the fact that her two prototypes of British Protestantism, the Episcopalian ministers Mr. Clinton and Mr. Herbert, do not represent the established Church of Scotland. Especially after the 1843 Divide, the heterogeneity of Scottish Protestantism was visible, with competition among the Church of Scotland, the Free Church, the United Presbyterians, the Episcopalians, and various others.[66] Sinclair's own prominent family illustrates some of the complex politics of religion in nineteenth-century Scotland. Her father, Sir John Sinclair, was a well-known politician, as was her brother, Sir George, much of whose political activity centered around religious questions. Catherine, like most of the rest of the family, was a member of the Church of Scotland. However, George became a member of the Scottish Free Church after the

1843 disruption. Another brother, John, joined the Church of England, becoming an Oxford divine, vicar of Kensington, and, finally, archdeacon of Middlesex. Within *Beatrice*, religious, ethnic, national, and political diversities are more extreme, belying Sinclair's claims for an authentic, homogeneous, Protestant Britain.

A potential inauthenticity is also shown to be endemic, not only to Britain but also to British men and women themselves. Sinclair argues that Protestants have refused to see both the foreign element that is secretly invading their shores and their own internal foreignness. Catholicism appeals precisely to this inauthenticity: "Children delight in being anything but themselves . . . and those who make religion a mere piece of scenic representation, thus at once recommend themselves to the natural craving of sinful man, whose object is to hide himself from himself." "Theatricality" was, as Nina Auerbach has shown, "a rich and fearful word in Victorian culture. . . . Reverent Victorians shunned theatricality as the ultimate, deceitful mobility."[67] In the theater of Catholicism, performers are seen to abdicate their identities – as family members, as Protestants, and as British subjects.

Romanism's appeals to theatricalized and theatricalizing selves come in the forms of beautiful music, pretty illustrated books, decorated churches, and vivid pageants, "all that tinsel and velvet, painting, gilding, vestments, perfumes, stained glass, and music can do to render a church like a theatre." Drummond and Bulloch describe the way that the traditionally austere Scottish services began, at mid-century, to shift in places towards a fascination with liturgical worship. Catholicism is an art that works on the body. "There is a gross materialism in your religion," Beatrice tells Lady Anne, "not only in the solid and monstrous idols you worship, but also in the scourging and maltreating of your own bodies." "As the deepest sorrows and sufferings of a martyr – the sorrows of the mind – cannot be painted, I greatly prefer to blend my sympathy for his bodily and mental torments together in my own imagination, without seeing one divided from the other in scenic representations." The naturally healthy Protestant body nurtured by a life of pleasant, wholesome moderation is, at the same time, an incipiently Catholic body, whose innate appetite for the unnatural and unhealthy makes it a body that longs to be a corpse – a gross materialism indeed. "The Popish faith is so suited to the natural inclinations of sinful human nature," Sinclair declares, "that in one respect it resembles the small-pox." Herself so scarred by a smallpox inoculation as to be considered unmarriageable, Catherine Sinclair knows well how willingly the body accepts the virus that is its enemy.[68]

Sinclair makes her case against Catholicism largely by means of such physical evidence – the tortured, broken bodies of Catholicism's victims. (Appropriately, while Sinclair references Kingsley's work throughout *Beatrice*, her touchstone is not *Westward, Ho!*, but his 1848 *Saint's Tragedy*, which graphically details Elizabeth of Hungary's torture by her confessor.) The emaciated bleeding bodies of Father Eustace's penitents evoke the image of an archaic and anachronistic patriarchal authority. Anti-Catholicism insistently and repeatedly reproduces such images as an argument for an alternative religious, political, and cultural model of the self and its regulation. In one telling example, Sinclair describes a nun who has had to chew a piece of window-glass as punishment for rinsing her teeth before taking Communion. When the amused Beatrice suggests that there is "no harm in brushing your own teeth," the nun replies, "Nothing is mine. We never say my, or mine, of anything. All is in common, – all is ours, nothing mine." Physicalized here, this erasure of selfhood extends in the novel to the legal selves of Englishmen and women, as the Jesuits wrest inheritances, votes, children, and spouses from their victims. Although Beatrice is amused by this instance of forbidden oral hygiene, the novel's ritualized beatings and tortures clearly enact an extreme masochism, a complete ceding of the self. "You are here to serve your masters. . . . At the first word or sign from anyone you will drop whatever you are doing and ready yourself for what is really your one and only duty: to lend yourself. Your hands are not your own, nor are our breasts, nor most especially any of your orifices," O is told in Pauline Reage's *Story* of sadomasochism. As Jessica Benjamin explains "O is to lose all subjectivity, all possibility of using her body for action; she is to be merely a thing."[69] Sinclair takes the dynamic of power, recognition, and submission that structures so much of Protestant polemic to its logical conclusion: the Catholic believer, mired in masochism, who can locate her identity only in the sadistic recognition of the priestly Other, literally becomes a "thing" – that is, a corpse.

The corporal punishments of the fathers literally and figuratively destroy the self; in their place, Sinclair offers the "disciplinary intimacy" that we have seen earlier in Frances Trollope's descriptions of mothers and daughters. Unlike *Westward, Ho!*'s litany, which praised England's Queen at the expense of Heaven's, *Beatrice*'s study of female rule is concerned primarily with the middle-class home. Lord and Lady Eaglescairn, who expect their titles, wealth, and autocratic manners to command compliance, meet with disrespect and rebellion. In contrast, the "mother" of Allan and Beatrice, Lady Edith, is, despite her title, the widow of a clergyman, who lives throughout most of the novel in a simple cottage. Although the major characters are, finally, all members of the aristocracy, Sinclair's model and audience, as her preface makes clear, are middle class. Like Kingsley, Sinclair focuses on female influence by making her primary mother character a single parent. In her relations with both Alan and Beatrice, Lady Edith creates a realm of loving intimacy in which she "seemed to have a sort of magnetic influence over their feelings, by the successful endeavour she constantly made to attach them to herself, and by the benefits she conferred while enlightening their understandings and improving their hearts." Allan, because he is a male, turned over to tutors and sent away to school, loses the benefit of these maternal lessons in self-discipline through love. But Beatrice follows Lady Edith to the small cottage that becomes her home after Lord Evan's death. And it is in this humble domestic paradise that the lessons of British Protestantism are fully implemented. Beatrice becomes an adherent of Lady Edith's "creed . . . of active energy":[70] sewing, studying, gardening, walking, visiting the poor, succoring the sick, and, above all, reading the Bible together.

In stressing this shared reading, Sinclair at once evokes a standard Protestant complaint (Catholics are "forbidden" to read the Bible) and demonstrates the effect that she hopes her own book will have on its readers, awakening them to "the enlightened happiness derived from the religion of England, founded on the Bible, contrasted with the misery arising from the superstition of Italy, founded on the Breviary."[71] The Breviary, the book of priests, is a series of prayers, hymns, and psalms that those in orders are required to recite at the canonical hours. In contrast, Protestants read (rather than recite by rote) the Bible, the book of the people, in its entirety. As the Breviary's name implies, it is an abbreviation of the Bible, in Sinclair's eyes, a savage truncation of the wholeness of God's Word that corresponds to Catholicism's violation of its adherents' selves. Suggestive here is Bhabha's elaboration of how the Other's "partial" presence menaces British authenticity:

In the ambivalent world of the "not quite/not white," on the margins of metropolitan desire, the *founding objects* of the Western world become the erratic, eccentric, accidental *objets trouvés* of the colonial discourse – the part-objects of presence. It is then that the body and the book loose [*sic*] their representational authority. Black skin splits under the racist gaze, displaced into signs of bestiality, genitalia, grotesquerie, which reveal the phobic myth of the undifferentiated whole white body. And the holiest of books – the Bible – bearing both the standard of the cross and the standard of the empire finds itself strangely dismembered. In May 1817 a missionary wrote from Bengal: Still everyone would gladly receive a Bible. And why? – that he may lay it up as a curiosity for a few pice; or use it for waste paper.[72]

The subalterns' use of the Bible reduces the wholeness of the Word, its fully immanent divinity, to scraps of waste paper, and the integrity of the white body is dismembered as it is mimed. So, too, Catholicism grotesquely breaches the book and the body, the Word and the self.

Further tying the representations of the book, the body, and the self, is the fact that the scene of reading in *Beatrice* is, as in Trollope, *the* scene of normative female development. Lady Edith proves herself as mother by reading with Beatrice; in turn, reading becomes for Beatrice an act of filial piety; and *Beatrice* offers its readership "the transaction by which a near one opens a world of sympathy and through that act carries authority deep inside."[73]

The fundamental antipathy of the Catholicism that Sinclair portrays to this readerly culture can be seen in its alternative model of mothering. The Jesuits' strongest weapons in the battle for Beatrice are their secret offers to restore her lost mother to her. By means of these private communications, the "fathers" create what Sinclair calls "a small dark closet in the mind of Beatrice . . . that Lady Edith was not to enter," an image of an inner sanctum or identity which evokes both the confessional and the convent cell. In 1853, Sinclair's critique of the "extralegal" status of Roman Catholic convents in Britain – "A convent is the only spot in her Majesty's wide dominions to which the law of British liberty does not extend"[74] – was part of the growing popular and legislative challenge to Catholic Church jurisdictions (see Chapter 5 for fuller discussion of this topic). Here, she images Beatrice's burgeoning Catholic consciousness as itself an alien realm. The very existence of this private space or self, hidden from the maternal gaze of surveillance, threatens to destroy the English relations between Lady Edith and her "daughter."

However, the fathers' contempt for the mother undoes their efficacy here. Plotting to wrest away Beatrice's inheritance, they insist that they have discovered her true mother: a Spanish nun, a "cold automaton" who has taken a vow of silence. Briefly displayed at a distance like a statue of the Blessed Virgin, she presents no possibility for the physical intimacy, the complete and open communication, the shared activities and experiences that Lady Edith practices and that domestic ideology defines as the marks of maternal and filial love. The disembodied Catholic "mother," her sexuality erased or perverted, contrasts with Lady Edith, who, as a widow and thus, like Kingsley's Mrs. Leigh, a participant in normalized heterosexuality, prepares her "children" for marriage, not unnatural celibacy. And she does so by providing "the best part of education, so strangely neglected by many mothers in our day, the familiar companionship and conversation of one whose experience in life can direct her judgment for future years," Sinclair admonishes, stressing, like Kingsley, the need at mid-century for a renewed attention to the maternal. Asked to choose between her two mothers, Beatrice demonstrates that her identity as a Protestant Englishwoman is constituted by her love and loyalty for a Protestant English mother: "Through life I have known but one mother and one friend. Whatever I am, she formed me; whatever I know, she taught me; whatever I possess, she gave me."[75]

In rejecting her unknown relative, Beatrice asserts her integrity; in reclaiming the youth of Scotland to Protestantism, Sinclair defends the Empire's: at the novel's end, Allan McAlpine, his body healed and his mind restored, determines on a career in Parliament because "those who value the existence of British institutions, of moral worth, of natural conscience, of human virtue and of human feelings, must unite in Parliament as one man in resisting this onset of Jesuitism in England." Yet what the novel has shown us are not one man and one England, but broken men and women and a fragmented Britain. Allan's decision itself reflects what his future wife describes as a state of division and a lack of (phallic) presence: "you must fill the old family seat in Parliament, to support the Protestant principle, and keep the Irish brigade of papists from casting the balance on every question. We want more stirring Scottish members."[76]

Westward, Ho! ends with an image of an England physically chastised by God, with the body of Amyas Leigh, blinded by lightning; the victims of Sinclair's foreigners, on the contrary, are all restored to health. Both novels finish, conventionally, with marriages – in *Beatrice's* case with three couples being united in a Protestant rite. Yet I would argue that, despite Sinclair's assertively happy ending, her depiction of Britain's invasion by Jesuitical Thugs has revealed, in the course of the novel, the covert presence of the primitive foreigner within both Britain and the British. Eagerly consuming Thug narratives, British readers in the thirties and forties learn to see Thugs everywhere. In 1852, Sinclair renders one uncanny figure – the Jesuit – as another – the Thug – linking these two images of repressed atavism. In a period of perceived Papal Aggression, of growing religious and demographic diversity, of increased immigration, and of imperialist expansion, *Beatrice* displays cultural fears about the return of Protestant's past and a counter-invasion of the conquered.

Westward, Ho! and *Beatrice*, one an adventure tale set largely in the New World, the other a domestic drama situated in England's ancient but non-English home, focus on national boundaries and their permeability and on how heterogeneity threatens national character. Like American nativist novels of the fifties, *Westward, Ho!* and *Beatrice* work hard to narrate nation in a period of expansion, even as they express anxieties about its integrity. Idiosyncratic as they are, neither Kingsley's nor Sinclair's stories are anomalous. Extremely popular in Great Britain, both *Westward, Ho!* and *Beatrice* were also repeatedly published and avidly read in the United States (Mott lists the former as a "better-seller," and DeWitt's 1860s edition of the latter is marked "30th ed."),[77] indicating the appetite of transatlantic audiences for narratives that (re)iterate the imperialist nature of Roman Catholicism. I want to close this chapter by suggesting how pervasive anti-Catholicism is in the fictional expression of American and British nativism and nationalism at mid-century by looking briefly at two more novels from the fifties, Augusta Evans's *Inez: A Tale of the Alamo* (1855) and Charlotte Bronte's *Villette* (1853). Doing so underscores and performs the work of my study as a whole – exploring both transatlantic connections and the contiguity of forgotten popular with canonical nineteenth-century fictions.

BORDER WARS

Inez had at least three nineteenth-century British publications, in addition to dozens of U.S. ones, indicating, perhaps, that Evans's domesticized and feminized nativism was more palatable to overseas audiences than the raw violence of *The Jesuit's Daughter* and its ilk. Written in 1855, ten years after Texas joined the United States, *Inez* depicts the battles of the Alamo and Goliad in which Texans of Anglo-American descent fought to secede from Santa Anna's Mexican rule. Evans views both battles as episodes in the history of American patriotism. Like Kingsley in *Westward, Ho!* and the authors of *The Countess, One Link in the Chain of Apostolic Succession*, and *The Princess of Viarna*, Evans uses the historical novel form to trace a masculine national lineage. *Inez* is dedicated "To The Texan Patriots, Who Triumphantly Unfurled and Waved Aloft The 'Banner of the Lone Star!' Who Wrenched Asunder the Iron Bands of Despotic Mexico! And Wreathed the Brow of The 'Queen State' With the Glorious Chaplet of 'Civil and Religious Liberty!'" Yet the novel's setting – the colony of Texas in 1836 – compares interestingly with Sinclair's Scotland, – that wild primitive land within Britain's borders. For, despite Evans's hindsight, the territory that she describes in *Inez* is not only not part of the United States, its inhabitants are not even working towards such a goal. The Texans who fought to secede from Mexico sought to set up an independent state; only in 1845, when that endeavor had failed, did Texas join the Union. Indeed, in a footnote, Evans acknowledges the arbitrariness of the label "American" in

1836 Texas: it "appears absurd to confine the title of 'Americans' to the few citizens of the United States who emigrated to Texas, when all who inhabit the continent are equally entitled to the appellation."[78] (A Southern writer, Evans points to the incohesiveness of the "United" States as well in *Inez's* defense of black slavery.) The national ideal that is defended in this novel, then – defended against Mexican despotism and Catholic tyranny – is a historical anachronism. The border territory of *Inez* proves, instead, an apt setting in which to stage yet another vexed Protestant effort to draw lines around nation, religion, and self.

In remembering the Alamo, Evans details both the immediate 1836 Mexican threat to "American" independence and the continuing dangers of Romanism. Catholicism is represented in *Inez* not by the Mexican Church but by an Italian Jesuit, Padre Alphonso Mazzolin, who, conventionally, hovers around deathbeds, threatens and controls his flock through the confessional, preys on young women, and schemes to obtain riches for Rome and to further his own ambition (also conventionally, "a cardinal's cap"[79]). In this, *Inez* resembles the work of other nativist novelists like Belisle and Buntline who locate Catholicism's true threat in the traditional Southern European Jesuit villain rather than the local clergy. *Inez* was clearly recognized as sharing the anti-Catholic discourse with groups like the Know-Nothings. The April 1855 issue of *Godey's Lady's Book* reviewed Evans's novel on the same page as *The Sons of the Sires*, and the language and judgments of the reviews are markedly similar. Of *Sons of the Sires*, *Godey's* says: "This handsome volume will doubtless attract very general attention during the prevalence of the politico-religious excitement which at present agitates the country." Of *Inez*: "Like other works of the same class, it will doubtless have a good run during the present excited state of the public mind on the vexed questions of religious faith and observances." Reading both volumes as topical excurses on politics and religion, *Godey's* accurately predicts their popularity, a popularity based in audience "excitement."[80] Evans's narrative is understood as participating legitimately in the contemporary debate over what constitutes America and American.

Yet, despite its affinities with the rhetoric of Know-Nothingism and although it is dedicated to the Texas revolutionaries, Evans's novel does not center around a struggle between a brotherhood of young male nativists and a foreign father. Titled with a woman's name and plotted around the lives and loves of women, *Inez* uses the war for independence primarily as a backdrop for female drama. In this her first novel, started when she was just fifteen, Evans begins to develop the independent female character for which she later became famous in *St. Elmo* (1866).

Barred by her ethnicity – Evans would say her "race" – from marriage to the American man she loves, Inez De Garcia becomes a heroic, tragic, figure who is compared to both Joan of Arc and Antigone. Indeed, the figure of Inez allows Evans a latitude which she is not yet ready to grant to her white characters. Inez substitutes for her Protestant counterparts (Mary Irving and Florence Hamilton), enacting their adventures – sexualized pursuit by the priest, threatened imprisonment in a convent, escape in male guise, loss of religious faith – and thus sparing their femininity.[81] Inez especially twins Florence, whose own vulnerability to Rome figures the precarious nature of Texas's American-ness. Florence's father succumbs on his deathbed to the blandishments of Padre Mazzolin; dying, Mr. Hamilton instructs his daughter to convert to Catholicism and obey the priest in all things. From the vantage of 1855, Evans can see American failures at the Alamo and Goliad as chapters in Texas's progress towards American statehood. But with the Hamiltons she also depicts the growing nation's vulnerability to "foreign" forces. Incorporating a Catholic territory into the Union may be part of America's triumphant expansion, but it also introduces a dangerous – perhaps contagious – heterogeneity. Evans's plot ostensibly resolves these problems by having the foreign female take Florence's place in the war against Catholicism, allowing the white maiden to return to Protestantism, marriage, and domesticity. Significantly, Inez, who has crossed national, religious, and gender borders, is felled on the battlefield, contracting an infection as she rescues her beloved's body, and is buried with her fallen love. Unlike Kingsley's Ayacanora, the Spanish maiden who becomes an English imperial subject, domesticated and Anglicized, Inez, the Mexican maiden who rebels against both God and country in her love for "American" Texans, dies, unregenerate, buried secretly and without rites in a howling storm. Evans's closing chapters return her remaining characters to happy plantation life in the American South, but this conventional ending does not fully elide the troubling presence and meaning of Inez/*Inez*'s story of America's foreignness.

As in the escaped nun's stories of the 1830s, then, a woman marks the point of American vulnerability to foreign influence. However, in the later novel the alien female offers an ambiguous, alternative figure of resistance, rejecting both the Catholic tyranny that is her heritage and the circum-scribed role of the American Protestant girl. And Wilson's border-crossing character is not unique. An Inez appears in *Stanhope Burleigh*. Again, the foreign woman (in this case Italian) is a brave, passionate counterpart to a victimized American girl. We last see this Inez escaping in male dis-guise, provoking our speculation about her future adventures. For American nativist writers, concerned with preserving national integrity, the character of Inez offers a space for narrative free play and emblematizes the attractions and dangers of the liminal.

In Charlotte Bronte's *Villette*, "Brussels" provides a similar realm. Suggestive here is Clark-Beattie's observation that *Villette* "is structured by what might be called a colonialist impulse," that is, rather than attack directly the British social structure that oppresses Lucy, Brontë places her heroine in a foreign country which supplies a safely non-British oppressor, in the form of the Catholic Church.[82] Like Kingsley, then, Brontë externalizes a problem within British culture, making a national division (between, for example, the desires of British women and the possibilities that they are offered in British society) into an international antagonism. But these novelists at the same time repeatedly undermine that division, showing how the foreign is in fact familiar.

The anti-Catholicism of Charlotte Brontë's *Villette* (1853), noted in its earliest reviews (e.g., that of Harriet Martineau), has received recent critical treatment in the work of Susan Bernstein, Rosemary Clark-Beattie, Michael Schiefelbein,[83] and others. In glancing briefly at *Villette*, I offer, not a new reading of the novel, but a suggestion about how Brontë's seemingly iconoclastic book in fact comports generically not only with anti-Catholic literature, but also with a specific form that that literature takes in Britain in the 1850s. Bernstein situates the novel within the anti-Catholic rhetoric of the Papal Aggression pamphlets and traces its resemblances to the escaped nun's tale. I would argue, further, that *Villette*'s response to the perceived Catholic threat to British national integrity is of a piece with novels like *Westward, Ho!* and *Beatrice*, as is its ambivalence about British colonialism. What critics have identified as *Villette*'s "paranoid structure" is, at least in part, a cultural symptom, a paranoia not merely personal but Protestant.[84]

Brontë's characterization of Catholicism is, by now, a familiar one, and one with specific resemblances to "mimetic" religion that Sinclair and Kingsley describe in the 1850s. Romanism is a system of espionage, of intimacy violated by spies. Brontë repeats the clichés about the materialism and materiality of Catholic culture, with its accompanying sensualism. In contrast to the internalized system of Protestant morality exemplified by Brontë's heroine, Lucy Snowe, Catholic girls are depicted as having no conscience – their morality lies in their superiors' ability to control them through rules and surveillance. Catholic culture tolerates – even cultivates – duplicity. As a teacher, Lucy experiences the pervasiveness of Catholic ignorance and mental laziness. Brontë represents priests wielding the power of the confessional to prey upon the weak and vulnerable. She insists throughout *Villette* that Catholicism is, in both essence and detail, un-English – indeed, anti-English.

Yet despite Brontë's and her heroine Lucy Snow's virulent hatred of Catholicism, this "foreign" religion has its attractions, as Lucy's desire for the confessional (which echoes Brontë's own), her doubling in the figure of the nun, and her love for the Catholic M. Paul indicate. As Père Silas seductively explains, Catholicism offers Lucy, the single British female, the shelter and support that her native Protestantism does not. Brontë's depiction of Catholicism, thus, is, through a now familiar strategy, an implicit critique of Protestantism.

The connection between the Catholic and the colonial is made more directly through M. Paul's exile to "Basseterre in Guadaloupe," a place name that represents on its surface the structure of colonialism. Here, Lucy's lover is sent to manage the estate of the Catholic matriarch Madame Walravens, powerful and "hideous as a Hindoo idol."[85] As in *Beatrice*, a discourse of paganism and primitivism pervades the novel, a discourse that intensifies at the home of Madame Walravens with its aura of the occult and its association with the Church of the Three Magi. The Catholic matriarch herself appears, dressed in blue brocade, laden with jewels, like one of the adorned Catholic statues so scorned by Protestants as idolatrous. (Brontë also links loyalty to Justine Marie, Madame Walravens's granddaughter, with devotion to the Madonna.)

If the house of Madame Walravens, Justine Marie, and Père Silas stands for the secret history that drives the actions of M. Paul, the future of that house depends upon the Walravens estate in Guadaloupe. As in *Jane Eyre*, exotic New World islands are perceived as the potential economic saviors of European life. In sending Lucy's lover to this particular colonial estate Brontë is obviously not commenting on *British* imperialism as such. Nonetheless, her text reflects the ways in which normalized life in Europe is supported and threatened by the colonies. So necessary are the West Indies to the economy of Catholic European existence, that Madame Walravens and her holy father, like the Rochester patriarch of *Jane Eyre*, willingly sacrifice their "son" to the uncivilized, unChristian world of the West Indies, an act that reveals their own corruption. Lucy's modest, neat English-style school is, notably, begun, not with money that M. Paul sends from Guadaloupe, but with his and then her earnings from teaching and from a belated English inheritance. Nonetheless, only by submitting to a Catholic, colonialist martyrdom, can M. Paul earn his true Protestant bride, a paradox played out in the novel's double ending.

Like Kingsley and Sinclair, Brontë writes a narrative whose vehement condemnation of Catholicism as foreign nonetheless adumbrates British vulnerability to, and simultaneous interest in, infiltration and conversion. At mid-century, Britain's international political situation is such that the rhetorics of anti-Catholicism and colonialism interpenetrate. Catholics are figured as rival colonial forces, as thugs, as foreign spies.

CHAPTER 5

Under which lord? Ritualism, marriage, and the law

Central to Lucy Snowe's encounter with Rome is her visit to a confessional.[1] This moment of intimacy with the holy father occurs when Lucy is most threatened by Catholicism – by the possibility that she will be kidnapped into a convent, as well as by her own longing for love and authority, for direction and forgiveness, and for intimacy. The scene resonates with Charlotte Brontë's own deeply ambivalent feelings about t he confessional. In a letter to her sister Emily on September 2, 1843, Brontë described how, lonely, she entered the cathedral of Ste. Gudule:

I took a fancy to change myself into a Catholic and go and make a real confession to see what it was like. Knowing me as you do, you will think this odd, but when people are by themselves they have singular fancies. . . . I was obliged to begin, and yet I did not know a word of the formula with which they always commence their confessions. It was a funny position. I felt precisely as I did when alone on the Thames at midnight. I commenced with saying I was a foreigner and had been brought up a Protestant. The priest asked if I was a Protestant then. I somehow could not tell a lie and said "yes." He replied that in that case I could not "*jouir du bonheur de la confesse*"; but I was determined to confess, and at last he said he would allow me because it might be the first step towards returning to the true church. I actually did confess – a real confession. When I had done he told me his address, and said that every morning I was to go to the rue du Parc – to his house – and he would reason with me and try to convince me of the error and enormity of being a Protestant!!! I promised faithfully to go. Of course, however, the adventure stops there, and I hope I shall never see the priest again. I think you had better not tell papa of this.[2]

Brontë and Lucy Snowe each evinces a daughterly, shamefaced attraction to the confessional. Solitude drives these women not to a traditional admission of sin, but to a recounting of the self, a demand for authoritative recognition and response. Yet both fear that confession also entails a dangerous ceding of the self.

This penitential scene's complex usefulness for Charlotte Brontë is only one example of how the traditional Protestant abhorrence of the confessional is enlisted at different historical moments. American narratives of the 1830s, as we have seen, depict the confessional as a site of abduction and rape for the woman, while British fictions from the same period describe confession as an infantilizing loss of autonomy for the male. In this chapter, I look at British novels of the 1860s, 1870s, and 1880s in which the trope of the confessional is used to mobilize resistance to the Ritualist movement in the Church of England (Plate 10), a movement widely perceived as an insidious Catholic corruption of Protestantism. Susan Bernstein argues that after the 1850s "women's confessions [in Victorian fiction] are most frequently secularized and domesticated, unfastened from the virulent moorings of anti-Catholic rhetoric." Recognizing the ways in which that rhetoric is mobilized in the Ritualist controversy calls Bernstein's chronology into question. Nonetheless her careful analysis of the figure of the familial confessor as rival to the domestic power of husbands and fathers illuminates the sensation novels I examine here. The trope of the national family so important to Sewell and Trollope comes to be represented by a triangulated marriage plot, whose conflicts are, in turn, understood and represented in legal terms. The confessional becomes a site for cultural tensions regarding contemporary juridical conflicts about matters as seemingly diverse as changes in English marriage laws, the newly declared doctrine of papal infallibility, and the contemporary controversy over vivisection. The legal cases and questions that pervade the anti-Ritualist novel underscore how thoroughly the movement and its opposition were understood within a legal framework (by contrast, the furor over Tractarianism is framed in theological and educational terms). Although Catholicism, supposedly reincarnated in this period as Ritualism, continues to be viewed as foreign, focus switches in these novels from the imperial anxieties manifested in Kingsley and Sinclair to domestic matters – domestic not just in the sense of familial, but also as internal to the nation. Indeed, it is around the crossing of these two domesticities, in the public regulation of the private, that Frederick William Robinson, in *High Church* (1860),[3] Charles Reade, in *Griffith Gaunt; or, Jealousy* (1866), Emma Jane Worboise,[4] in *Overdale; or, The Story of a Pervert: A Tale for the Times* (1869), Eliza Lynn Linton, in *Under Which Lord?* (1879), and Robert Buchanan, in *Foxglove Manor* (1884), structure their narratives.

Identified early on as the successor to eighteenth-century gothic fiction, the British sensation novel has, more recently, been the subject of studies that work to recapture nineteenth-century reviewers' sense of the intense

Plate 10   The Catholic confessor and his female victim. *Punch*, 1850.

topicality of these novels, uncovering their uses of contemporary newspaper reports and legal cases. Recognizing the role that religion plays in a particular group of sensation novels allows us to connect the two bodies of critical work. Anti-Catholicism, central to the gothic from its inception, as well as a lively force in nineteenth-century culture, has, on the whole, been overlooked as a factor in these writings. Yet, I will argue, it holds a peculiar – and representative – place. To the list of events "standard" to sensation novels – blackmail, murder, madness – we can add the introduction of Ritualism to the English parish and the intrusion of the Ritualist priest into the English marriage. While many earlier anti-Catholic fictions address the state of contemporary Protestantism by turning to arguments about origins and antiquity, these novels focus more directly on the problems of the present.

Anti-Ritualist fiction is a striking example of the density and complexity of sensation fiction's shaping immersion in cultural controversies. To realize the topicality of sensation fiction is, as these five novels underscore, not merely to recognize references, but to trace the interpenetration of frames of reference, discourses, attitudes, and assumptions. Critics like Jonathan Loesberg and Ann Cvetkovich have worked to chart the ideology of the sensation novel's narrative form. Recognizing the subgenre of the anti-Ritualist novel extends that work and emphasizes, as well, the fact that cultural beliefs (and anxieties) do not exist in segregation but, rather, in the social equivalent of Darwin's tangled bank, a structure visible in the tangled plots of these fictions.[5]

The husband–wife–priest triangle at work in these anti-Ritualist novels represents a variation on what Geraldine Jewksbury identified in 1864 as a characteristic British narrative strategy: "Heroes and heroines of the present generation of novels rarely dispense with the marriage ceremony altogether . . . but illegal marriages and supernumerary ceremonies are the order of the day."[6] Unable – or unwilling – to employ the adultery plot so pervasive in French fiction of the period, British sensationalist novelists create the bigamy plot – a story structure at once titillating and "moral." The notorious legal case that triggered the rash of bigamy novels in the 1860s, Theresa Longworth's suit against Major Yelverton, accusing him of bigamy, interestingly suggests the possibility of a religious rendering of the plot: Longworth was dressed as a Catholic Sister of Charity when she met with Yelverton, and they visited in her convent cell. Perhaps with this hint in mind, anti-Ritualist fiction depicts the intrusion of a priestly third into the marriage relation, (re)discovering another safely sensational way to rewrite the adultery plot. Readers' presuppositions and suspicions about Romanist lasciviousness are brought to bear in scenes of religious and sexual intimacy – like those in confessionals – but without, in these five novels at least, actual consummation.

The anxiety about authority that was displayed by the Oedipal plots of anti-Catholic fiction in the first half of the century is adumbrated in these later novels as a shifting sense of the validity, as well as the appropriate place, of law in the religious and personal lives of British subjects and especially of the legal and moral standing of the clerisy in the homes and churches of Britons. An "infallible," uncurbed clergy is represented as violating family intimacy and personal privacy and eroding individual and husbandly authority. Robinson, Reade, Worboise, Linton, and Buchanan join, through their fiction, contemporary debates about whose authority governs English religious practices and about what rights women retain in marriage. Under what circumstances must the members of the Church of England obey their ministry? Who governs those ministers? – the bishop? the Privy Council? the Parliament? Should the woman legally "disappear" in marriage? If not, how can the unity of the husband and wife be guaranteed? Does the married woman retain the right of private judgment? Are children entitled to such rights? Are there private areas inaccessible to religious authority? – the home? the marriage bed? Inaccessible to the law? – the convent? the confessional? These questions become linked to uncertainty about the regulation of science and scientists – for some, the age's new religion and clergy. Given the superior and specialized knowledge of scientists, which lay persons could, validly, assert authority over them? Was the lab a space subject to the law and its inspections? These questions were asked both explicitly and implicitly in the Parliament, law courts, popular press, pamphlets, and parlors of the time. To them, I would add another: how and why does Ritualism provide the occasion for fictional engagement with such queries?

The roots of Ritualism can be traced to Tractarianism – indeed, in popular nineteenth-century writing the terms are sometimes used interchangeably. In this sense, anti-Ritualist fiction is the counterpart to the anti-Tractarian writings discussed in Chapter 2. However, while Sewell's and Trollope's fiction attacked Roman Catholicism directly, anti-Ritualist novels are more focused on Catholicizing tendencies within Anglicanism. And, Ritualism itself is distinct from Tractarianism, both in its characteristics and its historical significance. Ritualists were, by definition, of the High Church party, but they did not rest easily with either the conservative High and Dry practices of the past or even with Tractarian modifications. Pusey himself repeatedly sought to distinguish the work of the Tractarians from later Ritualist innovations.

Starting from the Tractarian assumption that the Church of England should be restored to its ancient power and practices, Ritualists went much further. Referring always to the *Catholic* Church of England – "Protestant" being a term of disapprobation – Ritualists initiated the architectural and decorative restoration of churches and the reinstitution of elaborate vestments. Gilding, embroidery, flowers, lit candles, stained glass, and incense abounded; occasionally a crucifix even replaced the Protestant cross. Standing before the altar (no longer a communion table), the Ritualist priest (no longer a minister) faced eastward, with his back to the congregation, chanted or intoned the service, and invoked the Real Presence in the Eucharist. Services themselves multiplied, saints' days and festivals were observed, frequent communion was urged. The Ritualist organized a choir, encouraged fasting and other penitential practices, set up charitable sisterhoods. Most controversially, Ritualists favored celibacy, introduced auricular confession, and insisted upon the Church's, and especially the priest's, dogmatic authority.

Ritualists were denounced in the popular press, disciplined by the Anglican church hierarchy, condemned by Queen Victoria, and tried in the law courts of the land. So violent was the reaction to Ritualist practices, that minor alterations in the dress or practice of a minister assumed major significance. For example, when the vicar at Northmoor Green began wearing vestments, drunken parishioners pelted him with eggs. This "Romanization" of the Church of England was perceived as indicative of the decaying of national values, as a devolution in Englishness itself. Bentley points out that the Dean of Canterbury was not alone in seeing "[e]very success in the introduction of ritual" as "a step in the deterioration of the national character." Controlling ritualistic practices proved difficult, given the broadness of Church of England formularies. The fact that the ranks of the Ritualists were made up largely of rich young men, graduates of Oxford or Cambridge, made the situation even more alarming. Wealth freed them of dependency on preferment. Queen Victoria declared herself "'shocked and grieved' to see 'the higher classes and so many of the young clergy tainted with this leaning toward Rome!'"[7] Not just the future of the Church of England, but that of England itself seemed at stake.

Well-educated, wealthy Ritualists sought congregations in London, where the growing population could warrant the building of new Ritualist churches. Operative too was the assumption that the urban poor would be drawn to elaborate rituals and ceremonies addressed to the senses. Certainly, some of the negative reaction to Ritualism was based on this association. However, ritual's efficacy in drawing the poor seems to have been largely conjectural. As Chadwick observes, "though the ritualistic churches began by aiming at the working class, they succeeded especially among the middle classes."[8] The fictional reaction to, and representation of, Ritualism tends to be set, not among the urban poor, but among the genteel residents of provincial parishes.

Reflected in these texts is an uncertainty about the role of clerical authority in the lives of the upper and middle classes. As Chadwick explains,
with the abolishment of church rates in 1868, lay parishioners no longer
held authority over parish governance: "[w]e enter the most clerical age
of English life, clerical in the sense that the parson had more individual power in his parish church than ever before." The domineering figure
of the Ritualist priest is represented fictionally as transforming independent Protestant parishioners into a stupefied, demoralized flock who obey
unquestioningly a religious despot. Linton describes how a wealthy parish
family, the Molyneuxes, allow themselves to be dominated by the Reverend
Lancelot Lascelles: "He disposed of their time, their property, their persons,
their actions, as if independence and self-respect were words without meaning in English life; and they obeyed him as if they had been born into slavery
and knew nothing higher than the docility of dogs following at the heel
of the master."⁹ The Molyneuxes abandon their heritage, training, and
legal status as freeborn English persons, devolving into the animal existence of the non-English. Linton, her fellow novelists, and, presumably,
their readerships, find the Ritualist perversion of such formerly powerful
and respectable church members more horrific – and more interesting –
than the ministry to impoverished Londoners.

While Ritualist priests claimed nearly unlimited sacerdotal power, they
simultaneously rejected both episcopal and secular authority. Bentley notes
that, "In the end the ritualists developed a technique of deciding for themselves when a bishop was behaving as a bishop and when he was not. As
a sympathetic historian of the movement put it, if a bishop attempted to
prohibit what they were doing, they 'knew he would not be acting as a
bishop of the Catholic Church.'"¹⁰ Cardinal Manning, head of the Roman
Catholic Church in Britain, himself observed that "Ritualism is private
judgement in gorgeous raiment, wrought about with divers colours. It is, I
am afraid, a dangerous temptation to self-consciousness. . . . Every fringe
in an elaborate cape worn without authority is only a distinct and separate
act of private judgement."¹¹

Tricked out in an overwrought cloak of private judgment, these sacerdo-
talists, significantly, claim unconditional power in England at the same
period that the Vatican Council of 1870 is outraging Englishmen and
women by making Papal Infallibility a matter of dogma. No obscure theological fine point, the proclamation of infallibility was threatening enough
to arouse Gladstone's public attack in an "Essay on Ritualism" in *Contemporary Review* in October 1874 and a pamphlet on "The Vatican Decrees" in
November. Gladstone, who was so High Church and so much the political
friend of English Catholics that he had often been accused of secret popery,

declared that no Englishman could now convert to Roman Catholicism "without renouncing his moral and mental freedom, and placing his civil loyalty and duty at the mercy of another." Like Linton's critique of the Molyneuxes' Ritualism, Gladstone's attack on the Catholic Church asserts the psychological and legal incompatibility of English subjecthood with Romanism. Gladstone shares the popular apprehension that the Vatican Decrees seem bent on returning modern Europe to the Middle Ages.[12] As Norman explains, "Modern learning, science, individual freedom, and the liberal state: the council fathers appeared determined to outlaw every aspect of the nineteenth century which British Protestantism had come to espouse as of the essence of enlightenment in the new age." However, using the rhetorics of racialism, nationalism, and imperialism familiar from Kingsley, Gladstone asserts his confidence in the Englishman and his destiny: "a strong-headed and sound-hearted race will not be hindered, either by latent or by disavowed dissents, due to the foreign influence of a caste, from the accomplishment of its mission in the world."[13]

The Church Association, a Protestant organization formed in 1865, brought suit against a number of clergymen for Ritualist practices without success. The queen and Lord Shaftesbury both voiced the popular opinion that if current law could not curb these outrageous practices, then the law should be changed. Victoria wrote: "She thinks a *complete Reformation* is what we want. But if *that is impossible*, the archbishop should have the *power* given him by *Parliament*, to *stop all* these ritualistic practices, dressings, bowing, etc., and everything of that kind, and *above all, all* attempts at *confession*." The passing of the Public Worship Regulation Act in 1874 was aimed specifically at suppressing Ritualist practices and controlling Ritualist priests. Trials under the Act were to be heard by a lay judge (James Plaisted, Baron Penzance), with appeals to the Judicial Committee of the Privy Council. But the Ritualists saw all such regulation as Erastian. The Act was met with open defiance and a refusal to recognize the government's authority to decide upon church matters. Numerous suits were initiated and, after a series of widely publicized trials, five Ritualist clergymen were imprisoned for contempt of court. The Ritualist controversy dragged on through the 1890s and the trial of Edward King, the Bishop of Lincoln.[14]

These contemporary battles over religious rights are taken up directly by the novelists of the period. For Eliza Lynn Linton, the Ritualist is an "irresponsible ruler, neither paying obedience nor acknowledging superiority." Her character Lancelot Lascelles is described as "his own pope and college of cardinals all in one; absolute by right of ordination, and owing no submission to the heads of the Church whereof he was an inferior member, nor to the laws of the country whereof he was a citizen, should either displease him."[15] So, too, the Reverend Geoffrey Stone in Robinson's *High Church* stubbornly persists in his Ritualist practices even when they lead to rioting and brawling during services and, finally, to the burning of his church.

These critical depictions of the Ritualist priest represent a modern variation on the powerful primitive Catholic father figure, for example, Pearce in *Hawkstone* and Alexander Borgia in American nativist fiction. The Ritualists were, both fictionally and historically, young men who had taken up what was perceived as the latest theological style, who contemptuously disregarded the long-established religious practices of their elders. (Bentley cites Bishop Magee's characterization of Ritualists "'scratching and biting their elderly kindly nurses (the bishops)' and trying to kick over the supper table because they could not have the cloth and dishes set out exactly as they liked."[16]) Yet unlike American antebellum sensationalist fiction, which takes the side of the rising generation in its battle against the fathers, British sensation novels describe a battle within the generation that has come of age. The male rivalry depicted in anti-Ritualist fiction is between clerical and lay men, between those who wield ecclesiastical authority and those who rule domestically. These novels represent both the Ritualist scandal in the established church and the contemporary legal controversy about English marriage as a clash between private feeling and public regulation.

Ironically, the ecclesiastical authority that intrudes into the domestic circle is depicted as less a matter of institutional regulation and more the arbitrary will of the individual priest. Anti-Ritualist fiction portrayed Ritualists as rejecting the limitations placed on Roman Catholic priests by a church hierarchy and the doctrine of obedience, claiming, like the Pope, to speak for, and eventually as, God. "You had to choose your master. Which was it to be – God or man? – the Church or your home? – your Saviour or your husband? – me as your guide in the way of salvation or him as your leader into inevitable destruction?" demands Lascelles, arrogating divine authority to himself. Eustace Aylmer in *Overdale* speaks constantly of his priestly "authority," and declares all who disagree guilty of "schism." Buchanan, Robinson, and Worboise all suggest that this obsessive need for total authority rests on doubt. Indeed, Chadwick argues that Ritualism, like Tractarianism, is initially motivated in part by "the strong Anglican desire for due obedience to authority."[17] The nostalgic longing for submission to authentic authoritative rule that pervades Protestant discourse in the nineteenth century can be discerned both in the Ritualists' turn to ever-more observant practices and, paradoxically, in their insistence on unquestioning obedience to clerical commands. Faced with religious uncertainty, these modern clergymen do not rest with what Sewell saw as fundamentally British collegial, circumscribed rule of "Christian Paternalism," nor do they submit themselves to a higher patriarchal (papal) command. Instead, the Ritualists assert their own absolute authority.

Robinson's, Reade's, Worboise's, and especially Linton's and Buchanan's novels frame the controversy over religious rights as a marital crisis. So well-understood is the cultural meaning of the husband–wife–priest triangle in the second half of the century, that Charles Reade begins *Griffith Gaunt* with a generic set piece that needs no introductory explanation:

> "Then I say, once for all, that priest shall never darken my doors again."
> "Then I say they are my doors, and not yours, and that holy man shall brighten them whenever he will."
> The gentleman and lady who faced each other pale and furious, and interchanged this bitter defiance, were man and wife, and had loved each other well.

Depicting this religious dispute between wife and husband over issues of property, authority, and legality, Reade evokes the contemporary discussion about the state of marriage in England.[18] Impelled initially by the Law Amendment Society and the writings of Caroline Norton, and later by the campaigning of Victorian feminists like Barbara Leigh Smith and other members of the Langham Place Circle, Parliament sought to reform and regularize British marriage laws, enacting, in turn, the Divorce Act of 1857, the Married Women's Property Acts of 1870 and 1882, the Infant Custody Acts of 1873 and 1886, the Matrimonial Causes Act of 1878, and the Summary Jurisdiction (Married Women) Act of 1895.[19] Underlying all of these efforts was, as Shanley points out, an attack on the common law doctrine of coverture.[20] Under common law, a woman, in most instances, ceased to exist as a legal entity after marriage. She was "covered" by (that is, subsumed into) her husband before the law. As William Blackstone famously asserted: in law husband and wife are one person, and the husband is that person. "By marriage, the very being or legal existence of a woman is suspended, or at least incorporated or consolidated into that of the husband, under whose wing, protection, or cover she performs everything, and she is therefore called in our law a *feme covert*." This is precisely the doctrine that reformers attacked, pointing out that the "civil death" women underwent in marrying made them the legal equivalents of children, idiots, and criminals. Legislative attempts were made to give married women control over their selves, their children, and their property.

Under Which Lord? provides the most overt example of the ways in which the legal battle over religious rights and practices seemed entangled with the contemporary controversy over marriage reform. Eliza Lynn Linton (1822–98), journalist and author of over twenty-two novels, is now best known for her *Saturday Review* essays on the Woman Question, especially "The Girl of the Period" (1868), a satiric attack on modern women that created a major controversy. A vitriolic critic of the modern woman and opponent of women's suffrage, Linton was nonetheless early on a supporter of marriage reform, including the Married Woman's Property Acts, perhaps reflecting her own position as a self-supporting authoress (having broken with her father, she remained unmarried until she was thirty-six and soon separated from her husband).

By 1879 Linton finds that reforms aimed at protecting the institution of marriage and women as the weaker sex have instead, by subscribing to modern nonsense about women's rights, undermined marriage and injured both men and women. *Under Which Lord?* raises with its title itself the issue of the law: under which lord, which authority, is the married woman? "Love or religion – her husband's control or her Director's authority – the obligations of marriage or the ordinances of the Church – which would win? Under which Lord would she finally elect to serve?" wonders Linton's narrator about Hermione Fullerton. When the Ritualist priest, Lancelot Lascelles arrives in the parish, his insidious suggestions induce Hermione to speak of, and eventually claim, her "rights."[21] As her husband points out, the introduction of that word, with its assertion of individuality, marks the end of their English marriage union:

> There can be no discussion between you and me, my wife, on your rights. . . . Our life of harmony and oneness has not been tyranny on my side and enforced submission on yours, but so perfect a welding together that our two wills have been one, needing only one voice to express and one action to embody. And that voice and action have naturally been mine, because I am the stronger man. . . . As soon as there comes to be a divided will . . . yours has all right.[22]

Richard's voice is the voice of common law tradition which asserts that there are *not* two individuals in a marriage. Linton, despite her early advocacy of married women's property rights was warning in 1891 that "the pendulum is swinging too far the other way" and quoting Blackstone approvingly, "the old saying is true: – When two people ride on one horse one must sit behind."[23] In *Under Which Lord?* her spokesperson Richard discovers that this definition of marriage is not, in fact, upheld by the law or supported by the Church. In order to obtain more and more resources for his priestly ambition, Lascelles convinces Hermione to act against her husband, to take control of her property back from Richard. At her priest's behest, the wife drains and finally destroys the estate.

'*Let us understand each other, Mr. Lascelles.*'

Plate 11   The husband confronts the priest. *Under Which Lord?*, Eliza Lynn Linton, 1879.

Hermione owns her property not because of recent legal reforms, but because her father, using a strategy traditionally available to the wealthy, tied up her inheritance in a "separate estate" unavailable to her husband. Thus, Linton's critique is less of married women holding property and more of clergymen's manipulation of the law in order to interfere between man and wife. Linton may well have in mind the sensational 1871 ruling in *Cox v. Manners* in which a husband lost his legal challenge to his wife's right to make bequests to two convents. In depicting Richard Fullerton's helpless attempts to control the family property (representative of his marriage, his wife, and his family), Linton reveals the way that an arrogant, unchecked priesthood substitutes individual clerical "rights" for those of both husband and wife (Plate 11). Asserting the legitimacy of his unlimited authority, Lascelles reiterates the question of "under which lord?" by asking Hermione whether she will submit to "the rights given by confession or the duties owing to marriage," to the confessor or to the husband.[24]

In *Under Which Lord?* the Ritualist priest clearly introduces the issue of the wife's rights as an expedient means of securing her money. Hermione's independence is merely a sham, a cover for another man. While Hermione's financial independence is the direct result of her father's dislike of her husband, the primary contest in these anti-Ritualist novels is not between father and husband, but between husband and priest. Like "father" and "son" in the American nativist novels of the 1850s, "husband" here is a nationalized term, a trope made explicit in insistent and repeated descriptions of the spouse as a large, healthy, "English-looking" gentleman – the nineteenth-century avatar of Amyas Leigh. A *Punch* cartoon from June 26, 1858, makes the national stakes of this marital structure explicit in depicting a sturdy John Bull protecting British womanhood from unsavory-looking confessors' intrusions into the home (Plate 12).[25]

As this cartoon and as Lancelot Lascelles's claiming of "the rights of confession" illustrate, the rite of confession is viewed as the primary tool whereby the Ritualist substitutes his rights for all others', and, in particular, for those of the husband. Nowhere are the apparently unlimited claims and illegitimate authority of the Ritualist revealed more vividly than in depictions of the confessional. Tractarians, Keble in particular, began the reintroduction of auricular confession, but not until Ritualism does the practice become widespread and, thus, Protestant protest voluble and violent.[26] Public outrage peaked with the discovery of a manual for confessors, titled *The Priest in Absolution* (1866, 1870), which had been created by the Society of the Holy Cross, an Anglican order founded by Charles Lowder, one of the best-known Ritualists, in 1855. Critics seized on this revelation of Ritualism's

RELIGION À LA MODE.

Mrs. Bull. "NO, NO, MR. JACK PRIEST! AFTER ALL I HAVE GONE THROUGH, I'M NOT SUCH A FOOL AS TO STAND ANY OF THIS DISGUSTING NONSENSE!"

Plate 12   John Bull protects British womanhood. *Punch*, 1858.

"secrets," focusing on the questions that the priest was instructed to ask about sexual sins and even more particularly on the pages devoted to interrogation of the married woman. Norman estimates that "By the end of the year, 145,000 copies had been printed, 120,000 of them in a popular edition. . . . Every paper reproduced extracts from the pamphlet and from leading replies as they came in." Innumerable anti-Ritualist pamphlets responded, many of them titled *The Priest in Absolution* and containing selections from and summaries of the manual. Outraged Protestants, including the Home Secretary, Lord Redesdale, protested loudly at Church of England ministers using "obscene literature" as a guidebook for the spiritual direction of their flock. (So well known was this scandal about priests' professional violation of privacy that when, some twenty years later, Robert Buchanan criticized the press's treatment of Parnell during the O'Shea divorce, he titled his article "The Journalist in Absolution".[27])

In a *Quarterly Review* article in 1868, Benjamin Shaw explained why auricular confession was, for most Englishmen, Ritualism's worst offence: "Vestments and ceremonies may offend our religious feelings, but the practice of confession threatens our domestic peace." Penetrating into marriage and the family, the confessional made the private public, disclosing, according to Archbishop Thomson, "the sacredness of the hearth to a prying and often morbid curiosity." Many turned to Michelet's *Du Prêtre, de la femme, de la famille* (1845) for "documentation" about confessional practices in Catholic France.[28] The image of an extralegal power menacing the nation at home is invoked by Sir William Harcourt in an 1874 letter to *The Times* in which he quotes "the boast of a confessor who told the King of Spain, 'I hold your God in my hand, and I have your wife at my feet.'" This threat, Murray argues, is a modern one: the "subtle but more terrible despotism" of the contemporary confessor far exceeds that of "the old heathen priest."[29] This new generation of Romanized clergy operates in the intimate space of the confessional, rather than the dungeons of the Inquisition, inflicting psychological, rather than physical torture.

In all five of the novels under discussion, confession to a priest is represented as incompatible with the institution of marriage. With the exception of Worboise, who portrays the husband as the abject penitent, these novelists share the public consensus that women are more attracted to the confessional than men. However, in a break with the Protestant tradition exemplified by the American novels of the 1830s and 1850s, British anti-Ritualist writers are relatively unconcerned about confessors violating their female penitents' innocence. Instead of the usual outrage about the rape or seduction of "the young person," these novels demonstrate a more subtle suspicion: the fear that the confessional gives another man access to the married women, to that inner self who should be known only by the husband *to whom it belongs*. Victorian convention dictated that marriage created the woman's sexuality at the same time that it subsumed the individual woman into the identity "wife"; "wife," in turn, being subsumed by "husband." Only in the context of such unity can confession safely take place. As Martin Chester insists in *High Church*, "It shall be your husband for the one confessor on earth." What confession to a priest, like female control of property, implies is that the wife exists not within (or, in Blackstone's formulation, "behind") but beside her husband. Like the arguments for married women's property, confession to another man asserts the wife's separateness and autonomy (albeit a false autonomy, as the priest's ability to dominate her demonstrates). Linton is explicit here: both Hermione and her confessor recognize "the gift . . . she had made him of her wifehood." And Robert understands immediately that Hermione's confession makes her no longer his: "Confession – absolute obedience – suffering another man to come between husband and wife – to rob the parents of their child – giving to another man, call him priest or what you will, the most sacred feelings of your heart, the deepest and strongest of your love – you, a wife, submitting to the indelicacy of inquisitorial questions, to the indignity of regulations."[30]

Robert Fullerton's characterization of the confessor as robbing the parents of their child is not meant to be an exaggeration. In both of the novels in which the married couple have children (*Under Which Lord?* and *Overdale*), the daughter follows her parent into the confessional. Once there, she is no longer her parents' child, but the creature of her "more than father," the confessor. If nativist novels of the American 1850s literalized the conventional "father" "daughter" language of Catholicism by telling stories of incest, anti-Ritualist fiction, written amidst court battles about the regulation of public worship and controversies about the statutory redefinition of marriage, represents the relationship in legal terms, emphasizing the priestly abrogation of parental rights. Robert Fullerton finds that his family is at the mercy of a Law that says that an atheist has no legal claim to his child. Lascelles cites (without naming) *Shelley v. Westbrooke* (1817), the case in which Percy Shelley's atheism had cost him custody of his child. "We have not only Divine Command, but Parliament and the Law Courts, on our side," Lascelles taunts the husband and father.[31] The family is subject to clerical, not paternal, authority.

Along with the Shelley case, this secondary daughter's plot invokes the legal controversy over English convents. The transatlantic traffic in renegade nuns lessened somewhat in the second half of the nineteenth century but remained persistent. As late as the 1890s, a flyer advertises a lecture in Kalamazoo, Michigan, on "Convent Life Exposed" by Margaret L. Shepherd, "Nee Sister Magdalene Adelaide," "Late Consecrated Penitent of Arnos Court Nunnery, Bristol, England" (previous appearances apparently included Chicago, Syracuse, and New Castle, Pennsylvania). And American tales of escaped nuns had continued to be read avidly by British audiences: Josephine Bunkley's *Testimony of an Escaped Novice* was published in London in 1863, as was *The Escaped Nun*; Monk's *Awful Disclosures* saw 1851 and 1853 British editions (American editions were available on both sides of the Atlantic through the end of the century). And American books like *Helen Mulgrave* (1852) and *Sister Agnes* (1854) depicted the dangers of English convents as well. British interest in such narratives was fueled by the proliferation of Catholic convents within the realm: Arnstein counts seventy-one convents founded in Great Britain between 1863 and 1870.[32] Such institutions were viewed suspiciously as independent sovereign entities located within Britain's boundaries, ruled despotically and immune to government regulation. Critics insisted that convents be made open to inspection, and the rabidly anti-Catholic member of Parliament Charles Newdegate introduced legislation to that effect repeatedly in the 1860s (such a "Nunnery Committee" had been formed by the Massachusetts legislature in 1855).[33] He was finally successful in 1870 when, on the heels of the sensational case of *Saurin v. Star*, in which the "secrets" of convent life were eagerly published in *The Times*, Parliament constituted a Select Committee to investigate convent and monastic life in Britain. Newdegate's arguments were not anomalous, as Arnstein's figures for the number of petitions requesting government inspection of convents attest: "Ninety-five petitions bearing more than sixteen thousand signatures had been submitted during 1865; a comparable number had been sent in 1869; 134 petitions bearing over thirty-three thousand signatures had been submitted early in 1870." Newspaper after newspaper lauded the formation of Newdegate's committee, arguing that the rights of Englishwomen should not disappear at the convent door. The *Morning Advertiser* employed a popular analogy in inquiring "If lunatic asylums are bound to admit a Government inspector, why should a nunnery, which is but another sort of lunatic asylum, be left altogether uncared for and unwatched?"[34] Like the madhouse in Wilkie Collins's *The Woman in White* and *Armadale*, the convent serves sensation novelists' need for a secret realm at once inside and outside of Britain. The "lost" daughters in Linton's and Worboise's novels – unrecoverable by their parents' love and authority – image the fears that Newedegate continued to campaign against (Plate 13).

' *Her hands outstretched to her child.*'

Plate 13   The bereft mother barred from her daughter, now a nun. *Under Which Lord?*,
Eliza Lynn Linton, 1879.

In this fiction, as in parliamentary proceedings, pamphlets and petitions, as well as newspaper accounts, British families are represented as at the mercy of an arrogant clerisy, unchecked by either law or decency. So savage is the Ritualist assault on the English family structure that, at the height of her involvement with the Ritualist priest, Hermione Fullerton is repeatedly described in language that echoes Sinclair's characterization of Catholicism's "Hindoo" paganism, as a widow performing suttee: "their victim and widow was cajoled into completing the sacrifice already begun – prevented from leaping off the funeral pyre which they had laid for her best womanhood, her highest fidelity, her purest love."[35] In a reversal of the legal disappearance of the *woman* into marriage, Linton presents here the clerical erasure of the *wife*. Sacrificed on the marital pyre is not the trivial, useless self of Hermione's "independence" but her marriage. Accordingly, it is the faithful husband Richard, not Hermione, who dies at the end of *Under Which Lord?*.

While Hermione Fullerton's metaphorical "suttee" plays on the idea of Catholicism's primitivism, the violence that Ritualism wreaks upon the British family is also depicted by Linton, Buchanan, and Robinson as distinctly modern. All three novelists accuse Ritualist priests of "moral/ psychological vivisection." By using this language, they signal their engagement with several ongoing debates within the culture. Protestants objected to confessors' probings into their penitents' privacy, especially given the consensus that the confessional was especially attractive to females. The Roman Catholic response, echoed word-for-word by the Ritualists, was that, just as a doctor could – indeed, should – examine his patients' private parts with propriety, so, too, should the "physician[ ] of the soul" probe into the most hidden places in their souls (Ada Chester in *High Church* specifically calls her minister a "physician[] of the soul"[36]). With the public publication of *The Priest in Absolution*, this analogy was extended still further. Defenders of the manual argued that just as the doctor must study the wide variety of diseases in order to diagnose and thus heal, so the priest must study the forms of sin, in order to identify each soul's specific sickness.

Most Protestant critics rejected this analogy, refusing to grant priests such authority, but some, like John Murray took up the trope, declaring that the confessor practices "an audacious spiritual quackery," administering the equivalent of patent medicines. Eliza Lynn Linton, too, takes the Ritualists at their words when she describes Lancelot Lascelles as "neither moved nor warmed, neither disordered nor elated. He was only the vivisector studying phenomena and interpreting symptoms; only the priest binding his victim to the horns of the altar; the fisher of men hauling in his net with his prize."

Linton, who supported experimental vivisection of *animals* and who makes the noble, manly Richard Fullerton an agnostic student of science, laments that, unfortunately, "experiments in *moral* vivisection [of women] cause no outcry."[37] The Ritualist is not the scientist searching impersonally for truth nor the husband learning within an intimate exchange in which participants make themselves vulnerable. He is a killer, not a healer. The frivolous Hermione is appalled at her good husband's scientific inquiries, but regards the Ritualist priest's more dangerous human experiments as sacramental.

In calling male characters "vivisectionists," these novelists invoke yet another contemporary controversy with special associations for women. Male vivisectionists had attempted to position themselves as a "New Priesthood." Claude Bernard's influential *Introduction to the Study of Experimental Medicine* (1865) employs biblical and sacerdotal rhetoric throughout, for example, calling the frog the "Job of physiology." Bernard describes vivisection as a kind of sacrifice made impersonally at the hands of a high priest:

The physiologist is no ordinary man: he is a scientist, possessed and absorbed by the scientific idea that he pursues. He does not hear the cries of the animals, he does not see their flowing blood, he sees nothing but his idea, and is aware of nothing but an organism that conceals from him the problem he is seeking to resolve.[38]

Opposing this male priesthood was an antivivisectionist movement largely composed of women. Coral Lansbury has shown that "Women were the most fervent supporters of antivivisection, not simply for reasons of humanity but because the vivisected animal stood for vivisected woman: the woman strapped to the gynaecologist's table, the woman strapped and bound in the pornographic fiction of the period."[39] This identification is, Lansbury argues, literally emplotted in the novels of the period that represent vivisection (Wilkie Collins's 1883 *Heart and Science* is perhaps the best known example), each of which begins with the wife's horrified discovery of her husband's experiments on animals and ends with her final victimization by his cold cruelty.

The indifference to pain, the gradual hardening of the heart that Victorian antivivisectionists condemned, is precisely the cold impersonality characteristically ascribed to the confessor. In depicting the Ritualist, Linton deploys the image of the inhuman celibate Jesuit, immune to the claims of domestic love, an image of maleness unsoftened by need for women, familiar from incarnations like Frances Trollope's Jesuit General Scaviatoli. Celibacy exempts these men from the vulnerabilities of marriage, allows them to know the other without revealing themselves, grants them preternatural control and power. Linton overlays this figure with the contemporary image of the vivisector, seeking to overdetermine her audience's reactions.

For Linton, the Ritualist confessor is the vivisector; women are fools for crying over experiments on "the old brown dog" even as they acquiesce in the destruction of wifehood and marriage. But Buchanan, poet, playwright, controversialist, and an ardent antivivisectionist, as well as Linton's opponent on the subject of "Magdalen" or "fallen women," represents the *husband* in *Foxglove Manor* as the heartless scientist who wields the knife.[40] While Linton shows a marriage ruined by a priest's plotting and a woman's weakness, Buchanan describes a woman destroyed by two men, a sensuous priest, Charles Santley (in whom we can recognize clerics from Maria Monk's rapists to Rose Salterne's persecutor in *Westward, Ho!* to the avatars of Alexander Borgia that haunt American nativism), and a coldly rational husband, George Haldane. Their scientific readings and resulting materialism (Haldane builds his lab in a chapel; Santley has two secret shrines in his study, one filled with scientific books, the other with a colored plaster statue of the Madonna) have cost both men their belief in God's and woman's goodness, beliefs that Buchanan sees as intimately intertwined. This depiction of priest and scientist united in their destruction of the spiritual and the feminine is echoed in Buchanan's description elsewhere of the scientist Thomas Huxley as "only our old friend the Priest in another guise, as unsympathetic, as bigoted, as retrograde as anyone who ever wore a *soutane* or cowl." Such characterizations of maleness are part of Buchanan's ongoing analysis of contemporary gender politics. In 1889, Buchanan and Linton argued in the pages of the *Daily Telegraph*, Linton censuring fallen women, and Buchanan countering that "Magdalens" were the victims of men and the martyrs of society, a controversy reprinted by Buchanan as "Is Chivalry Still Possible?"[41]

Buchanan answers his own question negatively in *Foxglove Manor*. When the scientist-philosopher Haldane becomes suspicious of his wife Ellen's relationship with the Ritualist priest Charles Santley, he positions himself as a scientific observer:

I am about to set down, in as concise a manner as possible . . . certain events which have lately influenced my domestic life. Were it not that even a professed scientist might decline to publish experiments affecting his own private happiness, the description of the events to which I allude might almost form a chapter in my slowly progressing "Physiology of Ethics," and the description would be at least as interesting as many of Ferrier's accounts of vivisection on dumb animals. But, unfortunately, I am unable, in this case, to apply the dissecting knife to my neighbour's heart, without laying bare the ugly wound in my own.

"I had to conquer my struggling tenderness, and watch," Haldane asserts, analogizing the "cure" that he plans for his wife to a mastectomy that he has seen performed on an unanaesthetized woman: "For the moral cancer also, the knife may be the only remedy; and it will be, as in the other case, kill or cure." This self-described "moral physiologist" then designates himself as a "physician" to his rival: "You have had your own heart vivisected [by me], and have thus been made conscious of its disease; you have suffered terribly, as all patients must suffer, under the knife," he taunts Santley.[42] With one stroke of the scalpel, the scientist/physician/husband excises the moral cancers of both priest and penitent.

The scalpel is, of course, metaphoric here; but Haldane's performance as deadly man of science is nothing if not material. It is on his wife's body that Haldane performs his experimental operation, following a protocol that suggests he received his medical training under Nathaniel Hawthorne. From a book written by "a Castilian monk, Sebastiono" Haldane reads to his wife and rival the tale of an alchemist's revenge on *his* wife and her priest. Then, with the help of Baptisto, his cunning Spanish manservant, Haldane gives Ellen an "elixir of death," discovered by a French scientist through his work in "dissections and vivisections." The elixir renders Ellen temporarily lifeless – "even *rigor mortis* is simulated." The scientist husband confronts his priestly rival over the body of their female victim: "In one corner stood the white, cold bed, snowy sheeted, snowy curtained; and there, stretched out chill and stark, lay something whiter and colder – the marble bust of what had once been a living creature."[43] The legal principle of *feme covert* is gothically literalized. The narrative of *Foxglove Manor* makes it clear that Ellen's spiritual and emotional needs are unrecognized by her husband and manipulated by her priest. If Linton represents Hermione Fullerton as culpable in her failure to rest her weakness in her husband's strength, Buchanan depicts his heroine in a way that laments, as he would in his defense of "Magdalens" against Linton's strictures, the lack of male chivalry in modern culture.

In *High Church*, too, it is the husband's cold distance that "murders" his wife. Married to the proud, rational Martin Chester, Ada satisfies her desperate need for spirituality by becoming involved with the Ritualist priest, John Stone. Robinson stresses the similarities between husband and priest, their "Napoleonic lower jaws," their firmness, their "vigorous power to resist. . . . Two such men opposed to one another would battle to the death," Ada thinks. The two men do battle, but the resulting death is Ada's not theirs. Martin analyzes the situation with a scientist's detached eye: "It is a delicate subject; it would require careful handling of the knife to cut away the moral cancer – and . . . it is no particular business of mine." Refusing even to engage in the medical rescue of his wife that he deems necessary, Martin separates himself from Ada, whose health is irrevocably broken by his abandonment. At her deathbed, Martin calls his wife "my poor murdered Ada." Robinson terms Ada Chester "victim of High Church,"[44] but makes it clear that her husband shares the blame for her death.

In *Overdale*, Agatha Aylmer is also the dual victim of her husband and a priest. However, Worboise rotates the marriage triangle, putting the husband, himself a Ritualist clergyman, at the center.[45] In a figuration that harks back to *Father Eustace*, the man is enslaved by his confessor, a cold, manipulative secret Jesuit, who, in this case, commands his penitent to put by his wife and children. Although Worboise does not use the term "vivisector," Father Vallance conforms to the ruthless scientist's image: "He looked to her [Agatha] like a man severed from all human ties, conscientious if erring, but stern, pitiless, uncompromising; a man also whose will you could not resist, any more than you could resist the waves of the incoming tide, when they break around your path and warn you to retire, if you would not speedily be drowned." Aylmer's relationship with Vallance becomes a direct threat to and substitution for his marriage. Holding the laws of Britain in defiance, Aylmer and Vallance invoke what they claim is a higher religious law. Faced with the annulment of her marriage ("But the Church of Rome cannot annul marriages . . . good British marriages?"), Agatha is urged – to no avail – to "stand by your rights as a married woman." Like Hermione Fullerton, Aylmer is described as performing a kind of suttee for the sake of the priest who has become the substitute spouse; Agatha accuses her husband of "self-immolation, and it is worse than that; for you cannot sacrifice yourself without sacrificing me." His surrender to his priest's rule is a "living death."[46] However, it is in fact the wife who dies as a result of the Ritualist priest's interference in her marriage.

As a group, and in some cases individually, then, these novels show husbands and priests as competing vivisectionists, facing one another over the body of a woman, vying for her soul. The novelists render a Solomonic judgment in depicting women as rent and, finally, destroyed by these male struggles (although the men too pay a terrible price). The fiction that is most relentlessly occupied with the topic of male jealousy and rivalry, the aptly subtitled, *Griffith Gaunt; or, Jealousy*, provides a provocative twist on this dynamic. Of the five novels in this group, *Griffith Gaunt* is least concerned with matters of theology (in fact, the cleric is an actual Roman Catholic, rather than a Ritualist, priest). The narrative developments chastise not so much a cleric's interference as a wife's pride and a husband's jealousy.

Nonetheless, certain elements of this sensation fiction presage those in later novels like *Under Which Lord?* and *Foxglove Manor*. After all, the Gaunts' marital trouble begins when Kate's traditional eighteenth-century-style confessor (coarse, practical, gluttonous) is replaced by a handsome, intensely religious priest of the new generation, a situation that caricatures the changes in Anglican ministerial practices. When Kate is tried for her husband Griffith's supposed murder, the judge points out that religious difference such as theirs "hath more than once embroiled a nation, let alone a single family,"[47] underscoring the fact that their dilemma is representative not just of the marital but also of the national. Perhaps most importantly, Reade makes it clear that the wife's independent ownership of property is a major cause of the terrible events of the novel. Her legal and economic autonomy fosters Kate's failure to identify her will with her husband's.

The conjunction of issues and discourses that prevail in *Under Which Lord?*, *High Church*, *Foxglove Manor*, and *Overdale* is prefigured so precisely in *Griffith Gaunt* that Reade even describes a kind of vivisection. When Kate lies dying after childbirth, she is brought back to life by an experimental, highly controversial transfusion of her husband's blood. Here, instead of the cold, indifferent experimental dissection of living bodies, we have the (literally) hot-blooded opening of the self to and for the loved one (characteristically, Griffith jealously insists that his blood, not the young doctor's, be given to Kate). Viewed in the context of fictional representations of religious and marital "vivisection," Reade's depiction of an operation on living flesh serves as a vivid counter-example. When Griffith Gaunt opens his body to his wife, when their flesh literally becomes one (after the operation, Kate claims mysterious powers of sympathy), he enacts marriage.

Griffith makes his wife dependent on him by weakening himself. This narrative strategy for limiting male power within marriage is familiar from novels like *Westward, Ho!* and *Jane Eyre*, in which the man is crippled (a condition often read as castrated) in order to make him less of a threat to the woman. What Reade stresses is not a man's wounding but the mutuality of marital vulnerability. In contrast, religious vivisection, the priest's clinical penetration of another's spouse, not only violates the marriage bond, parodying perversely the sexual intimacy of marriage, but it does so without an answering vulnerability. Those self-revelations that should only take place within the safe mutuality of marriage, in which both parties stand revealed to one another, are instead opened to the cold gaze of one who is not similarly exposed.

The attempt to control and eradicate Ritualism was, fundamentally, a juridical attempt, and the Ritualist priest serves as villain in these sensation novels insofar as he views himself as above the law. The Ritualist creates the confessional as an extralegal space in which he wields unlimited power – the confessional standing, in turn, for the church building and the parish. Yet, his penetration into marital intimacy ironically resembles the legal system that in these decades is, sensationally, making public the intimacies of marriage. In the figure of the Ritualist, novelists find a fertile interpenetration of ideas, stances, and issues, a site rich in case law and connections to contemporary court battles.

I have argued that nineteenth-century Protestant attacks on Catholicism are informed variously by a struggle for recognition – the masochistic desire for acknowledgment, however painful; the lure of submission to authority; the dangerously revelatory subaltern's gaze. In anti-Ritualist novels, marriage is imagined as a threatened space in which mutual recognition and revelation is possible – a realm that recalls Trollope's mother and daughter scenes of reading together – but it is a space that modern culture and law seem bent on destroying.

Alexander Welsh has shown how fictional representations of blackmail point to nineteenth-century anxieties about the rise of information culture, detailing especially the role that invasive newspaper reporting played in the development of the "right to privacy." I would suggest that the figures of penetration and exposure that recur in the anti-Ritualist novel indicate a related anxiety about marriage and the law. These novels imply that the law, reformed or not, misconstrues marriage. In *High Church* and in *Griffith Gaunt*, spouses are mistakenly tried for crimes of passion (while, in the latter case, bigamy goes unprosecuted). In *Foxglove Manor* love and marriage exist within a tangled web of breach of promise, mock murder, and blackmail, none of which is prosecuted or even discovered by the legal authorities. In *Overdale*, the sweet wife refuses to stand on her legal rights and sue her husband. In *Under Which Lord?*, the wife's assertion of those rights announces the end of her marriage.

The sensation novel can be said to be defined by the conjunction of the intensely private and its public exposure. Contemporary reviewers agreed that what Murray called "proximity" was essential to sensationalism. Sensationalist writers find horrors hidden away in ordinary homes; the Archbishop of York complained that "They want to persuade people that in almost every one of the well-ordered houses of their neighbours there [is] a skeleton shut up in some cupboard."[48] Sensational anti-Ritualist fiction too reveals a mystery hidden in plain sight. The widely publicized story of Ritualism is the story of secrecy: of hidden Romanism, of secret manuals, of illicit intimacy between priests and married persons. These novels insist that the threat is from within, from within the Church of England, from within the parish church, from within the British marriage – that it has penetrated into the most intimate recesses of British lives and selves. Romanism is not a wholly external force to be defended against but already part of the everyday fabric of British life. Yet how to combat that internal threat without violating the private lives of British men and women? *High Church, Griffith Gaunt, Overdale, Under Which Lord?*, and *Foxglove Manor* offer a picture of Victorian society seemingly obsessed with matters of privacy, authority, and regulation. Topical issues of an almost bewildering variety are represented as conjoined by concerns about the place of law in the home, the church, and the laboratory. Ritualism, controversial in itself, is also embedded in and stands for a set of questions that cuts across contemporary culture – a tangled bank indeed.

CHAPTER 6

Black robes, white veils, and foregone conclusions: Disraeli, Howells, and James

My final chapter looks at how some of the "foregone conclusions" of anti-Catholic narrative formula are used in the works of canonical authors. Expanding on the comparative work that the juxtaposed British and American chapters of this book have done, I here read novels by Benjamin Disraeli, William Dean Howells, and Henry James together. Discussion of *Lothair* (1870), *A Foregone Conclusion* (1874), and *The American* (1877) – only the first of which might be classified as an anti-Catholic novel *per se* – gives us further glimpses of this discourse's wide dispersion in Anglo-American non-polemical writing. And this reading moves the discussion of ideology more explicitly into the marketplace by showing anti-Catholicism's part in Disraeli's, and especially Howells's and James's, efforts to shape their professional writerly identities in the 1870s. Those efforts are complicated, as critics have recognized, by Howells's and James's positions as American writers dealing with international subject matter, as male authors in a period that was "edging women out,"[1] and as the resistant heirs of the Hawthornian legacy of romance. I want to identify specifically one of the discourses that counts as "romantic" for these writers and to suggest how their refusal (or inability) to depict religious feeling highlights Howells's and James's difficulties in shaping a new psychological realism. Disraeli, as ex-Prime Minister and Anglican "Jew," writing a *roman à clef* about the religious mores of British high society, is situated very differently vis à vis his audience, occupying a unique professional position. Reading Disraeli's 1870 novel, *Lothair*, through the critical and fictional reactions of William Dean Howells and Henry James in the seventies helps re-create the distinct "culture of letters," to use Richard Brodhead's term, that each author occupies – or aspires to – at that time. For the British ex-prime minister, describing Catholicism provides a means of expounding political philosophy and settling old scores. The American writers, on the other hand, depict Romanism as a way of discussing genre, of exploring and explaining their ideas about narrative.

The need for and fear of unquestioned authority that underlies the vivid sadism of so much antebellum anti-Catholic fiction, and that later sensation novelists like Linton and Buchanan reformulate in legal terms, is missing from these texts. While Lothair does seek to ground himself within an authoritative religious and political system, Disraeli regards his protagonist's quest lightly – depicting it finally as more a matter of geographic movement than of psychological struggle. And the nostalgia that troubles Howells's and James's novels is markedly literary, not religious. Yet their ambivalent look back to the realm of romance is refracted through the looking-glass of the uncanny. Questions of authenticity continue to trouble these two American writers – professional men at once atypical and surprisingly representative. Roman Catholicism provides a rhetoric and an imagery with which to explore those questions.

Lothair follows the recognizable pattern of many British anti-Catholic novels: focusing on Catholicism as an upper-class phenomenon, Disraeli sees the potential infection of the British upper classes and diversion of British wealth to the Vatican's coffers. Perhaps more surprisingly, the Catholicism that concerns the two American writers in these novels also focuses on the upper classes – rather than that of contemporary Irish and German immigrants. Unlike the American nativist novels of the 1850s, Howells's *A Foregone Conclusion* and especially James's *The American* treat Catholicism as a subject and a mode distinct from the gritty realism of the tenement and the streets. Despite the claims that realism held for both Howells and James at this time, both explicitly reject what Howells calls the literature of "Father O'Brien" in favor of narratives that represent Romanism as romance.[2] For James, Catholicism is part of the mysterious, inaccessible European elite circles to which he aspires. For Howells, it represents the temptations of a romance that is marked as feminine and elitist. T. Jackson Lears has identified the nostalgic attractions of Rome to aristocratic Americans who were losing their power and status in the face of industrialization and mass culture, its allure as a cult of high culture. While neither Howells nor James felt that allure as a matter of personal religious practices, Rome provides both with a complex, and usable, set of associations.[3]

Lothair is based on the young Marquess of Bute's 1868 conversion to Roman Catholicism. Elsewhere in his fiction – *Contarini Fleming* (1832), *Coningsby* (1844), *Sybil* (1845) – Disraeli depicted Catholicism admiringly, dwelling on its historicity and traditions, as well as the richness of its rituals. Indeed, Young England, with its focus on the revival of past values and practices, had shared much in sensibility with the early Tractarian movement, as Disraeli himself noted in the "General Preface" to the 1870 edition of his novels.[4] However, Newman's conversion to Roman Catholicism was, to Disraeli, "a mistake and a misfortune." Further, Disraeli's political experiences fostered his dislike and distrust of the Roman Catholic hierarchy, particularly Cardinal Manning, who, Disraeli felt, had betrayed him on the Irish Church Disestablishment controversy in 1868.

Despite Disraeli's early affinities and the positive representations of Roman Catholic characters in his previous novels,[5] *Lothair*'s international readership immediately understood the book as also belonging to the genre of anti-Catholic fiction: the *Morning-Post* suggested that a "Romance of No-Popery" should be the book's subtitle; the *Nation* identified "its object . . . to expose the arts and wiles of the Catholics." This first novel ever to be published by an ex-Prime Minister of Britain was an immediate popular success in both Britain and America: the initial English edition sold out in a week; 80,000 American copies were sold in five months; "a street, a perfume, two ships, two songs, a waltz and a *galoppe*, even a racehorse" were given names from the book.[6] Disraeli rewrote the Marquess of Bute's story giving it what was, from his and the majority of his readers' point of view, a happy ending: the young heir to one of Britain's great fortunes turns out *not* to have gone over to Rome. He marries an English Protestant and lives happily and safely ever after within the confines of the Church of England. Disraeli also took the occasion to settle a few old scores, especially one with Cardinal Manning (Grandison in *Lothair*).

James reviewed *Lothair* in August 1870 for the *Atlantic Monthly*, where Howells was the assistant editor. *Lothair* also prompted a distinctly American parody, Bret Harte's *Lothaw, or, The Adventures of a Young Gentleman in Search of a Religion* (1871); Harte's short imitation of Disraeli's "silver fork" tendencies was certainly known to both Howells and James. In 1874, Howells, now editor at *Atlantic Monthly*, wrote a novel criticizing the Church of Rome, *A Foregone Conclusion*. It was published first in *Atlantic Monthly* (July–December 1874), then in book form in 1875. *A Foregone Conclusion* was reviewed twice by James in January 1875, once in the *North American Review* and again in the *Nation*. Roman Catholicism and the conventions of Protestant anti-Catholicism figure prominently in James's own *The American*, published first in *Atlantic Monthly* (June 1876–May 1877), then in book form in 1877.[7] Having published *The American* under his editorship, Howells did not review the book. Howells was, however, the most important American champion of James's writing during this period, and his November 1882 "Henry James, Jr." repeatedly turns to *The American* for examples.

A Foregone Conclusion and *The American* are written, published, and read, then, within a common literary and commercial milieu.[8] Reading and reviewing one another, Howells and James sought to find and shape their own audiences of readers, as the tutelary tone of their reviews and letters makes clear. During the 1870s, Howells and James are struggling to define themselves as fiction-writers. Negotiating the boundaries of realism and romance, they represent themselves as a new generation of American authors. I want to argue that "Romanism" plays a role in Howells's and James's literary self-definition, as well as their response to and creative participation in their literary culture. Neither *A Foregone Conclusion* nor *The American* are direct replies to *Lothair*, but the ex-Prime Minister's example was vividly before the two young American writers, and reading these texts together illuminates the literary and national issues at stake in each.

James's self-consciously American review of *Lothair* is illustrative here, especially in its discussion of the interplay between genre and audience. He begins by defending *Lothair* against the British critics who have, he asserts, attacked the novel solely on the basis of their political disagreement with Disraeli: "Each of the Reviewers had evidently read the book in the light of a deep aversion to the author's political character." Americans, James argues, can judge *Lothair* more fairly because they need not take it so seriously: "we Americans may happily rejoice in the remoteness of the author's political presence and action." His primary judgment of *Lothair* centers around the genre question crucial to American, but not British, fiction at the time: the relative merits of the romance and the novel. Indeed, James's judgment of *Lothair* is a genre judgment. With its elegant characters and exotic settings, its dukes and duchesses, and descriptions of Rome, *Lothair* succeeds, James argues, as a light "*amusette*," an antidote to "the dreary realism, the hard, sordid, pretentious accuracy, of the typical novel of the period" like the work of Trollope and Collins.[9] James assumes, then, that audience expectations are not restricted to content (e.g., all Jesuits are spies) but also both formal (e.g., an *amusette* raises and satisfies different expectations than a realist novel) and environmental (e.g., Americans do not read as the British do). His analysis resonates with my argument throughout that ideology informs writing not in the iteration of certain positions, nor in a rigid one-to-one relationship between a given genre and, say, a specific political stance. Rather narratives' articulations of ideology are part of the making and remaking of cultural understanding, a process in which author and audience both participate. Hence the adaptability of anti-Catholic narrative, its varied usefulness to writers from "Maria Monk" to Benjamin Disraeli.

But it is as an anti-Catholic novel – a "novel with a purpose" – that James judges *Lothair* a failure. Disraeli does not take what James sees as his real subject – religious conflict – seriously. Uninterested in religious feeling or belief, Disraeli fails to capitalize on what should be the central structuring conflict of the fiction: "The motive of the romance is not quite what, on the basis of these *data* [a rich young orphan of noble blood, two guardians of opposing religious sympathies], it might have been. It is not the contest between opposing agents for the possession of a great prize, a contest rich in dramatic possibilities and in scenes and situations of striking interest."[10]

Not only does Disraeli fail to structure his plot around religious conflict, but he is also unable to represent the inner religious struggle of his main character. In part this is because that character barely exists: "One can hardly say that he is weak, for to be weak you must at least begin by being. Throughout the book Lothair remains but a fine name." But the primary reason that Disraeli cannot exploit the narrative potential of religion, James argues, is that the villain of *Lothair* is, like its hero, not really there. *Lothair*'s "ruling idea" – exposing "the secret encroachments of the Romish Church" – is flawed; Disraeli's "anti-Romish enthusiasm is thoroughly cold and mechanical."[11] Rather than convincing his readership of Rome's real threat, Disraeli depicts only a genteel after-dinner charade or a costume drama for children: "His ecclesiastics are lay-figures, – his Scarlet Woman is dressed out terribly in the table-cloth, and holds in her hands the drawing-room candlesticks."

James's analogy is a telling one, since he also uses this review as an occasion to read Disraeli's own character. According to James, *Lothair* shows Disraeli's almost "infantine joy in being one of the initiated among the dukes" with his too-casually dropped hints that he is acquainted with the habits of the elite. Bent on showing his readership that he is socially in the know, Disraeli is childishly dazzled by surface details of dress and manners. James implies that what interests "serious"[12] readers (like himself) are not dukes' dining habits nor nuns' religious robes but what lies beneath them: the psychology of privilege and, especially, of belief.

James's criticism of Disraeli, which comes at precisely the time that he himself is attempting to make his way into European social and literary circles, reveals perhaps as much about its author as its subject. Nonetheless, James's remarks are supported by Leslie Stephen, who notes that "When *Lothair* made its appearance, critics were puzzled, not only by the old problem as to the seriousness of the writer, but by the extraordinary love of glitter." Stephen delivers a left-handed defense of the ex-Prime Minister:

"Why should not a man have a taste for the society of dukes, or take a child's pleasure in bright colours for their own sake?" Underpinning these and other critical condescending remarks about Disraeli's love of "glitter" is the Protestant perspective that sees both the Jew and the Catholic as primitive and superficial in their religious practices. Operative, too, is the image of the Jewish social climber, a type that Disraeli exemplified for many in Anglo-American culture.[13]

But, beyond the anti-Semitism of James's and Stephen's characterizations of *Lothair* and its author, their description of the novel as a matter of surfaces is accurate in at least one important sense. Disraeli's depictions of Catholicism *are* superficial. Lothair is a traditional *Bildungsroman* protagonist insofar as his inexperience leads him into misadventures; learning about the world, Lothair moves the narrative towards its resolution. Part of this plot movement comes from Disraeli's depictions of his protagonist's religious vacillations. Yet, these vacillations are almost entirely externalized matters of plot: Lothair's progress is charted through his successive encounters with mentors and his meetings with desirable women rather than through his internal wrestlings with religious belief. Again, Leslie Stephen echoes James's reading of the novel: "Lothair reduces himself so completely to a mere 'passive bucket' to be pumped into by every variety of teacher, that he is unpleasantly like a fool."[14] Lothair's confused involvement in the Italian battle for liberation exemplifies the insignificance and superficiality of his principles. As a politician, Disraeli had no sympathy for contemporary Italian nationalism and had supported the Vatican's bid to retain temporal power. Thus, while Lothair does fight against the Vatican, his sole military motivation seems to be his crush on a beautiful woman, Theodora, who inspires the Italian republicans and their supporters. So unimportant is Lothair's soldiering that the Catholic clergy has no trouble successfully claiming that he fell *defending* the Pope.

Indeed, the moment in the novel in which Lothair's threatened conversion is taken most seriously occurs when, recovering from battle wounds in Rome, the young British aristocrat is entrammeled in a web of appearances and false reports. Tricked into marching in a procession at Saint Peter's, the gullible Lothair lends weight to gossip and newspaper accounts about his conversion. Making Lothair's "Catholicism" into nothing more than a showy parade, Disraeli literalizes the Protestant claim that popery is a religion of appearances, both in its idolatrous, sensual materiality and in its deceitful disregard for inner truth. Disraeli's elaborate descriptions of the procession's ornate vestments, gorgeous flowers, and intoxicating incense at once titillate his Protestant readership and confirm Catholic belief as simultaneously superficial and sensual; Lothair's unwitting participation in the rite illustrates how little genuine religious belief the practices of Catholicism entail.

Disraeli's Romanism is less a religion than a politics of plots and misrepresentations. While much of *Lothair* is satiric (e.g., the caricature of Lord Leighton as the aesthetic "Mr. Phoebus"), the machinations of the Catholic clergy are depicted without irony – and this despite their clichéd predictability. Disraeli trots out the standbys of anti-Catholic literature: priests taking advantage of the sick or dying, scheming to wrest the inheritances of the young and naive, and seducing youths through an unhealthy mixture of sexuality and mysticism; the popish emphasis on glittering pageantry; the Catholic clergy's willingness to justify any ends to their means; the Church's campaigns to undermine citizenship and patriotism.

In a dinner table conversation at the home of the Catholic Lord St. Jerome, Monsignore Berwick discusses the danger that increasing secularization poses to the Papacy's plans to increase its power in Scotland, Ireland, Malta, and France. The Monsignore then reassures the table: "But if the Holy Father keep Rome, these strange changes will only make the occupier of the chair of St. Peter more powerful. His subjects will be in every clime and country, and then they will be only his subjects. We shall get rid of the difficulty of the divided allegiance" – divided, that is, between loyalty to one's church and loyalty to one's country. While the Monsignore outlines a global strategy, *Lothair*'s concern is almost exclusively local: the Catholic Church hierarchy's attempt to snare one young wealthy man. For all of *Lothair*'s generic recognizability as a "Romance of No-Popery" and its use of anti-Catholic clichés, Disraeli's attack on the Church of Rome is decidedly circumscribed. *Lothair* does allude tangentially to Irish Catholicism's threat to British civil order when Lothair stumbles into a Fenian meeting, but the scene is anomalous. While Sewell and Trollope, at the height of the Tractarian controversy, describe an institutionalization of Romanism through the infiltration and corruption of the British educational system, Disraeli's later novel does not generalize from the Marquess of Bute's/Lothair's example. Nor is Disraeli joining the sensation novelists in attacking the Ritualist movement.[15] The localized nature of Disraeli's assault on Romanism accords both with his earlier attraction to the Church of Rome and his generic aims in this book: *Lothair* is pointedly a *roman à clef*, a means for Disraeli to display his insider's information about the British upper classes. Reading such a book, Disraeli's audience is meant to recognize the events, characters, and plot; identifying with or even understanding the protagonist's psychology is secondary at best.

Indeed, we might speculate that the novel's refusal to explore the psychology of religious conversion is tied to Disraeli's own growing status in the Anglo-American cultural imaginary as the crypto-Jew. As Michael Ragussis has shown, the sincerity of Disraeli's childhood conversion to Christianity was attacked increasingly through the 1870s. Some of this suspicion was fueled by the way Disraeli stressed the Hebraic origins of the Christian civilization in *Lothair*, as elsewhere in his speeches and writings. Yet Disraeli's historical argument is clearly one of religious teleology, insisting not on a return to Judaism but on the legitimacy of the Church of England. For Disraeli, the Church of England's strength lies in its character as the traditional and established church of England. By writing an anti-conversion novel, Disraeli asserts the validity and consistency of his own conversion; he demonstrates his Englishness and his conservatism. The anti-conversion narrative does the work of legitimation, as it does with the novels by which William Sewell and Charles Kingsley distanced themselves from their early Tractarian leanings. Thus, in rejecting Catholicism, Lothair proves the essential Englishness of the English gentleman. Even the "devout" Roman Catholic Lord St. Jerome refuses to go along wholly with the entrapment of Lothair. St. Jerome "was an English gentleman, and there was at the bottom of his character a fund of courage, firmness, and common sense." The positive depiction of Lord St. Jerome illustrates the way that Disraeli distances himself in *Lothair* from the polemical Protestant literature that he draws on. The novel itself was urbanely dedicated to the Catholic Duc d'Aumale, and, two years after its publication, Disraeli was one of the legal witnesses at the Marquess of Bute's wedding, performed by Cardinal Manning.[16]

Disraeli's opportunistic and partial use of the literature of anti-Catholicism is reflected in the nature of his hero. We can recognize in Lothair a version of the "middle-of-the-road hero" Lukács discerns in Scott's *Waverley*, a representative figure who is not the great man but who, moving among various political camps, exemplifies his historical and political era.[17] Lothair's weakness may be less an artistic failure and more a strategy of Disraeli's historical fiction. Unlike Kingsley, who sets his historical novel back in time and attempts to create in Amyas Leigh an epic hero, Disraeli describes a different order of "national individual." Amyas's epic defeat of the Spanish Armada contrasts markedly with Lothair's ineffectual participation in what Disraeli regards as Italy's internal skirmishes. If Kingsley's story expresses his nostalgia for a "Roman Catholicism" that is solely an external, foreign, physical enemy unlike the psychological and cultural weakness that he fears is infecting nineteenth-century England, Disraeli's later narrative portrays Romanism's threat as a matter of the Church hierarchy's political machinations rather than a disease in the national character.

While politics generally and the Italian Risorgimento in particular, enter into both Howells's and James's novels (the American writers, not surprisingly, sympathize with the Italian republicans), neither takes international politics as its central topic nor regards the Roman Catholic Church as a serious threat.[18] Unlike Disraeli, whose *Lothair* was categorized by contemporary readers as a "novel of No-Popery," Howells and James borrow from anti-Catholic plots and characters to write decidedly secular novels. Yet, both American writers show Catholicism as more intimately bound with the psychologies of their male Protestant protagonists than are the superficial vacillations of Disraeli's "representative" British peer. Attempting to write a realism that goes below the surface, Howells and James look to Roman Catholic faith as a possible means of representing the internal life of characters.

We can see evidence of this changed focus in James's review of *A Foregone Conclusion*. *A Foregone Conclusion* tells the story of Henry Ferris's hesitant and ambivalent relations with Florida Vervain, a young American woman living with her mother in Venice. Ferris is wary of Florida's "passionate" temperament and holds her at a distance. Throughout much of the novel, Ferris observes and tests the young woman, seeking to determine her true nature and worth. The third party in this modern romance is Don Ippolito, an Italian priest, who falls in love with Florida, to both her and Ferris's dismay. In a climactic, but ironic, "recognition" scene Ferris watches Florida's embrace of the priest, interpreting what is actually an affectionate act of compassion as proof of illicit passion and deception. Don Ippolito dies soon afterwards; Ferris returns to the States, fights, and is wounded in the Civil War. The novel ends with Ferris and Florida's reconciliation and marriage.

James finds Howells's anti-Romish novel successful precisely insofar as its portrait of the Church and its power is psychologically convincing. Discussing the writing of *A Foregone Conclusion* in a letter to James, Howells explained, "the hero is a Venetian priest in love with an American girl," although the protagonist in the finished novel is clearly the American ambassador Ferris. Following Howells's lead, James consistently refers to the book in correspondence as a novel about a "Venetian priest." And both of James's reviews focus on the character of that priest, Don Ippolito, rather than on Ferris, despite the fact that the latter is Howells's self-portrait and the obvious predecessor of Lambert Strether. James claims that "the story is Don Ippolito's. . . . It is the poor priest's property, as it were; we regret even the reversion of it to Mr. Ferris. We confess even to a regret at seeing it survive Don Ippolito at all."[19]

James was not alone among American readers in focusing on *A Foregone Conclusion*'s Italian priest. Even those who disagreed with Howells's assessment of the Catholic clergy took Don Ippolito seriously: Woodress reports that John Boyle O'Reilly, editor of the Catholic Boston *Pilot*, protested the depiction of the priesthood in the novel. On the other hand, Longfellow, Francis Child (professor of English at Harvard and Howells's Cambridge neighbor), John Hay, and Robert Dale Owen joined James in praising the characterization of Don Ippolito.[20]

James's detailed evocation of the figure of the priest suggests why this audience of postbellum American male intellectuals found Don Ippolito so compelling:

a real creation, – a most vivid, complete, and appealing one. . . . The poor caged youth, straining to the end of his chain, pacing round his narrow circle, gazing at the unattainable outer world, bruising himself in the effort to reach it and falling back to hide himself and die unpitied, – is a figure which haunts the imagination and claims a permanent place in one's melancholy memories.[21]

Habegger argues that this version of Don Ippolito is not at all Howells's but wholly James's – indeed wholly James.[22] Habegger sees this pathetic characterization as a figure for James's own inadequate masculinity and Americanness, which, in turn, account for the failure of James's realism. While rejecting Habegger's characterization of James and his writing as failed, I would second his connection of both Howells's text and James's reading of it to matters of gender, nationality, and genre. What is clear is that the Roman Catholic serves here, again, as an uncanny double for the Protestant self. The priest becomes a "permanent" fixture: a haunting memory of limitation and failure that is both claimed and projected onto another. James's characterization of Don Ippolito offers a suggestive glimpse of what appears to be a shared anxiety among this cohort of American male readers about provincialism and inutility.

Throughout his essay, James emphasizes the differences that nationality makes in reading. *Lothair*'s aristocratic British characters and beautiful Italian scenery would charm American readers, James predicted. Those same readers will come to *A Foregone Conclusion* already trained by such "light reading," as well as by Howells's travel writings. James is thinking here of *Venetian Life* (1866) and *Italian Journeys* (1867), as well as Howells's letters to the Boston *Advertiser*, and articles in the *Atlantic*, the *Nation*, the *New York Times*, the *North American Review*, and elsewhere. The readerly expectations Howells fostered with these Italian writings created, James argues, both advantages and disadvantages for him as a writer. James describes his friend as introducing

us again to that charming half-merry, half-melancholy Venice which most Americans know better through his pages than through any others. He did this, in a measure, we think, at his risk; partly because there was a chance of disturbing an impression which, in so far as he was the author of it, had had time to grow very tranquil and mellow; and partly because there has come to be a not unfounded mistrust of the Italian element in light literature. Italy has been made to supply so much of the easy picturesqueness, the crude local color of poetry and the drama, that a use of this expedient is vaguely regarded as a sort of unlawful short-cut to success.[23]

Positioning both Howells and himself as modern, James claims that the growing refinement of the romancer's art makes the use of "Italy" now seem suspect, out of date – it smacks of "Mrs. Radcliffe." Analogizing reading to playing chess, James comments that, for an author to pull this "Italian move" is enough to make the reader fold up the board and go home. What James's analogy implies is the negotiations involved in writing and reading texts. Playing according to the agreed upon rules, with regulation board and pieces, the author relies on a repertoire of known conventions, as well as unexpected, original moves. Howells's task is to take advantage of all that "Italy" offers without reproducing the same tired combinations, without resting on even the moves that he himself has originated in the past – a dilemma that we can recognize as especially important for writers drawing on the traditions and techniques of anti-Catholicism. Howells runs the risk of cliché by setting his novel in Venice. But doing so is worth the risk because Venice supplies the romance that lifts *A Foregone Conclusion* above the quotidian realism – "the hard, sordid pretentious accuracy" – of the contemporary British novel.

James's praise of *A Foregone Conclusion* is qualified by his sense that despite the evocative portrait of Don Ippolito, Howells has finally failed to make psychological religious conflict into narrative structure. Because he makes the priest a religious skeptic, Howells cannot depict a struggle between faith and love. On the other hand, James recognizes that Howells's Protestant readership would not have accepted a "consenting priest": "he might have been in a way more picturesque, he would not have been more interesting; and the charm of the portrait is in its suffering us to feel with him, and its offering nothing that we find mentally disagreeable, – as we should have found the suggestion of prayers stupidly mumbled and of the *odeur de sacristie*." Howells fails to make the psychology of the priest his subject, James asserts, because neither the American writer nor his audience can take Catholic belief seriously. James's arch tone is telling here: "we" refined nineteenth-century readers should turn up our noses at the primitive scent of a believing Catholic priest.[24] The disgusted reaction of the American girl, Florida Vervain, to Don Ippolito's declaration of love is, for James, normative: "he is of necessity, as a lover, repulsive" and "is greeted with the inevitable horror provoked by such a proposition from such a source." This sort of automatic response is a topic of discussion in the novel itself, as when Florida muses, "I wonder why there is always something so dreadful to us in the idea of a priest." Ferris agrees, "They *do* seem a kind of alien creature to us Protestants."[25] Identifying with Howells's predominantly Protestant readership, James assumes a shared set of reactions: priestly sexuality is at once comic and threatening – comic because threatening? The urbane irony that James adopts here in representing the priest, coupled with the haunting image of a caged and chained Don Ippolito, hints that 1870s "modernity" has progressed only incompletely beyond the perceived primitivisms of both Catholicism and anti-Catholicism.

Yet, while validating the stereotypical Protestant response to priestly sexuality, James deliberately praises the scene in *A Foregone Conclusion* that was received by American audiences as scandalous – that of Florida kissing Don Ippolito's head. "There are really some readers who are in urgent need of a tonic regimen!,"[26] James pronounces, using one of his infrequent exclamation points. Unwittingly anticipating the reaction that his own "Daisy Miller" will receive in 1878, James here derides unthinking reactions by readers – especially insofar as they pertain to sexuality. James will make this case more thoroughly in "The Art of Fiction" (1884); for now, he describes Howells as rewriting a stock situation into a nuanced, modern psychological study.

The American artist's struggle to avoid, on the one hand, a clichéd, unbelievable fantasy and, on the other, a heavy-handed realism is depicted not just in James's review but also within Howells's novel itself. In *A Foregone Conclusion* Howells raises problems of representation and genre, as well as the question of Catholicism's place in modern (Protestant) art by foregrounding the problem of depicting the Italian priest. Don Ippolito's apartment is explicitly a representation of the priest himself ("The whole place was an outgrowth of himself, it was his history as well as his character" [32]), and with his discussion of that homology Howells details the uses that "an Italian priest" will serve in his narrative. Don Ippolito has painted his ante-room to look like a grape-arbor, yet his painting replicates, not country vines, but Venetian arbors created as entrances to restaurants or as decorations for palace doors. Similarly, the paintings in the priest's parlor are copies of prints of masterpieces, "hard . . . in line, fixed in expression, and opaque in color."

We can read the priest's rooms as an indictment of Catholicism, a religion which, according to Protestant polemic, forces its clergy into celibacy, condemns them to an artificial imitation of life, experiencing nature at second hand, and stunts their imaginations, confining them to a crude idolatrous literalism,[27] a reading for which Howells's earlier attack on priestly celibacy in the *New York Times* gives warrant. However, Howells's image of the priest's decorations is directed not just at religion, but also at the representation of religion. If the apartment means "priest," "priest," then, stands for the bad art which Howells will strive to avoid: an archaic notion of representation, wholly conventionalized, its rigid fidelity to a fixed "truth" ironically dictating an endless reproduction of clichés.

Yet, in describing the workshop, Howells seems to deliberately draw on a different set of clichés, invoking the gothic demonized figure of the "black-robed" priest leagued with the dark side in the pursuit of secret knowledge.

It seemed from some peculiarities of shape to have once been an oratory, but it was now begrimed with smoke and dust from the forge which Don Ippolito had set up in it; the embers of a recent fire, the bellows, the pincers, the hammers and the other implements of the trade gave it a sinister effect as if the place had been invaded by mocking imps, or as if some hapless mortal in contract with the evil powers were here searching by the help of the adversary, for the forbidden secrets of the metals and of fire. (33)

Reading about an oratory transformed into an inventor's workshop in 1874, Howells's Victorian readership might expect to see this magic modernized into science. But the inventor is a Roman Catholic priest, an anachronism for "modern" Protestant Americans, a conjuror who transports the place of religion and prayer further back in time into an alchemist's laboratory. Like Victor Frankenstein, isolated from the community of modern thought, he is trapped in a dead end.

Don Ippolito is a figure from the past not only because of his religious faith and his ties to the gothic. The Roman Catholic priest also allows Howells access to his predecessor Hawthorne, himself a writer who recognizes how "a by-gone time" conveys romance.[28] The most direct literary precedents for Don Ippolito's workshop are found in stories like "The Birthmark" and "Rappaccini's Daughter" (1846). Hawthorne's shadow has appeared earlier in the novel when Howells's narrative voice refers to Ferris as his "predecessor" in the Venetian ambassadorship. (While Hawthorne did not, strictly speaking, precede Howells's service as consul in Venice [1861–64], he did serve as an American consul abroad – in Liverpool – following which he lived in Italy for two years. In 1863, Howells and his wife made a pilgrimage to the house in Florence where Hawthorne had stayed.)

In *Lothair*, Disraeli chooses to write an "amusette." But the choice of genre is more fraught for the antebellum American author, in part because of the strong precedent of American romance writing, embodied for Howells and James in the figure of Hawthorne. Cady points out that Howells designated *A Foregone Conclusion* "My first novel," despite having published previous books of fiction (189). Howells is, Cady argues, declaring his choice of genre: he has progressed as a writer from the romance to the novel. Michael Davitt Bell, Alfred Habegger,[29] and others have described an anxiety about gender in Howells's choice of realism as his literary mode at this point in his career, a means of distancing himself from what he perceived as the feminized genre of romance. Yet, in making that choice, Howells does not simply reject Hawthornian romance and all that it represents. Rather, he delineates the functional role that these earlier American models for art play in the making of the modern man of letters.

What is striking about the Hawthornesque romantic picture of the isolated artist in *A Foregone Conclusion* is that it is one which the protagonist deeply desires, yet painfully refuses, to paint:

In those days, Ferris was an uncompromising enemy of the theatricalization of Italy, or indeed of anything; but the fancy of the black-robed young priest at work in this place, appealed to him all the more potently because of the sort of tragic innocence which seemed to characterize Don Ippolito's expression. He longed intensely to sketch the picture then and there, but he had strength to rebuke the fancy as something that could not make itself intelligible without the help of such accessories as he despised.

Rebuking fancy, Ferris schools himself into painting Don Ippolito without "accessories." Ferris's portrait will not be, he insists, an allegorical genre painting nor a stylized Catholic picture of a saint, where identity rests on pose and props. But there are risks to such stripped-down realism.[30]

Florida Vervain makes those risks plain, asking Ferris, "why do you paint him simply as a priest? . . . I should think you would want to make him the centre of some famous or romantic scene." "You're no worse than the rest," Ferris snaps. Florida here becomes the representative of the vulgar audience, demanding conventions (Ferris is so enraged that he lists these: a priest administering extreme unction to a victim of the Council of Ten, a priest stepping into a confessional and leering at the young female penitent, gondolas, the Bridge of Sighs). Florida retorts that "people will wonder why you came so far to paint Father O'Brien" unless Ferris includes "some sort of symbol . . . of a Venetian priest." That is, for Americans, unless a priest is clearly designated as Italian, set in what Hawthorne calls "a sort of poetic or fairy precinct," he is a figure with whom they are all too familiar: at best, a vulgar, ill-educated immigrant; at worst, a demagogue leading his flock in a fight against good American citizens (recalling the dynamic of earlier nativist novels in which Irish clergy were depicted as mere minions of powerful Italian or Spanish Jesuits). In *Becoming American*, historian Thomas Archdeacon underscores what Florida Vervain knows – that anti-Catholic and anti-Irish stories and stereotypes continued to be a feature of literate American life after the Civil War: "Calling attention to the social and political threat posed by the Irish became an obsession of the higher toned newspapers and periodicals of the late nineteenth century." Such anti-Irish warnings are frequent in Howells's nonfictional writings from this period, such as those gathered in *Suburban Sketches* (1870).[31] And, as editor of *Atlantic Monthly*, Howells knows well what his genteel readership thinks of Father O'Brien.

Genre choice, is, then, intimately involved with politics, with demography, with class. The American audience's understanding of "the real" – Father O'Brien and his apelike flock – like its expectations for the familiarly romantic – Mrs. Radcliffe – define Howells's dilemma. Like Ferris, Howells is committed to realism, but rejecting romantic clichés seems to leave Hawthorne's successors trapped in a two-dimensional imitative literalism. The romance of Roman Catholicism attracts the American artist because of its ability to point to the mysterious – what Sarah Josepha Hale called, in *Traits of American Life*, "the unknown." Think of Hawthorne's complaint about America: "no shadow, no antiquity, no mystery, no picturesque and gloomy wrong."[32] After the war, both Howells and James regard ambivalently the romantic knowledge that hovers beyond us – the balloon cut free from earth, to use James's famous metaphor.[33]

What is Ferris's alternative artistic vision? Nothing more, it turns out, than a list of alternate types: the pagan, the martyr, the rebel, the Jesuit. Ferris's "priest" is as clichéd as Florida's "Venetian priest." And Ferris's finished picture, tainted by his presuppositions about Italian priests, "*is*," as Ferris admits, "conventional, in spite of everything." Don Ippolito astutely remarks: "I suppose that it resembles me a great deal . . . and yet I do not *feel* like that. . . . It is as I should be if I were like other priests, perhaps?"[34]

Exposing conventions, even as he draws on them, Howells gives us multiple pictures of Don Ippolito – both those that Ferris creates and those that he rejects: while Ferris may not depict the Hawthorne scene of Don Ippolito in his oratory, Howells certainly does. Although he does not see Hawthorne's authority at work in *A Foregone Conclusion*, Richard Brodhead aptly characterizes the dynamics of his influence on Howells: "part of Howells's understanding of realism comes from his facing of what Hawthorne represented, both as model and as challenge to this work." Just as Howells needs Hawthorne as his point of reference, *A Foregone Conclusion* needs "a priest," needs Roman Catholicism, as well as the conventions, types, and plots of anti-Catholicism. But the modern novelist can only safely replicate these clichéd plots and figures by ironizing them. (Of course – ironically – in ironizing his relationship with the past and its plots, Howells is only following Hawthorne more precisely.) "The tragedy of Don Ippolito"[35] is how terribly un-tragic he is. As a "modern" writer, Howells shows Catholicism as neither ennobling nor gothically destroying Don Ippolito's life, but wasting it, making him into a comic character.

Because he uses Don Ippolito to these ends, Howells only hints at what the "man" "trapped" in "a priest" might look like; as Don Ippolito says to Florida, "I have given you the slight outward events, not the processes of my mind." In making the priest comic, in refusing to explore the workings of belief, Howells denies himself a venue for psychological realism. Nonetheless, Howells does forge a new form of realistic writing in the priest's workshop by using the character of the priest to show us the processes not of Don Ippolito's but of *Ferris's* and *Florida's* minds. "Priest" is a medium for exploration – and shoring up – of American Protestant maleness, standing at once for the masculinity that Ferris fears he lacks and for that lack itself. The women in the novel see priest's clothing as a soldier's uniform for those "who fight the spiritual enemies," comparing Don Ippolito to the late Colonel Vervain. Ferris, by contrast, does not put on the uniform that, as Aaron argues, defines contemporary American maleness until the very end of the novel.[36]

In acting as American consul in Venice, Howells, like his character Ferris, avoided service in the Union Army. His biographers and critics have long noted Howells's continuing preoccupation with this failure to participate in the defining experience of mid-century American manhood.[37] Howells glosses his own situation in the opening sentence of *A Fearful Responsibility* (1881): "Every loyal American who went abroad during the first years of our great war felt bound to make himself some excuse of turning his back on his country in the hour of her trouble."

A Foregone Conclusion explores precisely this anxiety, not simply through Ferris's character alone, but through the triangulated relations among a man, a woman, and a priest. These relations clearly differ from the sensational British descriptions of religion's penetration of the marriage bond during the Ritualist crisis. However, both American and British writers use the triangle to explore male rivalry and masculine anxiety. Don Ippolito at once stands in contrast to and is deeply imbricated with the American male of Howells's and James's generation. The Italian priest caricatures two representative images of successful American maleness at mid-century – the inventor and the soldier. Yet the weapons that the priest invents are comically flawed; the priest's habit resembles not only a soldier's uniform but also a woman's "skirt," as we are repeatedly reminded. When Don Ippolito describes a night out dressed in lay clothing, Ferris's reaction is especially – even embarrassingly – telling: "[the] story affected Ferris like that of some girl's adventure in men's clothes. He was in terror lest Mrs. Vervain should be going to say it was like that; she was going to say something; he made haste to forestall her and turn the talk on other things" (52). In this revealing progression, Ferris's reaction to Don Ippolito's revelation that he exceeds the category "priest" becomes a narrative of cross-dressing and gender confusion, which is then attributed to the woman, causing a frantic attempt to silence and control the (his) female speaking self. Stringing together his clauses with semi-colons, Howells emphasizes his representation of the process – and the frenetic pace – of Ferris's thought.

This projective anxiety about what a woman thinks pervades *A Foregone Conclusion*, though its object is typically Florida, rather than her mother. While Howells does not depict Florida as tempted by the confessional like Hawthorne's Hilda or Brontë's Lucy Snowe,[38] he does show Ferris worriedly monitoring her "devoutness" (47), especially since she attends High Church services. Frightened by Florida's "passionate nature," Ferris seems eager, as the novel's title indicates, to read her as a character in a well-known story of female infidelity.[39] Howells's 1865 *New York Times* attack on priestly celibacy was not so much directed at clerical sexual abstinence as at what he sees as the illicit sexual activities that result from Italian priests being forbidden to marry. Like the author of *Rosamond*'s escaped nun story, Howells calls upon the imagination of his Protestant American readership, an imagination well versed in stories of priestly corruption, confidently assuming that: "The reader will readily figure these things to himself" (5). Allowing marriage among the priesthood "will do more than any other [step] to advance social purity and religious freedom and independence" in Italy, Howells declares. In *A Foregone Conclusion*, the woman's relationship with a priest – a relationship that Protestants already "know" all about – is represented by Howells as a test of the American woman's suitability for marriage.

The *Othello* speech that provides Howells with the phrase "a foregone conclusion" illustrates how revelatory female "guilt" is of *male* anxiety. Told by Iago of Cassio's supposed dream about Desdemona, Othello declares, "But this denoted a foregone conclusion. / 'Tis a shrewd doubt, though it be but a dream" (3.3.429). Othello's conclusion proceeds from pointedly sketchy evidence – the *report* of Cassio's *dream* of kissing Desdemona. Similarly, Ferris's foregone conclusions about "the priest" and Florida's love allow Howells's exploration of his American protagonist's anxious masculinity:

Ferris came back and looked dizzily at the priest, trying to believe that this unhuman, sacerdotal phantasm had been telling him that it loved a beautiful young girl of his own race, faith and language. . . . It was all a shapeless torment; it held him like the memory of some hideous nightmare prolonging its horror beyond sleep. (125–26)

Ferris experiences the priest's sexuality as at once foreign (a threat to one of "his own race, faith and language") and familiar ("like the memory"). The "unhuman" Don Ippolito resembles the figures of mechanical mimicry central to Freud's analysis of the uncanny, figures at once rejected and remembered. Don Ippolito is a "phantasm" or "nightmare," Ferris's fancy crossing over into the real, the repressed returning as an "it" not a "he." Such language encourages us to see the priest as a version or aspect of Ferris, fearful to himself. Don Ippolito's pathetic imitation of manhood has called into question his Protestant American rival's own masculinity. His "doom[]" limns the stigma of male failure in America: Early lack of success dooms an American man forever. Although newly established as the editor of the *Atlantic Monthly*, Howells still faced these fears in the early seventies. Perhaps Ferris and Howells, like the priest, will return only to find that they are the undead, that they have no place in modern America.

Don Ippolito's role as an antique mirror for contemporary American masculinity crystallizes in what we might call the novel's "primal scene." Here, the figure of the priest as the feminized male resonates with Howells's generational need to regard romance as "feminine" and realism as "masculine." Hawthorne and Don Ippolito, insistently denigrated as childish throughout *A Foregone Conclusion*, nonetheless father the American writer's sexuality. Howells succumbs to temptation in the garden, setting the moment of revelation in the realm of "Rappaccini's Daughter": Ferris sees Florida kiss Don Ippolito at a ruined fountain in the midst of a garden, a place where Ferris has earlier poisoned Florida's mind with an "ultimate drop of venom" (61). Watching, Ferris receives a traumatic and shaping shock to his masculinity:

Ferris stepped back again into the shadow of the tree from which he had just emerged, and clung to its trunk lest he should fall. Another seemed to creep out of the court in his person, and totter across the white glare of the campo and down the blackness of the calle. In the intersected spaces where the moonlight fell, this alien, miserable man saw the figure of a priest gliding on before him.[40] (139)

Howells's scene of sexual discovery (like so many in Hawthorne's, as well as James's, fiction) involves an adult – not a child – witnessing a male – not a female – wound. Seeing sexuality so unmans Ferris that he must hide. Howells underscores his protagonist's shame at revealed weakness by having "Ferris" disappear into syntactic ambiguity as the paragraph progresses ("Another . . . in his person . . . this alien miserable man"). The male identities cross and exchange across a topography of light and darkness, which figures exposure and repression, suggesting movement between consciousness and the unconscious. And the conventional "figure of a priest gliding" across the Hawthornian "intersected spaces where the moonlight fell" acts, again, as a vehicle for Howells to transverse the romantic and the real.

Yet this moment of confrontation is to a large extent repressed by the novel's conclusion. The occlusion results in part from Howells's acquiescence to demands from his audience and publisher for a happy ending. The American man must marry the American girl. In contrast, the Italian priest meets a feminized – or at least a de-masculinized – end: failing to win the woman, find work, or get to America, he returns to what is represented as his primitive, superstitious faith and dies of unrequited love.

Nonetheless, Howells hints at the Italian priest's necessity in the formation – and, as I have suggested, the formulation – of the modern American couple. Don Ippolito is said to pervade the couple's self-definition: "they spoke of Don Ippolito as if he were a part of their love" (169). The heterosexual happy ending is imbricated with and rests on another, remembered story – that of the frightening and comic Catholic priest. Ferris and Florida are, in fact, reunited by the painting of Don Ippolito, a work which the penniless Ferris is vainly trying to sell.

In addition to its role in *A Foregone Conclusion's* final plot mechanics, the portrait of Don Ippolito serves here, as it did earlier, as a vehicle for Howells's delineation of his artistic dilemma in 1874. Ferris, faced with the conflict between his realist esthetic and his audience's (and his own) preconceptions regarding "an Italian priest" paints only a failed portrait that satisfies neither. Howells tries to solve the problem differently. He gives us romance – "the tragedy of Don Ippolito" – as well as the happily ending love story that his audience demanded, but tries to do so within the parameters of a realist novel. One way for Howells to have his romance and snub it too is through an uneven, ironic narratorial tone, a tone that pervades *A Foregone Conclusion*, but is especially marked in the novel's closing pages.

The mildly mocking narrative voice maintains *A Foregone Conclusion*'s readers at a careful distance from the novel's concluding resolution of the protagonist's professional and personal dilemmas. Ferris is portrayed as overly insistent in his attempts to belittle Don Ippolito. Lolling on the cushions of a gondola, Ferris snipes, "That story he told you of his child-hood and of how he became a priest: didn't it strike you at the time like rather a made-up, melodramatic history?" In an all too familiar American-ist formulation, Ferris claims that, in blaming circumstances rather than looking to himself, the priest revealed his "inadequacy" (170). This failure to make his own way and self, to be like Holgrave of *The House of the Seven Gables* or a Horatio Alger character, is, Ferris implies, a failure to be male in a recognizably American way.

But this is a criticism, the narrator has let us know, that might just as easily be made of Ferris himself. Although he has become, in one sense, the complete American man, having acquired a uniform, a war wound, and a wife, these achievements have been drawn into question. Ferris does not work for a living nor is he a professional artist – even the all-important war wound is belittled ("to hear her [Florida] you would suppose no one else had ever been shot in the service of his country" [168]). Having destabilized both Ferris's success story and the happy marriage plot, the narrative voice at once advances and undercuts the contemporary American artist's final dismissal of the Italian priest and all that he represents.

"People are never equal to the romance of their youth in after life," the narrator of *A Foregone Conclusion* punningly informs us (168). Howells positions himself both against and within a story of American success and failure in part by invoking and dismissing Hawthornian romance. The Italian priest, associated with the past, with the feminized man, and with the literary father, is an overdetermined figure for the fears facing an American male writer of Howells's generation.

No priest figures prominently in the Catholic world of *The American*. The dark secret of Europe's past involves no lascivious monk. Christopher Newman does not watch, horrified, as Claire de Cintré enters a scheming Jesuit's confessional. Nonetheless, Newman is one of James's important explorations of American masculinity, and Roman Catholicism is a vehicle for that exploration. However, both because the previous analysis of *A*

Foregone Conclusion treats the issue of gender at length and because there has been so much recent excellent work on Newman's vexed masculinity,[41] my emphasis in discussing *The American* will be more on how Catholicism, and anti-Catholicism, are integral to James's struggles in this novel with genre.

The American is one of the generically unstable early novels in which James attempts to move his writing from external action to internal psychological plots. Critics, taking their cue from James's preface ("I had been plotting arch-romance without knowing it," he admits forty years later) have long treated the genre of *The American* as a problem. Peter Brooks declares that "One can in fact read in *The American* and its differing modes an allegory of James's uncertain choices among different available forms of 'the novelistic,' his testing of them serially, and, implicitly, his search to define and create what would be the properly Jamesian form."[42] James's repeated allusions to and uses of romance and melodrama in the novel have been well documented. What I want to point to here is the particular sort of sensationalist plots and characters that Newman draws on in order to understand the Bellegardes. Identifying these particulars does not simply uncover a series of specific allusions or sources. Rather, it suggests how Catholicism and anti-Catholicism afford James a whole strain of writing, a set of audience associations, a range of references and techniques that he can turn to his purposes. Anti-Catholicism contributes crucially to the generic polyphony that is *The American*.

When Newman is outraged at the story of Claire de Cintré's forced first marriage, Tom Tristram declares that the same thing goes on in New York: "The Mysteries of the Fifth Avenue! Someone ought to show them up." Tristram alludes here to the extremely popular American sensation novel, *The Mysteries and Miseries of New York* (1848) by Ned Buntline. Itself modeled on Eugene Sue's *Les Mystères de Paris* (1842–43), Buntline's novel spawned a series of American imitators (*The Mysteries of Lowell*, *The Mysteries of Troy*, etc.). Sue's, Buntline's, and many of the other "mysteries of the city" novels, like the nativist sensation novels of the 1850s, contained standard anti-Catholic plots and characters: girls kidnapped into convents, assaults in confessionals, scheming Jesuits. Although Newman claims elsewhere not to read novels, his response – "I don't believe it" – makes his familiarity with sensationalist literature clear, as do his observations that the Bellegardes' house "answered to Newman's conception of a convent"; "It is like something in a play . . . ; that dark old house over there looks as if wicked things had been done in it, and might be done again." When Newman actually does see Claire's convent, he thinks, "at present it was not a reality to him. It was too strange and too mocking to be real; it was like a page torn out of a romance, with no context in his own experience." Catholicism represents a foreign discourse with its own plots and scenes.[43]

Newman cannot assimilate the "romance" of Catholicism into the register of his realism. His understanding of romance is the vulgar one that James dismisses in the preface to *The American* – "a matter indispensably of boats, or of caravans, or of tigers, or of 'historical characters,' or of ghosts, or of forgers, or of detectives, or of beautiful wicked women, or of pistols and knives"[44] – a story of long ago and far away.

But Catholicism is also *The American's* vehicle for the sort of romance that James *does* endorse in the preface. Attempting to explain the unexplainable, the unnamable, the unknowable, Claire de Cintré says to Newman, "It's like a religion." ("It's" antecedent is ambiguous: her fear of knowing; her need to obey; the terrible, half-glimpsed secrets of her family.) "Religion" here is connate with "romance," as James himself famously defines it: "the things that, with all the facilities in the world, all the wealth and all the courage and all the wit and all the adventure, we never *can* directly know; the things that reach us only through the beautiful circuit and subterfuge of our thought and our desire." Like the painting of Don Ippolito that Ferris longs but refuses to paint, Catholicism here stands for the plots, characters, conventions that the romantic realist uses, resists, ironizes.[45]

In *A Foregone Conclusion*, this disruption is the attractive nuisance that I have called "Hawthorne." Like all of James's writing, *The American* shows Hawthorne's influence – the brash Yankee who intrudes into an ancient house to woo the innocent young woman, the secret family murder which curses and haunts succeeding generations. However, Hawthorne is not a primary figure in the writing of *The American*, as comparison with *Roderick Hudson*, an anxious revision of *The Marble Faun*[46] written just a year before *The American*, makes clear.[47]

Nonetheless, a central site for romance in *The American* is a gothic figure that James and other nineteenth-century American readers would know as Hawthorne's: the veil. What does Newman see of the Catholic religion? "an object unknown to Newman, and covered with a white napkin," "genuflections and gyrations," "the screen behind the altar," a "pale, dead, discolored wall." This use of emblematic Roman Catholic items sounds suspiciously like what James derided as Disraeli's Scarlet Woman, draped in a tablecloth and waving a candlestick. Yet James implies that, rather than the hackneyed trappings of a Protestant scarecrow, the signs of Catholicism signify what Newman cannot know. The novel repeatedly draws attention to the white cloth – the distinctive long, loose, soft, white dresses and cloaks that cover Claire's body, marking her innocence and desirability. By *The American*'s conclusion, when Claire retreats behind a convent wall, her white dresses are exchanged for a Carmelite nun's white veil: "But still Newman hardly understood. 'You are going to be a nun,' he went on, 'in a cell – for life – with a gown and white veil?'" Taking her vows as "Veronica," the woman whose veil bears witness to a man's murder, Claire at once covers and reveals her family's secret. In obscuring, the veil asserts interiority.[48] In contrast to the minutely detailed clarity that is the defining technique of nineteenth-century realism, Claire's Catholic veil can be read as a trope for the suggestive obscurities of romance – what Hawthorne calls "mystery" or "shadow."

James's use of the veil illustrates the duality of the traditional Protestant suspicion of Catholicism as a religion of surfaces. The glittering veneer of the Church of Rome ensnares its childlike flock in a superficial religion. Yet nineteenth-century writers and readers continue to be allured by the way that Catholicism's surfaces seem to mark a mysterious depth.

For Newman, however, that depth remains inaccessible. He cannot read Claire's white writing[49] – the body beneath the veil, the "illogic" of her belief. He turns instead to the Protestant Mrs. Bread's vulgarly "romantic" sensational story of M. de Bellegarde's death. (Before he listens to the story, Newman checks Mrs. Bread's credentials: "Are you a Catholic?") Like "priest" for Ferris, the veils of Catholicism are signs which remain opaque and inert for Newman. John Rowe has explored how Newman's ignorance of European history makes for his failure to understand the significance of the Bellegardes' ultramontanism, the politics of their religion.[50] I want to emphasize the fact that Newman also fails to understand the religiousness of the Bellegardes' religion, the meaning and experience of Catholic belief. Christopher Newman is, like Lothair, an orphan who comes from a relatively "uncivilized" region yet represents the best his society has to offer and comes up against Catholicism's plots through his attraction to a woman named Claire (Clare) who eventually disappears into a convent. Whether or not Newman matures through the course of *The American*, one thing he certainly does not come to understand is Catholic belief. This is why, despite the expectations raised by Christopher Newman's nominal association with the nineteenth-century's most famous convert to Catholicism, John Henry Newman, *The American* is *not* a conversion novel.[51] When Newman is first introduced, we are told that "If he was a muscular Christian, it was quite without knowing it." Newman's distance from Catholicism lies not in a conscious Protestant conviction like Charles Kingsley's, but in his lack of receptivity to religious faith.[52]

As Brooks argues, the melodrama of *The American* moves inwards, into consciousness, and into "the realm of epistemology." This is what James suggested Disraeli and Howells should have done with *Lothair* and *A Foregone Conclusion* by centering the novels around a character's struggle with belief. Yet James accomplishes the movement Brooks describes by ignoring his own advice. Rather than exploiting the dramatic possibilities of internal religious conflict, *The American* depicts the unbeliever's inability to comprehend, even to recognize, belief. Catholicism represents the ways in which the other is romantic to us by dramatizing the inaccessibility of faith.[53] And, as in *A Foregone Conclusion*, as well as *Foxglove Manor, High Church*, and *Under Which Lord?*, this position is gendered male, instantiating the cultural perception that, as the nineteenth century progresses, religion becomes an increasingly feminized realm. Trying to understand another's belief, James implies, is like staring at a veiled woman, like standing outside the convent wall. This psychologizing of romance means that Newman makes no attempt to scale the convent wall armed with the "pistols and knives," nor does Claire become an escaped nun fleeing through a secret gate. Instead, with the image of the convent wall James figures blocked knowledge and thwarted desire.

This is an image James continues to reimagine throughout his career: looking over a garden wall, staring at the outside of a building, longing for knowledge and intimacy. In *The American*, James moves romance from the literalism of melodrama to the realm of the psychological, but, as the matter of religious belief implies, he still locates romance largely between, rather than within, characters. Comparison of Newman's plight with that of Maggie Verver in *The Golden Bowl* illustrates my point. Newman gazes at the wall that hides his lover; Maggie circles the pagoda that figures her own relations with her father, husband, and friend.[54] Maggie's pagoda is a figure of and for her mind: what has she known? what does she think? Newman faces a literal barrier; the experience that he cannot even see, let alone understand, is another's.[55] On March 30, 1877, James wrote to Howells defending *The American*'s unhappy ending: "We are each the product of circumstances & there are tall stone walls which fatally divide us. I have written my story from Newman's side of the wall, & I understand so well how Mme de Cintré couldn't really scramble over from *her* side!"[56]

In positioning Newman outside the convent wall, James also draws on nineteenth-century genre painting, in which the walled garden represents the cloister as a (perhaps desirable) space of living death. In paintings like Collins's 1851 *Convent Thoughts* and Millais's 1859 *The Vale of Rest*, the traditional "*hortus conclusus* or enclosed garden of chastity" is made religious.[57]

Susan Casteras describes the voyeurism at work as the viewer glimpses the secret life of nuns behind the high convent walls which dominate the paintings. (James's protagonist is blocked from even this glimpse, though his imagination, fueled by Mrs. Bread's sensational hints, conjures up Claire's supposed suffering.) Marked by *memento mori* – skulls, tombstones, graves – Victorian paintings of cloistered nuns depict both the woman's death to the world and her imminent bodily death. The general Protestant perception of Roman Catholicism as archaic, decayed, and primitive is concretized in these icons.

Death marks the ultimate unknowability of the Other, its relegation to the past,[58] and in *The American* Catholicism is a way of death. Confronting the Bellegardes, Newman feels "as if the door of a sepulchre had suddenly been opened, and the damp darkness were being exhaled" (798). Valentin's death is represented as part of his Catholicism: he is wounded defending an honor as invisible to Newman as his belief; his seconds are chosen because they are good Catholics (veterans, with Valentin, of the Zouaves, the papal troops against whom Lothair fights); Newman is angry and puzzled by what appears to be the Catholic attitude towards death – "the doctor has condemned him. . . . But he will die in the best sentiments. . . . The curé was quite satisfied" (764); the American witnesses, uncomprehendingly, Valentin's last rites and Catholic funeral. Claire's retreat into the convent in the Rue de l'Enfer is repeatedly described as a death; Newman even terms himself a widower. The Protestant polemical association of Catholicism, the religion of the primitive past, with death, whether it be the death of the soul in formalized, empty ritual or bodily death through inquisitorial torture or self-destructive, celibate asceticism, is brought to bear in *The American*, where to be Catholic is to turn away from life.

James, along with Disraeli and Howells, represents the death-in-life of Catholicism with the figure of the Carmelite. Despite their willingness to borrow from anti-Catholic literature, Disraeli, Howells, and James disdain the conventional dark, gliding Jesuit (though he surfaces comically in their protagonists' overheated imaginations). Instead, for all three writers, the Carmelite represents Catholicism at its most extreme. "They tell me it's most dreadful, sir; of all the nuns in Christendom the Carmelites are the worst. You may say they are really not human, sir; they make you give up everything – forever," the horrified Mrs. Bread informs Newman (796). The order's recent activities made such an image readily available: a Carmelite convent was opened in England in 1865, and their Pugin-designed church was dedicated in 1866.[59] The symbolic resonances of Claire de Cintré's retreat into the Carmelite convent in the Rue de l'Enfer have been much noted; less recognized is the fact that there actually was a Carmelite convent in that street at the time. This detail illustrates the general point that I have tried to make throughout this chapter: the stories and images of Catholicism provide a shared vocabulary upon which Disraeli, Howells, and James draw. James's choice of the name "Rue de l'Enfer" is not just symbolically apt; it is historically specific and culturally resonant.

When Disraeli's Clare Arundel takes vows as a Carmelite, she may waste her womanly potential, but her retreat serves primarily as a plot device to reduce Lothair to one obvious marital choice. For Howells and James the image of the Carmelite is much more evocative and threatening. Strikingly, what the Carmelite threatens is masculinity. Although Don Ippolito dies before he can enter the Carmelites, he serves as a specter of death-in-life that is emphatically male: "A priest is a man under sentence of death to the natural ties between himself and the human race. He is dead to us. That makes him dreadful. The specter of our dearest friend, father or mother, would be terrible. And yet . . . a nun isn't terrible" (100). While *Newman* finds Claire as a nun terrible, what *James* shows is not the horrors of the conventional nun's story, like Maria Monk's (sadistic Mother Superiors, lascivious priests, imprisonment, torture, etc.), but the way in which this female retreat emblematizes male defeat. When Claire announces her intention to become a Carmelite, Newman "tremble[s] visibly."

That this superb woman, in whom he had seen all human grace and household force, should turn from him and all the brightness that he offered her – him and his future and his fortune and his fidelity – to muffle herself in ascetic rags and entomb herself in a cell, was a confounding combination of the inexorable and the grotesque. As the image deepened before him the grotesque seemed to expand and overspread it; it was a reduction to the absurd of the trial to which he was subjected. (790)

What Newman dismisses early in the novel as archaic melodrama disrupts the realistic narrative that he has planned as his life story.[60] As in *A Foregone Conclusion*, Roman Catholicism is the vehicle whereby the gothic becomes the grotesque and the realm of romance is rendered ludicrous. Don Ippolito is dismissed as comic; Newman finds his nineteenth-century fiancée transformed into a medieval mummified saint.

Martha Banta points out that the *Scribner's* review of *The American* argued that "James had failed as a writer by allowing Newman to do something so un-American as to fail in his endeavors." Later critics who have viewed the novel as more successful have nevertheless recognized the ways in which James's anxieties about money, publication, his identity as an

American in Europe, and his financial and emotional relations with his family are played out on the pages of *The American*. Like Howells, James positions himself both against and within a story of American masculine success and failure. And, as in the nativist novels of their (unacknowledged) American predecessors, the Catholic Church provides a familiar antagonist against which a rising generation of men attempt to prove themselves. But for postbellum writers like Howells and James, that struggle cannot be represented wholly seriously. What I would suggest is that the uneven and ambivalent tone with which both *A Foregone Conclusion* and *The American* describe their respective protagonists[61] is at least in part a function of the fact that their opponents are a man in a skirt and a woman in a veil, a "Scarlet Woman . . . dressed out terribly in the tablecloth." Romance, gliding into Howells's and James's fictions by means of the plots and figures of anti-Catholicism, is at once archaic, absurd, and necessary.

If Howells's and James's Catholic Churches finally resemble Disraeli's in their comic scariness, the differences between these particular American and British anti-Catholic fictions remain fundamental. To use a Jamesian distinction, *Lothair* is a novel of plot; *A Foregone Conclusion* and *The American* are novels of character. These specific examples from the 1870s reverse the pattern that has been descried elsewhere in this book, in which Americans write standard, sensational plots and British writers focus on the psychology of character. What separates Howells's and James's writing from Disraeli's here has also to do with how these authors regard themselves professionally at this point in their careers. *Lothair* is a story about being an insider; *A Foregone Conclusion* and *The American* describe what it is to be an outsider. In the 1870s, these American writers, just beginning to succeed, are defining for themselves what it means to be a modern American literary professional in part, as Brodhead has demonstrated, by modeling themselves on and against the past (the romantic, the Hawthornian, the novel of plot).[62] Roman Catholicism, the religion of what Jackson Lears calls "antimodernism," provides one means of engaging this task. By depicting Ferris and Newman as barred from an understanding of Catholic belief – stuck outside, staring uncomprehendingly at the figure of the priest, the nun's veil, the convent wall – Howells and James at once display and displace their anxiety. The ambiguity of tone that pervades both *A Foregone Conclusion* and *The American* is nowhere more marked than in these moments of incomprehension and narratorial distance. The closing sentence of James's review of *Lothair* provides a telling gloss on Howells's and James's own situation in the seventies: "Quite the most interesting point with regard to the work is this frequent betrayal of the possible innocence of one who has been supposed to be nothing if not knowing."[63] What this (supposedly knowing) remark reveals is not Disraeli's "infantine" "innocence" but that the reviewer is a young American writer, determined to make his mark. Here, as in *The American* and *A Foregone Conclusion*, it is James's and Howells's depictions of not knowing that are revelatory.

Reliquaries

At the century's close, anti-Catholicism becomes less and less manifest in British and American fiction. Plots and images endure (indeed, they continue to circulate in Anglo-American culture today), but they are less pervasive and become increasingly detached from the religious critique to which they were initially tied. A strong connection between anti-Catholicism and literature does appear late in the century in the attacks on the Decadent movement, with its interest in Anglo-Catholicism and association with homosexuality. Pre-existing perceptions of the Catholic priesthood as effeminate and perverse become part of public response to the culture of Pater and Wilde. Ellis Hanson and David Hilliard have analyzed in detail these connections and the responses to them, and I will not replicate their arguments here.[1] In any case, the turn-of-the-century critique of Decadence as Catholic, and Catholicism as decadent, comes largely in nonfictional form. Instead, my discussion of anti-Catholicism and nineteenth-century fiction closes by looking briefly at several turn-of-the-century fictions: Mary Wilkins Freeman's "A New England Nun" (1891), Alice Dunbar Nelson's "Sister Josepha" (1899), Edith Wharton's "The Bunner Sisters" (1916), and Mary Ward's *Helbeck of Bannisdale* (1898). While hardly an exhaustive catalogue of the lingering uses of anti-Catholic narratives, these texts, when read together, are a telling indication of how religious fiction becomes secularized at the end of the Victorian era.[2] Critics like Elizabeth Ammons, Richard Brodhead, Josephine Donovan, and Louis Renza have analyzed the strategies of regionalist women's writing at the turn of the century, describing the cultural, economic, professional, and writerly reasons behind female authors' choice of this "minor" mode.[3] I want to suggest why such writing seemed an appropriate genre for the remnants of anti-Catholic narrative.

With its title, "A New England Nun" situates itself as a story informed by Protestant conceptions of Catholicism. While Freeman's tale is hardly an attack on Catholicism, it draws upon its readership's narrative "knowledge" of convents, nuns, and Catholicism. Unlike the "involuntary" nuns who flee the Romish convents in which they are imprisoned by a predatory priesthood, Louisa Ellis's life is entirely of her own choosing. Louisa's last name echoes that of Sarah Stickney Ellis, whose 1838 *Women of England*, widely read on both sides of the Atlantic, described in detail the duties of woman's domestic sphere as wife and mother. Louisa's perfect solitary domesticity in an era of gender population imbalance both mimics and ironizes her predecessor's glorification of the female realm. Having spent fifteen years waiting for her fiancé, Joe Dagget, to make his way in the world, Louisa creates a "happy solitary life" of rigid order and decorum: an immaculate home with the books always piled exactly so on her table, not so much as a speck of dust on her floors or a twig on her garden path, her dress covered with a "company apron" preserved by a sewing apron protected by a garden apron, evoking the layers of cloth that comprise a nun's habit. Rather than a sexualized realm of sadism, Louisa's "convent" is overwhelmingly chaste – a pretty haven, an analogue for the self that she hedges round with aprons, protected from dirt, from passion, from intercourse with the world of men and women. When the time comes, Louisa finds that she cannot renounce her nun's cell which has become, like her needle and thimble "from long use and constant association, a very part of her personality." She gives up Joe Dagget and the life that he offers and represents:

If Louisa Ellis had sold her birthright she did not know it, the taste of the pottage was so delicious, and had been her sole satisfaction for so long. Serenity and placid narrowness has become to her as to the birthright itself. She gazed ahead through a long reach of future days strung together like pearls in a rosary, every one like the others, and all smooth and flawless and innocent, and her heart went up in thankfulness. Outside was the fervid summer afternoon; the air was filled with the sounds of the busy harvest of men and birds and bees; there were halloos, metallic clatterings, sweet calls, and long hummings. Louisa sat, prayerfully numbering her days, like an uncloistered nun.

Freeman's depiction of Louisa as a secular nun refuses the sensationalism of a Maria Monk tale. Captivity here is metaphorical: Louisa's chained dog and caged bird. "A New England Nun" does, however, resonate with Victorian critiques of religious sisterhoods as refusals of life and its duties in favor of sterility and self-absorption. Freeman emphasizes Louisa's self-pleasuring – her delight in sitting and sewing and resewing seams in her lap, her happiness as she "gloat[s] gently over her orderly bureau-drawers, with their exquisitely folded contents redolent with lavender and sweet clover and very purity."[4] Surrounded by the aromatic essences she distills, with her carefully prepared meals of sugared currants and little cakes, Louisa is a milder version of the nuns of anti-Catholic narrative who delight in the sensuality of Catholic incense, flowers, and elaborate decorations and whose sexuality manifests itself in childish greediness for sweets.

Sarah Josepha Hale's nun's tale, "The Catholic Convert," argued that the true female vocation is not an unnatural life of celibacy, but holy marriage. Freeman, in turn, details both the appeal and the limitations of a "nun's" calling. The woman who chooses marriage in the story, Lily Dyer (whose goodness, as well as her sexuality, are vividly imaged in her name), is clearly meant to represent a more "natural" model of female fecundity than Louisa Ellis's death-in-life. Nonetheless, Freeman makes it clear that Louisa's "narrow" retreat from the world offers an alternative, if lesser, female vocation. Hale's argument about women, religion, and marriage is situated within and motivated by her belief that Protestants needed to actively respond to Catholic immigration and missionary activity, that, as she insists in the *American Ladies' Magazine*, Protestant education for women is essential to such a response. A different demographic change informs Freeman's fiction: the shortage of men in New England that resulted from the Civil War and from migration to urban manufacturing centers. Joe Daggett, who must leave New England and go to Australia to make a living, returns to find that there are two women for one man. "Catholic" practices of celibacy thus offer a practical solution to the female surplus. (Although figured less explicitly as "Catholic," the celibate women who abound in the fictions of writers like Freeman and Sarah Orne Jewett, whether as solitary figures or as members of female communities, represent other versions of this solution). Louisa's retreat into the old-fashioned gentility of her conventual life constitutes a narrative reimagining of traditional nuns' stories. Unlike Frances Trollope's sensational *Father Eustace*, which also imagines celibacy as emblematic of a fantastic realm of female choice and autonomy, Freeman's story situates itself as ethnographic realism.

The title character of Alice Dunbar Nelson's "Sister Josepha" (1899) is less happily resigned to her conventual fate. Nelson depicts a young, lively, beautiful girl trapped in a sisterhood that stifles (and, we are led to believe, will sour and ruin) her. Abandoned at the convent door as a child, Camille spends her first years happily enough as "the pretty little tyrant" of the school. When she grows, at fifteen, into a "glorious tropical beauty of the type that matures early," a couple seek to adopt her. Unsettled by the man's "pronounced leers," she chooses instead to become a nun. However, "cooped up" in the convent, condemned to a dull daily routine, she rebels. Yet her plans to escape (triggered by the sight of a beautiful young man) are thwarted when she realizes that she knows neither "who" or "what" she is. The racial import of that "what" is unspoken but clear.

The racialized Other in earlier nineteenth-century anti-Catholic polemic is typically either the Southern European or the Irish. As foreigner, the Catholic appears at times as the figure for the colonial subject. And, in 1850s, black America and miscegenation surface in tales of the founding fathers. Here, Alice Dunbar uses a convent story (a failed escaped nun's tale) to raise the unspoken problem of race in America. Nelson's critique is not directed at the Catholic Church and its convents. What we see, instead, is postbellum America's refusal to deal with the reality of a mixed-race woman. When the "heavy door" closes behind Camille at the story's end, we understand that there is no life for her except the death-in-life of the convent. She is not trapped not by a kidnapping priest nor perverted parents; indeed, the convent serves as a place of refuge, albeit a "home of self-repression" for the young woman.[5] Yet its associations mark it as a place for the uneasy burial of the secrets and legacies of America's racism. The Convent du Sacre Cœur serves as a repository for the sins of the fathers, a place in which America's past is hidden. "Sister Josepha" illustrates that even in a non-polemical narrative, emptied of religion, "Catholicism" occupies a space in America's story of itself.

Anti-Catholic narrative functions more decidedly in Edith Wharton's "The Bunner Sisters." Written in 1892 (but not published until 1916), this novella presents itself as a relentlessly realistic – if not naturalistic – depiction of antebellum New York. Amy Kaplan has argued that "realism is a strategy for imagining and managing the threats of social change – not just to asset a dominant power but often to assuage fears of power-lessness." In "The Bunner Sisters" Wharton details the circumstances of a pair of genteelly impoverished Protestant women, ineptly coping with a changing New York. Although we might read the ritualized and circum-scribed sisterhood of the Bunners as a story of New York Nuns (note Ann Eliza's "sacramental black silk"), it is only after that celibate communion is broken by Evelina's marriage with the German immigrant Herman Ramey that "popery" and its evils intrude. For Ann Eliza, the revelation that her sister Evelina has secretly followed her husband into Roman Catholicism triggers an ingrained horror at all that "Papist" encompasses. Wharton depicts this reaction as ignorant prejudice on Ann Eliza's part – a mark of her old-fashioned sensibility. Yet, such attitudes seemingly persist into the twentieth century, for it is Wharton herself who casts the Roman Catholic Ramy as representative of the foreign in her story, associating him with sex-uality, physical abuse, secrets, and death. Romanism's sensual "drugging" of its adherents is presented both literally in Ramy's own opium addiction and metaphorically in the returning Evelina's ruined body and dying desire for a priest's daily ministrations "with that mysterious covered something in his hands." Catholicism simultaneously represents the decadence of the Old World and its modern intrusion into the United States; the genteel, proper life of the Bunner sisters is being replaced by the new world of the foreigner. We can recognize Ramy's role as that of the "priest" – the foreign intruder with a secret, the Roman Catholic who tricks the innocent, genteel Protestants out of their inheritance. Appropriately, when Evelina is dying, Ramy's place is taken by an actual Roman Catholic priest, who effectively bars Ann Eliza from her sister. Catholicism as such does not destroy the Bunner Sisters, but it does mark Evelina's regression as well as their final and enduring (even after death) separation. The Bunners themselves are the objects of the conflicted Whartonian nostalgia familiar to readers of *The Age of Innocence*; the bright, young shopgirl who represents Ann Eliza's replacement at the end of the story is a figure of thoughtless, ahistorical modernity (like *The Custom of the Country*'s Undine Spragg). Like Freeman and Dunbar, Wharton describes a world in which there is no place for the traditional female. The religious domesticity of which she was meant to be the locus seems no longer to exist. That this harmonious, homogeneous female realm was always only an ideal, as Wharton's own depictions of "the age of innocence" attest, perhaps only strengthens the nostalgia it evokes in this generation of women writers.[6]

The demographic changes played out in this group of fictions are specifically American; however, the laments for disappearing ways of life, the cultural shift towards secularism and, in particular, the sense that women were losing their place as arbiters of domesticized religion all find expression in an important British novel of 1898, Mary Ward's *Helbeck of Bannisdale*. *Helbeck* describes the doomed love of Laura Fountain, the daughter of a free-thinking Cambridge don, and Alan Helbeck, the scion of an old Catholic family. With this story, Ward returns to her immensely popular novel of religious doubt, *Robert Elsmere* (1888), by way of *Villette* and *Jane Eyre*.[7] That is, she puts a female figure at the center of her drama of belief. Laura Fountain's religious skepticism is rooted in loyalty to her freethinking father, a Cambridge don, yet Mr. Fountain never furnishes Laura with the modern education she needs to think through these issues: "as to women and their claims, he was old-fashioned and contemptuous; he would have been much embarrassed by a learned daughter." He raises her as a "a child of Knowledge, a child of Freedom, a child of Revolution – without an ounce of training to fit her for the part. It is like an heir – flung to the gypsies."[8]

Leaving Cambridge for Bannisdale in the Lake District, Laura thinks that she is moving back in time to a pastoral simplicity. *Helbeck*, with its extended descriptions of the District's landscapes (landscapes that Ward had come to love through her own trips there), serves as the reader's introduction to a part of England uneasily situated in relation to modernity: for the kindly peasant cousins she expects to meet turn out to be either narrowly superstitious or vulgarly enamored of the cheap and the new. The younger generation longs for the town, with its foundry and mass-produced consumer goods; the older is entrenched in archaic anti-Catholic bigotry. Surprised, Laura exclaims: "no one *hates* Catholics now. One may just – despise them."⁹ Alan Helbeck, however, proves difficult to despise. The Fountain cousins' ignorance is set against his learning, which is at once ancient and alien: having fallen under the spell of a Jesuit at Stonyhurst and continued his education at Louvain, he has rejected the moderate Catholicism of his family, following a rigid religious rule, selling off family portraits and treasures, giving over his ancestral home to the Church.

Falling in love with Alan Helbeck, Laura must base her resistance on what amounts to blind faith in her father and a powerful need to maintain her personal autonomy. Like Jane Eyre, Lucy Helbeck fears that union with her lover will mean a loss of identity. Catholicism, depicted as the religion of obedience and abnegation of the self, underscores the ways in which loving a man represents female submission. Helbeck's religion is an archaic system of austerity and male dominance. Far older than the girlish Laura, the stern Catholic man, whose vows have brought him to the brink of priesthood, issues parental admonitions and attempts to monitor her actions. Ward describes Catholicism, with its privileging of celibacy, its insistence on fasting and penance, its elaborate rituals for the dying, and, she insists, its disgust for the female body, as a cult of death rather than a way of life. Yet the new light of Protestant, female-centered spiritual domesticity that should have replaced this masculine hierarchy long ago is, by 1898, no longer viable. Turned relentlessly from religious belief by her father (and deprived of a mother's softening influence), Laura has no weapons with which to battle Alan, no alternative life, love, and home to offer him. Facing the priesthood of which Helbeck is all but a member, Laura asks, "What power have I besides theirs?" Laura is a New Woman manqué: "I wish I was a new woman," she laments, "But I'm not good enough – I don't know anything." The female is thrust into modernity deprived of belief but inadequately educated. Ward herself struggled to reconcile her "heretical" disbelief in the miraculous with her deep need for religious ritual and communion.

And the intellectual anxieties of this accomplished amateur scholar may also be reflected and exaggerated in Laura's situation. Certainly *Helbeck* presages Virginia Woolf's analysis of the poverty of female education in *A Room of One's Own*. Laura Fountain's only recourse is a flight that at once mimics and reverses that of an escaped nun, running from Catholic Bannisdale in secret, hiding from the lover who seeks to recover her. Laura's role as a representative figure for her generation is underscored in the final description of her suicide as an "awful spending of her young life – this blind witness to august things!"[10]

Caught between two worlds, Laura Fountain is caught between two men, between a father and a lover who serves as a father-figure. Mary Ward, whose father's conversion and reconversion to Roman Catholicism devastated their family life, wrote *Helbeck* to and about her father, revising the manuscript heavily in order to meet with his approval.[11] Sutherland argues, in fact, that in researching the novel Ward was herself considering conversion. The conflicted depiction of the Church in *Helbeck of Bannisdale* was reflected in the reviews and reactions to the novel, which ranged from accusing Ward of anti-Catholicism to complaining that she was promoting Romanism. What is striking about this father–daughter story, in light of its anti-Catholic predecessors, is its refusal of the uncanny, the monstrous. The local farmers who hate and fear Helbeck as a satanic representative of Catholicism's horrors are depicted as bigots and fools. Borrowing significantly from Charlotte Brontë in this novel,[12] Ward tellingly excludes the gothic elements so prominent in the earlier writer's work. Helbeck's first love is not locked in the manor's attic but living, by her own choice, in a convent. Bannisdale is not devastated by a symbolic fire but despoiled by Helbeck's selling off its contents to raise money for Catholic charities. Catholicism is neither hidden nor disguised but openly practiced. Even the female ghost that is explained away only at the end of *Villette* is, in *Helbeck*, debunked from the start.

Like fictions by Freeman, Dunbar-Nelson, and Wharton, then, Ward's old story about Catholicism indexes the diminishing power and unity of Protestantism, illustrates how demographic changes are weakening the ties between national and religious identities. By the end of the century, the forces of secularization are such that Catholicism, and the past that it represents, function in narrative fiction less as a violent threat and more as a pitiable retreat from the modern. The Church of Rome seems to no longer function in the cultural unconscious as a powerful figure of seduction and avoidance. The vestiges of anti-Catholic narrative that mark these fictions figure not the return of the repressed but the shared consciousness of an historical turn away from religion. If anti-Catholicism tells us about Protestantism, these stories relate its irrelevance. Discussing the role of the racial stereotype in colonial discourse, Homi Bhabha argues that "the same old stories of the negro's animality, the coolie's inscrutability or the stupidity of the Irish which *must* be told (compulsively) again and afresh, and is gratifying and terrifying each time."[13] While I have argued that the discourse of anti-Catholicism resonates with that of colonialism, by the turn of the century, the former's threat has so far weakened that it offers neither such deep gratifications nor such decided terrors.

This shift is reflected narratively: rather than being structured around a male generational, Oedipal struggle these fictions describe instead a female dilemma.[14] The nineteenth-century ideology that understood women as inherently more spiritual than men develops, in a period of growing doubt and secularization, into a focus on the female as a figure of loss. If the escaped nuns' tales of the thirties expressed fears about female religious power, the women who turn to Catholicism in turn-of-the-century narratives represent anxiety about modernity. The dangerous, ambivalent nostalgia for the religious certainty and dogma of the Church of Rome that earlier narratives warn the Protestant faithful against is now recast as attraction to a limited and limiting comfort that the modern culture of disbelief cannot offer.[15] Turn-of-the-century fiction rarely pits Catholic and Protestant theologies and practices against one another; more often, Catholicism comes to represent religious culture and belief as such.

Uninterested in attacking Roman Catholicism *per se*, these later fictions instead mobilize a set of associations familiar from earlier anti-Catholic writing, a tendency we can see prefigured in Disraeli's *Lothair*, Howells's *A Foregone Conclusion* and James's *The American*. For those male writers, the Protestant associations of Catholicism with the foreign and the feminine, with upper-class mysteries and secrets from which parvenu Protestant is excluded, provide structures through which to work out problems of gender, modernity, and national identity. Howells and James especially position themselves both against and within the genres of anti-Catholicism in constructing themselves as modern literary professionals. But Freeman, Dunbar, Wharton, and Ward depict a very different relationship with modernity. In drawing on anti-Catholic narrative, these female writers explore what a culture of secularism and doubt means for women. Their fiction shows the Victorian ideal of a feminized Christianity, centered in the woman's sphere of home and manifested in marriage and motherhood, as less and less imaginable at the turn of the century. Images of the Catholic nun and the foreign priest serve now to delineate woman's loss of privileged spirituality.

This sense of a lost woman's sphere is played out generically as well. Rome and Romanism serve as vehicles by which Disraeli, Howells, and James can enfold romance into their realism. By contrast, in the nineties and the teens, the "horrors" of Catholicism become for Freeman, Dunbar, Wharton, and Ward a means of writing a realism specifically recognizable as that of turn-of-the-century regionalism:[16] ethnography that details modes of life threatened with extinction. Even further removed than the three male writers from the heyday of religious polemical fiction, these women write "Catholic" and "Protestant" in the appropriately "minor" literature of regionalism. Here, the nineteenth-century Protestant understanding of Catholicism as retrograde and archaic is recast as its practices come to represent disappearing ways of life.[17] Unable any longer to imagine lives and households structured by Protestant beliefs and behaviors, these writers can only represent a religious life – albeit an isolated, dying one – by turning to Catholicism. Protestantism can no longer provide what is needed, but Catholicism offers only a retreat from the present and a refusal of the future.

As regionalist literature, then, Catholicism, at the turn of the century, continues to serve as a means of identity-making for populations of America and England in these texts, albeit on a reduced scale. Theorists of regional literature have demonstrated how the description of the local in this period can be read as part of what has been called an "imperialist nostalgia" that memorializes the very cultural practices that it is eradicating. Given the homogenizing forces of nationalism, particularly in an era of improved transportation and communication and of growing standardization and mobility of goods, information, and services, such nostalgia can be seen as operating within national boundaries as well. Regionalist writing exoticizes and memorializes the local for a national audience. This insistent memorialization is simultaneously part of the dominant culture's distancing, its narratives of progress.[18]

The vestigial traces of religious polemic, the continuing interpenetration of "Catholic" and "Protestant" in Protestant imaginings, support narratives that depict the relations between the local and the national multiply. "Sister Josepha," which uses Franglish dialect and is set in New Orleans, situates Catholic culture itself as an American "region." Freeman's "A New England Nun" describes a barren (albeit satisfying) way of life analogized as Catholic. "The Bunner Sisters" too depicts a disappearing female realm; however, Catholicism here is a force in its displacement and destruction. And for Ward Catholicism stands for the sheltering culture of belief and submission no longer available to the new woman. The mixture of nostalgia and triumphalism characteristic of regionalist narratives is played out differently in each of these scenarios.

The local, then, comes to serve as a literary reliquary. Created to hold a fragment of holiness which has been preserved from the past, a reliquary is a made thing: a casket, a shrine. The relic that it holds is not an idea, an abstraction, or a universal. It is physical, local (it must travel or be traveled to); it has a name, a history, a specificity (a piece of Veronica's veil, a splinter of the Cross). The reliquary brings its audience into proximity with the past, and, presumably, the divine. But the presence that it signals is always, of necessity, partial – not St. Theresa walking among us but her bone. What is partially preserved in works made by Freeman, Dunbar-Nelson, Wharton, and Ward is neither Catholicism nor Protestantism but the fragments of anti-Catholic discourse and with it, incongruously, the memories of an imaginary elsewhere in which women were centrally and wholly present. Throughout the nineteenth century, Protestant nationalisms' construction of "Romanism" as what Bhabha calls a "'partial' presence," at once incomplete and virtual, reflected fears about its own authenticity and integrity. Cast as the superficial mimicry of Christianity, Catholic surfaces threatened to reveal the Protestant America and Britain's fractures. By the century's close, religious identity itself appears to be in shards.

Near the end of *Helbeck of Bannisdale*, a relic of St. John of the Cross is sent to Alan's dying sister, Laura's stepmother. Laura, who is estranged from Alan at this point, has just been reading about the "mutilation" of St. Theresa of Avila's body by relic-hunters:

In a ruthless haste, these pious thieves had lifted the poor embalmed corpse from its resting-place at Alba; they had cut the old woman's arm from the shoulder; they had left it behind in the rifled coffin, and then hastily huddling up the body, they had fled southwards with their booty, while the poor nuns who had loved and buried their dead "mother," who had been shut by a trick into their own choir while the awful thing was done, were still singing the office, ignorant and happy.

The orphaned girl, remembering this passage and faced with her stepmother's death, looks into the reliquary and is visibly revolted by a "shrivelled horror." What Alan perceives as disdain prompts, in turn, his cold, stern reprimand, signaling to Laura the "break-down of the last vestiges and relics of the old relation."[19] This seemingly minor scene serves as a turning point for the novel. Unable to sustain his disapproval, Laura at last submits to Catholicism, proposing that she study for conversion and that she and Alan marry. The result of this submission is, ultimately, her suicide.

"Relic" here serves multiple purposes. Although Laura has been trained by her father to distrust all religions, her revulsion echoes that of the Protestant polemical characterization of Catholicism as a religion of "dead men's bones." The religious practices surrounding relics seemed vivid proof of the Catholic Church's refusal of enlightenment – rejecting reason and progress for a primitive superstition bound to the body. Laura shares the Protestant perception that relics are tokens of the Catholic's crude literalmindedness and gullibility (a credulous peasant tricked into worshipping shards and shreds) and of the Church's unclean obsession with the body and with death.

And yet the polemical critique of Catholicism implied by Laura's immediate disgust at the relic never appears in *Helbeck*. Instead, the relic first serves a plot function: a vehicle for the lovers' misunderstanding of one another. Their differing perceptions of the relic, and of each other, mark their distance. Ward next uses "relic" as an analogy for the persistence of Laura and Alan's past ("relics of the old relation"). Situated within yet another text – the life of St. Theresa that Laura has been reading – the relic conveys Laura's need to remain true to her dead father and to cope with her stepmother's dying. Finally, the invocation of St. Theresa would recall for Ward's 1898 audience another story of a young, badly educated woman casting about to make something meaningful of her life: Dorothea Brooke, "a Saint Theresa, foundress of nothing," thus reinforcing the sense that Laura is born into a world that has no place for her.

My point is that this relic is precisely a fragment torn from the body of Protestant belief that, though retroactively imagined as whole, was always fissured by Catholicism. Ward quickly de-consecrates the relic, but does not exorcise its associations. For what *is* it that Laura glimpses and that comes to Ward's aid as she finishes her novel? "A finger, was it? or a portion of one? Perhaps torn from some poor helpless one . . . ? And to such aids and helps must a human heart come in dying!"[20] Enclosed in a reliquary which is itself ensconced in a leather case, the relic harks back to those mysterious items covered with white cloth that priests carry through the passages of anti-Catholic novels, to the veiled bodies and faces that haunt their plots. Even when it is no longer a "threat" then, Catholicism lingers within Protestant nationalisms as a familiar yet partial presence reflecting the unstable identity of dominant cultures. A literary "leftover," turn-of-the-century anti-Catholicism points backwards to its earlier role as a disturbing excess. Persisting, vestigially, into the modern, stories of nuns and priests display Catholicism's stubborn failure to give way.

Notes

INTRODUCTION

1. Harriet Beecher Stowe, *My Wife and I, or Harry Henderson's History* (New York: Ford, 1872), p. 2.
2. See Jane Tompkins, *Sensational Designs: The Cultural Work of American Fiction, 1790–1860* (New York: Oxford University Press, 1985) for the most influential analysis of Stowe's rhetorical power.
3. Jonathan Loesberg, "The Ideology of Narrative Form in Sensation Fiction," *Representations* 13 (Winter 1986): 116.
4. Linda Colley and Walter Arnstein have both drawn attention to scholars' surprising tendency to dismiss evidence of eighteenth- and nineteenth-century anti-Catholicism as an "embarrassing and atavistic survival of an earlier age" (Colley, *Britons: Forging the Nation, 1707–1837* [New Haven: Yale University Press, 1992], p. 23) and a "retrospective sweeping under the carpet of Victorian propriety of one of the era's major sources of domestic disunity and disorder" (Arnstein, *Protestant Versus Catholic in Mid-Victorian England: Mr. Newdegate and the Nuns* [Columbia: University of Missouri Press, 1982], p. 1). One early exception to this denial is Billington's *The Protestant Crusade, 1800–1860: A Study of the Origins of American Nativism* (New York: Macmillan, 1961), still a standard study of American nativism. More recently, Arnstein, *Protestant Versus Catholic*; Edward Norman, *The English Catholic Church in the Nineteenth Century* (Oxford: Clarendon, 1984), and D. G. Paz, *Popular Anti-Catholicism in Mid-Victorian England* (Stanford: Stanford University Press, 1992), have contributed valuable historical work on nineteenth-century British anti-Catholicism.
5. Thomas J. Archdeacon, *Becoming American: An Ethnic History* (New York: Free Press, 1983).
6. E. R. Norman, *Anti-Catholicism in Victorian England* (New York: Barnes and Noble, 1968), p. 17.
7. See Dale Knobel, *America for the Americans: The Nativist Movement in the United States* (New York: Twayne, 1996); Paz, *Popular Anti-Catholicism*.
8. See, for example, the frontispiece to *The Princess of Viarna: Or, The Spanish Inquisition, in the Reign of the Emperor Charles the Fifth* (New York: Pudney & Russell, 1857), which reads: "To the Protestant community of this land of religious toleration, the following pages, aiming to elucidate, in a familiar manner,

the iniquities of priestcraft during a period of ecclesiastical supremacy over the mightiest of Roman Catholic empires, is fraternally dedicated by their author, in a fervent hope, that the historical experience of man's degradation in the past may forewarn enlightened children of Luther, that, although the Spanish Inquisition is nominally extinct, the religious spirit which created it, not only lives among us, but ardently struggles to re-erect, in every quarter of the globe, its blasphemous tribunal."

9. *Startling Facts for Native Americans called "Know-Nothings," or a Vivid Presentation of the Dangers to American Liberty, to be Apprehended from Foreign Influence* (New York: "Published at Nassau Street," 1855), p. 74.

10. William Sewell, *Hawkstone: A Tale of and for England in 184–* (London, 1845; New York: Garland, 1976), vol. 2, p. 380.

11. Indeed, Eugene Sue's widely read anti-Catholic novel, *The Wandering Jew* ([no city]: Chapman & Hall, 1844–45), becomes a resource for British and American writers. On the evolution of the image of the Wandering Jew, see George Anderson, *The Legend of the Wandering Jew* (Providence: Brown University Press, 1965).

12. See Colleen McDannell, *The Christian Home in Victorian America, 1840–1900* (Bloomington: Indiana University Press, 1986) on the differing material cultures of Protestant and Catholic homes.

13. Jenny Franchot, *Roads to Rome: The Antebellum Protestant Encounter with Catholicism* (Berkeley: University of California Press, 1994), p. 112.

14. *Ibid.*

15. James Parton, "Our Roman Catholic Brethren," *Atlantic Monthly* 21 (April 1868): 439–40; 21 (May 1868): 556.

16. John Maynard's work has prepared us to recognize the Victorian propensity to represent religious institutions as sexually marked and sexuality by means of religious discourse (*Victorian Discourses on Sexuality and Religion*, Cambridge: Cambridge University Press, 1993).

17. For a transatlantic study of the way these tensions manifested themselves in the nineteenth-century family, see Steven Mintz's discussion of the familial "prison of expectations" that demanded both autonomy and obedience (*A Prison of Expectations: The Family in Victorian Culture*, New York: New York University Press, 1983).

18. Benedict Anderson, *Imagined Communities: Reflections on the Origin and Spread of Nationalism*, rev. ed. (London: Verso, 1991), p. 195.

19. William Sewell, *Christian Politics* (Oxford: Parker, 1848), p. 74.

20. On the historical relation between the gothic and anti-Catholicism, see Sister Mary Tarr, *Catholicism in Gothic Fiction* (New York: Garland, 1979). See Priscilla Wald, *Constituting Americans: Cultural Anxiety and Narrative Form* (Durham, NC: Duke University Press, 1995) for a different reading of the role that the uncanny plays in the constituting of personal identity against and through official narratives of American nationhood.

21. Homi Bhabha, ed., *Nation and Narration* (New York: Routledge, 1990), p. 2.

22. Karen Halttunen, *Confidence Men and Painted Women: A Study of Middle-Class American Culture in America, 1830–1870* (New Haven: Yale University Press, 1982).

23. Robert Levine, *Conspiracy and Romance: Studies in Brockden Brown, Cooper, Hawthorne, and Melville* (Cambridge: Cambridge University Press, 1989), p. 12.

24. Bhabha, *Nation and Narration*, p. 4.

25. Thad Logan, *The Victorian Parlour* (Cambridge: Cambridge University Press, 2001), pp. 195–98.

26. See the subtitles for Charles Frothingham's *The Convent's Doom: A Tale of Charlestown in 1834*, 5th ed. (Boston: Graves & Weston, 1854) and *Six Hours in a Convent: or The Stolen Nuns! A Tale of Charlestown in 1834*, 1854, 8th ed. (Boston: Graves & Weston, 1855), Sewell's *Hawkstone*, and Emma Jane Worboise's *Overdale: or, the Story of a Pervert: A Tale for the Times* (London: Clack, 1869).

27. "Hard Church Novel," *The National Review* (July 1856): 131.

28. A few literary scholars have begun to examine the narratives of anti-Catholicism that were sketched out in early surveys by Margaret Maison, *Search Your Soul, Eustace: A Survey of the Religious Novel in the Victorian Age* (London: Sheed and Ward, [1961]), and Robert Lee Wolff, *Gains and Losses: Novels of Faith and Doubt in Victorian England* (New York: Garland, 1977), in particular, Franchot's *Roads to Rome*, and David Reynolds's work on religious and sensational fiction (*Faith in Fiction: The Emergence of Religious Literature in America*, Cambridge, MA: Harvard University Press, 1981), as well as Susan David Bernstein's study of the Victorian confessional (*Confessional Subjects: Revelations of Gender and Power in Victorian Literature and Culture*, Chapel Hill: University of North Carolina Press, 1997) and Robert Levine's suggestive exploration of the ties between conspiracy and American Romance (*Conspiracy and Romance*). Nancy Bentley's essay on anti-Mormon fiction looks at a different aspect of polemical religious fiction ("Marriage as Treason: Polygamy, Nation, and the Novel," in *The Futures of American Studies*, ed. Donald Pease and Robyn Wiegman, Durham, NC: Duke University Press, 2002).

29. Bhabha, *Nation and Narration*, p. 2.

30. Franchot, *Roads to Rome*, p. xvii.

31. Hawthorne's continuing importance to his (reluctant) heirs, William Dean Howells and Henry James, is a topic in my Chapter 6.

32. David Reynolds, *Faith in Fiction*.

33. Ellis Hanson, *Decadence and Catholicism* (Cambridge, MA: Harvard University Press, 1997); David Hilliard, "UnEnglish and Unmanly: Anglo-Catholicism and Homosexuality," *Victorian Studies* 25, no. 2 (1982): 181–210.

34. While *Anti-Catholicism and Nineteenth-Century Fiction* "rediscovers" some obscure and forgotten novels, it does not catalogue every example of anti-Catholicism in nineteenth-century fiction. Significant sources for such bibliography remain Billington's *Protestant Crusade*, Franchot's *Roads to Rome*, and Wolff's *Gains and Losses*, on which I have drawn extensively and in a number of cases supplement.

35. John Sutherland, *The Stanford Companion to Victorian Fiction* (Stanford: Stanford University Press, 1989), p. 1. Work like Bill Brown's anthology of dime novels, *Reading the West: An Anthology of Dime Westerns* (Boston: Bedford, 1997) and reprintings like the Schomburg Library of Nineteenth-Century Black Women Writers have, in recent years, helped to expand our scholarly scope.

36. Quoted in Miriam Allott, *The Brontës: The Critical Heritage* (London: Routledge, 1974), p. 174.

37. "The Catholic Question," *Western Monthly Magazine* 3 (1835): 379.

38. Surveys of nineteenth-century religious fiction, like those of Reynolds, *Faith in Fiction*, and Wolff, *Gains and Losses*, suggest some of this variety and, with it, areas for further study.

39. See Peter Brooks, "The Turn of *The American*," in *New Essays on* The American, ed. Martha Banta (Cambridge: Cambridge University Press, 1987), 43–67.

40. Elizabeth Barnes, *States of Sympathy: Seduction and Democracy in the American Novel* (New York: Columbia University Press, 1997), and James Twitchell, *Forbidden Partners: The Incest Taboo in Modern Culture* (New York, Columbia University Press, 1987), are among those who have discussed the prevalence of American tales of incest.

41. See Bernstein, *Confessional Subjects*, for another reading of *Villette* in the context of anti-Catholic literature.

42. In American Studies, see, for example, the 1998 "No More Separate Spheres" issue of *American Literature* edited by Davidson and the 1999 issue of *differences*, edited by Gould, on "Revisiting the 'Feminization' of American Culture." Scholars of British fiction and culture, like Daniel Bivona, *Desire and Contradiction: Imperial Visions and Domestic Debates in Victorian Literature* (New York: St. Martin's, 1990); Patrick Brantlinger, "What is 'Sensational' about the 'Sensational Novel'?," *Nineteenth-Century Fiction* 37, no. 1 (1982): 1–28; Deidre David, *Rule Britannia: Woman, Empire, and Victorian Writing* (Ithaca: Cornell University Press, 1995); and Gayatri Spivak, "Three Women's Texts and a Critique of Imperialism," *Critical Inquiry* 12 (1985): 246–61, have explored the interpenetration of the imperial and the domestic.

43. See Carolyn Porter's essay, "What We Know That We Don't Know: Remapping American Literary Studies," *American Literary History* 6, no. 3 (1994): 467–526, for a survey of work on the literature of the Americas, an area that has become a growing field.

44. Lawrence Buell, "American Literary Emergence as a Postcolonial Phenomenon," *American Literary History* 4 (1992): 411–42, lists the handful of works on Anglo-American literary relations, concluding, "This work, however, has not yet seriously affected the way Americanists conduct business as usual," p. 414.

45. Thus, my study in some ways resembles more closely the work of scholars like David Shields, *Oracles of Empire: Poetry, Politics, and Commerce in British America, 1690–1750* (Chicago: University of Chicago Press, 1990), who are exploring the earlier literature of "British America."

46. According to Vernon Bogdanor, ed., Introduction, *Lothair*, by Benjamin Disraeli (New York: Oxford University Press, 1975), pp. vii–xvii, "15,000 copies [of *Lothair*] were sold on the first day of publication, and it was said that no book had been so popular since *Uncle Tom's Cabin*" (ix). Frank Luther Mott, *Golden Multitudes: The Story of Best Sellers in the United States* (New York: Macmillan, 1947) lists *Lothair* among his "better-sellers."

47. Anti-clericalism was, of course, a powerful force in other European cultures, French and Spanish in particular. Indeed, nineteenth-century British and American polemical writers borrow heavily from the work of Jules Michelet and Eugene Sue. See Bernstein, *Confessional Subjects*; Franchot, *Roads to Rome*; and Chapter 4 of this study.

48. I borrow the term from Brown's Introduction to his edition of dime novels (*Reading the West*).

49. Lauren Berlant, *The Anatomy of National Fantasy* (Chicago: University of Chicago Press, 1991), p. 5.

50. See Franchot, *Roads to Rome*; McDannell, *The Christian Home*.

51. *The Arch Bishop: Or, Romanism in the United States* by Orvilla S. Belisle (Philadelphia: Smith, 1855); *The Convict: Or, The Conspirator's Victim. A Novel, Written in Prison* (New York: Dick & Fitzgerald, 1854); and *The Jesuit's Daughter: A Novel for Americans to Read* (1854, Reprint, New York: Burgess and Day, 1863) by Ned Buntline (Edward Zane Carroll Judson); *Stanhope Burleigh: The Jesuits in Our Home* (New York: Stringer and Townsend, 1855) by Helen Dhu (Charles Edwards Lester); *The Countess: or, The Inquisitor's Punishments. A Tale of Spain* (Boston: Gleason's, 1847) by William Engolls; *New York: Its Upper Ten and Lower Million* (1853, Reprint, Upper Saddle River: Literature House, 1970) by George Lippard; *One Link in the Chain of Apostolic Succession; or The Crimes of Alexander Borgia* (Boston: Hinks, 1854); and *The Princess of Viarna: or, The Spanish Inquisition in the Reign of Charles the Fifth* (New York: Pudney & Russell, 1857).

52. See Spivak's breakthrough work ("Three Women's Texts") on how *Jane Eyre* evidences Brontë's participation in the colonialism of her time.

53. For a recent study of sensationalism, marriage and the law, see Marlene Tromp, *The Private Rod: Marital Violence, Sensation, and the Law in Victorian Britain* (Charlottesville: University Press of Virginia, 2000).

54. [H. L. Mansel], "Sensational Novels," *Quarterly Review* 113 (April 1863): 251–68. Quoted in Patrick Brantlinger, "What is 'Sensational' about the 'Sensational Novel'?", p. 7.

55. Howells and James thus provide a late example of the connection that Levine, *Conspiracy and Romance*, explores between conspiracy and romance in antebellum fiction.

56. On gender and genre in nineteenth-century America, see Michael Davitt Bell, *The Development of American Romance: The Sacrifice of Relation* (Chicago: University of Chicago Press, 1983), and Alfred Habegger, *Gender, Fantasy, and Realism in American Literature* (New York: Columbia University Press, 1982).

57. T. Jackson Lears, *No Place of Grace: Antimodernism and the Transformation of American Culture, 1880–1920* (New York: Pantheon, 1981), 183–215.

58. Nina Baym, "Melodramas of Beset Manhood," *American Quarterly* 33 (1981): 123–39.

59. Nancy Cott, *The Bonds of Womanhood: "Woman's Sphere" in New England, 1780–1835* (New Haven: Yale University Press, 1977); Jane Tompkins, *Sensational Designs*.

60. Susan Mizruchi, ed., *Religion and Cultural Studies* (Princeton: Princeton University Press, 2001), p. x. A special issue of *Victorian Literature and Culture*, 31, no. 1 (2003) which appeared after this manuscript had been completed, is a promising sign that this work is being taken up.

61. "Religious Stories," *Fraser's Magazine* 38, no. 224 (Aug. 1848): 150.

1 AWFUL DISCLOSURES: THE ESCAPED NUN'S TALE

1. Levine, *Conspiracy and Romance*, pp. 107–08.

2. Billington, *Protestant Crusade*, pp. 367, 345–51.

3. Franchot, *Roads to Rome*.

4. Archdeacon, *Becoming American*; David H. Bennett, *The Party of Fear: From Nativist Movements to the New Right in American History* (Chapel Hill: University of North Carolina Press, 1988); Billington, *Protestant Crusade*; Halttunen, *Confidence Men*; Alice Felt Tyler, *Freedom's Ferment: Phases of American Social History from the Colonial Period to the Outbreak of the Civil War* (New York: Harper, 1944).

5. On the connection between the public school movement and anti-Catholicism, see David Nasaw, *Schooled to Order: A Social History of Public Schooling in the United States* (New York: Oxford University Press, 1979); David Tyack and Elizabeth Hansot, *Managers of Virtue: Public School Leadership in America, 1820–1980* (New York: Basic, 1982).

6. See, for example, Thomas Ford Caldicott, *Hannah Corcoran: An Authentic Narrative of Her Conversion From Romanism, Her Abduction From Charlestown, and The Treatment She Received During Her Absence* (Boston: Gould and Lincoln, 1853); Frothingham, *Convent's Doom* and *Six Hours*; Harry Hazel [Justin Jones], *The Nun of St. Ursula, Or The Burning of the Convent. A Romance of Mt. Benedict* (Boston: Gleason, 1845).

7. Franchot, *Roads to Rome*, p. 162.

8. Sales figures are from Billington, *Protestant Crusade*, and Mott, *Golden Multitudes*. Edition is a vexed term in studies of nineteenth-century publishing; nonetheless, these multiple "editions" indicate substantial sales. David S. Reynolds's *Beneath the American Renaissance: The Subversive Imagination in the Age of Emerson and Melville* (Cambridge, MA: Harvard University Press, 1988) discusses canonical authors' reading and rewriting of popular anti-Catholic literature.

9. On women's shaping influence on American Protestantism, see Cott, *Bonds of Womanhood*; Ann Douglas, *The Feminization of American Culture* (New York:

Knopf, 1977); Mary Ryan, *Cradle of the Middle Class: The Family in Oneida County, New York, 1790–1865* (Cambridge: Cambridge University Press, 1981); and Kathryn Kish Sklar, *Catharine Beecher: A Study in American Domesticity* (New York: Norton, 1976).

10. See Nina Baym, *Woman's Fiction: A Guide to Novels by and about Women in America, 1820–1870* (Ithaca: Cornell University Press, 1978).

11. Reynolds, *Faith in Fiction*, p. 181.

12. Mott, *Golden Multitudes*.

13. Levine, *Conspiracy and Romance*, p. 110.

14. Rosamond Culbertson, *Rosamond: or, a Narrative of the Captivity and Sufferings of an American Female Under the Popish Priests, in the Island of Cuba With a Full Disclosure of Their Manners and Customs, Written by Herself*, 2nd ed. (New York: Leavitt, Lord, 1836), p. 14.

15. *Ibid.*, p. 2.

16. On convents as priests' brothels, see, for example, Andrew Cross, *Priests' Prisons For Women, Or A Consideration of the Question, Whether Unmarried Foreign Priests Ought To Be Permitted To Erect Prisons, Inot* [sic] *Which, Under Pretence of Religion, To Seduce Or Entrap, Or By Force Compel Young Women to Enter, And After They Have Secured Their Property, Keep Them in Confinement, And Compel Them, As Their Slaves, To Submit Themselves To Their Will, Under The Penalty Of Flogging Or The Dungeon?* (Baltimore: Sherwood, 1854), as well as William Hogan, "a former Roman Catholic priest," whose works were extremely popular (*Auricular Confession and Popish Nunneries*, 1845, 3rd ed. [London: Arthur Hall, 1847]; *A Synopsis of Popery, As It Was and As It Is* [Boston: Saxton & Kelt, 1845]).

17. For an extended discussion of the Charlestown burning, see Nancy Lusignan Schultz, *Fire and Roses: The Burning of Charlestown Convent, 1834* (New York: Free Press, 2000).

18. Franchot, *Roads to Rome*, p. 138.

19. See Billington, *Protestant Crusade*, pp. 53–84, for a fuller account of these events.

20. Beecher's most popular anti-Catholic sermon was published as *A Plea for the West* (1835, Reprint, New York: Arno, 1977). His son, Edward Beecher, who was also involved in anti-Catholic activities, published *The Papal Conspiracy Exposed and Protestantism Defended in the Light of Reason* in 1855 (New York: Arno, 1977). On his daughter Harriet Beecher Stowe's shifting attitudes towards Catholicism, see Joan Hedrick, *Harriet Beecher Stowe: A Life* (New York: Oxford University Press, 1994).

21. Rebecca Theresa Reed, *Six Months in a Convent, or, The Narrative of Rebecca Theresa Reed, Who was Under the Influence of the Roman Catholics about Two Years, and an Inmate of the Ursuline Convent on Mount Benedict, Charlestown, Mass., Nearly Six Months, in the Years 1831–32 With Some Preliminary Suggestions by the Committee of Publication* (1835, Reprint, New York: Arno, 1977), p. 13.

22. Mary Anne Ursula Moffatt [Sister Mary Edmund St. George], *Answer to Six Months in a Convent, Exposing Its Falsehoods and Manifold Absurdities by The Lady Superior with Some Preliminary Remarks* (Boston: Eastburn, 1835).

23. Billington, *Protestant Crusade*.

24. Because I want to focus on fears about religion in America in this chapter, I do not discuss fictions written and published in America that describe convents and escapes set in England or continental Europe, for example, *Helen Mulgrave; or, Jesuit Executorship: Being Passages in the Life of a Seceder from Romanism. An Autobiography* (New York: De Witt & Davenport, 1852) and *Sister Agnes; or The Captive Nun. A Picture of Convent Life. By a Clergyman's Widow* (New York: Riker, Thorne, 1854).

25. Reynolds, *Faith in Fiction*, p. 183.

26. *Ibid.*

27. Theodore Dwight, *Open Convents: Or Nunneries and Popish Seminaries Dangerous To The Morals, And Degrading To The Character Of A Republican Community* (New York: Van Nostrand and Dwight, 1836), p. 116.

28. *Six Months*, p. 22.

29. *Six Hours*, p. 5.

30. Christopher Looby, "George Thompson's 'Romance of the Real': Transgression and Taboo in American Sensation Fiction," *American Literature* 65 [1993]: 651–72. Looby's idea is borne out in the antebellum exposé par excellence: the slave narrative. For example, Jean Yellin describes Harriet Jacobs's use of fictional formulae in *Incidents in the Life of a Slave Girl Written by Herself*, ed. Jean Fagan Yellin (Cambridge, MA: Harvard University Press, 1987, pp. xiii–xxxiv), and Harriet Beecher Stowe documents the factual basis of *Uncle Tom's Cabin; or, Life Among the Lowly* (ed. Kathryn Kish Sklar, New York: Library of America, 1982) in prefatory remarks, in narrative intrusions, and in the subsequently published *A Key to Uncle Tom's Cabin; Presenting the Original Facts and Documents upon Which the Story is Founded. Together with Corroborative Statements Verifying the Truth of the Work* (Boston: Jewett, 1853).

31. Alexander Welsh, *Strong Representations: Narrative and Circumstantial Evidence in England* (Baltimore: Johns Hopkins University Press, 1992), pp. ix, 42.

32. Reed, *Six Months*, p. 40.

33. *Ibid.*, pp. 64, 105, 107.

34. Maria Monk, *Awful Disclosures of The Hotel Dieu Nunnery of Montreal, Revised, with an Appendix* (1836, Reprint, New York: Arno, 1977), p. 253; Caldicott, *Hannah Corcoran*, p. iii.

35. On the juridical history of this claim, see Welsh, *Strong Representations*, pp. 1–42.

36. Reed, *Six Months*, p. 264.

37. Welsh, *Strong Representations*, p. 9.

38. Culbertson, *Rosamond*, pp. 10, 23, 28, 23.

39. On the importance of probability, see Welsh, *Strong Representations*, p. 69.

40. Reed, *Six Months*, pp. 146–47.
41. William Earle Binder, *Madelon Hawley, or, The Jesuit and His Victim. A Revelation of Romanism* (New York: Dayton, 1857), pp. 172–73.
42. Culbertson, *Rosamond*, p. 58.
43. Norwood Damon [Mary Magdalen], *The Chronicles of Mount Benedict. A Tale of the Ursuline Convent. The Quasi Production of Mary Magdalen* (Boston: Printed for the Publisher, 1837), pp. xiii, 117, 118.
44. Reed, *Six Months*, pp. 40; Hogan, *Synopsis of Popery*, pp. 9–10, 100.
45. Monk, *Awful Disclosures*, pp. 71, 354.
46. Davidson, *Revolution and the Word: The Rise of the Novel in America* (New York: Oxford University Press, 1986), p. 127. On nineteenth-century American women and publicity, see Nina Baym, *American Women Writers and the Work of History, 1790–1860* (New Brunswick: Rutgers University Press, 1995) and *Woman's Fiction*; Richard Brodhead, *Cultures of Letters: Scenes of Reading and Writing in Nineteenth-Century America* (Chicago: University of Chicago Press, 1993); Mary Kelley, *Private Woman, Public Stage: Literary Domesticity in Nineteenth-Century America* (New York: Oxford University Press, 1984).
47. Reed, *Six Months*, p. 13.
48. Caldicott, *Hannah Corcoran*, p. 128; Culbertson, *Rosamond*, p. 10; Monk, *Awful Disclosures*, pp. 4, 5; Franchot, *Roads to Rome*, p. 112.
49. Billington reproduces this epigraph in the 1962 facsimile edition (*Awful Disclosures of Maria Monk* [1836, Reprint, Hamden, Conn.: Archon Books, 1962]; the Arno reprint omits the frontispiece (Monk, *Awful Disclosures*).
50. Halttunen, *Confidence Men*, p. 58.
51. See Lionel Trilling, *Sincerity and Authenticity: The Charles Eliot Norton Lectures, 1969–1970* (Cambridge, MA: Harvard University Press, 1971); see Welsh, *Strong Representations*, on sincerity.
52. Reed, *Six Months* p. 35.
53. Mrs. Lucinda Larned, *The American Nun; or The Effects of Romance* (Boston: Otis, Broaders, 1836), p. 117.
54. See Caldicott, *Hannah Corcoran*, p. 129: "The only thing concerning which there can be any serious question in the minds of the candid will be the propriety, righteousness or lawfulness, of divulging that which Hannah promised to keep secret."
55. *The Escaped Nun: Or, Disclosures of Convent Life; And The Confessions Of A Sister Of Charity. Giving A More Minute Detail of Their Inner Life, And A Bolder Revelation Of The Mysteries And Secrets Of Nunneries, Than Have Ever Before Been Submitted To The American Public* (New York: De Witt & Davenport, 1855), pp. 214–15.
56. Culbertson, *Rosamond*, p. 105.
57. See Ruth Bernard Yeazell on fainting in *Pamela* (p. 85) and on the connections among women's chastity, modesty, and unconsciousness (*Fictions of Modesty: Women and Courtship in the English Novel* [Chicago: University of Chicago Press, 1991]).

58. Culbertson, *Rosamond*, p. 106.
59. See Jones, *Nun of St. Ursula*, as well as *The Escaped Nun*, whose protagonist describes herself as an "involuntary nun": "They disposed of me all this morning as they pleased, for I was insensible of its lapse. I neither knew what was done nor what was said. . . . I pronounced some vows, but I have no recollection of them, and I became a nun as unconsciously as I was made a Christian" (p. 52).
60. Billington, *Protestant Crusade*, p. 108.
61. My point is not, of course, that Monk's story is true but that both nineteenth- and twentieth-century commentators consider her sexual status a relevant test of the story's truth.
62. Lizzie St. John Eckel Harper, *Maria Monk's Daughter: An Autobiography* (New York: United States Publishing, 1874), pp. 170–71.
63. Monk, *Awful Disclosures*, p. 4.
64. [Mr. De Potter], *Female Convents. Secrets of Nunneries Disclosed* (New York: Appleton, 1834), p. ix.
65. Larned, *American Nun*, p. v. Both David Brion Davis, "Some Themes of Counter-Subversion: An Analysis of Anti-Masonic, Anti-Catholic, and Anti-Mormon Literature," *Mississippi Valley Historical Review* 47 (1960–61): 205–24, and Bennett, *Party of Fear*, suggest that in describing sexual profligacy, these stories are expressing contemporary concern about declining moral standards, even as they provide a medium for fantasy. Bennett also links the sadism of these narratives to Protestant men's insecurity during this period.
66. Billington, *Protestant Crusade*, p. 69; Franchot, *Roads to Rome*, pp. 135–41.
67. Billington, *Protestant Crusade*, p. 69.
68. I have not located circulation figures for 1835, but J. C. G. Kennedy, *Catalogue of the Newspapers and Periodicals Published in the United States* (New York: Livingston, 1852), lists the 1850 circulation as 10,200.
69. "The Ursuline Convent," *Christian Watchman* March 20, 1835: 46.
70. Of the fourteen parents who write, only one is a woman.
71. "Another Effort of Papal Benevolence, Rendered Abortive by Protestant Obstinacy," *Baltimore Literary and Religious Magazine* 5, no. 9 (Sept. 1839): 422.
72. "Review of the Correspondence Between the Archbishop and the Mayor of Baltimore," *Baltimore Literary and Religious Magazine* 5, no. 11 (Nov. 1839): 485.
73. "Review of the Case of Olevia Neal the Carmelite Nun, Commonly Called Sister Isabella," *Baltimore Literary and Religious Magazine* 5, no. 10 (Oct. 1839): 441.
74. See, for example, Cott, *Bonds of Womanhood*; Douglas, *Feminization of American Culture*; Ryan, *Cradle of the Middle Class*; Sklar, *Catharine Beecher*.
75. Tompkins, *Sensational Designs*, p. 142.
76. Larned, *American Nun*, pp. v, vi. Narratives that directly attack the practice of sending American Protestant girls to convent schools include Rachel

Macrindell's *The School Girl in France; or, The Snares of Popery: A Warning to Protestants against Education in Catholic Seminaries* (Philadelphia: Hooker, 1843) (also published as *The Protestant Girl in a French Nunnery*) and Pamela Cowan's *The American Convent as a School for Protestant Children* (New York: Protestant Episcopal Society for the Promotion of Evangelical Knowledge, 1870).

77. Nina Baym, "Onward Christian Women: Sarah J. Hale's History of the World," *New England Quarterly* 63 (1990): 249–70; *eadem, American Women Writers*; Tonkovich, "Rhetorical Power in the Victorian Parlor: *Godey's Lady's Book* and the Gendering of Nineteenth-Century Rhetoric," in *Oratorical Culture in Nineteenth-Century America: Transformation in the Theory and Practice of Rhetoric*, ed. Gregory Clark and S. Michael Halloran (Carbondale: Southern Illinois University Press, 1993), pp. 158–83.

78. E.g., Cott, *Bonds of Womanhood*; Douglas, *Feminization of American Culture*; Sklar, *Catharine Beecher*; Tompkins, *Sensational Designs*.

79. Baym, *American Women Writers*; Franchot, *Roads to Rome*; Hedrick, *Harriet Beecher Stowe*.

80. For an analysis of Hale's construction of her *Godey's* readership as "conversational partners" (p. 167), see Nicole Tonkovich, "Rhetorical Power," pp. 158–83.

81. Baym, *American Women Writers*, pp. 46–66.

82. Sarah Josepha Hale, "The Ursuline Convent," *American Ladies' Magazine* 7 (Sept. 1834): 422, 418, 425.

83. Sara Josepha Hale, "How to Prevent the Increase of Convents," *American Ladies' Magazine* 7 (Nov. 1834): 519.

84. Nicole Tonkovich Hoffman, "*Legacy* Profile: Sarah Josepha Hale," *Legacy* 7, no. 2 (1990): 49.

85. Hale, "How to Prevent," p. 521.

86. *Ibid.*, p. 561. Hale would later support the efforts of Catherine Beecher (Lyman's daughter) to educate young women, serving as a member of her American Woman's Educational Association (Sklar, *Catherine Beecher*, p. 224).

87. Hale, "How to Prevent," pp. 563, 561, 564. On Hale's support for female missionaries, see Baym, "Onward."

88. Hale also makes some minor revisions, including changing the last name of the father in the story from M'Leod to Marshall.

89. Sarah Josepha Hale, *Traits of American Life* (Philadelphia: Carey, 1835), p. 51.

90. *Ibid.*, p. 52.

91. *Ibid.*, pp. 53, 52.

92. On this transformation, see George Forgie, *Patricide in the House Divided: A Psychological Interpretation of Lincoln and His Age* (New York: Norton, 1979), and Karen Halttunen, *Confidence Men*. Clark and Halloran's volume, *Oratorical Culture in Nineteenth-Century America: Transformations in the Theory and Practice of Rhetoric* (Carbondale: Southern Illinois University Press, 1993), charts the rhetorical changes that accompany this ideological shift.

93. Hale, *Traits*, pp. 54–55.

94. This is a project that Hale shares with the writers and painters of the Hudson River schools. While there is a substantial scholarship on canonical authors' engagement with the work of storying the American landscape, it is symptomatic of the gender divide that still obtains in American studies that little attention has been paid to women writers' share in this task. On male writers' and painters' work, see for example, James Callow, *Kindred Spirits: Knickerbocker Writers and American Artists, 1807–1855* (Chapel Hill: University of North Carolina Press, 1967); Robert Ferguson, "William Cullen Bryant: The Creative Context of the Poet," *NEQ* 53 (1980): 31–63; Blake Nevius, *Cooper's Landscapes: An Essay on the Picturesque Vision* (Berkeley: University of California Press, 1976); Barbara Novak, *Nature and Culture: American Landscape and Painting, 1825–75* (New York: Oxford University Press, 1980); and Donald Ringe, *The Pictorial Mode: Space and Time in the Art of Bryant, Irving, and Cooper* (Lexington: University of Kentucky Press, 1971). See Baym, *American Women Writers*, pp. 67–91, for a discussion of how "topographical" poems written by women historicized local sites. See Brodhead, *Cultures of Letters*, for connections between travel literature, local-color writing, and women writers in the second half of the nineteenth century.
95. Hale, "The Romance of Travelling," p. 187.
96. Quoted in Tonkovich, "Rhetorical Power," p. 158.
97. *Ibid.*
98. Hale, *Traits*, p. 56.
99. *Ibid.*, pp. 58, 62.
100. See, for example, Cowan, *American Convent*, and Larned, *American Nun*.
101. Hale, *Traits*, pp. 85, 86, 109.
102. *Ibid.*, p. 87. Franchot, *Roads to Rome*, p. 108, also delineates the Jesuit as an "alternatively constructed masculine power" who rivals and threatens the Protestant father.
103. On the depiction of nuns in nineteenth-century paintings, see Susan Casteras, "Virgin Vows: the Early Victorian Artists' Portrayal of Nuns and Novices," *Victorian Studies* 24 (1981): 157–84. For nineteenth-century attitudes towards sisterhoods, see Franchot, *Roads to Rome*, and Martha Vicinus, *Independent Women: Work and Community for Single Women, 1850–1920* (Chicago: University of Chicago Press, 1985).
104. Hale, *Traits*, pp. 65, 73.
105. McDannell, *The Christian Home*, pp. 152, 132, 152, 154.
106. Hale, *Woman's Record; or, Sketches of All Distinguished Women from the Creation to A.D. 1854. Arranged in four eras. With selections from female writers of every age*, 2nd ed. (New York: Harper, 1855), p. 152. On *Woman's Record* as Protestant women's history, see also Baym, "Onward" and "Sarah Hale, Political Writer," in *Feminism and American Literary History* (New Brunswick: Rutgers University Press, 1992), pp. 167–82.
107. Hale, *Traits*, p. 90.
108. Brodhead, *Cultures of Letters*; Tompkins, *Sensational Designs*.
109. Hale, *Woman's Record*, p. 152.

110. Anderson, *Imagined Communities*, p. 7.
111. Baym, *American Women Writers*, p. 47.
112. Franchot, *Roads to Rome*, p. 128.

2 THE DEAD FATHER AND THE RULE OF RELIGION:
THE OXFORD MOVEMENT

1. Vicinus, *Independent Women*.
2. Sewell, *Hawkstone*, 2: 39.
3. Other anti-Tractarian novels include Charles Maurice Davies, *Philip Paternoster. A Tractarian Love-Story* (1858, Reprint, New York: Garland, 1975); Anne Howard, *Mary Spencer: A Tale for the Times* (1844, Reprint, New York: Garland, 1975); and Lady Catherine Long, *Sir Roland Ashton. A Tale of the Times* (1844, Reprint, New York: Garland, 1975).
4. Both novelists express tolerance for what they see as the mistaken, but relatively benign, Catholicism of the older British families who had long been recusant; their enmity is reserved for the virulent new strain of "Romanism" or "popery" infecting the Church of England through Oxford as well as, in Sewell's case, by what he sees as an uncivilized Irish Catholic mob invading England. On the general distinction made in nineteenth-century England between the newly conspicuous "Roman" Catholic party and the "Old" or "English" (Roman) Catholics, see Edward Norman, *English Catholic Church*, pp. 1–28.
5. Exceptions to this rule include Joseph Ellis Baker, *The Novel and the Oxford Movement* (Princeton: Princeton University Press, 1932); Elisabeth Jay, *Faith and Doubt in Victorian Fiction* (London: Macmillan, 1986); U. C. Knoepflmacher, *The Victorian Novel of Religious Humanism: A Study of George Eliot, Walter Pater, and Samuel Butler* (Princeton: Princeton University Press, 1970).
6. As Paz, *Popular Anti-Catholicism*, p. 19, has argued, "there were varieties of anti-Catholicisms that served several purposes, social, political, and theological, according to the needs and histories of specific groups and locales."
7. See, for example, William Sewell's defense of "Oxford Theology," *Quarterly Review* 63 (March 1839): 526–72.
8. Arnstein, *Protestant Versus Catholic*, pp. 40–42. On the threat of Irish Catholics in England, see Paz, *Popular Anti-Catholicism*; John Wolffe, *The Protestant Crusade in Great Britain, 1829–1860* (Oxford: Clarendon, 1991); as well as the discussion of Sinclair in Chapter 4.
9. Owen Chadwick, *The Victorian Church*, vol. 1, 1966 (London: SCM, 1987), pp. 167–211, 41.
10. David Roberts, *Paternalism in Early Victorian England* (New Brunswick: Rutgers University Press, 1979), p. 2.
11. Sewell, *Christian Politics*, p. 74.
12. *Ibid.*, p. 206.
13. Paz, *Popular Anti-Catholicism*, p. 51.

14. Sewell, *Hawkstone*, 2: 380.

15. *Ibid.*, 1: 334, 335. See Chapter 4 for how Mary Stuart continued to stand for the Catholic threat in the nineteenth-century Protestant imagination.

16. Sewell, *Christian Politics*, pp. 389, 388; Herbert Sussman, *Victorian Masculinities: Manhood and Masculine Poetics in Early Victorian Literature and Art* (Cambridge: Cambridge University Press, 1995), pp. 55–61.

17. Roberts, *Paternalism in Early Victorian England*, p. 38; Lionel James, *A Forgotten Genius: Sewell of St. Columba's and Radley* (London: Faber, 1945), p. 46, traces Sewell's focus on teaching England's youth to his break with the Tractarians: "Sewell, driven in upon himself, concentrated more and more on the educational side."

18. Lionel James, *Forgotten Genius*, p. ix; Sewell quoted in Lionel James, pp. 143, 294. In *Christian Politics*, p. 59, Sewell asks: "How can the same person be both greater and less, master and subject, in relation to another? It is possible, because there are two distinct elements of moral authority in the human mind, – one, power, and force and energy; the other weakness."

19. John Chandos, *Boys Together: English Public Schools 1800–1864* (New Haven: Yale University Press, 1984).

20. Richard Brodhead, *Cultures of Letters*. See Mintz, *Prison of Expectations*, for a discussion of the transatlantic ubiquity of this ideal.

21. Sewell quoted in Chandos, *Boys Together*, p. 343.

22. Sewell quoted in Lionel James, *Forgotten Genius*, p. 293.

23. Sewell, *Hawkstone*, 2: 307.

24. *Ibid.*, 1: 168, 2: 345, 1: 208.

25. Sewell, *Christian Politics*, p. 74.

26. Sewell, *Hawkstone*, 1: 241–42, 242.

27. *Ibid.*, 1: 319, 320.

28. Sewell, *Christian Politics*, p. 61; *Hawkstone*, 1: 248.

29. Sewell, *Hawkstone*, 1: 251, 3: 414, 1: 336, 337.

30. Sigmund Freud, *Totem and Taboo. The Standard Edition of the Complete Psychological Works of Sigmund Freud*, trans. James Strachey, vol. 13 (London: Hogarth, 1953), pp. 141–42.

31. *Ibid.*, pp. 143, 146.

32. *Ibid.*, p. 141.

33. Sewell, *Hawkstone*, 1: 326, 1: 107–08, 2: 327.

34. E.g., Wolff, *Gains and Losses*.

35. Sewell, *Hawkstone*, 2: 421–22.

36. Arnstein, *Protestant Versus Catholic*; G. F. A. Best. "Popular Protestantism in Victorian Britain," in *Ideas and Institutions of Victorian Britain*, ed. Robert Robson (London: Bell, 1967).

37. William Sewell, "Romanism in Ireland," *Quarterly Review* 67 (Dec. 1840): 135. On the stereotype of the Jew as vengeful, see Harley Erdman, *Staging the Jew: The Performance of an American Ethnicity, 1860–1920* (New Brunswick: Rutgers University Press, 1997).

38. On the Christian theologies at work in stories of the Wandering Jew, see George Anderson, *Legend of the Wandering Jew* (Providence: Brown University Press, 1965).

39. Sewell, *Hawkstone*, 2: 405, 421, 422.

40. See Jessica Benjamin's argument, *The Bonds of Love: Psychoanalysis, Feminism, and the Problem of Domination* (New York: Pantheon, 1988), that sado-masochism is driven by the desire for recognition.

41. Sewell, *Hawkstone*, 2: 39. On Protestant conceptions of Roman Catholicism as Oriental, see Chapter 4.

42. On Trollope's industrial fiction, see Rosemarie Bodenheimer, *The Politics of Story in Victorian Social Fiction* (Ithaca: Cornell University Press, 1988); Catherine Gallagher, *The Industrial Reformation of English Fiction, 1832–1867* (Chicago: University of Chicago Press, 1985); Joseph Kestner, *Protest and Reform: The British Social Narrative by Women, 1827–1867* (Madison: University of Wisconsin Press, 1985). Helen Heineman, *Mrs. Trollope: The Triumphant Feminine in the Nineteenth Century* (Athens, OH: Ohio University Press, 1979), pp. 107–09, 230–31. In his survey of Victorian religious fiction, Wolff, *Gains and Losses*, p. 40, describes *Father Eustace* as "readable" and "arresting as a piece of popular psychology."

43. Arnstein, *Protestant Versus Catholic*, p. 214.

44. Francis Milton Trollope, *Father Eustace: A Tale of the Jesuits*. 3 vols. (1847, Reprint, London: Garland, 1975), 1: 328.

45. Sutherland, *Stanford Companion*, pp. 638–39.

46. Teresa Ransom, *Fanny Trollope: A Remarkable Life* (New York: St. Martin's, 1995), p. 166; Lucy Poate Stebbins and Richard Poate Stebbins, *The Trollopes: The Chronicle of a Writing Family* (New York: Columbia University Press, 1945), p. 120.

47. Frances Eleanor Trollope, *Frances Trollope: Her Life and Literary Work*, 2 vols. (London: Bentley, 1895), 2: 84.

48. Tamar Heller, *Dead Secrets: Wilkie Collins and the Female Gothic* (New Haven: Yale University Press, 1992), pp. 19–21; Trollope, *Father Eustace*, 2: 275–76.

49. Arnstein, *Protestant Versus Catholic*; Best, "Popular Protestantism"; Norman, *Anti-Catholicism*. Chadwick, *The Victorian Church*, 1: 503–04. For more on the confessional, see Chapter 5.

50. Trollope, *Father Eustace*, 1: 162.

51. Best, "Popular Protestantism"; Maison, *Search Your Soul, Eustace*; Wolff, *Gains and Losses*; Chadwick, *The Victorian Church*, 1: 177, 196.

52. Pusey quoted in James Eli Adams, *Dandies and Desert Saints: Styles of Victorian Manhood* (Ithaca: Cornell University Press, 1995), p. 90; p. 95.

53. Trollope, *Father Eustace*, 1: 162, 1: 241, 2: 81.

54. For more extended discussions of the confessional, see Bernstein, *Confessional Subjects*; Jules Michelet, *Priests, Women, and Families*, trans. C. Cocks, 12th ed. (London: Longman, Brown, Green, and Longmans, 1847); and my Chapter 5.

55. Both Heineman, *Frances Trollope* (Boston: Twayne, 1984), and Wolff, *Gains and Losses*, note the novel's focus on obedience.

56. John Henry Newman's (mis)education of young men remained a Protestant concern long after he had left Oxford, as Charles Kingsley's 1864 "What, Then, Does Dr. Newman Mean?" illustrates. Newman, *Apologia Pro Vita Sua*, ed. David J. DeLaura (New York: Norton, 1968), pp. 310–40. Susan Chitty, *The Beast and the Monk: A Life of Charles Kingsley* (London: Hodder and Stoughton, 1974), Maynard, *Victorian Discourses*, and others have argued convincingly that Kingsley's attack has its roots in his own early attraction to Tractarianism. I take up Kingsley's anxieties about celibacy, the homosocial, and homosexuality in relation to Victorian ideas of brotherhood in Chapter 4.

57. Trollope, *Father Eustace*, 1: 234–35.

58. Quoted in Ransom, *Fanny Trollope*, p. 166.

59. Trollope, *Father Eustace*, 2: 182–83, 3: 95, 2: 178.

60. The celibacy of Roman Catholic clergy was a traditional point of Protestant attack. Scholars have recently explored the way in which, especially in the later decades of the nineteenth century, Catholic and Anglo-Catholic celibacy was read as homosexuality. See, for example, Adams, *Dandies and Desert Saints*; Hanson, *Decadence and Catholicism*; Hilliard, "UnEnglish"; Maynard, *Victorian Discourses*.

61. Trollope, *Father Eustace*, 2: 295, 1: 261, 2: 80.

62. John Henry Newman, *Parochial and Plain Sermons* (1835, Reprint, Westminster, Maryland: Christian Classics, 1966), pp. 31, 135.

63. Trollope, *Father Eustace*, 1: 241, 3: 189, 2: 80, 181, 191.

64. *Ibid.*, 3: 242, 267.

65. *Ibid.*, 3: 317. From the start, *Father Eustace* suggests that obedience to the dead father kills daughters: "All that she [Juliana] had not, and could not have felt for her gloomy father during his life, seemed now to swell her heart almost to bursting; and she would gladly have given years of life to have possessed power at that moment to comply with every wish expressed by Father Ambrose in her father's name."

66. *Ibid.*, 1: 272.

67. *Ibid.*, 2: 264, 3: 205.

68. Brodhead, *Cultures of Letters*; Kate Flint, *The Woman Reader, 1837–1914* (Oxford: Clarendon Press, 1993), pp. 40–43; McDannell, *The Christian Home*.

69. Trollope, *Father Eustace*, 3: 323.

70. Flint, *Woman Reader*, pp. 40–43.

71. Trollope, *Father Eustace*, 3: 107. In this subplot, Trollope, *Father Eustace*, also alludes comically to stories of captive nuns. The beautiful but impoverished Fanny Clarence comes to live with her cousin, Adelaide Stansberry, whose Italian heritage has given her a violent temper. Adelaide forces Fanny to "veil" herself (wear a hideous muffler and bonnet at all times), so that she will not attract William Curtis, the man Adelaide plans to marry with the help of the novel's Jesuits. Juliana rescues Fanny from this Italian plot and arranges her marriage to William Curtis.

72. See Heineman, *Frances Trollope*, pp. 18–19.

73. Anthony Trollope, *An Autobiography*. intro. Bradford Allen Booth (Berkeley: University of California Press, 1947), pp. 11–12. For a discussion of Trollope's pre-Tractarian anti-Catholic novel, *The Abbess* (1833), see my "Revising the Popish Plot," *Victorian Literature and Culture* 31, no. 1 (2003): 279–93.

74. On *Villette*, see Chapter 4.

3 THE FOREIGN FATHER AND THE SONS OF THE SIRES: NATIVIST NOVELS OF THE 1850S

1. American interest in the Oxford Movement was widespread, although, unlike in Great Britain, very little reaction came in fictional form. See, for example, the following articles on "Puseyism": "Puseyism, or Ecclesiastical Authority Versus Protestantism," *Christian Examiner* 35, no. 3 (Jan. 1844): 273–302; "Puseyism, as characterized by Lord Winchilsea," *Christian Secretary* 12, no. 7 (20 April 1849): 2; "Puseyism," *Christian Secretary* 12, no. 31 (5 Oct. 1849): 1; "Puseyism gone mad!" *Liberator* 13, no. 32 (11 Aug. 1843): 128; "Puseyism," *Liberator* 13, no. 32 (11 Aug. 1843): 128; "Puseyism Examined," *Merchants' Magazine and Commercial Review* 8, no. 5 (May 1843): 491; and "Puseyism Examined," *Methodist Quarterly Review* 3, no. 11 (April 1843): 324. Billington, *Protestant Crusade*, also discusses the American reaction to the movement.

   Surprisingly, given Frances Trollope's fame, I have not found evidence of an American edition of *Father Eustace*. Of course, American readers could have read English editions of the work.

2. "Hawkstone: A Tale of and for England in 1840," *Literary World* 3, no. 17 (27 May 1848): 324.

3. See Bennett, *Party of Fear*; Billington, *Protestant Crusade*; Franchot, *Roads to Rome*; and Levine, *Conspiracy and Romance*.

4. Forgie, *Patricide in the House Divided*; Lawrence Friedman, *Inventors of the Promised Land* (New York: Knopf, 1975); Michael Paul Rogin, *Subversive Genealogy: The Politics and Art of Herman Melville* (New York: Knopf, 1983).

5. Michael Denning, *Mechanic Accents: Dime Novels and Working-Class Culture in America* (London: Verso, 1987), p. 73.

6. Loesberg, "Ideology of Narrative Form," pp. 116, 128.

7. Tyler Anbinder, *Nativism and Slavery: The Northern Know Nothings and the Politics of the 1850s* (New York: Oxford University Press, 1992), pp. 52–74; Billington, *Protestant Crusade*, 388–89; Bennett, *Party of Fear*, 115, 125.

8. Anbinder, *Nativism and Slavery*, p. 8.

9. For discussion of this threat to and defense against national identity and unity, see Bennett, *Party of Fear*; Franchot, *Roads to Rome*; and John Higham, *Strangers in the Land: Patterns of American Nativism, 1860–1925* (New Brunswick: Rutgers University Press, 1988). Levine, *Conspiracy and Romance*, analyzes the efficacy of the conspiracy plot.

10. Bennett, *Party of Fear*, p. 89.

11. Benedict Anderson, *Imagined Communities*, p. 6.

12. Bennett, *Party of Fear*, does go on to interpret a standard convent narrative plot, arguing that it reveals male anxiety about female power. Pioneering works

on the sometimes overlapping genres of American religious and sensation novels are: Denning, *Mechanic Accents*; Franchot, *Roads to Rome*; and Reynolds, *Beneath the American Renaissance.*

13. Benedict Anderson, *Imagined Communities*, pp. 204, 203.
14. McDannell, *The Christian Home.*
15. Ned Buntline, *The Jesuit's Daughter; A Novel for Americans to Read* (New York: Burgess and Day, 1863), p. 115.
16. Bennett, *Party of Fear*, p. 90.
17. Orvilla S. Belisle, *The Arch Bishop: Or, Romanism in the United States* (Philadelphia: Smith, 1855), pp. 99, 257; Edward Hinks, *One Link in the Chain of Apostolic Succession; Or, The Crimes of Alexander Borgia* (Boston: Hinks, 1854), p. vii.
18. Eugene Sue, *The Wandering Jew* (n.p.: Chapman & Hall, 1844–45), p. 110. The central villain of Sue's *Wandering Jew* is a Jesuit bent on stealing a fabulous inheritance, destroying republicanism and, particularly, fraternal working-men's organizations, and achieving political domination. For Sue's influence on English fiction, see Anne Humphries, "Generic Strands and Urban Twists: The Victorian Mysteries Novel," *Victorian Studies* 34 (1991): 455–72; Robert Maxwell, *The Mysteries of Paris and London* (Charlottesville: University Press of Virginia, 1992), and Chapter 4 of this book.
19. Mark C. Carnes, "Middle-Class, Men and the Solace of Fraternal Ritual," in *Meanings for Manhood: Constructions of Masculinity in American Literature*, ed. Mark C. Carnes and Clyde Griffen (Chicago: University of Chicago Press, 1990), p. 47. Indeed, the breakdown of the apprentice system meant that even the possibility of a workplace father-substitute was disappearing.
20. Forgie, *Patricide in the House Divided*; Levine, *Conspiracy and Romance*, p. 9; Belisle, *Arch Bishop*, p. 18.
21. E. Anthony Rotundo, *American Manhood: Transformations in Masculinity from the Revolution to the Modern Era* (New York: Basic, 1993), p. 26.
22. William Alfred Bryan, *George Washington in American Literature, 1775–1865* (New York: Columbia University Press, 1952), p. 19; Forgie, *Patricide in the House Divided*, p. 185; Levine, *Conspiracy and Romance*, pp. 3–5. Work on the Washington Monument began in 1848. The 1854 monument incident is yet another instance of the perceived dichotomy between the founding and foreign fathers: Pius IX, like other world leaders, donated a block of marble for the Washington Monument. Outraged Know-Nothings stole the block and took over the monument committee for several years. The work done on the obelisk during that period was so shoddy that it was later dismantled and replaced.
23. See Lawrence Friedman, *Inventors of the Promised Land*, for a fuller discussion of this logic and its implications.
24. Quoted in Friedman, *Inventors of the Promised Land*, pp. 57, 33; Rogin, *Subversive Genealogy*, p. 33.
25. Catherine Albanese, *Sons of the Fathers: The Civil Religion of the American Revolution* (Philadelphia: Temple University Press, 1976); Forgie, *Patricide in the House Divided*; Friedman, *Inventors of the Promised Land.*
26. Buntline, *Jesuit's Daughter*, pp. 16–17, 58–59; Hinks, *One Link*, p. ix.

27. *The Sons of the Sires; A History of the Rise, Progress, and Destiny of the American Party, and It's Probable Influence on the Next Presidential Election* (Philadelphia: Lippincott, 1855), pp. v, 10. See Forgie, *Patricide in the House Divided*, for an Oedipal reading of this figure which he finds dominant in the 1840s (pp. 89–122).

28. Belisle, *Arch Bishop*, p. 258.

29. *Sons of the Sires*, pp. 13–14.

30. Ned Buntline, *The Convict: Or, The Conspirator's Victim. A Novel, Written in Prison* (New York: Dick & Fitzgerald, 1854), p. 43.

31. Franchot, *Roads to Rome*, p. 109.

32. The cross represented in Hughes's ecclesiastical signature was the source of the nickname, "Dagger John."

33. "This work, a revelation of the Borgias, is dedicated to Archbishop Hughes, as a token of Eternal Enmity! with the hope that it will be instrumental in awakening Americans to their duty, and in forming a bulwark of defence against foreign and papal aggression around the rights of all Protestant Americans."

34. In calling Hughes "Eminence," the proper form of address for a cardinal, Buntline seeks to reveal the Archbishop's ambition. Most of the novels under discussion depict Hughes as plotting obsessively to become Cardinal and then Pope.

35. Lippard, *New York: Its Upper Ten and Lower Million* (Upper Saddle River: Literature House, 1970), p. 69.

36. See Richard Shaw, *Dagger John: The Unquiet Life and Times of Archbishop John Hughes of New York* (New York: Paulist Press, 1977). On Hughes's political activities, see also Anbinder, *Nativism and Slavery*.

37. Buntline, *The Convict*, p. 198.

38. Billington, *Protestant Crusade*, p. 290.

39. Bennett quoted in Richard Shaw, *Dagger John*, p. 256.

40. Barnum actually tried to get Hughes to endorse his museum: "I enclose a *free* ticket and will esteem it a favor if you will give this establishment a . . . critical examination. If found worthy of support I trust you will kindly recommend it to your friends," quoted in Shaw, *Dagger John*, p. 248.

41. John Hughes, *The Decline of Protestantism, and its Cause* (New York: Dunigan, 1850), pp. 15–16, 22, 19; see also Franchot, *Roads to Rome*, p. 218.

42. Joseph Berg, *Dr. Berg's Answer to the Lecture of Archbishop Hughes on the Decline of Protestantism* (Philadelphia: Peterson, 1850), pp. 5–6, 23.

43. *Ibid.*, pp. 11, 30.

44. *Ibid.*, 30.

45. Levine, *Conspiracy and Romance*, p. 112. For example, Charles Edwards Lester, a lawyer, Presbyterian minister, and descendant of Jonathan Edwards, who published *Stanhope Burleigh* under the pseudonym Helen Dhu, was an "ardent Democrat," who served as secretary of the treasury and consul at Genoa under Polk. Active in the anti-slavery movement, Lester wrote a number of books, including *The Glory and Shame of England* (1841) "an exposure of the hardships of British labor in factories and mines," and translations of Machiavelli, Ceba,

Alfieri, and Azeglio (1845), *The National Cyclopaedia of American Biography*, vol. 13 (New York: White, 1906), p. 111; Dumas Malone, *Dictionary of American Biography* (New York: Scribner's, 1933), pp. 189–90. Buntline's politics, on the other hand, were notoriously opportunistic. See also Lippard, *New York*; Denning, *Mechanic Accents*; and Reynolds, *Beneath the American Renaissance*.

46. *Jesuit's Daughter*, p. 43; *The Convict*, p. 169; *Stanhope Burleigh*, pp. 167, 338.

47. This strategy is evident in many nineteenth-century Protestant historical novels. See, for example, Harriet Beecher Stowe's claiming of Savonarola as a proto-Protestant in *Agnes of Sorrento* (1862).

48. *Princess Viarna*, p. 350; *One Link*, p. 142.

49. Jay Monaghan, *The Great Rascal: The Life and Adventures of Ned Buntline* (Boston: Little, Brown, 1951), p. 208; An advertisement bound in with *One Link* claims "This paper is circulated in every state in the Union. It enjoys alike the patronage and confidence of the various National American organizations throughout the country, and has already attained the unprecedented circulation of 80,000 copies weekly." Billington, *Protestant Crusade*, lists its dates of publication as 1854–55. Reynolds, *George Lippard*, p. 30.

50. Bennett, *Party of Fear*, pp. 106, 111; see also Anbinder, *Nativism and Slavery*, pp. 20–21.

51. Anbinder, *Nativism and Slavery*, pp. 34–42; Carnes, "Middle-Class Men"; see also Rotundo, *American Manhood*, pp. 201–02.

52. Compare Forgie's analysis of Lincoln's dilemma: "the only way that both ambition and filiopiety could be satisfied in a post-heroic age was if a good (rational, renunciatory, obedient) son were to rescue the fathers' institutions from some *other* ambitious person. Lincoln created this person out of undesirable wishes he could not recognize in himself," *Patricide in the House Divided*, p. 86. For Lincoln, Forgie claims, this person was Stephen Douglas.

53. *Arch Bishop*, p. 360. Forgie, *Patricide in the House Divided*, p. 25, discusses the Farewell Address's status as "an important founding document," in which "the father was speaking personally."

54. *Jesuit's Daughter*, p. 73.

55. On Hughes's opposition to the public schooling for Catholics, see Shaw, *Dagger John*. On the connections between the public school movement and anti-Catholicism, see David Nasaw, *Schooled to Order*; Tyack and Hansot, *Managers of Virtue*. See also Mann on *The Republic and the School: Horace Mann on the Education of Free Me*, ed. Lawrence A. Cremin (New York: Teachers College, 1957).

56. *One Link*, p. vii; *Stanhope Burleigh*, pp. 75, 173–74. See also *The Arch Bishop* in which those who sell their votes to Catholic influence suffer nightmares in which "their sires, long since mingled with the dust, passed mournfully before them, and they turned from their upbraiding eyes to encounter the cajoling visage of the Arch Bishop," Belisle, *The Arch Bishop*, p. 264.

57. Benedict Anderson, *Imagined Communities*, p. 198.

58. *Jesuit's Daughter*, pp. 64–65. While *The Princess of Viarna* depicts the Inquisition as the work of the Dominicans, most of these fictions represent the

Jesuits as controlling both the historical Inquisition and its supposed secret reestablishment in the nineteenth-century.

59. *The Countess*, p. 74; *Stanhope Burleigh*, p. 398.

60. Both the sadism of American sensation novels and the upsurge in fraternal societies have been read as negative reactions to the increasingly powerful culture of female domesticity, as well as to the agitation for women's rights. See Bennett, *Party of Fear*; Carnes, "Middle-Class Men"; Reynolds, *Beneath the American Renaissance*; Anthony Rotundo, *American Manhood*.

61. The daughter's de-feminization is sometimes represented by her dressing as a man, as Ines does throughout much of *Stanhope Burleigh*.

62. *Jesuit's Daughter*, pp. 154–55.

63. William Engolls, *The Countess: or, The Inquisitor's Punishments. A Tale of Spain* (Boston: Gleason's, 1847), p. 71.

64. To use another example, while we might explain away the Jesuit as a version of the confidence man, the contemporary villain discussed so ably by Halttunen, *Confidence Men*, and others, a more apt line of inquiry might ask why the ancient religious foe is resurrected in this new secular form.

65. Hinks, *One Link*, p. 78. Both the Catholic Church and its priests are repeatedly identified as vampires in these novels: see, for example, the passage from *The Arch Bishop*, p. 258, quoted above. See Reynolds, *Beneath the American Renaissance*, pp. 191–92, on blood-drinking in American sensation fiction.

66. American historians have tended to explain away instances of incest in sensation fiction as a simple side-effect of (benighted) Victorian repression (Thomas Archdeacon, *Becoming American*; Bennett, *Party of Fear*; Reynolds, *Beneath the American Renaissance*). Delineating the politics of a democratic ideal based on sympathy, Elizabeth Barnes, *States of Sympathy*, p. 3, has argued that in American novels "[i]ncest can . . . be read as a metaphor for a culture obsessed with loving familiar objects." In the nativist novels of the 1850s, however, incest functions more specifically to express both resentment towards "foreigners" who are usurping the rights of true American men and hostility towards the generation of the founding fathers.

67. At least two other Buntline fictions (neither of them anti-Catholic) center around father–son rivalry and father–daughter incest themes: "Love's Desperations, or The President's Only Daughter" (1848) and his novel about Lincoln's assassination, *The Parricides* (1865).

68. Franchot, *Roads to Rome*.

69. J. B. Bullen, *The Myth of the Renaissance in Nineteenth-Century Writing* (New York: Oxford University Press, 1994), analyzes a number of nineteenth-century depictions of Lucretia Borgia, all of which are extremely negative. A volume of Alexandre Dumas's popular *Crimes célèbres* (1840) had been devoted to the Borgias. American and British audiences would also have known her story as it was told by Donizetti's *Lucretia Borzia* (1833), itself a recasting of Victor Hugo's play *Lucrece Borgia* (1833). For counter-examples, see Sarah Josepha Hale's *Woman's Record* and "An Historical Sketch" in the 1853 *Southern Literary Messenger* which defends Lucretia Borgia (19, no. 4 [April 1833]: 208–13). My

thanks to an anonymous reader for Cambridge University Press for this latter reference.

70. On nineteenth-century culture's fascination with the figure of Beatrice Cenci, see Ginger Strand and Sarah Zimmerman, "Finding an Audience: Beatrice Cenci, Percy Shelley, and the Stage," *English Romantic Review* 6, no. 2 (1996): 246–68.

71. The great man is never identified. His name is said to be "familiar to the civilized world," Lippard, *New York*, p. 79, and his image is immediately recognizable to the characters. Jefferson and Washington are the most obvious candidates. Lippard, New York, 161.

72. As Anbinder, *Nativism and Slavery*, has shown, the racialist politics of nativism translated into a range of positions on slavery. Lippard was actively against slavery (see Denning, *Mechanical Accents*, pp. 114–17). Buntline's nativist politics were generally tolerant of slaveholders (after all, Washington was one), but he did eventually fight as a scout on the Union side. Lester, like Buntline early on, sees Abolitionism as a form of fanaticism that deflects national attention from the real problems of America (immigration, etc.) and calls slaveholding "this venerable institution, which numbers among its members the Father of his Country, and all his companions in arms, except Arnold, the traitor" (*Stanhope Burleigh*, p. 206).

73. The latter was, of course, another form of property right. See Michael Grossberg, *Governing the Hearth: Law and Family in Nineteenth-Century America* (Chapel Hill: University of North Carolina Press, 1985).

74. *Stanhope Burleigh*, p. 406.

4 MARIOLATRY, IMPERIAL MOTHERHOOD, AND MANHOOD

1. "The Know-nothings – American Prospects," *British Quarterly Review* 22 (1855): 62. Sussman, *Victorian Masculinities*, p. 2. Before 1889 there were five editions and eleven reprints of *Westward, Ho!* in Great Britain.

2. On Victorian ideas about British mothers' contributions to the Empire, as well as the conception of Victoria herself as its "mother," see David, *Rule Britannia*; Margaret Homans, *Royal Representations: Queen Victoria and British Culture, 1837–1876* (Chicago: University of Chicago Press, 1998); Margaret Homans and Adrienne Munich, Introduction, in *Remaking Queen Victoria*, ed. Margaret Homans and Adrienne Munich (Cambridge: Cambridge University Press, 1997), pp. 1–10; and Adrienne Munich, *Queen Victoria's Secrets* (New York: Columbia University Press, 1996).

3. Norman, *Anti-Catholicism*, p. 170.

4. See J. T. Tucker, "Popery as a Present Fact," *Boston Review* 5 (March 1865): 178–92, p. 190, and "The Religious Scarecrow of the Age," *National Magazine* 5 (Dec. 1854): 523–28, p. 524, for differing American assessments of the Immaculate Conception as a (male) Catholic move to strengthen Romish power. John Gatta, *American Madonna: Images of the Divine Woman in Literary Culture* (New York: Oxford University Press, 1997), p. 10, briefly discusses American resistance to the doctrine.

5. Sinclair, *Beatrice; or, the Unknown Relatives* (New York: Garland, 1975), 2: 37–38.

6. G. M. Young and W. D. Handcock, eds., *English Historical Documents, 1833–1874* (New York: Oxford University Press, 1956), p. 365.

7. Norman, *Anti-Catholicism*, p. 56. Lord Russell quoted in Norman, *English Catholic Church*, p. 104. "Papal Aggression," *The Times* (London) 22 Oct. 1850: 6. Norman, *Anti-Catholicism*, p. 61.

8. "Besides stimulating the growth of positive theology and the theory of doctrinal development, the definition of 1854 was significant as a kind of 'test case,' exhibiting the authority of the Church's *magisterium* in interpreting divine revelation . . . it did constitute an actual exercise of the authority that would be defined sixteen years later." Edward O'Connor, ed., *The Dogma of the Immaculate Conception: History and Significance* (Notre Dame: University of Notre Dame Press, 1958), p. viii.

9. Marina Warner, *Alone of All Her Sex: The Myth and the Cult of the Virgin Mary* (New York: Vintage, 1976).

10. Norman, *Anti-Catholicism*, p. 160.

11. Chadwick, *The Victorian Church*, I: 272.

12. See, for example, Kingsley's letter, *His Letters and Memories of His Life*, 2 vols. (London: Kegan Paul, 1880), on May 11, 1849, to a young man considering conversion to Roman Catholicism:

   Believe me, I can sympathise with you. I have been through it; I have longed for Rome, and boldly faced the consequences of joining Rome; and though I now have, thank God, cast all wish of change behind me years ago, as a great lying devil's temptation, yet I still long as ardently as ever to see in the Church of England much which only now exists, alas! in the Church of Rome. (vol. I: 162–63)

13. Kingsley himself disliked the term, which was coined by T. C. Sandars in the *Saturday Review*: "We all know by this time what is the task that Mr. Kingsley has made specially his own – it is that of spreading the knowledge and fostering the love of a muscular Christianity. His ideal is a man who . . . in the language which Mr. Kingsley has made popular, breathes God's free air on God's rich earth, and at the same time can hit a wood-cock, doctor a horse, and twist a poker round his fingers," quoted in Bruce Haley, *The Healthy Body and Victorian Culture* (Cambridge, MA: Harvard University Press, 1978), p. 108.

14. Chitty, *The Beast and the Monk*; Peter Gay, *The Tender Passion* (New York: Oxford University Press, 1986).

15. "Kingsley's Sexual *Via Media*" appears as the running head in his *Victorian Discourses*, pp. 85–140.

16. See Brantlinger, *Rule of Darkness: British Literature and Imperialism, 1830–1914* (Ithaca: Cornell University Press, 1988) on the validity of using the term "imperialism" to describe the attitudes and writings of mid-Victorians.

17. Adams, *Dandies and Desert Saints*, p. 150. On Kingsley's concern with the health of the English "race" in the nineteenth century, see Vance, *The Sinews of the Spirit: The Ideal of Christian Manliness in Victorian Literature and Religious*

Thought (Cambridge: Cambridge University Press, 1985); Michael Banton, "Kingsley's Racial Philosophy," *Theology* 78 (Jan. 1975): 22–29. Kingsley was an active worker in sanitary reform, testifying before the House of Commons in 1854. See also his "Speech on Behalf of the Ladies' Sanitary Association," *Miscellanies*, 2nd ed., 2 vols. (London: John W. Parker and Son, 1860), pp. 309–17. Part of Kingsley's outrage at British mismanagement in the Crimea resulted from reports on the gross inadequacy of the military hospitals and health care.

18. Anthony Froude, the brother of Hurrell, one of the leaders of the Oxford Movement, had earlier authored the notorious *Nemesis of Faith* (1849). This somewhat autobiographical narrative of a clergyman's loss of belief so enraged William Sewell, then Senior Tutor at Exeter, that he tore up and burned a pupil's copy. Froude subsequently resigned his fellowship at Oxford, was disinherited, and ended up sheltering with the Kingsleys. There he met Fanny's sister Charlotte, a convert to Roman Catholicism who was about to enter the convent. She was saved from this fate (which had horrified Fanny and Charles) by falling in love with and marrying Froude. He went on to become a distinguished historian, authoring, among other works, *The History of England from the Death of Cardinal Wolsey to the Defeat of the Spanish Armada* (1856–70) (London: Parker & Sons, 1856).

19. In 1854, Kingsley had been rereading Hakluyt and going on long walks with Froude. See Froude's *Westminster Review* 58 (July 1852): 18–36 article on "England's Forgotten Worthies" and his "The Morals of Queen Elizabeth," *Fraser's Magazine* 48, nos. 286–287 (Oct. and Nov. 1853): 371–87, 489–505, for examples.

20. *Westward, Ho!*, p. 8; Robert Martin, *The Dust of Combat: A Life of Charles Kingsley* (New York: Norton, 1960), 178, makes a similar point about maleness and femaleness in Kingsley. See also Nancy Armstrong, *Desire and Domestic Fiction: A Political History of the Novel* (New York: Oxford University Press, 1987), and Nina Auerbach, *Woman and the Demon: the Life of a Victorian Myth* (Cambridge, MA: Harvard University Press, 1982), on how Victorians used a female iconography to define maleness.

21. Margaret Homans and Adrienne Munich, Introduction to *Remaking Queen Victoria*, ed. Homans and Munich (Cambridge: Cambridge University Press, 1997), p. 2; Macaulay quoted in Nicola J. Watson, "Gloriana Victoriana: Victoria and the Cultural Memory of Elizabeth I," in *Remaking Queen Victoria*, ed. Margaret Homans and Adrienne Munich (Cambridge: Cambridge University Press, 1997), p. 94. On Victoria and Elizabeth, see also Homans, *Royal Representations*.

22. So strong was this association that Maison's 1961 study of nineteenth-century religious fiction, *The Victorian Vision*, was initially published in England as *Save Your Soul, Eustace*.

23. *Westward, Ho!*, pp. 480, 481.

24. Warner, *Alone*, 254; *Westward, Ho!*, p. 65. See also Martin, *The Dust of Combat*, p. 178.

25. Kingsley, *Letters*, I: 210.

26. Newman, *Apologia*, p. 298.

27. *Westward, Ho!*, p. 51.

28. *Westward, Ho!*, pp. 51, 52; Kingsley, *Letters* I: 204; *Westward, Ho!*, pp. 467–68, 468, 65, 118.

29. *Westward, Ho!*, pp. 469, 29. Elizabeth Langland, *Nobody's Angels: Middle-Class Women and Domestic Ideology in Victorian Culture* (Ithaca: Cornell University Press, 1995); David, *Rule Britannia*.

30. Kristeva, "Stabat Mater," in *Contemporary Critical Theory*, ed. Dan Latimer (New York: HBJ, 1989), pp. 580–603, has argued that the Immaculate Conception, by structuring the economy of gender, performed the cultural work of allowing man to "surmount[] death . . . by postulating maternal love . . . the spectrum of auditory, tactile, and visual memories that precede language" (p. 594). In *Westward, Ho!* this work is accomplished, not by the image of a divine virgin-mother, but by an earthly bodied maternity. In contrast to my focus on the relationship of the male to the Immaculate Conception, Kristeva's primary interest in this essay is on how Mary seemed to offer empowerment to females.

31. See Munich, *Queen Victoria's Secrets*.

32. *Westward, Ho!*, p. 25. "They were calling each other mother and daughter then?" Kingsley's narrator asks rhetorically, "Yes. The sacred fire of sorrow was fast burning out all Ayacanora's fallen savageness; and, like a Phoenix, the true woman was rising from those ashes, fair, noble, and all-enduring, as God had made her" (495). On Kingsley's interest in male pain, see Adams, *Dandies and Desert Saints*, p. 112.

33. *Westward, Ho!*, p. 544.

34. James Anthony Froude, "The Morals of Queen Elizabeth," p. 385.

35. *Westward, Ho!*, p. 288. Both Froude and Kingsley stress that Elizabeth was constantly threatened with assassination and thus in need of male protection.

36. Homans, *Royal Representations*, pp. 11–12.

37. Kingsley, *Westward, Ho!*, pp. 49, 73, 166, 249, 222.

38. *Ibid.*, p. 472.

39. *Ibid.*, pp. 379, 394, 399, 397, 399. Adams, *Dandies and Desert Saints*, p. 125, reads the jaguar wholly as an avatar of the natural world. See Maynard, *Victorian Discourses*, pp. 132–33, for a discussion of this scene similar to my own that, in addition, emphasizes Kingsley's own violent reaction to his imagination of sexual liberty.

40. *Westward, Ho!*, p. 508.

41. Amy Kaplan, *The Social Construction of American Realism* (Chicago: University of Chicago Press, 1988), p. 672. Although Kaplan's is an analysis specific to American novels and culture, the standard plot she analyzes recalls *Westward, Ho!* at a number of points.

42. *Westward, Ho!*, pp. 422, 446, 468.

43. *Ibid.*, pp. 495, 544, 455.

44. *Ibid.*, pp. 14, 54–55.
45. Hanson, *Decadence and Catholicism*; Hilliard, "UnEnglish"; Sussman, *Victorian Masculinities*, p. 6.
46. The scene's resemblance to *Jane Eyre*'s depiction of the unmanned Rochester leaning on Jane has not gone unnoticed in the critical literature.
47. The epithet is taken from the title of Nicola J. Watson's essay, "Gloriana Victoriana: Victoria and the Cultural Memory of Elizabeth I."
48. Sally Mitchell, ed., *Victorian Britain: An Encyclopedia* (New York: Garland, 1988), p. 724. *Beatrice* was not Sinclair's only anti-Catholic work. In 1852, she published *Popish Legends and Bible Truths* and, in 1855, *Cross-Purposes*.
49. *Beatrice*, 3: 344; Murray G. H. Pittock, *Celtic Identity and the British Image* (Manchester: Manchester University Press, 1999), pp. 42–43, 42.
50. *Beatrice*, 3: 81, 2: 42–43.
51. In the 1830s: Charles E. Trevelyan, "Ramaseeana; or a Vocabulary of the Peculiar Language of the Thugs," *Edinburgh Review* 130 (Jan. 1837): 189–210 (this is a review of Sleeman's original documents on Thuggee, which were published only in Calcutta); Edward Thornton, *Illustrations of the History and Practice of the Thugs* (London: Allen, 1837); Sir William Sleeman, *History of the Thugs or Phansigars of India* (Philadelphia: Carey & Hart, 1839). Sleeman went on to write a number of reports and memoirs, including, *Report on the Depredations Committed by the Thug Gangs of Upper and Central India* (Calcutta: Huttman, 1840); *A Journey through the Kingdom of Oudh in 1849–50* (London: Bentley, 1858); *Rambles and Recollections of an Indian Official*, ed. V. A. Smith (Westminster: Constable, 1893). As late as 1901, Sleeman's books were receiving attention in "A Religion of Murder," *Quarterly Review* 194 (1901): 506–13. Sutherland, *The Stanford Companion*, p. 620, describes Taylor's book as "an instant success with the English public (Queen Victoria was an early and avid reader)." Sutherland also credits *Confessions* with introducing "the word 'thug' into general English usage" (p. 145). Important critical readings of the story of Thuggee include Brantlinger, *Rule of Darkness*, and David, *Rule Brittania*, which both discuss the disciplinary structures of the narrative.
52. David Rapoport, "Fear and Trembling: Terrorism in Three Religious Traditions," *The American Political Science Review* 78 (1984): 664. In addition to his analysis of Thuggee, Rapoport provides a useful bibliography on the topic.
53. David, *Rule Britannia*, pp. 135, 141.
54. "The popularity of *Le Juif errant* was enormous, not only in France but throughout Europe" (George Anderson, *Legend of the Wandering Jew*, p. 235). It was quickly translated into English, published in London and New York, and reprinted many times. Given the variety and number of translations and reprints, I will give volume and chapter number for quotations from *The Wandering Jew*. The translation from which I am quoting is that of the original Chapman and Hall edition (1844–45).

For another study that analyzes Sue's nineteenth-century English influence (and influences), see Humphries, "Generic Strands and Urban Twists." British anti-Catholicism's use of French "authorities" can also be seen in the case of Jules Michelet, whose writings on the Jesuits are widely quoted in British novels, pamphlets, speeches, etc. One English translation of Michelet's *Du Prêtre, del la Femme, de la Famille* (1845) had seen twelve "editions" by 1847.

55. The clerisy in general and the Society of Jesus in particular are the favorite targets of French anti-Catholicism. George Anderson, *Legend of the Wandering Jew*, p. 231, gives a succinct summary of the Society's French history: "expelled from France in 1765, suppressed by papal decree in 1773, restored to grace after the defeat of its enemy Napoleon in 1814, and dispersed once again after the popular revolution in France in 1830."

56. Between 1850 and 1853, Landor also published the anti-Catholic "Ten Letters Addressed To His Eminence The Cardinal Wiseman By A True Believer" (pp. 103–34). The argument that Catholics craftily misused toleration was widespread. See, for example, "The Know-Nothings."

57. *Beatrice*, 2: 41.

58. *Ibid.*, 1: 42. "[T]he popish half of our village looks as if a fragment of some such countries as we have seen abroad, beggared by a grasping priesthood; as if a morsel of Spain, or Portugal, or Ireland, were transplanted into the Highlands" (*Ibid.*, 1: 129–30).

59. *Ibid.*, 1: 318, 1: 316.

60. On the problems that Irish immigration created in Scotland, see Hugh Kearney, *The British Isles: A History of Four Nations* (Cambridge: Cambridge University Press, 1989).

61. *Beatrice*, 3: 121.

62. Colley, *Britons*, p. 6; *Beatrice*, 1: 292–93.

63. Bhabha, "Mimicry," p. 126; Benedict Anderson, *Imagined Communities*, p. 93; Bhabha, "Mimicry," pp. 128, 129, 132.

64. Bhabha, "The Other Question: Difference, Discrimination, and the Discourse of Colonialism," in *Literature, Politics and Theory: Papers from the Essex Conference, 1976–84*, ed. Francis Barker, Peter Hulme, Margaret Iversen, and Diana Loxley (London: Methuen, 1986), p. 159; *Beatrice*, p. xvi.

65. *Beatrice*, 2: 212, 3: 117.

66. On the church history of nineteenth-century Scotland, see Andrew Drummond and James Bulloch, *The Church in Victorian Scotland, 1843–1874* (Edinburgh: St. Andrew Press, 1975). On the multiplicity of cultures within Scotland in particular and the British Isles in general, see Kearney, *History of Four Nations*. See Benedict Anderson, *Imagined Communities*, pp. 88–90, on the reasons for the lack of a Scottish nationalist movement.

67. *Beatrice*, 3: 42–43; Auerbach, *Private Theatricals*, p. 4. For a general account of anti-theatricality, see Jonas Barish, *The Antitheatrical Prejudice* (Berkeley: University of California Press, 1981).

68. *Beatrice*, 2: 76; Drummond and Bulloch, *The Church in Victorian Scotland*, p. 210; *Beatrice*, 3: 70, 73; see also Bhabha, "Mimicry," pp. 132–33; *Beatrice*, 1: 281. According to Sutherland, *Stanford Companion*, p. 580, Sinclair's father had all of his daughters inoculated for smallpox, "which ruined their complexions and their marriage chances." (Interestingly, Sleeman, *History of the Thugs*,

identifies Kali as the goddess of smallpox.) Throughout *Beatrice*, Catholicism is represented as a highly contagious disease: Sinclair warns of "that pestilence walking in darkness, which seems about to overshadow the happy land of her birth" (p. xxxiv); Lord Iona states that he "thought it a duty to myself to avoid his [Allan's] society, for these things are so catching that the victims should be put under quarantine" (2: 28); Lady Edith decries "the gradual increase of the Popish fever in our families" (3: 252); Mr. Clinton experiences "the delirium of a typhus fever" (3: 173), etc. Sinclair may also be remembering Sue's *Wandering Jew* in which Ahasuerus is the carrier of cholera.

69. *Beatrice*, 3: 115. *Story* quoted in Benjamin, *The Bonds of Love*, p. 56.

70. *Beatrice*, 1: 119, 1: 207.

71. *Ibid.*, 1: v.

72. Bhabha, "Mimicry," pp. 132–33.

73. Brodhead, *Cultures of Letters*, p. 47.

74. *Beatrice*, 2: 267, xviii.

75. *Ibid.*, 3: 59, 1: 109, 3: 18. This domestic ideology is reinforced by the example of the Clintons: when Mr. Clinton is perverted into Catholicism, he deserts his wife and sends his sons off to strange Catholic institutions of indoctrination. The boys escape to return to their mother's arms, only to be sent away again. Mrs. Clinton, brought near to death by the loss of her family, is restored only by their final physical and emotional homecoming.

76. *Beatrice*, 3: 289–90, 3: 287.

77. The *Dublin Review* quotes (disapprovingly) an advertisement that claims: "The unprecedented success of Miss Catherine Sinclair's works in America, has been known throughout the country these many years; but the reception given to 'Beatrice,' her last novel, has, in fact, exceeded that of 'Uncle Tom's Cabin' in England. Above one hundred thousand copies were sold in a few weeks. A pamphlet was published by twenty-eight clergymen of New York, advising that each of their congregation should possess a copy. It has been recommended from the pulpit, a written testimonial to its merits has been sent to the American publishers by Father Gavassi [a well-known and traveled "renegade" ex-priest], and favourable notices of 'Beatrice'; have appeared in above five hundred newspapers and magazines, all of which testify to the deep interest of the story, as well as to the very important object it has in view," "Our Ministry," 33, no. 69 (Sept. 1853): 199–229, p. 203.

78. Augusta Evans, *Inez: A Tale of the Alamo*, 1855 (New York: Harper, 1864), p. 94.

79. *Ibid.*, p. 34.

80. "Literary Notices," *Godey's Lady's Book* 50 (April 1855): 370.

81. American writers' tendency to pair dark and light women was, of course, first discussed at length by Leslie Fiedler, *Love and Death in the American Novel* (New York: Criterion, 1960). On this pairing in *Inez*, see also my "Defenders of the Faith: Women, Anti-Catholicism, and Narrative in 19th-Century America," in *Cambridge Companion to 19th-Century American Women*, ed. Dale Bauer and Phil Gould (Cambridge: Cambridge University Press, 2001), pp. 157–75.

82. Rosemary Clark-Beattie, "Fables of Rebellion: Anti-Catholicism and the Struc-
    ture of *Villette*," *English Literary History* 53 (1986), p. 825. Beattie goes on to
    argue that Brontë then subverts this division, showing the ways in which British
    social structures are implicated in Lucy's misery. Bernstein, *Confessional Sub-
    jects*, argues as well that "Lucy Snowe's narration deploys the Roman Catholic
    Church as a tyrannical institution to launch and to disguise a general critique
    of male domination and female subordination intrinsic to the structure of
    English Victorian society" (p. 61).
83. Bernstein, *Confessional Subjects*; Clark-Beattie, "Fables of Rebellion"; Schiefel-
    bein, "A Catholic Baptism for *Villette*'s Lucy Snowe," *Christianity and Literature*
    45, nos. 3–4 (1996): 319–29.
84. See Clark-Beattie's religious contextualizing of the novel's "conspiracy plot"
    ("Fables of Rebellion").
85. Charlotte Brontë, *Villette* (London: Dent, 1977), p. 420.

5 UNDER WHICH LORD? RITUALISM, MARRIAGE, AND THE LAW

1. For a more thorough reading of this scene, see Bernstein's fine analysis of
   Villette, which centers around the confessional (*Confessional Subjects*).
2. Charlotte Brontë, *The Letters of Charlotte Brontë*, ed. Margaret Smith (Oxford:
   Clarendon, 1995), p. 330. This attraction to the scene of the confessional, the
   intimate revelation of the self to a holy father, the giving up of the burden of
   autonomy is not unique to either Charlotte Brontë or Lucy Snowe. Nathaniel
   Hawthorne, for example, rewrites this confessional scene in *The Marble Faun*,
   echoing both his own desire to confess to a priest and the resistance that redi-
   rects that desire safely into the scene of watching a woman confess. See Susan
   Griffin, "The Discourse Within: Feminism and Intradisciplinary Study," *Arizona Quarterly* 44, no. 4 (1989): 1–13, and Franchot, *Roads to Rome*. Hawthorne
   spoke of these attractions in his *French and Italian Notebooks. The Centenary
   Edition of the Works of Nathaniel Hawthorne*, ed. Thomas Woodson, vol. 14
   (Columbus: Ohio State University Press, 1980), 59, 458.
3. Bernstein, *Confessional Subjects*, p. 71. Robinson, a former journalist, wrote
   over fifty novels, many on religious topics (Sutherland notes his repeated use
   of the word "Church" in his titles [*Stanford Companion*, p. 542]).
4. Worboise, who edited the *Christian World* from 1866 to 1887, was the
   author of some forty-one volumes of fiction (Sutherland, *Stanford Companion*,
   p. 680).
5. See Gillian Beer, *Darwin's Plots: Evolutionary Narrative in Darwin, George
   Eliot and Nineteenth-Century Fiction* (London: Routledge, 1983), p. 170, on the
   entangled bank as a narrative structure.
6. Jewksbury quoted in Jeanne Fahnestock, "Bigamy: The Rise and Fall of a
   Convention," *Nineteenth-Century Fiction* 36, no. 1 (1981): 57.
7. Chadwick, *The Victorian Church*, 2: 321–22; James Bentley, *Ritualism and Politics in Victorian Britain: The Attempt to Legislate for Belief* (Oxford: Oxford
   University Press, 1978), p. 36; Queen Victoria quoted in Bentley, p. 23.

8. Chadwick, *The Victorian Church*, 2: 316.

9. *Ibid.*, 2: 322. Linton, *Under Which Lord?* (New York: Garland, 1976), 2: 237.

10. Bentley, *Ritualism and Politics*, p. 25. Bentley is quoting from J. Embry, *The Catholic Movement and the Society of the Holy Cross* (London: Faith, 1931), p. 200. In contrast, Chadwick, *The Victorian Church*, 2: 310, argues that Ritualism reflected "the strong Anglican desire for due obedience to authority."

11. Cardinal Manning quoted in L. E. Elliott-Binns, *Religion in the Victorian Era*, 2nd ed. (London: Lutterworth, 1946), p. 231.

12. Gladstone, *Contemporary Review*, Oct. 1874: 674. See, for example, John Murray, "Sacerdotalism, Ancient and Modern," *The Quarterly Review* 136 (Jan. 1874): 55–70.

13. Norman, *Anti-Catholicism*, pp. 80, 221.

14. Queen Victoria quoted in Chadwick, *The Victorian Church*, 2: 321. For a description of King's trial, see Norman, *Anti-Catholicism*.

15. *Under Which Lord?*, 3: 54, 1: 27.

16. Bentley, *Ritualism and Politics*, p. 43.

17. *Under Which Lord?*, 2: 120; Chadwick, *The Victorian Church*, 2: 310.

18. *Griffith Gaunt*, p. 1. Although *Griffith Gaunt* is set in the eighteenth century, its sensational marriage plot marks its engagement with contemporary debates on marriage. *High Church* is also set in an indefinite earlier period.

19. For the history of these changes, see Mary Lyndon Shanley, *Feminism, Marriage, and the Law in Victorian England* (Princeton: Princeton University Press, 1989); Elizabeth Helsinger, Robin Lauterbach Sheets, and William Veeder, *The Woman Question: Society and Literature in Britain and America, 1837–1883*, 3 vols. (1983, Reprint, Chicago: University of Chicago Press, 1989); Avrel Erickson and Fr. John McCarthy, "The Yelverton Case: Civil Legislation and Marriage," *Victorian Studies* 14 (1971): 275–91.

20. Shanley, *Feminism*, p. 8.

21. *Under Which Lord?*, 3: 139. "Hermione flushed. How he [Lascelles] insisted on her rights! But, after all, she was what he said – she was something more than Richard's wife" (1: 52).

22. *Ibid.*, 1: 288.

23. Eliza Linton, "The Judicial Shock to Marriage," *Nineteenth Century* 39, no. 171 (May 1891): 697.

24. *Under Which Lord?*, 3: 162.

25. See also *Punch* cartoons on June 30, 1877, and October 9, 1858.

26. See Bernstein, *Confessional Subjects*, on popular confessional narratives at mid-century.

27. Norman, *Anti-Catholicism*, pp. 95, 109. See Robert Buchanan, *The Coming Terror and Other Essays and Letters*, 2nd ed. (London: Heinemann, 1891).

28. Benjamin Shaw, "Private Confession in the Church of England," *Quarterly Review* 124 (Jan. 1868): p. 87. Archbishop Thomson quoted in Bentley, *Ritualism and Politics*, p. 31. On the popularity of Michelet's anti-clerical writings in the United States and Britain, see Franchot, *Roads to Rome*, pp. 121–25, and Bernstein, *Confessional Subjects*, pp. 54–57.

29. Harcourt quoted in Bentley *Ritualism and Politics*, p. 34; Murray, "Sacerdotalism," p. 58.
30. *High Church*, 1: 266; *Under Which Lord?*, 3: 81, 60–61. After Bee Nesbitt accepts Ringrove Hardesty's proposal of marriage in *Under Which Lord?*, she "involuntarily, instinctively, . . . not knowing what she did" embraces him and speaks her love (3: 249). Linton's narrator comments: "Surely too a better kind of confession, warm, loving, natural as it was, than those made so often in the church where casuistry creates sins that do not exist in fact, and superstition bends its neck to acts of penitence that have neither warranty in reason nor cause in nature!" (3: 250).
31. *Under Which Lord?*, 2: 96, 2: 149.
32. Arnstein, *Protestant Versus Catholic*, p. 129. For a recent work on Anglican sisterhoods, see Susan Mumm, ed., *All Saints Sisters of the Poor: An Anglican Sisterhood in the Nineteenth Century* (Rochester: Boydell, 2001) and *Stolen Daughters, Virgin Mothers: Anglican Sisterhoods in Victorian Britain* (New York: Leicester, 1999).
33. See Billington, *Protestant Crusade*, pp. 413–15.
34. Arnstein, *Protestant Versus Catholic*, p. 129. *Morning Advertiser* quoted in Arnstein, p. 135.
35. *Under Which Lord?*, 3: 172.
36. *High Church*, 1: 247.
37. Murray, "Sacerdotalism," p. 69; *Under Which Lord?*, 1: 246, 3: 234, emphasis mine.
38. Coral Lansbury, *The Old Brown Dog: Women, Workers, and Vivisection in Edwardian England* (Madison: University of Wisconsin Press, 1985), p. 132; Bernard quoted in Lansbury, pp. 158, 157.
39. *The Old Brown Dog*, p. x.
40. Buchanan's and Linton's examples may seem exceptions to Lansbury's identification of antivivisection as a female cause, but, as her study shows, many men (especially working-class men) opposed vivisection as well, *The Old Brown Dog*.
41. Buchanan, *The Coming Terror*, p. 349. *Daily Telegraph* (22 March 1889, 27 March 1889, April 1889, 4 April 1889).
42. Robert Buchanan, *Foxglove Manor* (1884, Reprint, New York: Garland, 1975), 1: 225–26, 2: 9, 2: 100, 1: 226, 2: 348.
43. *Ibid.*, 1: 179–80, 2: 180, 2: 193.
44. *High Church*, 1: 65, 1: 20, 2: 307, 293.
45. For another novel from the period in which the husband is rent from his wife by a scheming priest, see Wilkie Collins's *The Black Robe* (New York: Fenelon Collier, 1881). As in Trollope's *Father Eustace*, the character of the Jesuit is split into two – in *The Black Robe*, the young, innocent disguised priest Penrose is the tool of the calculating Father Benwell, both of whom work successfully to estrange Lewis Romayne (and his estate) from his Protestant wife. Collins explicitly compares the priests' manipulation of the English marriage laws to the Papal Aggression. The novel is marked by male–male relations of

extraordinary intensity. On Collins's sensational uses of anti-Catholicism, see my "The Yellow Mask, the Black Robe, and the Woman in White: Wilkie Collins, Anti-Catholic Discourse, and the Sensation Novel," *Narrative* 12, no. 1 (2004): 55–73.

46. Emma Jane Worboise, *Overdale: or, the Story of a Pervert: A Tale for the Times* (London: Clack, 1869), pp. 183, 325, 432, 319, 413.

47. Charles Reade, *Griffith Gaunt, or, Jealousy* (1866, Reprint, Boston: Ticknor and Fields, 1866), p. 178.

48. Murray, "Sacerdotalism," p. 255; Archbishop of York quoted in Brantlinger, "What Is 'Sensational' about the 'Sensational Novel'?", p. 7.

6 BLACK ROBES, WHITE VEILS, AND FOREGONE CONCLUSION: DISRAELI, HOWELLS, AND JAMES

1. Gaye Tuchman, *Edging Women Out: Victorian Novelists, Publishers and Social Change* (New Haven: Yale University Press, 1989).

2. Speaking of antebellum America, Franchot, *Roads to Rome*, p. 201, says, "In an age when the term *romance* figured frequently to describe narrative prose, the Protestant identification of Rome with the seductive mysteries of the imagination endowed the church with the controversial powers of fiction."

3. Edwin Sill Fussell, *The Catholic Side of Henry James* (Cambridge: Cambridge University Press, 1993), disagrees, arguing that Catholicism held attractions for James.

4.

"Resting on popular sympathies and popular privileges, they held that no society could be durable unless it was built upon the principles of loyalty and religious reverence.

The writer and those who acted with him looked, then, upon the Anglican Church as a main machinery by which these results might be realised. . . . But these great matters fell into the hands of monks and schoolmen; and little more than a year after the publication of CONINGSBY, the secession of DR. NEWMAN dealt a blow to the Church of England under which it still reels. That extraordinary event has been 'apologised' for, but has never been explained. It was a mistake and a misfortune."

Benjamin Disraeli, "General Preface," *Novels and Tales by the Earl of Beaconsfield*, vol. 10 (London: Longmans, 1881), pp. xiv–xv.

5. On Disraeli's changing attitudes towards Roman Catholicism, see Robert Blake, *Disraeli* (New York: St. Martin's, 1967); Arthur H. Frietzsche, *Disraeli's Religion: The Treatment of Religion in Disraeli's Novels* (Logan: Utah State University Press, 1961); and Michael Ragussis, *Figures of Conversion: "The Jewish Question" & English National Identity* (Durham, NC: Duke University Press, 1995).

6. Edmund Quincey, "Lothair," *The Nation* 80 (1870), p. 372; Sarah Bradford, *Disraeli* (New York: Stein and Day, 1983), p. 290. So eager were the American public and publishers that "One [American] publishing company attempted to steal a march on its rivals by having the novel telegraphed across the Atlantic, and was deterred only by the cost. 15,000 copies were sold on the first day of

publication and it was said that no book had been so popular since *Uncle Tom's Cabin.*" Benjamin Disraeli, *Lothair*, ed. Bogdanor, p. ix.

7. As Fussell, *Catholic Side of Henry James*, has shown, Catholic characters appear in James's fiction throughout his career, including various works written in the 1870s. However, *The American* is the only novel from this period in which Roman Catholicism plays an important part and in which James draws on the characters and plots of anti-Catholicism.

8. See also *The School of Hawthorne* (New York: Oxford University Press, 1986), p. 108, where Brodhead says, "If we ask what the institutional setting is that James's writing presumes, the answer is that it is much the same as Howells's. James started publishing at almost exactly the same time as Howells, and through exactly the same organs."

9. Henry James, *Essays on Literature, American Writers, English Writers* (New York: Library of America, 1984), pp. 859, 862.

10. *Ibid.*, pp. 862, 860.

11. *Ibid.*, pp. 860, 861, 862.

12. *Ibid.*, pp. 863, 3.

13. Leslie Stephen, *Hours in a Library* (New York: Knickerbocker, 1907), pp. 320, 322. See Ragussis, *Figures of Conversion.*

14. Stephen, *Hours in a Library*, p. 295.

15. Disraeli, *Lothair*, ed. Bogdanor, p. 34. On Disraeli's somewhat reluctant support of legislation to discipline Ritualist clergy, see Blake, *Disraeli*, pp. 300, 550–51.

16. Frietzsche, *Disraeli's Religion*; *Lothair*, pp. 285, x, xvii.

17. György Lukács, *The Historical Novel*, trans. Hamah and Stanley Mitchell (Lincoln, NB: University of Nebraska Press, 1962), p. 37.

18. John Carlos Rowe, "The Politics of Innocence in Henry James's *The American*," in *New Essays on* The American, ed. Martha Banta (Cambridge: Cambridge University Press, 1987), pp. 69–97, does argue that politics – or rather ignorance of it – is central to *The American* insofar as Newman fails because he is unaware of ultramontane politics.

19. James, *Letters, Fictions, Lives: Henry James and William Dean Howells*, ed. Micheal Anesko (New York: Oxford University Press, 1997), pp. 79, 492–93.

20. James Woodress, *Howells and Italy* (Durham, NC: Duke University Press, 1952), p. 157.

21. James, *Essays*, pp. 488–89. Apparently it was a memory that lasted at least until the composition of *The Golden Bowl* (1904), where this image recurs in descriptions of Charlotte's situation.

22. Habegger, *Gender, Fantasy, and Realism*, pp. 246–47.

23. James, *Essays*, p. 486.

24. *Ibid.*, p. 488, 489. See Fussell, *Catholic Side of Henry James*, pp. 17–19, on James's use of the Protestant "we."

25. James, *Essays*, pp. 490, 487. William Dean Howells, *A Foregone Conclusion. Novels 1875–1886* (New York: Library of America, 1982), p. 99.

26. James, *Essays*, pp. 495–96.

27. Cf. Ferris's reaction: "they strongly appealed to the painter as the stunted fruit of a talent denied opportunity, instruction and sympathy." Howells, *A Foregone Conclusion*, in *Novels 1875–1886*, p. 34.
28. Nathaniel Hawthorne, *The House of the Seven Gables* (New York: Bantam, 1981), p. viii.
29. Bell, *The Development of American Romance*; Habegger, *Gender, Fantasy, and Realism*.
30. *A Foregone Conclusion*, p. 33. Resisting Hawthorne's pull is, then, resisting the desire to allegorize. See Paul K. Saint-Amour, "Transatlantic Tropology in James's *Roderick Hudson*," *Henry James Review* 18, no. 1 (1997): 22–42; William Veeder, "The Portrait of a Lack," in *New Essays on* The Portrait of a Lady, ed. Joel Porte (Cambridge: Cambridge University Press, 1985), pp. 95–121.
31. *A Foregone Conclusion*, pp. 49, 50; Archdeacon, *Becoming American*, p. 100. See Kenneth Lynn, *William Dean Howells: An American Life* (New York: Harcourt, 1971), pp. 201–12, on Howells's dislike of Irish immigrants.
32. On the connections between "mystery" and Catholicism in Hawthorne in particular and in antebellum literature generally, see Levine, *Conspiracy and Romance*.
33. In *Lothair*, this romance and mystery is supplied by the Syrian figure of the Paraclete.
34. *A Foregone Conclusion*, pp. 50, 118.
35. Brodhead, *School of Hawthorne*, p. 83; *A Foregone Conclusion*, p. 171.
36. *A Foregone Conclusion*, p. 92, 52; Franchot, *Roads to Rome*; Habegger, *Gender, Fantasy, and Realism*; Daniel Aaron, *The Unwritten War: American Writers and the Civil War* (Madison: University of Wisconsin Press, 1987).
37. E.g., Edwin Cady, *The Road to Realism: The Early Years, 1837–1885, of William Dean Howells* (Syracuse: Syracuse University Press, 1956); John Crowley, *The Mask of Fiction: Essays on W. D. Howells* (Amherst: University of Massachusetts Press, 1989); Lynn, *William Dean Howells*.
38. However, Howells does include an instance of a priest using a woman's confession against her husband in the story of the madman who curses Don Ippolito (147).
39. See Elizabeth Stevens Priouleau, *The Circle of Eros: Sexuality in the Work of William Dean Howells* (Durham, NC: Duke University Press, 1983), for an extended reading of the novel's sexual triangle.
40. Bell, *The Development of American Romance*; Habegger, *Gender, Fantasy, and Realism*.
41. E.g., Eric Haralson, "James's *The American*: A (New)Man is Being Beaten," *American Literature* 54, no. 3 (1992): 475–96; Leland Person, "Henry James, George Sand, and the Suspense of Masculinity," *PMLA* 106 (May 1991): 515–28.
42. Henry James, *French Writers, Other European Writers, The Preface to the New York Edition* (New York: Library of America, 1984), p. 1057; Brooks, "The Turn of *The American*," 46–47.

43. Henry James, *The American*. *Novels 1871–1880* (New York: Library of America, 1983), pp. 591, 555, 590, 831.
44. James, *French Writers*, p. 1063.
45. James, *The American*, p. 788, *French Writers*, p. 1063. "If James is willing to ironize melodrama and put quotation marks around the stagey, he is determined that he shall eventually have them straight as well." Brooks, "The Turn of *The American*," p. 61.
46. James's debt to, and struggle with, Hawthorne in *Roderick Hudson* has been long recognized. See Brodhead (*School of Hawthorne*) and Saint-Amour, "Transatlantic Tropology," for recent treatments of this topic.
47. Brooks, "The Turn of *The American*," argues that Balzac is the primary influence on *The American*; Oscar Cargill, *The Novels of Henry James* (New York: Macmillan, 1961) sees Dumas's *L'Étrangère* as the novel's prototype.
48. James, *The American*, pp. 777, 832, 867, 790. In an analysis of the "dialectic of depth and surface" deployed by the cinematic veil, Mary Ann Doane, "Veiling over Desire: Close-ups of the Woman," in *Feminism and Psychoanalysis*, ed. Richard Feldstein and Judith Roof (Ithaca: Cornell University Press, 1989), pp. 105–41, has suggested that in "the discourse of metaphysics, the function of the veil is to make truth profound, to ensure that there is a depth that lurks behind the surface of things" (pp. 118–19). Doane, in fact, argues that in cinema, the veil, by hiding and drawing attention to the woman's face, focuses the viewer on this eroticized image. That is, the veiled face becomes not a surface to be read for signs of interiority but an end in itself. I would argue that in James's fiction, and perhaps in fiction generally, where we do not, either literally or metaphorically, see beyond the veil, what is hidden is not flattened out in the manner Doane describes.
49. See Luce Irigaray, *The Sex Which is Not One*, trans. Catherine Porter, with Carolyn Burke (Ithaca: Cornell University Press, 1985).
50. Rowe, "Politics of Innocence."
51. James, *The American*, p. 803. I disagree with Fussell, *Catholic Side of Henry James*, who maintains that the novel posits Newman's conversion as a possibility. The only potential conversions – and even these fail to occur – are Claire and Valentin Bellegarde's "conversions" to Newman's Americanisms and Newman's possible "conversion" to the values and tactics of the Bellegardes.
52. James, *The American*, p. 516. For an analysis of the role that Kingsley plays in this novel, see Haralson, "James's *The American*."
53. Brooks, "The Turn of *The American*," p. 65. Even *Guy Domville*, James's play about a young Roman Catholic man destined for the priesthood, does not depict an internal struggle with belief. Like Lothair, Guy is a failed protagonist, what Stephen calls an "empty vessel."
54. Maggie is, of course, a Roman Catholic. However, *The Golden Bowl* is concerned with matters of belief that are other than religious.
55. James does at one point in *The American* introduce the wall as a mental image: "As to what such sacrifice was now to be made to, here Newman stopped short before a blank wall over which there sometimes played a shadowy imagery."

56. James, *Letters*, pp. 126–27.
57. Casteras, "Virgin Vows," p. 172.
58. See James's other meditations on this topic in "The Altar of the Dead" (1895), "The Turn of the Screw" (1898), and *The Sense of the Past* (1917), among others.
59. Peter-Thomas Rohrbach, *Journey to Carith: The Story of the Carmelite Order* (New York: Doubleday, 1966).
60. See Brooks, "The Turn of *The American*."
61. Martha Banta, Introduction to *New Essays on* The American, ed. Martha Banta (Cambridge: Cambridge University Press, 1987), p. 25; Leon Edel, *The Conquest of London* (New York: Avon, 1978). Vol. 2 of *The Life of Henry James*. On narratorial tone in these novels, see, for example, Priouleau, *Circle of Eros*, on Howells, and Haralson, "James's *The American*," on James.
62. See Brodhead, *School of Hawthorne*; Jacobson, *Henry James and the Mass Market* (University: University of Alabama Press, 1983); Anesko, *"Friction with the Market": Henry James and the Profession of Authorship* (New York: Oxford University Press, 1986); Veeder, "Portrait of a Lack."
63. James, *Essays*, p. 863.

RELIQUARIES

1. Hanson, *Decadence and Catholicisim*; Hilliard, "UnEnglish."
2. Mary Wilkins Freeman, "A New England Nun," in *A New England Nun and Other Stories* (New York: Harper, 1891); Alice Dunbar Nelson, "Sister Josepha," in *The Goodness of St. Rocque and Other Stories* (Freeport: Books for Libraries, 1971), pp. 155–72; Edith Wharton, "The Bunner Sisters," in *Collected Stories, 1911–1937* (New York: Library of America, 2001), pp. 166–246; Mary Ward, *Helbeck of Bannisdale* (London: Penguin, 1983). For an example of a more "traditionally" polemical anti-Catholic novel published at the end of the century see *The Convent of the Sacred Heart* by Hudson Tuttle (Philadelphia: Carter, 1892), which seeks to "tell a tale of truth that is stranger than the wildest flight of fiction. . . . To expose the infamous depths of depravity, that the sham and pretence of the Catholic church may be known" (p. 3).
3. Ammons, *Conflicting Stories: American Women Writers at the Turn into the Twentieth Century* (New York: Oxford University Press, 1991); Brodhead, *Cultures of Letters*; Josephine Donovan, *New England Local Color Literature: A Women's Tradition* (New York: Ungar, 1983); Louis A. Renza, *"A White Heron" and the Question of Minor Literature* (Madisons University of Wisconsin Press, 1984).
4. Freeman, "A New England Nun," pp. 9, 3, 1, 17, 9.
5. Nelson, "Sister Josepha," pp. 158–59, 156, 171, 172, 168.
6. Kaplan, *Social Construction*, p. 10; Wharton, "The Bunner Sisters," pp. 168, 243. Ammons, *Conflicting Stories*, argues that "turn-of-the-century women writers found themselves, often in deep, subtle ways, emotionally stranded between worlds. They floated between a past they wished to leave (sometimes ambivalently, sometimes defiantly) and a future that they had not yet gained," p. 10.

7. On Ward and Brontë, see Beth Sutton-Ramspeck, "The Personal is Poetical: Feminist Criticism and Mary Ward's Reading of the Brontës," *Victorian Studies* 34 (1990): 55–75.
8. Ward, *Helbeck*, pp. 58, 315.
9. *Ibid.*, p. 102.
10. *Ibid.*, pp. 272, 145, 389.
11. See John Sutherland, *Stanford Companion*, for a full description of the family's religious history.
12. *Ibid.*, pp. 194, 158. See Sutton-Ramspeck, "The Personal is Poetical."
13. Bhabha, "The Other Question," p. 164.
14. This female pattern was not, of course, exclusive. See, for example, Harold Frederic's *Damnation of Theron Ware* (Chicago: Stone and Kimball, 1896) in which Catholicism figures familiarly as "the pornography of the Puritan." The Church of Rome provides an occasion of sin for the Protestant minister, yet his "knowledge" of the "usual" relations between women and priests proves mistaken. When he wrongly accuses the woman with whom he is infatuated with an affair with her confessor, she spurns him, sending him into a downward spiral of disbelief and cynicism.
15. See Lears, *No Place of Grace*, pp. 184–215, on antimodernism and "Catholic" taste in turn-of-the-century America.
16. Freeman and Dunbar-Nelson are typically categorized as regional writers. Wharton actively resisted such a designation and Ward, as a British writer, operates in a different literary culture. However, Nancy Bentley, among others, has demonstrated the ethnographic stance of Wharton's writing ("Marriage as Treason"). And I would argue that the fading "old New York" world of the genteel Bunner sisters, conveyed through Wharton's careful description of Ann Eliza and Evelina's peculiar milieu with its ritualized behaviors, as well as her use of dialect, allow us to view "The Bunner Sisters" as local color fiction. Ward's situation obviously differs greatly from that of her American counterparts, and I do not mean to conflate the situations of American and British writers at the time. However, *Helbeck of Bannisdale*, with its loving and detailed description of the Lake District, its dialect characterizations, its interest in local customs, and particularly its evocation of a disappearing way of life, can rightly be viewed as part of the rise in regional fiction experienced in Britain starting in the 1880s. See K. D. M. Snell, ed., *The Regional Novel in Britain and Ireland, 1800–1990* (Cambridge: Cambridge University Press, 1998), pp. 23–27.
17. See Brodhead, *Cultures of Letters*, Chapter 4, for a discussion of regionalism and ethnography as associated with the disappearance of the local.
18. See Brodhead, *Cultures of Letters*.
19. Ward, *Hellbeck of Bannisdale*, p. 369.
20. *Ibid.*

Bibliography

Aaron, Daniel. *The Unwritten War: American Writers and the Civil War.* Madison: University of Wisconsin Press, 1987.

Adams, James Eli. *Dandies and Desert Saints: Styles of Victorian Manhood.* Ithaca: Cornell University Press, 1995.

Albanese, Catherine L. *Sons of the Fathers: The Civil Religion of the American Revolution.* Philadelphia: Temple University Press, 1976.

Allott, Miriam, ed. *The Brontës: The Critical Heritage.* London: Routledge, 1974.

Ammons, Elizabeth. *Conflicting Stories: American Women Writers at the Turn into the Twentieth Century.* New York: Oxford University Press, 1991.

Anbinder, Tyler. *Nativism and Slavery: The Northern Know Nothings and the Politics of the 1850s.* New York: Oxford University Press, 1992.

Anderson, Benedict. *Imagined Communities: Reflections on the Origin and Spread of Nationalism.* Rev. ed. London: Verso, 1991.

Anderson, George K. *The Legend of the Wandering Jew.* Providence: Brown University Press, 1965.

Anesko, Michael. *"Friction with the Market": Henry James and the Profession of Authorship.* New York: Oxford University Press, 1986.

"Another Effort of Papal Benevolence, Rendered Abortive by Protestant Obstinacy." *Baltimore Literary and Religious Magazine* 5, no. 9 (Sept. 1839): 421–23.

Archdeacon, Thomas J. *Becoming American: An Ethnic History.* New York: Free Press, 1983.

Armstrong, Nancy. *Desire and Domestic Fiction: A Political History of the Novel.* New York: Oxford University Press, 1987.

Armstrong, Nancy, and Leonard Tennenhouse. "The American Origins of the English Novel." *American Literary History* 4 (1992): 386–410.

Arnstein, Walter. *Protestant Versus Catholic in Mid-Victorian England: Mr. Newdegate and the Nuns.* Columbia: University of Missouri Press, 1982.

Auerbach, Nina. *Private Theatricals: The Lives of the Victorians.* Cambridge, MA: Harvard University Press, 1990.

Woman and the Demon: the Life of a Victorian Myth. Cambridge, MA: Harvard University Press, 1982.

Baker, Joseph Ellis. *The Novel and the Oxford Movement.* Princeton: Princeton University Press, 1932.

Banta, Martha. Introduction to *New Essays on* The American, ed. Martha Banta. Cambridge: Cambridge University Press, 1987. 1–42.

Banton, Michael. "Kingsley's Racial Philosophy." *Theology* 78 (Jan. 1975): 22–29.

Barish, Jonas. *The Antitheatrical Prejudice*. Berkeley: University of California Press, 1981.

Barker, Benjamin. *Cecilia: or the White Nun of the Wilderness. A Romance of Love and Intrigue*. Boston: Gleason, 1845.

Barnes, Elizabeth. *States of Sympathy: Seduction and Democracy in the American Novel*. New York: Columbia University Press, 1997.

Baym, Nina. *American Women Writers and the Work of History, 1790–1860*. New Brunswick: Rutgers University Press, 1995.

Feminism and American Literary History. New Brunswick: Rutgers University Press, 1992.

"Melodramas of Beset Manhood." *American Quarterly* 33 (1981): 123–39.

"Onward Christian Women: Sarah J. Hale's History of the World." *New England Quarterly* 63 (1990): 249–70.

Woman's Fiction: A Guide to Novels by and about Women in America, 1820–1870. Ithaca: Cornell University Press, 1978.

Beecher, Edward. *The Papal Conspiracy Exposed and Protestantism Defended in the Light of Reason*. 1855. Reprint, New York: Arno, 1977.

Beecher, Lyman. *A Plea for the West*. 1835. New York: Arno, 1977.

Beer, Gillian. *Darwin's Plots: Evolutionary Narrative in Darwin, George Eliot and Nineteenth-Century Fiction*. London: Routledge, 1983.

Belisle, Orvilla S. *The Arch Bishop: Or, Romanism in the United States*. Philadelphia: Smith, 1855.

Bell, Michael Davitt. *The Development of American Romance: The Sacrifice of Relation*. Chicago: University of Chicago Press, 1983.

Benjamin, Jessica. *The Bonds of Love: Psychoanalysis, Feminism, and the Problem of Domination*. New York: Pantheon, 1988.

Bennett, David H. *The Party of Fear: From Nativist Movements to the New Right in American History*. Chapel Hill: University of North Carolina Press, 1988.

Bentley, James. *Ritualism and Politics in Victorian Britain: The Attempt to Legislate for Belief*. Oxford: Oxford University Press, 1978.

Bentley, Nancy. "Marriage as Treason: Polygamy, Nation, and the Novel." In *The Futures of American Studies*, edited by Donald Pease and Robyn Wiegman. Durham, NC: Duke University Press, in press.

Berg, Joseph F. *Dr. Berg's Answer to the Lecture of Archbishop Hughes on the Decline of Protestantism*. Philadelphia: Peterson, 1850.

Berlant, Lauren. *The Anatomy of National Fantasy*. Chicago: University of Chicago Press, 1991.

Bernstein, Susan David. *Confessional Subjects: Revelations of Gender and Power in Victorian Literature and Culture*. Chapel Hill: University of North Carolina Press, 1997.

Best, G. F. A. "Popular Protestantism in Victorian Britain." In *Ideas and Institutions of Victorian Britain*, edited by Robert Robson. London: Bell, 1967.

Bhabha, Homi. "Of Mimicry and Man: The Ambivalence of Colonial Discourse." *October* 28 (Spring 1984): 125–33.

"The Other Question: Difference, Discrimination, and the Discourse of Colonialism." In *Literature, Politics and Theory: Papers from the Essex Conference, 1976–84*, edited by Francis Barker, Peter Hulme, Margaret Iversen, and Diana Loxley. London: Methuen, 1986. 148–72.

Bhabha, Homi, ed. *Nation and Narration.* New York: Routledge, 1990.

Billington, Ray Allen. Introduction to *Awful Disclosures of Maria Monk.* 1836. Reprint, Hamden, CT: Archon Books, 1962.

The Protestant Crusade, 1800–1860: A Study of the Origins of American Nativism. New York: Macmillan, 1961.

Binder, William Earle. *Madelon Hawley, or, The Jesuit and His Victim. A Revelation of Romanism.* New York: Dayton, 1857.

Viola; Or The Triumphs of Love and Faith. A Tale of Plots and Counterplots. New York: Evans, 1858.

Bivona, Daniel. *Desire and Contradiction: Imperial Visions and Domestic Debates in Victorian Literature.* New York: St. Martin's, 1990.

Blake, Robert. *Disraeli.* New York: St. Martin's, 1967.

Bodenheimer, Rosemarie. *The Politics of Story in Victorian Social Fiction.* Ithaca: Cornell University Press, 1988.

Bogdanor, Vernon, ed. Introduction to *Lothair*, by Benjamin Disraeli. New York: Oxford University Press, 1975. vii–xvii.

Bourne, George. *Lorette. The History of Louise, Daughter of a Canadian Nun, Exhibiting the Interior of Female Convents.* 2nd ed. 1833. Reprint, New York: Small, 1834.

Boyle, Thomas. *Black Swine in the Sewers of Hampstead: Beneath the Surface of Sensationalism.* London: Hodder and Stoughton, 1991.

Bradford, Sarah. *Disraeli.* New York: Stein and Day, 1983.

Brantlinger, Patrick. *Rule of Darkness: British Literature and Imperialism, 1830–1914.* Ithaca: Cornell University Press, 1988.

"What is 'Sensational' about the 'Sensational Novel'?" *Nineteenth-Century Fiction* 37, no. 1 (1982): 1–28.

Brodhead, Richard. *Cultures of Letters: Scenes of Reading and Writing in Nineteenth-Century America.* Chicago: University of Chicago Press, 1993.

The School of Hawthorne. New York: Oxford University Press, 1986.

Brontë, Charlotte. *The Letters of Charlotte Brontë.* Ed. Margaret Smith. Oxford: Clarendon, 1995.

Brontë, Charlotte. *Villette.* London: Dent, 1977.

Brooks, Peter. "The Turn of *The American.*" In *New Essays on* The American, edited by Martha Banta. Cambridge: Cambridge University Press, 1987. 43–67.

Brown, Bill. *Reading the West: An Anthology of Dime Westerns.* Boston: Bedford, 1997.

Bryan, William Alfred. *George Washington in American Literature, 1775–1865.* New York: Columbia University Press, 1952.

Buchanan, Robert. *The Coming Terror and Other Essays and Letters*. 2nd ed. London: Heinemann, 1891.

Foxglove Manor. 1884. New York: Garland, 1975.

Buell, Lawrence. "American Literary Emergence as a Postcolonial Phenomenon." *American Literary History* 4 (1992): 411–42.

Bullen, J. B. *The Myth of the Renaissance in Nineteenth-Century Writing*. New York: Oxford University Press, 1994.

Bunkley, Josephine M. *The Testimony of an Escaped Novice. From The Sisterhood of St. Joseph, Emmettsburg, Maryland, The Mother-House of the Sisters of Charity in the United States*. Philadelphia: Harper, 1855.

Buntline, Ned [Edward Zane Carroll Judson]. *The Convict: Or, The Conspirator's Victim. A Novel, Written in Prison*. New York: Dick & Fitzgerald, 1854.

The Jesuit's Daughter; A Novel for Americans to Read. New York: Burgess and Day, 1863.

Cady, Edwin. *The Road to Realism: The Early Years, 1837–1885, of William Dean Howells*. Syracuse: Syracuse University Press, 1956.

Caldicott, Thomas Ford. *Hannah Corcoran: An Authentic Narrative of Her Conversion From Romanism, Her Abduction From Charlestown, and The Treatment She Received During Her Absence*. Boston: Gould and Lincoln, 1853.

Callow, James T. *Kindred Spirits: Knickerbocker Writers and American Artists, 1807–1855*. Chapel Hill: University of North Carolina Press, 1967.

Cargill, Oscar. *The Novels of Henry James*. New York: Macmillan, 1961.

Carnes, Mark C. "Middle-Class Men and the Solace of Fraternal Ritual." In *Meanings for Manhood: Constructions of Masculinity in American Literature*, edited by Mark C. Carnes and Clyde Griffen. Chicago: University of Chicago Press, 1990. 37–52.

Secret Ritual and Manhood in Victorian America. New Haven: Yale University Press, 1989.

Casteras, Susan P. "Virgin Vows: The Early Victorian Artists' Portrayal of Nuns and Novices." *Victorian Studies* 24 (1981): 157–84.

"The Catholic Question." *Western Monthly Magazine* 3 (1835): 375–90.

Chadwick, Owen. *The Victorian Church*. 2 vols. 1966. London: SCM, 1987.

Chandos, John. *Boys Together: English Public Schools 1800–1864*. New Haven: Yale University Press, 1984.

Chaplin, Mrs. Jane Dunbar [Hyla]. *The Convent and the Manse*. Boston: Jewett, 1853.

Chitty, Susan. *The Beast and the Monk: A Life of Charles Kingsley*. London: Hodder and Stoughton, 1974.

Clark, Gregory, and S. Michael Halloran, eds. *Oratorical Culture in Nineteenth-Century America: Transformations in the Theory and Practice of Rhetoric*. Carbondale: Southern Illinois University Press, 1993.

Clark-Beattie, Rosemary. "Fables of Rebellion: Anti-Catholicism and the Structure of *Villette*." *English Literary History* 53 (1986): 821–47.

Colley, Linda. *Britons: Forging the Nation, 1707–1837*. New Haven: Yale University Press, 1992.

Collins, Wilkie. *The Black Robe*. New York: Fenelon Collier, 1881.

Cott, Nancy. *The Bonds of Womanhood: "Woman's Sphere" in New England, 1780–1835*. New Haven: Yale University Press, 1977.

Cowan, H. Pamela. *The American Convent as a School for Protestant Children*. New York: Protestant Episcopal Society for the Promotion of Evangelical Knowledge, 1870.

Cross, Andrew B. *Priests' Prisons For Women, Or A Consideration of the Question, Whether Unmarried Foreign Priests Ought To Be Permitted To Erect Prisons, Inot* [sic] *Which, Under Pretence of Religion, To Seduce Or Entrap, Or By Force Compel Young Women to Enter, And After They Have Secured Their Property, Keep Them in Confinement, And Compel Them, As Their Slaves, To Submit Themselves To Their Will, Under The Penalty Of Flogging Or The Dungeon?* Baltimore: Sherwood, 1854.

Crowley, John W. *The Mask of Fiction: Essays on W. D. Howells*. Amherst: University of Massachusetts Press, 1989.

Culbertson, Rosamond. *Rosamond: or, a Narrative of the Captivity and Sufferings of an American Female Under the Popish Priests, in the Island of Cuba With a Full Disclosure of Their Manners and Customs, Written by Herself*. 2nd ed. New York: Leavitt, Lord, 1836.

Cvetkovich, Ann. *Mixed Feelings: Feminism, Mass Culture, and Victorian Sensationalism*. New Brunswick: Rutgers University Press, 1992.

Damon, Norwood [Mary Magdalen]. *The Chronicles of Mount Benedict. A Tale of the Ursuline Convent. The Quasi Production of Mary Magdalen*. Boston: Printed for the Publisher, 1837.

David, Deirdre. *Rule Britannia: Woman, Empire, and Victorian Writing*. Ithaca: Cornell University Press, 1995.

Davidson, Cathy N. *Revolution and the Word: The Rise of the Novel in America*. New York: Oxford University Press, 1986.

Davies, Charles Maurice. *Philip Paternoster. A Tractarian Love-Story*. 1858. New York: Garland, 1975.

Davis, David Brion. "Some Themes of Counter-Subversion: An Analysis of Anti-Masonic, Anti-Catholic, and Anti-Mormon Literature." *Mississippi Valley Historical Review* 47 (1960–61): 205–24.

De Laura, David. "O Unforgotten Voice: The Memory of Newman in the Nineteenth Century." In *Sources for Reinterpretation: The Use of Nineteenth-Century Literary Documents*, edited by Harry Ransom. Austin: Dept. of English and Humanities Research Center, 1975. 23–55.

[Mr. De Potter]. *Female Convents. Secrets of Nunneries Disclosed*. New York: Appleton, 1834.

Denning, Michael. *Mechanic Accents: Dime Novels and Working-Class Culture in America*. London: Verso, 1987.

Dhu, Helen [Charles Edwards Lester]. *Stanhope Burleigh: The Jesuits in Our Homes*. New York: Stringer and Townsend, 1855.

Dictionary of American Biography. Ed. Dumas Malone. New York: Scribner's, 1933.

Disraeli, Benjamin. "General Preface." *Novels and Tales by the Earl of Beaconsfield.* Vol. 10. London: Longmans, 1881. vii–xx.

Disraeli, Benjamin. *Lothair.* Ed. Vernon Bogdanor. London: Oxford University Press, 1975.

Doane, Mary Ann. "Veiling over Desire: Close-ups of the Woman." In *Feminism and Psychoanalysis,* edited by Richard Feldstein and Judith Roof. Ithaca: Cornell University Press, 1989. 105–41.

Donovan, Josephine. *New England Local Color Literature: A Women's Tradition.* New York: Ungar, 1983.

Douglas, Ann. *The Feminization of American Culture.* New York: Knopf, 1977.

Drummond, Andrew L., and James Bulloch. *The Church in Victorian Scotland, 1843–1874.* Edinburgh: St. Andrew Press, 1975.

Dwight, Theodore. *Open Convents: Or Nunneries and Popish Seminaries Dangerous To The Morals, And Degrading To The Character Of A Republican Community.* New York: Van Nostrand and Dwight, 1836.

Edel, Leon. *The Conquest of London.* New York: Avon, 1978. Vol. 2 of *The Life of Henry James.*

Elder, George [Philemon Scank]. "The Ursuline Convent." In *A Few Chapters to Brother Jonathan, Concerning "Infallibility, &c." or, Sticturees [sic] on Nathan L. Rice's "Defence of Protestantism," &c. &c. &c.* Louisville, KY: Published for the Author, 1835.

Eliot, George. *Middlemarch.* Edited by Bert G. Hornbeck. New York: Norton, 1977.

Elliott-Binns, L. E. *Religion in the Victorian Era.* 2nd ed. London: Lutterworth, 1946.

Embry, J. *The Catholic Movement and the Society of the Holy Cross.* London: Faith, 1931.

English Historical Documents, 1833–1874. Ed. G. M. Young and W. D. Handcock. New York: Oxford University Press, 1956.

Engolls, William. *The Countess: or, The Inquisitor's Punishments. A Tale of Spain.* Boston: Gleason's, 1847.

Erdman, Harley. *Staging the Jew: The Performance of an American Ethnicity, 1860–1920.* New Brunswick: Rutgers University Press, 1997.

Erickson, Avrel B., and Fr. John McCarthy. "The Yelverton Case: Civil Legislation and Marriage." *Victorian Studies* 14 (1971): 275–91.

The Escaped Nun: Or, Disclosures of Convent Life; And The Confessions Of A Sister Of Charity. Giving A More Minute Detail of Their Inner Life, And A Bolder Revelation Of The Mysteries And Secrets Of Nunneries, Than Have Ever Before Been Submitted To The American Public. New York: De Witt & Davenport, 1855.

Evans, Augusta. *Inez: A Tale of the Alamo.* 1855. New York: Harper, 1864.

Fahnestock, Jeanne. "Bigamy: The Rise and Fall of a Convention." *Nineteenth-Century Fiction* 36, no. 1 (1981): 47–71.

Ferguson, Robert A. "William Cullen Bryant: The Creative Context of the Poet." *NEQ* 53 (1980): 31–63.

Fiedler, Leslie A. *Love and Death in the American Novel.* New York: Criterion, 1960.

Flint, Kate. *The Woman Reader, 1837–1914.* Oxford: Clarendon, 1993.

Forgie, George B. *Patricide in the House Divided: A Psychological Interpretation of Lincoln and His Age.* New York: Norton, 1979.

Franchot, Jenny. *Roads to Rome: The Antebellum Protestant Encounter with Catholicism.* Berkeley: University of California Press, 1994.

Frederic, Harold. *The Damnation of Theron Ware.* Chicago: Stone and Kimball, 1896.

Freeman, Mary E. Wilkins. *A New England Nun and Other Stories.* New York: Harper, 1891.

Freud, Sigmund. *Totem and Taboo. The Standard Edition of the Complete Psychological Works of Sigmund Freud.* Trans. James Strachey. Vol. 13. London: Hogarth, 1953.

Friedman, Lawrence J. *Inventors of the Promised Land.* New York: Knopf, 1975.

Frietzsche, Arthur H. *Disraeli's Religion: The Treatment of Religion in Disraeli's Novels.* Logan: Utah State University Press, 1961.

Frothingham, Charles W. *The Convent's Doom: A Tale of Charlestown in 1834* also *The Haunted Convent.* 5th ed. Boston: Graves & Weston, 1854.

Six Hours in a Convent: or The Stolen Nuns! A Tale of Charlestown in 1834. 1854. 8th ed. Boston: Graves & Weston, 1855.

Froude, James Anthony. "England's Forgotten Worthies." *Westminster Review* 58 (July 1852): 18–36.

The History of England from the Death of Cardinal Wolsey to the Defeat of the Spanish Armada. London: Parker & Sons, 1856.

"The Morals of Queen Elizabeth." *Fraser's Magazine* 48, nos. 286–287 (Oct. and Nov. 1853): 371–87, 489–505.

Fussell, Edwin Sill. *The Catholic Side of Henry James.* Cambridge: Cambridge University Press, 1993.

Gallagher, Catherine. *The Industrial Reformation of English Fiction, 1832–1867.* Chicago: University of Chicago Press, 1985.

Gatta, John. *American Madonna: Images of the Divine Woman in Literary Culture.* New York: Oxford University Press, 1997.

Gay, Peter. *The Tender Passion.* New York: Oxford University Press, 1986. Vol. 2 of *The Bourgeois Experience: Victoria to Freud.*

Giles, Paul. *Transatlantic Insurrections: British Culture and the Formation of American Literature, 1730–1860.* Philadelphia: University of Pennsylvania Press, 2001.

Transnational Fictions and the Transatlantic Imaginary. Durham, NC: Duke University Press, 2002.

Gladstone, William. "Ritualism and Ritual." *Contemporary Review* (October 1874): 663–81.

Griffin, Susan M. "The Black Robe of Romance: Hawthorne's Shadow and Howells's Italian Priest." In *Roman Holidays: 19th-Century American Writers Abroad*, edited by Robert K. Martin and Leland Person. Iowa City: University of Iowa Press, 2001. 191–205.

" 'The Dark Stranger': Sensationalism and Anti-Catholicism in Sarah Josepha Hale's *Traits of American Life.*" *Legacy* 14, no. 1 (1997): 13–24.

"Defenders of the Faith: Women, Anti-Catholicism, and Narrative in 19th-Century America." In *Cambridge Companion to 19th-Century American Women*, edited by Dale Bauer and Phil Gould. Cambridge: Cambridge University Press, 2001. 157–75.

"The Discourse Within: Feminism and Intradisciplinary Study." *Arizona Quarterly* 44, no. 4 (1989): 1–13.

"Revising the Popish Plot." *Victorian Literature and Culture* 31, no. 1 (2003): 279–93.

"Scar Texts: Tracing the Marks of Jamesian Masculinity." *Arizona Quarterly* 53, no. 4 (Winter 1997): 61–82.

"Screening the Father: Strategies of Obedience in Early James." In *Refiguring the Father: New Feminist Readings of Patriarchy*, edited by Patricia Yaeger and Beth Kowaleski-Wallace. Carbondale: Southern Illinois University Press, 1989. 39–57.

"The Yellow Mask, the Black Robe, and the Woman in White: Wilkie Collins, Anti-Catholic Discourse, and the Sensation Novel." *Narrative* 12, no. 1 (2004): 55–73.

Grossberg, Michael. *Governing the Hearth: Law and Family in Nineteenth-Century America.* Chapel Hill: University of North Carolina Press, 1985.

Habegger, Alfred. *Gender, Fantasy, and Realism in American Literature.* New York: Columbia University Press, 1982.

Hale, Sarah Josepha. "Convents are Increasing." *American Ladies' Magazine* 7 (Dec. 1834): 560–64.

"How to Prevent the Increase of Convents." *American Ladies' Magazine* 7 (Nov. 1834): 517–21.

Traits of American Life. Philadelphia: Carey, 1835.

"The Unknown." *Ladies' Magazine* 3 (Aug.–Sept. 1830): 338–53, 385–93.

"The Ursuline Convent." *American Ladies' Magazine* 7 (Sept. 1834): 418–26.

Woman's Record; or, Sketches of All Distinguished Women from the Creation to A. D. 1854. Arranged in four eras. With selections from female writers of every age. 2nd ed., rev. New York: Harper, 1855.

Haley, Bruce. *The Healthy Body and Victorian Culture.* Cambridge, MA: Harvard University Press, 1978.

Halttunen, Karen. *Confidence Men and Painted Women: A Study of Middle-Class American Culture in America, 1830–1870.* New Haven: Yale University Press, 1982.

Hanson, Ellis. *Decadence and Catholicism.* Cambridge, MA: Harvard University Press, 1997.

Haralson, Eric. "James's *The American*: A (New)Man is Being Beaten." *American Literature* 54, no. 3 (1992): 475–96.

"The Hard Church Novel. *The National Review* (July 1856): 127–46.

Harper [Mrs. L. St. John Eckel]. *Maria Monk's Daughter; An Autobiography.* New York: United States Publishing, 1874.

Harte, Bret. *Lothaw, or, The Adventures of a Young Gentleman in Search of a Religion.* London: J. C. Hotten, 1871.

"Hawkstone: A Tale of and for England in 1840." *Literary World.* 3, no. 17 (27 May 1848): 322–25.

Hawthorne, Nathaniel. *French and Italian Notebooks. The Centenary Edition of the Works of Nathaniel Hawthorne.* Ed. Thomas Woodson. Vol. 14. Columbus: Ohio State University Press, 1980.

Hazel, Harry [Justin Jones]. *The Nun of St. Ursula, Or the Burning of the Convent. A Romance of Mt. St. Benedict.* Boston: Gleason, 1845.

The House of the Seven Gables. New York: Bantam, 1981.

Hedrick, Joan D. *Harriet Beecher Stowe: A Life.* New York: Oxford University Press, 1994.

Heineman, Helen. *Frances Trollope.* Boston: Twayne, 1984.

Mrs. Trollope: The Triumphant Feminine in the Nineteenth Century. Athens, OH: Ohio University Press, 1979.

Helen Mulgrave; or, Jesuit Executorship: Being Passages in the Life of a Seceder from Romanism. An Autobiography. New York: De Witt & Davenport, 1852.

Heller, Tamar. *Dead Secrets: Wilkie Collins and the Female Gothic.* New Haven: Yale University Press, 1992.

Helsinger, Elizabeth K., Robin Lauterbach Sheets, and William Veeder. *The Woman Question: Society and Literature in Britain and America, 1837–1883.* 3 vols. 1983. Reprint, Chicago: University of Chicago Press, 1989.

Higham, John. *Strangers in the Land: Patterns of American Nativism, 1860–1925.* New Brunswick: Rutgers University Press, 1988.

Hilliard, David. "UnEnglish and Unmanly: Anglo-Catholicism and Homosexuality." *Victorian Studies* 25, no. 2 (1982): 181–210.

Hinks, Edward W. *One Link in the Chain of Apostolic Succession; Or, The Crimes of Alexander Borgia.* Boston: Hinks, 1854.

Hoffman, Nicole Tonkovich. "*Legacy* Profile: Sarah Josepha Hale." *Legacy* 7, no. 2 (1990): 47–55.

Hofstader, Richard. *The Paranoid Style in American Politics and Other Essays.* 1965. Reprint, Chicago: University of Chicago Press, 1979.

Hogan, William. *Auricular Confession and Popish Nunneries.* 3rd ed. London: Arthur Hall, 1847.

A Synopsis of Popery, As It Was and As It Is. Boston: Saxton & Kelt, 1845.

Holcombe, Lee. *Wives and Property: Reform of the Married Women's Property Law in Nineteenth-Century England.* Toronto: University of Toronto Press, 1983.

Homans, Margaret. *Royal Representations: Queen Victoria and British Culture, 1837–1876.* Chicago: University of Chicago Press, 1998.

Homans, Margaret, and Adrienne Munich. Introduction to *Remaking Queen Victoria,* edited by Margaret Homans and Adrienne Munich. Cambridge: Cambridge University Press, 1997. 1–10.

Howard, Anne. *Mary Spencer: A Tale for the Times.* 1844. Reprint, New York: Garland, 1975.

Howells, William Dean. *A Fearful Responsibility and Tonelli's Marriage*. London: Hamilton, Adams, and Company, 1882.

A Foregone Conclusion. Novels 1875–1886. New York: Library of America, 1982. 1–171.

"Henry James, Jr." In *Discovery of a Genius: William Dean Howells and Henry James*, edited by Albert Mordell. New York: Twayne, 1961. 112–22.

"Marriage among the Italian Priesthood." *New York Times* 19 Oct. 1865: 4+.

Hughes, John. *The Decline of Protestantism, and its Cause*. New York: Dunigan, 1850.

Humphries, Anne. "Generic Strands and Urban Twists: The Victorian Mysteries Novel." *Victorian Studies* 34 (1991): 455–72.

Inez: A Tale of the Almo. *Godey's Lady's Book* 50 (1855): 370.

Irigaray, Luce. *The Sex Which is Not One*. Trans. Catherine Porter, with Carolyn Burke. Ithaca: Cornell University Press, 1985.

Jacobs, Harriet. *Incidents in the Life of a Slave Girl Written by Herself*. Ed. Jean Fagan Yellin. Cambridge, MA: Harvard University Press, 1987.

Jacobson, Marcia. *Henry James and the Mass Market*. University: University of Alabama Press, 1983.

James, Henry. *The American. Novels 1871–1880*. New York: Library of America, 1983. 513–872.

Essays on Literature, American Writers, English Writers. New York: Library of America, 1984.

French Writers, Other European Writers, The Preface to the New York Edition. New York. Library of America, 1984.

Letters, Fictions, Lives: Henry James and William Dean Howells. Ed. Michael Anesko. New York: Oxford University Press, 1997.

James, Lionel. *A Forgotten Genius: Sewell of St. Columba's and Radley*. London: Faber, 1945.

Jay, Elisabeth. *Faith and Doubt in Victorian Fiction*. London: Macmillan, 1986.

Jenner, Stephen. *Steepleton; or, High Church and Low Church: Being the Present Tendencies of Parties in the Church, Exhibited in the History of Frank Faithful*. London: Longman, Brown, Green, & Longmans, 1847.

Kaplan, Amy. *The Social Construction of American Realism*. Chicago: University of Chicago Press, 1988.

Kearney, Hugh. *The British Isles: A History of Four Nations*. Cambridge: Cambridge University Press, 1989.

Kelley, Mary. *Private Woman, Public Stage: Literary Domesticity in Nineteenth-Century America*. New York: Oxford University Press, 1984.

Kelso, Isaac. *Danger in the Dark: A Tale of Intrigue and Priestcraft*. 1854. 31st ed. Cincinnati: Rulison, Queen City Publishing House, 1855.

Kennedy, J. C. G. *Catalogue of the Newspapers and Periodicals Published in the United States*. New York: Livingston, 1852.

Kestner, Joseph. *Protest and Reform: The British Social Narrative by Women, 1827–1867*. Madison: University of Wisconsin Press, 1985.

Kingsley, Charles. *His Letters and Memories of His Life*. 2 vols. London: Kegan Paul, 1880.

"Speech on Behalf of the Ladies Sanitary Association." In *Miscellanies*. 2nd ed. 2 vols. London: John W. Parker and Son, 1860. 309–17.

Westward, Ho! New York: Airmont, 1969.

Knobel, Dale T. *America for the Americans: The Nativist Movement in the United States*. New York: Twayne, 1996.

Knoepflmacher, U. C. *The Victorian Novel of Religious Humanism: A Study of George Eliot, Walter Pater, and Samuel Butler*. Princeton: Princeton University Press, 1970.

"The Know-nothings – American Prospects." *British Quarterly Review* 22 (1855): 45–75.

Kristeva, Julia. "Stabat Mater." In *Contemporary Critical Theory*, edited by Dan Latimer. New York: HBJ, 1989. 580–603.

Landor, Walter Savage. *The Complete Works of Walter Savage Landor*. Vol. 12. Ed. T. Earle Welby. London: Chapman & Hall, 1931.

Langland, Elizabeth. *Nobody's Angels: Middle-Class Women and Domestic Ideology in Victorian Culture*. Ithaca: Cornell University Press, 1995.

Lansbury, Coral. *The Old Brown Dog: Women, Workers, and Vivisection in Edwardian England*. Madison: University of Wisconsin Press, 1985.

Larned, Mrs. Lucinda. *The American Nun; or The Effects of Romance*. Boston: Otis, Broaders, 1836.

Lears, T. Jackson. *No Place of Grace: Antimodernism and the Transformation of American Culture, 1880–1920*. New York: Pantheon, 1981.

Levine, Robert S. *Conspiracy and Romance: Studies in Brockden Brown, Cooper, Hawthorne, and Melville*. Cambridge: Cambridge University Press, 1989.

Linton, Eliza. "The Judicial Shock to Marriage." *Nineteenth Century* 39, no. 171 (May 1891): 691–700.

Under Which Lord? New York: Garland, 1976.

Lippard, George. *New York: Its Upper Ten and Lower Million*. Upper Saddle River: Literature House, 1970.

"Literary Notices," *Godey's Lady's Book* 50 (April 1855): 370.

Loesberg, Jonathan. "The Ideology of Narrative Form in Sensation Fiction." *Representations* 13 (Winter 1986): 115–37.

Logan, Thad. *The Victorian Parlour*. Cambridge: Cambridge University Press, 2001.

Looby, Christopher. "George Thompson's 'Romance of the Real': Transgression and Taboo in American Sensation Fiction." *American Literature* 65 (1993): 651–72.

Long, Lady Catherine. *Sir Roland Ashton. A Tale of the Times*. 1844. New York: Garland, 1975.

"Lucretia Borgia. An Historical Sketch." *Southern Literary Messenger* 19, no. 4 (April 1853): 208–13.

Lukács, György, *The Historical Novel*. Translated by Hannah and Stanley Mitchell. Lincoln and London: University of Nebraska Press, 1962.

Lynn, Kenneth. *William Dean Howells: An American Life*. New York: Harcourt, 1971.

Macrindell, Rachel. *The School Girl in France; or, The Snares of Popery: A Warning to Protestants against Education in Catholic Seminaries.* Philadelphia: Hooker, 1843.

Maison, Margaret. *Search Your Soul, Eustace: A Survey of the Religious Novel in the Victorian Age.* London: Sheed and Ward [1961].

The Victorian Vision: Studies in the Religious Novel. New York: Sheed and Ward, 1961.

Malone, Dumas. *Dictionary of American Biography.* New York: Scribner's, 1933.

Mann, Horace. *The Republic and the School: Horace Mann on the Education of Free Men.* Ed. Lawrence A. Cremin. New York: Teachers College, 1957.

Martin, Robert Bernard. *The Dust of Combat: A Life of Charles Kingsley.* New York: Norton, 1960.

Martineau, Harriet. *Harriet Martineau's Autobiography.* Vol. 2. London: Smith, 1877.

Maxwell, Robert. *The Mysteries of Paris and London.* Charlottesville: University Press of Virginia, 1992.

Maynard, John. *Victorian Discourses on Sexuality and Religion.* Cambridge: Cambridge University Press, 1993.

McDannell, Colleen. *The Christian Home in Victorian America, 1840–1900.* Bloomington: Indiana University Press, 1986.

Michelet, Jules. *Priests, Women, and Families.* Trans. C. Cocks. 12th ed. London: Longman, Brown, Green, and Longmans, 1847.

Miller, D. A. *The Novel and the Police.* Berkeley: University of California Press, 1988.

Mintz, Steven. *A Prison of Expectations: The Family in Victorian Culture.* New York: New York University Press, 1983.

Mitchell, Sally, ed. *Victorian Britain: An Encyclopedia.* New York: Garland, 1988.

Mizruchi, Susan, ed. *Religion and Cultural Studies.* Princeton: Princeton University Press, 2001.

Moffatt, Mary Anne Ursula. [Sister Mary Edmund St. George]. *Answer to Six Months in a Convent, Exposing Its Falsehoods and Manifold Absurdities by The Lady Superior with Some Preliminary Remarks.* Boston: Eastburn, 1835.

Monaghan, Jay. *The Great Rascal: The Life and Adventures of Ned Buntline.* Boston: Little, Brown, 1951.

Monk, Maria. *Awful Disclosures of The Hotel Dieu Nunnery of Montreal, Revised, with an Appendix.* 1836. New York: Arno, 1977.

Mott, Frank Luther. *American Journalism: A History of Newspapers in the United States Through 250 Years, 1690–1940.* New York: Macmillan, 1941.

Golden Multitudes: The Story of Best Sellers in the United States. New York: Macmillan, 1947.

Mumm, Susan. *Stolen Daughters, Virgin Mothers: Anglican Sisterhoods in Victorian Britain.* New York: Leicester, 1999.

Mumm, Susan, ed. *All Saints Sisters of the Poor: An Anglican Sisterhood in the Nineteenth Century.* Rochester: Boydell, 2001.

Munich, Adrienne. *Queen Victoria's Secrets.* New York: Columbia University Press, 1996.

Murray, John. "Sacerdotalism, Ancient and Modern." *The Quarterly Review* 136 (Jan. 1874): 55–70.

Nasaw, David. *Schooled to Order: A Social History of Public Schooling in the United States.* New York: Oxford University Press, 1979.

The National Cyclopaedia of American Biography. Vol. 13. New York: White, 1906.

Nelson, Alice Dunbar. "Sister Josepha." In *The Goodness of St. Rocque and Other Stories.* Freeport: Books for Libraries, 1971. 155–72.

Nevius, Blake. *Cooper's Landscapes: An Essay on the Picturesque Vision.* Berkeley: University of California Press, 1976.

Newman, John Henry. *Apologia Pro Vita Sua.* Edited by David J. DeLaura. New York: Norton, 1968.

Parochial and Plain Sermons. 1835. Reprint, Westminster, MD: Christian Classics, 1966.

Norman, E. R. *Anti-Catholicism in Victorian England.* New York: Barnes and Noble, 1968.

The English Catholic Church in the Nineteenth Century. Oxford: Clarendon, 1984.

Novak, Barbara. *Nature and Culture: American Landscape and Painting, 1825–75.* New York: Oxford University Press, 1980.

O'Connor, Edward Dennis, ed. *The Dogma of the Immaculate Conception: History and Significance.* Notre Dame: University of Notre Dame Press, 1958.

"Our Ministry of Public Instruction." *Dublin Review* 33, no. 69 (Sept. 1853): 199–229.

"Papal Aggression." *The Times* (London) 22 Oct. 1850: 6.

Parton, James. "Our Roman Catholic Brethren." *Atlantic Monthly* 21 (April 1868): 432–51; 21 (May 1868): 556–74.

Paz, D. G. *Popular Anti-Catholicism in Mid-Victorian England.* Stanford: Stanford University Press, 1992.

Person, Leland. "Henry James, George Sand, and the Suspense of Masculinity." *PMLA* 106 (May 1991): 515–28.

Pittock, Murray G. H. *Celtic Identity and the British Image.* Manchester: Manchester University Press, 1999.

Poovey, Mary. *Uneven Developments: The Ideological Work of Gender in Mid-Victorian England.* Chicago: University of Chicago Press, 1988.

Porter, Carolyn. "What We Know That We Don't Know: Remapping American Literary Studies." *American Literary History* 6, no. 3 (1994): 467–526.

The Princess of Viarna: Or, The Spanish Inquisition in the Reign of the Emperor Charles the Fifth. New York: Pudney & Russell, 1857.

Priouleau, Elizabeth Stevens. *The Circle of Eros: Sexuality in the Work of William Dean Howells.* Durham, NC: Duke University Press, 1983.

"Puseyism." *Christian Secretary* 12, no. 31 (5 Oct. 1849): 1.

"Puseyism, as characterized by Lord Winchilsea." *Christian Secretary* 12, no. 7 (20 April 1849): 2.

"Puseyism, or Ecclesiastical Authority Versus Protestantism." *Christian Examiner* 35, no. 3 (Jan. 1844): 273–302.

"Puseyism gone mad!" *Liberator* 13, no. 32 (11 Aug. 1843): 128.

"Puseyism." *Liberator* 13, no. 32 (11 Aug. 1843): 128.

"Puseyism Examined." *Merchants' Magazine and Commercial Review* 8, no. 5 (May 1843): 491.

"Puseyism Examined." *Methodist Quarterly Review* 3, no. 11 (April 1843): 324.

Quincey, Edmund. "Lothair." *The Nation* 80 (1870): 372–73.

Ragussis, Michael. *Figures of Conversion: "The Jewish Question" & English National Identity*. Durham, NC: Duke University Press, 1995.

Ransom, Teresa. *Fanny Trollope: A Remarkable Life*. New York: St. Martin's, 1995.

Rapoport, David C. "Fear and Trembling: Terrorism in Three Religious Traditions." *The American Political Science Review* 78 (1984): 658–77.

Reade, Charles. *Griffith Gaunt, or, Jealousy*. 1866. Reprint, Boston: Ticknor and Fields, 1866.

Reed, Rebecca Theresa. *Six Months in a Convent, or, The Narrative of Rebecca Theresa Reed, Who was Under the Influence of the Roman Catholics about Two Years, and an Inmate of the Ursuline Convent on Mount Benedict, Charlestown, Mass., Nearly Six Months, in the Years 1831–32 With Some Preliminary Suggestions by the Committee of Publication*. 1835. Reprint, New York: Arno, 1977.

"A Religion of Murder." *Quarterly Review* 194 (1901): 506–13.

"The Religious Scarecrow of the Age." *National Magazine* 5 (Dec. 1854): 523–28.

"Religious Stories." *Fraser's Magazine* 38, no. 224 (Aug. 1848): 150–66.

Renza, Louis. *"A White Heron" and the Question of Minor Literature*. Madison: University of Wisconsin Press, 1984.

"Review of the Case of Olevia Neal the Carmelite Nun, Commonly Called Sister Isabella." *Baltimore Literary and Religious Magazine* 5, no. 10 (Oct. 1839): 433–46.

"Review of the Correspondence Between the Archbishop and the Mayor of Baltimore." *Baltimore Literary and Religious Magazine* 5, no. 11 (Nov. 1839): 481–96.

Reynolds, David S. *Beneath the American Renaissance: The Subversive Imagination in the Age of Emerson and Melville*. Cambridge, MA: Harvard University Press, 1988.

——— *Faith in Fiction: The Emergence of Religious Literature in America*. Cambridge, MA: Harvard University Press, 1981.

——— *George Lippard, Prophet of Protest*. New York: Lang, 1986.

Ringe, Donald A. *The Pictorial Mode: Space and Time in the Art of Bryant, Irving, and Cooper*. Lexington: University of Kentucky Press, 1971.

Roberts, David. *Paternalism in Early Victorian England*. New Brunswick: Rutgers University Press, 1979.

Robinson, Frederick William. *High Church*. 1860. Reprint, New York: Garland, 1975.

Rogin, Michael Paul. *Subversive Genealogy: The Politics and Art of Herman Melville*. New York: Knopf, 1983.

Rohrbach, Peter-Thomas. *Journey to Carith: The Story of the Carmelite Order*. New York: Doubleday, 1966.

Romero, Lora. *Home Fronts: Domesticity and Its Critics in the Antebellum United States*. Durham, NC: Duke University Press, 1997.

Rotundo, E. Anthony. *American Manhood: Transformations in Masculinity from the Revolution to the Modern Era.* New York: Basic, 1993.

Rowe, John Carlos. "The Politics of Innocence in Henry James's *The American.*" In *New Essays on* The American, edited by Martha Banta. Cambridge: Cambridge University Press, 1987. 69–97.

Ryan, Mary P. *Cradle of the Middle Class: The Family in Oneida County, New York, 1790–1865.* Cambridge: Cambridge University Press, 1981.

Sadlier, Michael. *XIX Century Fiction: A Bibliographical Record Based on His Own Collection.* 2 vols. Cambridge: Cambridge University Press, 1951.

Saint-Amour, Paul K. "Transatlantic Tropology in James's *Roderick Hudson.*" *Henry James Review* 18, no. 1 (1997): 22–42.

Schiefelbein, Michael. "A Catholic Baptism for *Villette*'s Lucy Snowe." *Christianity and Literature* 45, nos. 3–4 (1996): 319–29.

Schultz, Nancy Lusignan. *Fire and Roses: The Burning of the Charlestown Convent, 1834.* New York: Free Press, 2000.

Sekora, John. "Black Message/White Envelope: Genre, Authenticity, and Authority in the Antebellum Slave Narrative." *Callaloo* 10 (1987): 482–515.

Sewell, William. *Christian Politics.* Oxford: Parker, 1848.

    Hawkstone: A Tale of and for England in 184–. 2 vols. London, 1845. New York: Garland, 1976.

    "Oxford Theology." *Quarterly Review* 63 (March 1839): 526–72.

    "Romanism in Ireland." *Quarterly Review* 67 (Dec. 1840): 118–71.

Shanley, Mary Lyndon. *Feminism, Marriage, and the Law in Victorian England.* Princeton: Princeton University Press, 1989.

    "'One Must Ride Behind': Married Women's Rights and the Divorce Act of 1857." *Victorian Studies* 25, no. 3 (1982): 355–76.

Shaw, Richard. *Dagger John: The Unquiet Life and Times of Archbishop John Hughes of New York.* New York: Paulist Press, 1977.

Shaw, Benjamin. "Private Confession in the Church of England." *Quarterly Review* 124 (Jan. 1868): 83–116.

    "Convent Life Exposed: Great Lectures on Romanism." Margaret L. Shepherd. Flyer for lecture. [1890].

Shields, David S. *Civil Tongues and Polite Letters in British America.* Chapel Hill: University of North Carolina Press, 1997.

    Oracles of Empire: Poetry, Politics, and Commerce in British America, 1690–1750. Chicago: University of Chicago Press, 1990.

Silverman, Kaja. *Male Subjectivity at the Margins.* New York: Routledge, 1992.

Sinclair, Catherine. *Beatrice; or, the Unknown Relatives.* New York: Garland, 1975.

Sister Agnes; or The Captive Nun. A Picture of Convent Life. By a Clergyman's Widow. New York: Riker, Thorne, 1854.

Six Months in a House of Correction, Or, The Narrative of Dorah Mahony, Who Was Under the Influence of the Protestants About A Year, And An Inmate of the House of Correction, in Leverett St., Boston, Massachusetts, Nearly Six Months, In The Years 18–. Boston: Mussey, 1835.

Sklar, Kathryn Kish. *Catharine Beecher: A Study in American Domesticity*. New York: Norton, 1976.

Sleeman, William. *History of the Thugs or Pansigars of India*. Philadelphia: Carey & Hart, 1839.

    A Journey Through the Kingdom of Oudh in 1849–50. London: Bentley, 1858.

    Rambles and Recollections of an Indian Official. Ed. V. A. Smith. Westminster: Constable, 1893.

    Report on the Depredations Committed by the Thug Gangs of Upper and Central India. Calcutta: Huttman, 1840.

Snell, K. D. M., ed. *The Regional Novel in Britain and Ireland, 1800–1990*. Cambridge: Cambridge University Press, 1998.

The Sons of the Sires; A History of the Rise, Progress, and Destiny of the American Party, and It's Probable Influence on the Next Presidential Election. Philadelphia: Lippincott, 1855.

Spivak, Gayatri. "Three Women's Texts and a Critique of Imperialism." *Critical Inquiry* 12 (1985): 246–61.

Startling Facts for Native Americans called "Know-Nothings" or a Vivid Presentation of the Dangers to American Liberty to be Apprehended from Foreign Influence. New York: "Published at Nassau Street," 1855.

Stebbins, Lucy Poate, and Richard Poate Stebbins. *The Trollopes: The Chronicle of a Writing Family*. New York: Columbia University Press, 1945.

Stephen, Leslie. *Hours in a Library*. New York: Knickerbocker, 1907.

Stowe, Harriet Beecher. *A Key to Uncle Tom's Cabin; Presenting the Original Facts and Documents upon Which the Story is Founded. Together with Corroborative Statements Verifying the Truth of the Work*. Boston: Jewett, 1853.

    My Wife and I, or Harry Henderson's History. New York: Ford, 1872.

    Uncle Tom's Cabin; or, Life Among the Lowly. Ed. Kathryn Kish Sklar. New York: Library of America, 1982.

Strand, Ginger, and Sarah Zimmerman. "Finding an Audience: Beatrice Cenci, Percy Shelley, and the Stage." *English Romantic Review* 6, no. 2 (1996): 246–68.

Sue, Eugene. *The Wandering Jew*. [no city]: Chapman & Hall, 1844–45.

Sussman, Herbert. *Victorian Masculinities: Manhood and Masculine Poetics in Early Victorian Literature and Art*. Cambridge: Cambridge University Press, 1995.

Sutherland, John. *The Stanford Companion to Victorian Fiction*. Stanford: Stanford University Press, 1989.

Sutton-Ramspeck, Beth. "The Personal is Poetical: Feminist Criticism and Mary Ward's Reading of the Brontës." *Victorian Studies* 34 (1990): 55–75.

Tarr, Sister Mary Muriel. *Catholicism in Gothic Fiction*. New York: Garland, 1979.

Thomas, Ronald. *Dreams of Authority: Freud and the Fictions of the Unconscious*. Ithaca: Cornell University Press, 1990.

Thornton, Edward. *Illustrations of the History and Practice of the Thugs*. London: Allen, 1837.

Tompkins, Jane. *Sensational Designs: The Cultural Work of American Fiction, 1790–1860*. New York: Oxford University Press, 1985.

Tonkovich, Nicole. "Rhetorical Power in the Victorian Parlor: *Godey's Lady's Book* and the Gendering of Nineteenth-Century Rhetoric." In *Oratorical Culture in Nineteenth-Century America: Transformation in the Theory and Practice of Rhetoric*, edited by Gregory Clark and S. Michael Halloran. Carbondale: Southern Illinois University Press, 1993. 158–83.

Trevelyan, Charles E. "Ramaseeana; or a Vocabulary of the Peculiar Language of the Thugs." *Edinburgh Review* 130 (Jan. 1837): 189–210.

Trilling, Lionel. *Sincerity and Authenticity: The Charles Eliot Norton Lectures, 1969–1970*. Cambridge, MA: Harvard University Press, 1971.

Trollope, Anthony. *An Autobiography*. Intro. Bradford Allen Booth. Berkeley: University of California Press, 1947.

Trollope, Frances Eleanor. *Frances Trollope: Her Life and Literary Work*. 2 vols. London: Bentley, 1895.

Trollope, Frances Milton. *The Abbess: A Romance*. 3 vols. London: Whittaker, Treacher, 1833.

   Father Eustace: A Tale of the Jesuits. 3 vols. 1847. Reprint, London: Garland, 1975.

Tromp, Marlene. *The Private Rod: Marital Violence, Sensation and the Law in Victorian Britain*. Charlottesville: University of Virginia Press, 2000.

Tuchman, Gaye. *Edging Women Out: Victorian Novelists, Publishers and Social Change*. New Haven: Yale University Press, 1989.

Tucker, J. T. "Popery as a Present Fact." *Boston Review* 5 (March 1865): 178–92.

Tuttle, Hudson. *The Convent of the Sacred Heart*. Philadelphia: Carter, 1892.

Twitchell, James B. *Forbidden Partners: The Incest Taboo in Modern Culture*. New York, Columbia University Press, 1987.

Tyack, David, and Elizabeth Hansot. *Managers of Virtue: Public School Leadership in America, 1820–1980*. New York: Basic, 1982.

Tyler, Alice Felt. *Freedom's Ferment: Phases of American Social History from the Colonial Period to the Outbreak of the Civil War*. New York: Harper, 1944.

   "The Ursuline Convent." *Christian Watchman* March 20, 1835: 46.

Vance, Norman. *The Sinews of the Spirit: The Ideal of Christian Manliness in Victorian Literature and Religious Thought*. Cambridge: Cambridge University Press, 1985.

Veeder, William. "The Portrait of a Lack." In *New Essays on* The Portrait of a Lady, edited by Joel Porte. Cambridge: Cambridge University Press, 1985. 95–121.

Vicinus, Martha. *Independent Women: Work and Community for Single Women, 1850–1920*. Chicago: University of Chicago Press, 1985.

Victorian Literature and Culture 31, no. 1 (March 2003).

Wald, Priscilla. *Constituting Americans: Cultural Anxiety and Narrative Form*. Durham, NC: Duke University Press, 1995.

Ward, Mary Elizabeth. *Helbeck of Bannisdale*. London: Penguin, 1983.

Warner, Marina. *Alone of All Her Sex: The Myth and the Cult of the Virgin Mary*. New York: Vintage, 1976.

   From the Beast to the Blonde: On Fairy Tales and Their Tellers. New York: Farrar, Straus and Giroux, 1995.

Watson, Nicola J. "Gloriana Victoriana: Victoria and the Cultural Memory of Elizabeth I." In *Remaking Queen Victoria*, edited by Margaret Homans and Adrienne Munich. Cambridge: Cambridge University Press, 1997. 79–104.

Weisbuch, Robert. *Atlantic Double-Cross. American Literature and British Influence in the Age of Emerson*. Chicago: University of Chicago Press, 1986.

Welsh, Alexander. *Strong Representations: Narrative and Circumstantial Evidence in England*. Baltimore: Johns Hopkins University Press, 1992.

Wharton, Edith. "The Bunner Sisters." In *Collected Stories, 1911–1937*. New York: Library of America, 2001. 166–246.

Wolff, Robert Lee. *Gains and Losses: Novels of Faith and Doubt in Victorian England*. New York: Garland, 1977.

Wolffe, John. *The Protestant Crusade in Great Britain, 1829–1860*. Oxford: Clarendon, 1991.

Woodress, James L., Jr. *Howells and Italy*. Durham, NC: Duke University Press, 1952.

Worboise, Emma Jane. *Overdale: or, the Story of a Pervert: A Tale for the Times*. London: Clack, 1869.

Yeazell, Ruth Bernard. *Fictions of Modesty: Women and Courtship in the English Novel*. Chicago: University of Chicago Press, 1991.

Yellin, Jean Fagan. *Incidents in the Life of a Slave Girl*, by Harriet A. Jacobs. Cambridge, MA: Harvard University Press, 1987. xiii–xxxiv.

Index

Note: Italicized page numbers refer to illustrations.

Printed in the United Kingdom
by Lightning Source UK Ltd.
135862UK00003B/53/P